The Cultural Politics of Food, Taste, and Identity

Also Available from Bloomsbury:

The Emergence of National Food, edited by Atsuko Ichijo, Venetia Johannes, and Ronald Ranta
Food Values in Europe, edited by Krista Harper and Valeria Siniscalchi
Taste, Politics, and Identities in Mexican Food, edited by Steffan Igor Ayora-Diaz

The Cultural Politics of Food, Taste, and Identity

A Global Perspective

Edited by
Steffan Igor Ayora-Diaz

BLOOMSBURY ACADEMIC
LONDON • NEW YORK • OXFORD • NEW DELHI • SYDNEY

BLOOMSBURY ACADEMIC
Bloomsbury Publishing Plc
50 Bedford Square, London, WC1B 3DP, UK
1385 Broadway, New York, NY 10018, USA
29 Earlsfort Terrace, Dublin 2, Ireland

BLOOMSBURY, BLOOMSBURY ACADEMIC and the Diana logo are trademarks of
Bloomsbury Publishing Plc

First published in Great Britain 2021
Paperback edition published 2023

Copyright © Steffan Igor Ayora-Diaz and contributors, 2021

Steffan Igor Ayora-Diaz has asserted his right under the Copyright, Designs and
Patents Act, 1988, to be identified as Editor of this work.

For legal purposes the Acknowledgments on p. vii constitute an extension
of this copyright page.

Cover design: Terry Woodley
Cover image © Taylor Simpson/Unsplash

A catalogue record for this book is available from the British Library.

A catalog record for this book is available from the Library of Congress.

ISBN: HB: 978-1-3501-6272-3
PB: 978-1-3502-3740-7
ePDF: 978-1-3501-6273-0
eBook: 978-1-3501-6274-7

Typeset by Deanta Global Publishing Services, Chennai, India

To find out more about our authors and books visit www.bloomsbury.com and
sign up for our newsletters

Contents

Acknowledgments

This volume follows the steps of *Taste, Politics and Identities in Mexican Food* (Ayora-Diaz 2019). This has been possible thanks to the interest and support of Lucy Carroll and Lily McMahon, at Bloomsbury Academic. My sincere thanks to them. Of course, all the authors in this volume spent hours writing our first drafts under the unfavorable conditions resulting from the SARS-CoV-2 pandemic, an event that drastically affected our everyday lives; many of us had to improvise and shift from classroom to online interaction with our students, and deal with the resulting, stressing circumstances. For their dedication, and for their commitment to this project, I sincerely thank all the contributors to the volume.

Unfortunately, as now it often happens under global budgetary restrictions, there were no institutional funds of any type to support this volume. However, before the pandemic, some of us had the opportunity to enjoy face-to-face interaction: in July of 2018, Gabriela Vargas Cetina, Walter Little, and I took part in a session on taste I organized with Ramona Perez for the International Congress of Americanists in Salamanca, Spain, which facilitated the transition from the previous volume to this one. Also, Rossella Galletti, Cristina Grasseni, Shingo Hamada, Yoshimi Osawa, and I had the opportunity to meet and introduce our work to each other at the National Museum of Ethnology in Osaka, Japan, between March 18 and 20, 2019, during the international symposium "Making Food in Human and Natural History," organized by Atsushi Nobayashi and Hironao Kawai. I thank all colleagues and friends for their positive comments and encouragement.

Steffan Igor Ayora-Diaz
U. Autónoma de Yucatán
Volume Editor

Map

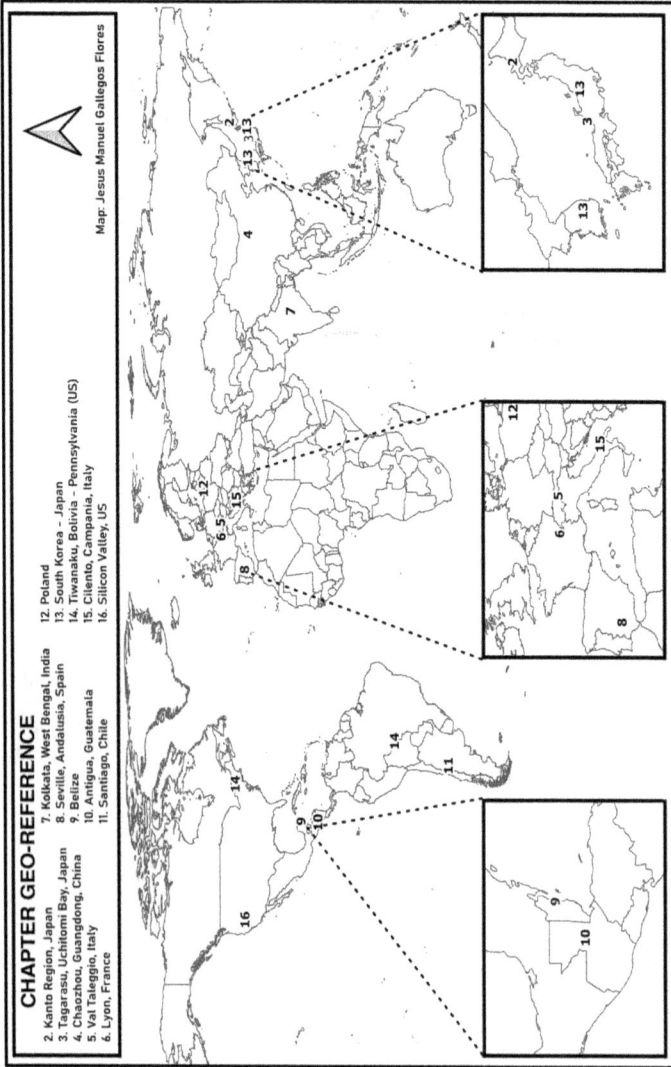

CHAPTER GEO-REFERENCE

2. Kanto Region, Japan
3. Tagarasu, Uchitomi Bay, Japan
4. Chaozhou, Guangdong, China
5. Val Taleggio, Italy
6. Lyon, France

7. Kolkata, West Bengal, India
8. Seville, Andalusia, Spain
9. Belize
10. Antigua, Guatemala
11. Santiago, Chile

12. Poland
13. South Korea – Japan
14. Tiwanaku, Bolivia – Pennsylvania (US)
15. Cilento, Campania, Italy
16. Silicon Valley, US

Map: Jesús Manuel Gallegos Flores

Chapter Geo-Reference. Drawn by Jesús Manuel Gallego Flores.

Introduction

The Cultural Politics of Taste in Global Perspective

Steffan Igor Ayora-Diaz

The Politics of Taste

The first time I ate white truffles in Italy I was unable to distinguish them from the other flavors in my meal. Years later, also in Italy, Roman friends took me and my wife to a restaurant in Tuscany. Surrounding the table, my happy friends and I engaged in the convivial experience of a Sunday meal and ordered pasta with truffes. My friends told me what it was I was eating, explained how truffles are collected and the seasonal changes they undergo in flavor and aroma, then praised the aromas and flavors of the different ingredients, the truffles included, and taught me to distinguish them in my meal, initiating me into the many tastes of truffles, an ingredient new for me. As I experienced the subjective pleasure of consuming this meal, this episode also highlighted the social and cultural aspects that constitute the taste of food and its experience. It has been often pointed out that taste is a capacity that most humans possess to perceive the flavor of things. The human sensorial apparatus has the capability to detect different properties in the objects that surround us. This apparatus and its experiences are complemented by cognitive abilities that allow humans to distinguish among flavors and to prefer some tastes over others and to experience pleasure or disgust during their consumption (Perullo 2016; Plakias 2018). This explanation, however, still falls short, because taste is an even more complex phenomenon: taste mobilizes our sensorial body into *seemingly* subjective experiences which, in fact, are intersubjective, social, and, of course, political, and fluid—one that changes over time and with context—(Counihan and Højlund 2018); furthermore, taste has an important historical dimension which is enhanced by the memory of meals (Von Hoffmann 2016).

In general, food summons our symbolic capacity, and we recognize foods as edible or inedible on religious, political, ethnic, gendered, and social grounds that are rendered more complex when the state or transnational institutions such as UNESCO, FAO, and the World Bank, for example, intervene to determine or establish which food habits and traditions deserve protection, which ones need to be promoted, or (tacitly) which ones are not deserving of attention and care. This complexity often leads us to contradicting or, minimally, equivocal relations with food. For example, FAO promotes the nutritious consumption of insects to expand our edible universe, despite the fact that their meaning can be highly ambivalent at the local level (e.g.,

Cohen and Schuster 2019; Van Huis et al. 2013). In addition, as we have seen in the context of the current pandemic of Covid-19, the consumption of unusual (for the consumers from North Atlantic societies) animals and insects can trigger emotional and moral disgust toward a country's whole diet, as when China and the Chinese are morally condemned because some ethnic groups include in their diet some species of bats and pangolins (see, e.g., Zhang 2020).

Food is generally charged with different symbolic meanings. Religion has been one important social foundation for dietary restrictions and preferences. For example, when Muslims and Hindus confront their preferences and negotiate, sometimes violently, their cultural boundaries. The same can be said of the differences between Christians and Jews, and of the influence of Buddhism on food preferences. Of course, religion can be used to draw boundaries that signal belonging, especially through commensality (Taussig 2009). In addition, gender differences are mediated, produced and maintained through food, as when women are socially expected to be more inclined to the consumption of salads and wine, while men's preferences are expected to be mostly for meat and beer (Adams 2015). Also, this far, men are the ones who control most professional kitchens in renowned restaurants, while women are relegated to domestic cooking or subordinated within restaurant kitchens (Haddaji, Albors-Garrigós and García-Sigovia 2017; Leschziner 2015: 183). It is noteworthy that, for example, Netflix series on chefs available in 2020 feature more men than women, while shows focusing on street foods tend to privilege the stories of female cooks. In many instances, it is the claim to ethnic, regional, or national authenticity that is used to add market value to a cuisine, but also to affirm group identities though the taste of food and the social and cultural practices of cooking and sharing meals (Julier 2013; Ray 2016). There is, of course, no natural disposition to explain these differences but, rather, different preferences are socially shaped, and have been turned into common stereotypes deployed to collapse whole cuisines into a single meal, or even an ingredient. Taste is the sensorial marker attributed to food that is usually used to explain these *naturalized* dispositions; that is, although they are the product of historical and social processes, these are usually bracketed, and thus lead to the perception of taste preferences as "natural" (Ayora-Diaz 2012).

The authors in this volume think of taste as an intersubjective experience in which historic, social, cultural, and economic processes converge, that we are all inclined to examine the political dimension of taste. That is, we are concerned with analyzing the sociocultural and historic mechanisms that involve taste (its production, preference, and appropriation) and find expression in the production and reproduction of social, economic, cultural, and thus political differences and inequality among different groups. This is an aspect that, as I explain in Chapter 1, has been inspired by Bourdieu's work on social distinction (1984): individual and group preferences for food, restaurants, and localities to eat signal social class and, at the same time, their choices mark in return foods and establishments as "belonging" into their system of preferences. In this sense, the contemporary world encompasses societies which, to a larger or lesser extent, communicate with each other. Hence, local processes that apparently demonstrate and affirm the "identity" of a group through its food and taste, result in meals, cuisine, and taste that simultaneously distinguish the members of one group from others, and signal different positions within the cultural political structure. For example, when French cuisine is recognized as more "sophisticated" than others, which are placed in a hierarchy below French cooking (Ferguson 2004). Alternatively, the value hierarchy may be established along with criteria of exoticism and authenticity, and consumers' preferences mark their food choices as more knowledgeable and informed than those of others (Heldke 2003; Johnston and Baumann 2010). We find, in consequence, that the simultaneous affirmation of identity and otherness, of membership and exclusion, has effects on food choices and preferences. By cooking, eating, and sharing (or not) a meal we are actively performing and representing our identity and rejecting that of the social and cultural "other."

Food, Taste, and the Politics of Identity

Food and its taste, we show in this volume from different disciplinary perspectives, are connected to different forms of everyday politics of identity. Although identities are dynamic and fluid, the common understanding of "identity" is that of an imagined self-sameness and permanence. Hence, safeguarding the identity of a people, its food, and its taste preferences conveys the image of unchanging food habits, as well as of historical continuity in taste preferences and cooking practices. Cultural representations, those produced either by scholars from different disciplines or by groups of people, have strong political meanings that support the identities of groups and signal difference and unequal positions within diverse social structures. Important for food studies is acknowledging that one important dimension in the everyday politics of representation and identity is the different ways in which different actors engage in the essentialization of cultural attributes. As Vargas-Cetina (2013: 1) argues, "In a world marked more than ever by the politics of identity, where access to resources is often predicated in establishing a clear membership in recognizable groups, anthropologists everywhere are showing the contingent construction of 'truth' while taking sides in local struggles." Today, I would add, this is a predicament shared by all the disciplines in the social sciences and humanities that is revealed as we continue to examine the strategies whereby food is deployed to affirm identities and belonging, and to exclude other people.

In this discussion, the language used by different social actors gains importance in the contemporary world, as it is placed within networks of information such as social media, the press, television, radio, and other media charged with the task of representing different cultural practices (Dürrschmidt and Kautt 2019). As Hall, Evans, and Nixon suggested (2013: 21): "Language is one of the 'media' through which thoughts, ideas and feelings are represented in culture," and sounds, written words, images, and, we would add, food and taste, can be used to stand for people and their cultural preferences. Food-related practices, as much as the choice of clothes, music, and bodily practices, "say something" about persons or groups; that is, food has the power to represent a group and its others.

When we examine the ways in which food is signified and how important it is in defining the identity of many groups, we find that it often has political implications.

Sharing the taste preference for a certain fermented vegetable, for smoked flavors, or for a type of dashi, fish, or cheese frequently highlights group commonalities and belonging. Food, also, when it is displayed as part of the cultural heritage of a group, establishes identities (of people, product, and territory), and their conflation may be used as a springboard when the group's cuisine seeks to secure a niche in the global market of "ethnic," "exotic," and "authentic" ingredients, meals, cuisines, and cooking and eating practices. For example, French chefs emphasize their cooking practices as the foundation of Lyons's gastronomic importance; highland producers in the Alps brand their cheese as cultural heritage distinguishable from the cheese produced in lowland regions, and the Mediterranean Diet is valued differently in Seville, Spain, or in Campania, Italy. "Tradition" and "modernity" are regularly turned into meaningful markers of food, sometimes revealing ambivalent tensions mediated by ingredients and meals. Foods, furthermore, are inscribed with political meanings that signal particular identities and become objects and practices that are, at the same time, culturally fragmenting instruments in the global economy (Ayora-Diaz 2013: 50).

In this volume we take the different meanings of food ingredients (their production, use, and consumption), recipes, meals, culinary codes, cooking practices, and modes of consumption as vehicles of everyday forms of political strategies of identity formation. It is in this sense that the politics of taste do not necessarily involve confrontational tactics, but often take the form of negotiations of meaning among actors who occupy different positions in the social and economic structure; food choices become cultural vehicles to carry the identity of a group vis-à-vis other groups, national and supranational institutions. Hence, locality, terroir, ethnicity, authenticity, heritage, and other values become markers with which groups seek to reposition themselves within the local, regional, national, and global foodscape.

Structure of this Volume

Following the publication of *Taste, Politics, and Identities in Mexican Food* (Ayora-Diaz 2019), the authors in this volume saw the need to explore how taste articulates multiple meanings around tradition, modernity, authenticity, nostalgia, terroir and locality, heritage, regionalism, and nationalism in a global context. In global society, all nation-states, regions, and local cultures share a market of food in which different values are variously negotiated by people with their own local, national, or international institutions. "Heritage," for example, means something different for different social groups. Inspecting the UNESCO list of Intangible Cultural Heritage, several of us find cooking practices, social modes of consumption, single ingredients or meals, or, like in Mexico, a localized indigenous culinary code writ large to encompass the whole country's diverse cuisines. In contrast, other groups of people define their food as their "heritage" because it has been handed from one generation to the next, but instead of looking for institutional recognition, they seek to arouse the appetite of consumers. Likewise, different groups consider their cooking and food to be either "traditional" or "modern," and in each instance their meaning must be negotiated. How different people taste their food and the food of others translates into different modes of everyday politics, from the tacit denial of value of a group's taste preferences to the affirmation of the trueness of one's group's taste preferences. These, in turn, may lead to the outright rejection of other people's food and even to direct physical confrontation, as we see in different chapters of this book. The chapters in this volume examine these issues by looking at food and taste in Asia, Europe, and the Americas (for cases related to Mexico, see Ayora-Diaz 2019). Following this introduction, the book is divided into three parts, followed by a Postface.

Part I: Taste and the Politics of Identity

The book starts with Chapter 1, "Food, Taste, and Identity in the Global Arena," by Ayora-Diaz. Here we find a conceptual-theoretical discussion that locates taste in the field of everyday cultural politics. This chapter emphasizes the need to examine historic, social, cultural, and economic processes as they intersect with the politics of identity. It emphasizes the intersubjective nature of our perception of taste. Taste, furthermore, relies on historical, social memories that help constitute and make it recognizable, turning it into an important marker of social distinction. This chapter also emphasizes the need to look at the everyday aesthetic, sensorial-sensual experience of food as a condition to more fully examine the politics of food taste and its relationship with cultural values such as "exoticism," "authenticity," "heritage," and "nostalgia," as they are tied to a sometimes fragmented global market of food and local, ethnic, regional, and national identities. In Chapter 2, "Centralization and Standardization of Taste: Dashi in Japan," Yoshimi Osawa argues that to understand the taste of *washoku* (Japanese food) we need to examine the complex relationship between the umami taste and the manufacture of dashi (stock). She demonstrates the effects of the nationalist policy aimed at highlighting the importance of both umami and dashi in Japanese cooking and taste on the state-led standardization of dashi taste. However, she shows, there is great regional diversity in cooking techniques and ingredients used in the preparation of this stock. Hence, there exists a constant negotiation between the homogenized flavor fostered by industrially produced stocks and those made at home with local ingredients. As she demonstrates, UNESCO has played an important part in shaping the politics of dashi taste in including *washoku* in the list of Intangible Cultural Heritage.

In Chapter 3, "Heritagization of Fermented Taste in Southwestern Fukui, Japan," Shingo Hamada underscores the meaning of food heritage as knowledge transmitted through generations. In this instance, the people in the Uchitomi Bay affirm that the manufacture of fermented food is dependent on terroir and seasonality. It is an important local product and their producers seek consumers' recognition by deploying the value of "authenticity" in the locally produced fermented mackerel against similar competing mackerel which is commercially and industrially produced. Local producers emphasize the virtues of local variability, the taste effects of using different ingredients, the importance of terroir, and the insistence on how taste preferences have been instituted though time, from generation to generation. In Chapter 4, we move to China. In "The Changing Landscapes of *Gongfu Cha* Tea Culture in Contemporary

China," Lanlan Kuang describes the *gongfu cha* tea ceremony both in its place of origin and its de- and reterritorialization elsewhere in China, Taiwan, and France. She discusses the part played by the local understanding of this ceremony as local heritage as it faces the emergence of commercialized practices. She demonstrates how this ceremony is inflected by aesthetic choices (on the recipients, the tea, the water, the smokeless wood, the serving cups, and the rules to taste the tea), which are, in turn, shaped by religious values. She describes how this tea ceremony and the objects required for its performance are framed by Buddhist values strongly linked to the cultural identity of people in Chaozhou, in the Guangdong province of China. Similarly, to the case of mackerels, in the previous chapter, the practice of this ceremony appeals to "heritage," an asset important in the context of a global market of edible (and drinkable) commodities.

Chapters 5 and 6 take us to Europe. In Chapter 5, "Italian Cheese in the Global Heritage Arena," Cristina Grasseni discusses how heritage must be negotiated among different social actors. In Val Taleggio, on the Italian Alps, negotiations over Protected Designation of Origin (PDO) recognize the cultural value of cheese manufacture among highlands pastoralists over that made in the lowlands, even though both cheeses should be understood as the product of transhumant practices. Furthermore, heritagization leads to standardization and local empowerment over cheese production as villagers claim the cultural authority to reinvent their PDO cheese (*Strachitunt*) against other cheeses they define as outsiders' "invention" seeking to industrially replicate the value of the local cheese. In Chapter 6, "The Gastronomic Capital of the World: Food, Politics, and Identity in Lyon," Rachel Black focuses on national-regional politics as it converges with social class and gender politics in the representation of the city's gastronomy. Thus, Lyon's cuisine is pitted against the cuisine of Paris, the former as living demonstration of the richness of French regional cuisine, and the latter as hegemonic but homogeneous, characterless food. It was in this context, Black argues, that, historically, female cooks maintained the regionalist values of French cuisine. Yet, she shows, their recipes, which were already the bourgeois interpretation and upscaling of rural recipes, have been appropriated by male chefs. Currently, at least before the pandemic, privileging the region and its flavors, Lyon hosts restaurants in which foreign influences are adopted and have continued transforming regional gastronomic practices and values.

Part II: Translocal and Transnational Politics of Taste and Identity

Part II encompasses five chapters in which we find the politics of nation and regions or the position into which ethnic groups (not necessarily minorities, demographically speaking) are located. Although values such as "authenticity" and "patrimony" can be deployed, food, in these instances, mediates identity claims to support the taste of the ruling groups, nationalist constructions, and representations of popular culture, ethnic or religious taste preferences, which explain, morally and politically, the subordination of some groups. In Chapter 7, "Fetid Flesh and Fragrant Fare: Food, Scandal, and Identity in Contemporary Bengal," Ishita Banerjee-Dube examines the negotiation of meanings among right-wing nationalist Indian Hindus and Bengalis. In Kolkata, there was, she shows, a media scandal triggered by the sale of rotten meat to restaurants and eateries. The discovery of this illegal market put in play upper-caste Hindu vegetarian values and invoked the Bengali Muslim inclination for flesh consumption. This characterization was compounded by a politics of language through which Hindi was asserted as the national language and Bengali people revendicated Bangla as their own language. Hence, food, its taste as either fresh or rotten, became explicitly tied to religion, caste, language, and nationalist versus regionalist identities. In Chapter 8, "Tasting 'Innovation': The Politics of Taste in Contemporary Restaurant Food in Seville, Spain," Steffan Igor Ayora-Diaz and Gabriela Vargas-Cetina demonstrate how the taste of food in the city of Seville, Spain, is the product of historic, translocal connections that allow the coexistence of two different culinary taste preferences: that of fish and seafood, and that of stews (cocidos, ladle meals). This duality is compounded by the fact that during the last thirty years the northern regions of Spain have become paradigmatic centers of gastronomic innovation and young chefs in Seville must decide to what extent they will seek innovation or the preservation of "traditional" taste. The politics of identity are displayed at different scales: Spanish vis-à-vis French and Nordic gastronomy, national and regional cuisines, and cooks' and chefs' alliances with either "innovation" or "tradition."

In Chapter 9, "Of Corn and Coconuts: Taste and the Cultural Politics of Gastronationalism in Belize," Lyra Spang argues that the taste of Belize is shaped by gastronationalist politics. In fact, in a country occupied by people of African, Asian, Caribbean, Central and North American, and European origins, she demonstrates how the definition of "Belizean" food is largely informed by its Kriolization, that is, its full appropriation by Kriol cooking. Consequently, although corn is one important ingredient for the Maya people of the region, the centrality of coconuts, an Afro-Caribbean ingredient, is what defines national Belizean cuisine, and corn as well as other Maya ingredients can only become "Belizean" when they have been adopted into the national culinary canon. Remaining within Central America, in Chapter 10, "Street Food to Restaurant: Politics of Eating and Cultural Heritage in Antigua, Guatemala," Walter Little argues that, in contrast to Mexico's cuisine, Guatemala's is not internationally recognized. In fact, within the country it is the invocation of "heritage" that confers upon street food the ability to convey what the taste of Guatemala's food is. This highlights a particular ambivalence for the people of Antigua who inhabit a city listed on UNESCO's list of material heritage, but the listing does not include the food. Still, in the context of tourism promotion, the Government of Guatemala can be seen as appropriating the taste of street food to promote restaurants as the sites to try local food. To complete Part II, Isabel Aguilera and Alejandra Alvear, in Chapter 11, "Popular Urban Taste and Mass Culture: *Chancho* and *Terremoto* in Chile," argue that the display of taste is a marker of urban social distinction. To demonstrate this relationship between food and distinction, in Santiago, Chile, they show how a drink (*terremoto*) and pork (*chancho*) meals commonly associated with working and popular classes also carry cultural ambivalence, as they become appropriated by other social classes during national celebrations and are turned into objects of consumption in "slum tourism" when upper- and middle-class people take guests to food stands where they serve foods and drinks associated with the popular mass of people. However, Aguilera and Alvear show, these pork-based meals and cheap drinks acquire positive connotations when they are taken to embed national cultural preferences, showing how the value of authenticity is blurred during these national festive moments of consumption.

Part III: The Global-Local Politics of Taste

This last part also encompasses five chapters. The chapters show different ways in which food "traditions" are locally constructed under conditions of global mobility and the circulation of global values. Local foods may be the outcome of different cultures succeeding each other or overlapping in what we today recognize as a "national" territory. At other times, under colonial conditions, the people and their food travel from the dominant to the subordinate regions, or the other way around: colonized people travel with their foods into hegemonic societies. In each case, foods have to be adapted to become accepted. The global market of national, ethnic, authentic, and traditional foods and ingredients locally imposes market values that legitimize people's claims to protect the existence and persistence of their food traditions. Issues such as modernization, industrialization, and the international market of edible commodities bring again into relief values such as nostalgia, memory, heritage, and authenticity as positive signifiers of taste preferences, with clear significance in the global market of edible commodities.

In Chapter 12, "Foreign Influences in Polish Culinary Taste during the Twentieth Century," Katarzyna Cwiertka takes us back to Europe. She argues that Poland has gone through different political transformations in which different powers imposed their representations of Polish people and affected national food dispositions. She argues that the construction of a national cuisine bridges regional and local differences spawning an identifiable "Polish" taste. She demonstrates how contemporary Polish cuisine is the amalgamation of tastes of the different groups that make up Polish society, and the industrialization of ingredients and food in general highlights the importance of some tastes such as smoked and acidic (from pickles): local recipes and food industries reciprocally influence each other. Back in Asia, in Chapter 13, "Kimchi's Transnational Journey: Tastes of Authenticity and Ambiguity," Sonia Ryang focuses on kimchi to illustrate the conceptual limitations of the notion of "national" cuisines. She discusses the transformations of kimchi through time, the historical impact of Japanese colonialism over Korea and Korean taste, and the travel of kimchi from Korea to Japan and then to the world. Hence, as a consequence of its global (and Japanese) appropriation, the Korean government obtained the inclusion of *kimjang* (making of kimchi) in the UNESCO list of Intangible Cultural Heritage, leading to its institutional standardization and the silencing of its local variability. This, she argues, forces local producers to strengthen their claims to authenticity. In Chapter 14, "Tasting Quinoa: From Indigenous Food to 'Healthy' US Dining," Christina Morris and Clare Sammells take us through a journey similar to that of kimchi. They show how an "indigenous," "traditional" ingredient in Bolivia, quinoa, which is locally associated with the diet of the poor rural inhabitants of the Andes, adopts a different commodity value in the United States and the world at large. Marketed as a "superfood," consumers do not always like the taste, but recognize it as healthy. In fact, in the Pennsylvania college where they conducted research, quinoa is associated with gender and class, losing the "indigenous" and "poor" qualifications the grain has in Bolivia. Here, in this college, although not exclusively, it is middle- and upper-class white women who are seen as favoring its consumption.

In Chapter 15, "The Taste of Mediterranean Diet: Food, Taste, and Identity in the Campania Region, South Italy," Rossella Galletti argues that the inclusion of the Mediterranean Diet in the UNESCO list of Intangible Cultural Heritage obeys global trends that tend to naturalize the ties between people and diet through time. Using information collected among elderly people in Cilento, Campania, she shows how local taste is rooted in an experience of poverty and hard peasant work, and food preferences among younger generations are changing as other ingredients not comprised in the paradigmatic definition of the Mediterranean Diet are gaining favor. This change creates a paradoxical situation whereby the diet of poor peasants is promoted by FAO as the possible solution to world hunger. Finally, in Chapter 16, "Soylent: The Cultural Politics of Functional and Tasteless Food," Andrew Ofstehage presents us with a puzzling case in which tastelessness, instead of a particular "authentic," "traditional" taste steers individuals' actions. Looking at the tech community in Silicon Valley, he describes a group of people who place a greater value on "nutrition" rather than on taste. The value here is placed not on a meal with which large groups of people can identify, but rather within a selected few who can bio-hack their bodies and whose "community" is found online rather than around the table. The politics they express is the power some people have to represent themselves as living "outside" social relations. While food and commensality depend on and reproduce social relations, for these consumers in Silicon Valley the important dimension is their anti-food stance (which, in turn, is based on an online "community"). Tastelessness becomes their mark of distinction vis-à-vis those who depend on the cultural aspects of taste preferences. To conclude the volume, in "Postface: Heritage Making after the US Century," Krishnendu Ray focuses on the ways in which heritage is used in the contemporary global arena to strengthen nationalist and ethnic politics leaden to the cultural, social, and even bodily erasure of different minorities.

In sum, this volume brings together eighteen specialists on food studies, from different disciplinary persuasions, to demonstrate that taste is not a subjective, "natural" power, humans have. Taste is shaped by everyday politics of gender, ethnicity, religion, nationality, regionalism, and other forms of cultural (self)representation. Hence, taste is not only intersubjective but is also shaped through negotiations between individuals, between groups of individuals, and between individual and social, cultural, economic, and political institutions. In some instances, UNESCO, and the recognition it grants, may be of paramount importance. In other cases, the globalized language of "heritage," "authenticity," "exoticism," and "otherness" has been appropriated locally, regionally, or nationally, and this makes it possible for people to validate their taste preferences.

Food, drinks, and cooking and serving practices are all vehicles for the actualization of power relations. We all hope that these chapters will be an invitation to look more closely into taste, often overlooked because of being thought of as a "natural" bodily property, instead of the social construct it actually is.

References

Adams, C. J. (2015 [1990]), *The Sexual Politics of Meat: A Feminist Vegetarian Critical Theory*, London: Bloomsbury Academic.

Ayora-Diaz, S. I. (2012), *Foodscapes, Foodfields and Identities in Yucatán*, Amsterdam and New York: Cedla and Berghahn.

Ayora-Diaz, S. I. (2013), "Yucatecan Food and the Postcolonial Politics of Representation," in G. Vargas-Cetina (ed.), *Anthropology and the Politics of Representation*, pp. 49–65, Tuscaloosa: University of Alabama Press.

Ayora-Diaz, S. I., ed. (2019), *Taste, Politics and Identities in Mexican Food*, London: Bloomsbury Academic.

Bourdieu, P. (1984), *Distinction: A Social Critique of the Judgment of Taste*, trans. R. Nice, Cambridge, MA: Harvard University Press.

Cohen, J. and P. K. Schuster (2019), "To Eat *chapulines* in Oaxaca, Mexico: One Food, Many Flavors," in S. I. Ayora-Diaz (ed.), *Taste, Politics and Identities in Mexican Food*, pp. 131–44, London: Bloomsbury Academic.

Counihan, C. and S. Højlund, eds. (2018), *Making Taste Public: Ethnographies of Food and the Senses*, London: Bloomsbury Academic.

Dürrschmidt, J. and Y. Knautt, eds. (2019), *Globalized Eating Cultures: Mediation and Mediatization*, Cham: Palgrave Macmillan.

Ferguson, P. P. (2004), *Accounting for Taste: The Triumph of French Cuisine*, Chicago: University of Chicago Press.

Haddaji, M., J. Albors-Garrigós, and P. García-Sigovia (2017), "Women Professional Progress to Chef's Position: Results on an International Survey," *Journal of Culinary Science and Technology*, August 2017. DOI: 10.1080/15428052.2017.1363109

Hall, S., J. Evans, and S. Nixon, eds. (2013 [1997]), *Representation*, Second edition, London: Sage.

Heldke, L. (2003), *Exotic Appetites: Ruminations of a Food Adventurer*, London: Routledge.

Johnston, J. and S. Baumann (2010), *Foodies: Democracy and Distinction in the Gourmet Foodscape*, London: Routledge.

Julier, A. P. (2013), *Eating Together: Food, Friendship, and Inequality*, Urbana: University of Illinois Press.

Leschziner, V. (2015), *At the Chef's Table: Culinary Creativity in Elite Restaurants*, Stanford: Stanford University Press.

Perullo, N. (2016), *Taste as Experience: The Philosophy and Aesthetics of Food*, New York: Columbia University Press.

Plakias, A. (2018), "Putting Our Morals Where Our Mouths Are: Disgust and Food Ethics," in N. Strohminger and V. Kumar (eds.), *The Moral Psychology of Disgust*, pp. 195–209, London: Rowman and Littlefield.

Ray, K. (2016), *The Ethnic Restaurateur*, London: Bloomsbury Academic.

Taussig, H. (2009), *In the Beginning Was the Meal: Social Experimentation and Early Christian Identity*, Minneapolis: Fortress Press.

Van Huis, A., J. Van Itterbeeck, H. Klunder, E. Mertens, A. Halloran, G. Muir, and P. Vantomme (2013), *Edible Insects: Future Prospects for Food and Security*, Rome: Food and Agricultural Organization of the United Nations (FAO).

Vargas-Cetina, G. (2013), "Introduction: Anthropology and the Politics of Representation," in G. Vargas-Cetina (ed.), *Anthropology and the Politics of Representation*, pp. 1–15, Tuscaloosa: University of Alabama Press.

Von Hoffmann, V. (2016), *From Gluttony to Enlightenment: The World of Taste in Early Modern Europe*, Urbana: University of Illinois Press.

Zhang, J. G. (2020), "Pinning Coronavirus on How Chinese People Eat Plays into Racist Assumptions," *Eater*, January 31, 2020. https://www.eater.com/2020/1/31/21117076/coronavirus-incites-racism-against-chinese-people-and-their-diets-wuhan-market, last accessed July 10, 2020.

Part I

Taste and the Politics of Identity

1

Food, Taste, and Identity in the Global Arena

Steffan Igor Ayora-Diaz

The Politics of Food, Taste, and the Senses

Every day we find evidence that food not only is meaningful but also has a close relationship to people's sense of identity and belonging, and thus, political importance. Despite its apparent banality, we find repeating assertions, often loaded with affective charge, of what a food *is* or *ought to be*. These pronouncements are often deployed as defense against perceived attacks on the integrity of an ethnic, regional, or national cuisine. A common global debate I find in social media is whether pineapple belongs in pizza or not. For most of my Italian friends (but not all), it is a disrespect to Italian cuisine and sense of taste. They just don't go together. Foreigners, in contrast, tend to see pizza as just a type of bread that accommodates whatever one pleases (and that is the way pizza delivery services market it). Something similar happens within academic circles when food specialists join local or national efforts to obtain UNESCO recognition of a food as intangible cultural heritage. This is particularly the case, as for example, when scholars debate whether the Mediterranean Diet has "ancestral" roots or not (Medina 2017). Food is evidently political, especially as it plays an important part strengthening the ties between a cuisine and different modes of identity (ranging from local to cosmopolitan).

It is in this context that we must remind ourselves that food is good to think with. The field of food studies has been rapidly growing during the last three decades. A number of volumes have provided directions to follow within anthropology, cultural studies, and history (e.g., Counihan and van Esterik 2013; Flandrin and Montanari 1999; Klein and Watson 2016; Lebesco and Naccarato 2018; Pilcher 2012). Remarkable monographs which became highly influential in spawning questions and shaping the field of food studies have included Sidney Mintz's *Sweetness and Power* (1985) and David Sutton's *Remembrance of Repasts* (2001) in anthropology, Harvey Levenstein's *Revolution at the Table* (1988), Priscilla P. Ferguson's *Accounting for Taste* (2004), and Rebecca Spang's *The Invention of the Restaurant* (2003) in history, to mention just a few. It would exceed the purpose of this chapter to review the bibliography pertaining to the entire field but there is no question that during the twenty-first century the literature on food studies has rapidly grown in the social sciences and the humanities (see, e.g., Ayora-Diaz 2015; Mintz and Du Bois 2002; Phillips 2006; Pilcher 2006).

Food and cooking, we agree now, contribute to structure everyday social relations and cultural practices through the inscription of meanings in their modes of production, circulation, and consumption. In addition, food and cooking have political symbolic meanings that both produce and mirror structures of social inequality. Multiple studies have shown how food is tied to different politics of identity in which it mediates the groups' representations of self and others (Banerjee-Dube 2016; Coleman 2011; Poulain 2017). Taking into account the global context, in this chapter I am concerned with discussing the part played by food and cooking in the structure of power and social inequality, and how they relate to the politics of identity in different societies; that is, how culinary practices are turned into mechanisms productive of difference between members and outsiders of any given group. One very important and generative aspect of taste—its social, cultural, and economic entanglements with social differentiation—has been pursued by scholars inspired by Bourdieu's *Distinction* (1984). His analysis privileges the ways in which the consumption of goods (food among them) inscribes and is inscribed by the consumers' social class. This conceptual position has influenced many authors focusing on the consumption of food and how these practices convey social distinction.

Focusing on the political dimension of food and cooking, Arjun Appadurai (1981) examined the ways in which food is used to shape power inequalities between men and women and among social and religious groups in Hindu India. He proposed that food plays an important part in social and religious conflicts in different arenas of social and political competition (1981: 495). Similarly, while advocating a more sensual ethnography (and an anthropology of the senses), Stoller and Olkes (1989) illustrated how a woman among the Songhay was able to defy, albeit momentarily, the gender and social unequal structure by intentionally cooking a defective sauce that, through its sour/bitter flavor, symbolically critiqued the prevalent gender dynamics of the group. The association between gender and food constitutes a privileged site in which unequal power structures are displayed and deserve close anthropological and historical attention (Counihan 1999; Counihan and Kaplan 1998; Pite 2013). Different meanings of food are, in the context of modern capitalism and postcolonial conditions, continuously deployed in strategies seeking to reposition different groups within society at large. Significant contributions have focused on the politics of identity to examine the relationship between food and cooking practices and ethnic, local, regional, and national identities (e.g., Farquhar 2002; Holtzman 2009; Ichijo, Johannes, and Ranta 2019; Ichijo and Ranta 2016; Roy 2010). Nonetheless, in these studies the *taste* of food is either downplayed in importance or not taken into account. Here I argue that it is important to recognize the contributions of the anthropology, history, and other sociocultural studies on the senses and being to bring the perception of flavor to prominence in scholarly work on food.

The Politics of Food and the Senses

An important challenge in the analysis of the politics of taste is the question of how to take into account the different ways in which the senses act jointly to produce, explain, and give meaning to our taste for food *and* the taste of food. In anthropology, David E. Sutton (2010) has argued for the development of a gustemological approach to recognize the synergic interaction of all the senses involved in cooking and eating and the part played by memory in the construction of our sociocultural and political perception of taste (see below). In consequence, we must recognize that a first dimension (and prejudice) of our shared understanding of the politics of the senses is their historically given position within a hierarchy. This positioning began with the writings of philosophers in ancient Greece, particularly Aristotle and Plato. It was later revisited by Roman and Christian thinkers and theologians. This hierarchy privileged the "distant" senses of sight and hearing, while taste, touch and smell, considered "proximal" senses, were undervalued. Scholars favored the distant senses because they provided an objective appraisal of the material world, while they considered the others subjective and, thus, unreliable (Agamben 2017; Gronow 1997; Howes and Classen 2014; Korsmeyer 1999). However, most authors usually recognize that this hierarchy is marred with ambiguities and ambivalence, and while continuously reproduced, it has also been questioned in different quarters. This hegemonic representation of the senses has led, among other things, to restricting the significance of "taste" to the description and marking of social distinctions, in Bourdieu's meaning of the term.

Calls for an anthropology, for historical, literary, social, and cultural studies of the senses, have progressively received a favorable response. However, with some exceptions (Ackerman 1990; Le Breton 2017; Jütte 2005), as a nascent interest, most studies have focused on the analysis of the social and cultural significance of each sense separate from the others. In fact, some monographs, such as those of Ackerman and Le Breton, even when discussing the five hegemonic senses, they examine them separately. Similarly, the different contributors in Howes' *Empire of the Senses* (2005b) call for taking the study of the senses seriously, and while the chapters in this volume claim for the recognition of this field of studies, their authors did not propose clear analytical strategies to integrate them. An exception to this limitation is Howes' own chapter on *hyperesthesia*, where he discusses how the production of commodities during late capitalism seeks to stimulate in the consumer as many senses as possible to make commodities desirable (Howes 2005a). Consequently, his approach privileges the material object and its capacity to invoke and stimulate all the senses, rather than analyzing how the senses act in common to know the world.

Many studies have been dedicated to the social, cultural, historical, and political aspects related to sound (Feld 2012; Samuels et al. 2010), touch (Classen 2012; Paterson 2007), smell (Classen 1993), taste (Korsmeyer 1999), and sight (Korsmeyer and Sutton 2011). The remaining question is how to approach the multisensorial perception of the world, and within it, of food. Fiona Macpherson (2011), from a philosophical angle, recognizes that even though for analytical purposes we have separated the senses, they act together. In the first place, she challenges the notion that we have five senses. She suggests that other senses are not properly recognized (such as proprioception and the sense of balance) and are usually excluded from discussion. Also, she points out, each sense is complex, as different modalities exist for each of them. For example, touch modalities include the perception of temperature, pressure, and pain, and a given experience of touch, as those who cook know, may involve all of these different modalities. Also, she argues, all senses act in common. We hear what people say, but some sounds are alike, and it is often the case that because we can see the other person's mouth, we can recognize the sound. Hence, we also need to take into account that we use different senses in our relation to the world and there are multi- and cross-modal sensory perceptions. This is similar to what anthropologist David Sutton has been calling *synesthesia*.

In his influential review, Sutton (2010) proposes that we adopt a *gustemological* approach. These, Sutton suggests, are "approaches that organize our understanding of a wide spectrum of cultural issues around taste and other sensory aspects of food" (p. 215). In this sense, he argues that the taste of food plays an important part in the construction of place. He suggests that we must also look at the synesthetic elements articulated by food. As he defines it, "synesthesia is not a faculty, but a rather cultivated skill, developed in particular practices and linguistic devices. Food is often a vehicle for such synesthetic practices" (p. 218). I would suggest that all chapters in this volume, even if not explicitly, adopt a synesthetic approach to the different food and culinary practices we describe. In fact, the multiple cooking practices, ingredients, and foods discussed in this book are shown to engage different bodily senses, including sensorial and social memories that give meaning to the taste of food and drinks. It is in these sense that, as Sutton argues (Korsmeyer and Sutton 2011), when we examine synesthetic experiences, we must also include the question of how memory supports and signifies the interaction among different bodily senses and our perception of food's taste (see also Holtzman 2006, 2009). Thus, for example, if I eat a *paella* today, I am relying on my senses of sight, smell, touch, and taste to experience the meal, but its taste is supplemented and given meaning by my memories of paellas I ate along with my family, with friends, and at renowned restaurants in different parts of the world. And for some, especially those who in their families learned to appreciate the *socarrat* (the burned rice that sticks to the bottom of the paella pan), the sound of a spoon scooping it out augments the experience of the meal's taste.

Aesthetics and the Politics of Taste

I also argue that our current concern with taste must be understood within the context of our changing understanding of "aesthetics" (Ayora-Diaz, Vargas Cetina, and Fernández Repetto 2016). First, I must point out that Bourdieu's important work on *Distinction* contributed to shape much of the discussion around the value of food as a marker of social status. In general, I suggest that Bourdieu shares the understanding that aesthetics places first and foremost the values of beauty and the sublime. It is the recognition and possession of these attributes that distinguish between the music, clothing, and food preferences of the elites and the working classes. Following suit, many studies have looked at how the preference for different types of food ingredients and cuisines mark consumers as belonging to specific social classes. In the discussion as to whether food can be seen as an art, or as part of art, we can find affirmative answers when food is understood as embodying the senses of beauty and the sublime, or sometimes because it is endowed with shocking value (Kirshemblatt-Gimblett

1999; Sweeney 2018; Vercelloni 2016). Hence, haute cuisine, *nouvelle cuisine*, fusion, molecular, and other modernist innovative cuisines are consumed by people seeking beauty, wonder (even shock), and novelty in the meals, while, in contrast, working and lower social classes favor filling, "traditional" meals (e.g., Ferguson 2004; Finn 2017; Lane 2014; Leschziner 2015; Strong 2011). When the upper classes choose to consume a food seen as tied to a "popular," peasant, or immigrant culinary code, they mark it with the sign value of upper-class distinction, often adapting it to fit the dominant modernist aesthetics, and by consuming it they make it unavailable, or expensive and rare, for the social classes that had hitherto depended on it.

Nevertheless, during the last thirty years, other approaches to aesthetics have emerged challenging the hegemonic primacy of the sublime and beautiful. Leddy (2012) remarks that even in Kant's work there was an appreciation for the everyday sensual pleasures, and thus an aesthetics of the everyday. Other authors have sought to explain the ways in which aesthetics can be used to encompass sensual-sensorial experiences not usually included among the dominant values (Featherstone 1991). The need to address everyday aesthetics has been tied to the growth in consumer studies. In this context, Yukio Saito (2007) argues that an everyday aesthetics generates multiple codes that make possible the articulation and expression of emotions and the experience of beauty in the material world along lines different from canonical philosophical definitions of the beautiful. Hence, we find an aesthetic sense of appreciation when people define objects, practices, and other stuff, with values such as cute, quaint, clean, ordered, interesting, eccentric, bizarre, and kitsch (e.g., Harris 2000; Ngai 2012; Sturken 2007). Yet, we must also note that "kitsch" and some of the other values just listed may contribute to maintain the class-distinctive meaning of these terms, as when the "food of modernity" (Jell-O, spam, canned fruits, and other industrialized edibles) or the food of subordinate classes is characterized as "kitsch" (Sheldon 2004).

In this context, we need to reclaim the concept of everyday aesthetics to incorporate in the analysis the sensual-sensorial dimension of food-related practices. Following a long tradition of thought that focus on praxis as politics (Adorno 1973; Habermas 1973; Heller 1984), I consider that these food-related practices are eminently political because they reinforce social differences and inequality. For example, there is a strong visual component involved in selecting our fruit, meat, and other produce we harvest or purchase for our consumption. There is, of course, a history of visual manipulation on the part of the food industry that has helped to institute the color of "freshness" and that reproduce gender politics when it ascribes women with the power (and duty) to identify and select the "right" products for the family kitchen and table (Hisano 2019). Sight is supplemented by the sense of touch, as when in different countries we are allowed to touch the produce in markets and supermarkets or must touch them in the field to establish ripeness and the right time to harvest. When a person must cook, touch turns out to be important during the selection of ingredients, for which we need to feel their texture, and during the process of cooking, when we feel them to decide whether or not they have reached the right texture or density (of a sauce, of bread dough, of mayonnaise, or a stew, for example). In addition, while cooking we can perceive the aroma of spices, meats, and other ingredients. And we can also derive pleasure from the material characteristics of a knife sharp or dull, a wooden board, a copper casserole, or a cast-iron skillet someone inherited from her great-grandmother. In their materiality they possess color, weight, and surface traits, which may impart flavor upon our meals. This becomes most relevant when, as Perez (2019) explains, food cooked in earthen pots is associated with "authenticity" among Oaxacan migrants, or when in India, as several domestic cooks explained to me in Mumbai, Delhi, Jaipur, and Agra in 2018, people choose specific metal dishes and utensils to cook and then serve particular foods. We humans hear the water or broth when boiling or simmering, hear–see–smell the fat change when frying, and see–touch–hear–smell the mortar and pestle when grinding spices or herbs.

All of these everyday culinary acts have an aesthetic dimension that is often disregarded probably, and partly, because cooking is usually women's work performed in the private, enclosed space of the kitchen. These sensual-sensorial, hyperesthetic experiences are undoubtedly supplemented by the memory of cooking, either by the grandmother or parent or by the chef at a school or the open kitchen of a restaurant, as well as by remembrances of the commensality events in which these meals were or are consumed and shared. The effects of these memories on taste can also be illustrated by the reading of cookbooks that stimulate our memory of meals and suggest old, new, or improvised cooking practices (Counihan 2004; Sutton 2001). Yet, even when we acknowledge the everyday aesthetics of food, we also know that within society at large food critics, be they professional or amateur, tend to privilege the visual aspects of plating and food composition served at the table in places like *elBulli*, *NOMA*, or the *Osteria Franciscana*, paradigmatic examples of beautiful and novel food. It is in this context that the figure of the amateur can, in some instances, be used to understand the active process of acquiring expertise and "taste," in the double sense of a differentiating knowledge and the acquisition of the ability (and practice) to perceive, identify, and produce new flavors in food (Hennion 2005; Tell and Hennion 2004).

Food Taste and the Politics of Identity

Food, both as ingredients and as gastronomic codes, has been found tied to different politics of identity that sustain regionalism, nationalism, ethnic, and other local identities. For example, different authors have demonstrated the importance of a single ingredient for national identities: rice, in different varieties, is fundamental, among others, for Japanese and Vietnamese identities, corn and maize for indigenous Mesoamerican culture, and corn and wheat have had wavering importance in the construction of Mexican National identity (Avieli 2012; Ohnuki-Tierney 1994; Pilcher 1998; Sandstrom 1991). Also, in the context of global mobility, certain foods have become clichéd markers of national and ethnic identity: sushi for the Japanese, pizza and pasta for Italians, paella for Spaniards, kimchi for Koreans, chop suey for the Chinese, pad Thai for Thailanders, and curry for Indians (La Cecla 2007; Issenberg 2007; Medina 2005; Padoongpatt 2017; Pettid 2008; Ray and Srinivas 2012; Roberts 2002; Ryang 2015). A few national cuisines and gastronomic systems have also been granted this generalized recognition: French, Italian, Japanese, Chinese, Korean,

Indian, and Thai are now so common in the global market that they, for knowing consumers, transcend their identification with single meals and are recognized as distinct gastronomic codes encompassing a variety of dishes; amateur aficionados and foodies even aim at recognizing regional differences within these larger cuisines (Cwiertka 2006, 2012; Ferguson 2004; Mennell 1985; Padoongpatt 2017; Parasecoli 2014; Spencer 2002).

The performance of cultural politics through food as "authentic" and/or "traditional" is crossed by the historically constructed personal and group preferences in food taste, aromas, modes of preparation, and symbolic meanings in at least four different but interrelated ways (presented here in an arbitrary order, since I am not assuming that they keep a lineal relation, but rather that they reciprocally produce each other):

- First, regional or national cuisines are presented and represented as "authentic" in the world market of food and gastronomy, often veiling the multinational origins of their ingredients.
- Second, state officers and cultural promoters purposefully seek to define a cuisine as "national," generally silencing the power struggles within which the diversity of regional and local cuisines and of particular dishes must seek to be repositioned and redefined. As a result, colonial relations, including internal colonialism, are hidden in the particular dishes and groups of dishes that are made to stand for "national traditions" of cuisine and food. For example, in the definition of *washoku* as the "authentic" Japanese cuisine, foreign influences are assimilated into the hegemonic gastronomic code.
- Third, the personal or group affirmation of food preferences draws boundaries around *naturalized* culinary inclinations attributed to different national groups. For instance, at the beginning of the twentieth century, northern Italians were though to prefer polenta, while southerners were thought to favor the consumption of pasta.
- Fourth, ways of cooking and consuming food may be based on a distinction between "modern and rational" systems, on the one hand, and, on the other, what seems to be dishes that come assorted in configurations lacking an internal structure. For example, the historically recent trend that has located the innovation of Spanish cooking in Catalunya and the Basque country turns, by the same movement, all local and regional cuisines into unsystematic cooking traditions.

Of course, these representations are often contested, but kept in the social imaginary of these societies. In consequence, consumers' and critics' recognition of "authenticity," "national gastronomies," "local gastronomies," and "ethnic food" preferences engage in profoundly political practices of cultural representation involving one or more of these dimensions, sometimes purposely. These political aspects of food are also closely tied to the politics of identity manifested at different social scales: local, ethnic, regional, national, and migrant culinary traditions that depart from their "original" versions in their places of origin. This political dimension forces us to look at and examine different processes that occur on a global scale, albeit with localized manifestations.

Mobility and the Identity Politics of Food

All throughout humanity's history people have moved from one place to another. While moving they carry the foods they know and favor. During the expansion of global capitalism and empires, spices and different fruits and animals were imported into, or extracted from, different regions of the world. Today we are enjoying (some are fearing) the culinary effects of the international and global displacement of people. Although important for the people who carry them, most often these different culinary traditions have had to go through slow processes of adaptation, adoption and appropriation (Denker 2003; Gabaccia 1998; Ray and Srinivas 2012; Roberts 2002; Wu and Cheung 2002). The process of inscribing "foreign" cuisines in new sites is not an easy one, and it is often laden with conflicts that signal struggles in a field that recognizes or denies recognition of the immigrants' and their food's identity and cultural value (Garcia, Dupuis, and Mitchell 2017).

The cuisines of immigrants, even when granted a different value, are now part of the global foodscape and have become part of the gastronomic-culinary choices for consumers everywhere. As Lisa Heldke (2003) argues, in most cities we have access to the food of the "other" and engage in a mode of local culinary tourism whereby consumers are in a constant quest for "exotic" meals—even though what one day is exotic, in a few years becomes localized and exotic-no-more. Some foods that consumers experienced first at a restaurant may become integrated in the domestic menu, as the home cook purchases, say a wok, bamboo ladles, Chinese noodles and sauces, and cookbooks of Chinese recipes to cook at home. Culinary tourism was a nascent category at the beginning of this century. It was taken for granted that when tourists travel, they must eat. However, a new group of consumers has emerged in larger numbers: people who travel to different places with the main purpose of consuming the food in its place of origin (Hjalager and Richards 2002; Long 2010). And yet, it is more common to practice culinary tourism within the boundaries of one's place of residence, where an individual can exercise different modes of gastro-nomadism (the practice of consuming food from many different gastronomic traditions) and gastro-sedentarism (consuming food only thought of as "local") (Ayora-Diaz, Vargas Cetina, and Fernández Repetto 2016: 136–43).

Within this global foodscape, consumers appreciate the exotic value of meals, but also seek, more often, authentic versions of ethnic, national, local, and regional cuisines. The Parisian *gastronomade*, who navigates the foodscape following *Michelin* stars, pursues authentic restaurants and meals in French rural villages. He or she belongs with the consumers claiming connoisseurship. Today, followers of electronic apps such as Tripadvisor, Yelp, Tinder, Twitter, and Instagram pursue the same goal following other consumers' opinions when choosing a restaurant where to eat, and often, among them, "authenticity" is a highly valued recognition (Rousseau 2012). We inhabit a globalized culinary-gastronomic foodscape in which the past becomes highly valued, as modern consumers structure their worldview with a nostalgic approach to food—the food of our forebearers, or the food of the countryside, or the food of "ethnic" groups unpolluted by "modernity" (Berliner 2020; Comaroff and Comaroff 2009).

The Politics of Heritage

The articulation of modern values and nostalgia, with a growing market for cultural objects branded as authentic and ethnic and for exotic cultural practices, finds institutional expression in the UNESCO lists of material and intangible heritages. As David Lowenthal (1998) has argued, contemporary societies are engaged, among other things, in what he calls a "heritage crusade." Present-day political groups seek to validate their identity and self-representation through UNESCO's recognition. The inclusion of cultural culinary practices in the UNESCO list of Intangible Cultural Heritage mobilizes and forces the negotiation of people's ambivalence and ambiguity regarding foods and their social, cultural, and political meanings (Ayora-Diaz 2019a). While I cannot discuss here the intricacies of these politics of heritage (see, for example, Bak-Geller Corona, Matta, and de Sureiman 2019; Brulotte and Di Giovine 2014; Brumann and Berliner 2016), it is important to point out the valuation of different ingredients, meals, culinary procedures, and gastronomic traditions as *unique*, in addition to their perceived status as endangered. As the chapters in this volume demonstrate, producers and consumers in different societies emphasize the uniqueness of their foods, culinary practices, and preferences. This uniqueness can be rooted in the territory that favors certain virtues in the ingredients, in the cooking techniques, technologies, and practices, and in the particularities of a people's culinary or gastronomic code. Karpik (2010: 3), for example, argues that as consumers in the current capitalist economy we are flooded with a mass of objects, and, in response, producers must highlight the uniqueness of their goods, seeking to position them over other "undifferentiated" objects. At the same time, consumers must also come in agreement while defining and selecting objects that they can recognize as "unique."

In the world of culinary and gastronomic heritage, products must be characterized by unique traits to be granted recognition. Their heritageization underlines what makes the product "special" and different from other similar objects. The literature on such products is growing, and thus we can find that cheese in the Alps is a unique product; that the Neapolitan pizza has been recognized on the grounds of detailed and certified ingredients, techniques, and technologies; that there is an authentic Japanese cuisine (*washoku*) distinguished from foreign foods within Japan; that French commensality is unique as well; and that Mexican cuisine (the Michoacan paradigm, in fact) is an authentically indigenous culinary system in need of protection, and the Mediterranean Diet is a universally valuable culinary system (Ayora-Diaz 2019a; Cwiertka 2020; Grasseni 2017; Moro 2014; UNESCO 2020). The "authenticity" of many of these "traditions" has been challenged, so their meaning must be constantly renegotiated in a world in which they are also accorded economic importance by the people who keep or reinvent these traditions. Here as in other volumes we look at the strategies deployed by different groups in their attempt to obtain recognition for their food as their own cultural heritage (Ayora-Diaz 2019b). The recognition they seek does not have to come necessarily from UNESCO, but from their own nation-state, or from consumers in the market of "traditional," "ethnic" specialty foods.

Local people articulate differently politics for the recognition of their food as valuable. The notion of *terroir* has become fundamental in this local food politics

(Trubek 2008). Often, a meal or ingredient can be found in different places, but local activists may claim that the soil, the water, the air, give their food a special flavor, color, aroma, texture that makes it different *and better* than those of other regions. Italy, for example, has a long list of products with certified origin. As Capatti and Montanari (2000) argue, different regions are recognized by the vegetables, fish, or meat that they produce (in 2005, Davide Paolini published an encyclopedia, 681 pages-long, of Italian "typical" products). Counihan (2018), for example, has shown how different claims in favor of Sardinian local foods are centered on the *terroir*, and Smith (2016) has examined the importance of these claims for legitimizing the product and identity of winegrowers in the Languedoc in France. The sites where terroir is invoked are abundant, and several examples are discussed in this volume.

Conclusion: Taste is a Political Issue

In this chapter, I have argued that taste and the political aspects of taste are constituted through the complex articulation of different social, cultural, political, and economic phenomena and processes. The taste of food is the outcome of cooks' labor in bringing together history and memory, social relations, political inequalities, as well as multiple meanings mobilized by ingredients, techniques, and technologies and meals that convey a certain taste (or sometimes, disguise it). Hence, taste should not be reduced to only one of its defining dimensions. Perceiving flavor and the taste of food is possible not only because human bodies have the sensorial apparatuses necessary for the perception of flavors, colors, aromas, textures, and sounds (among other possible modes of perception) but also because we have the cognitive abilities to sort out our physical experiences and the psychological instruments to make sense of this experience. However, I (like the contributors to this volume) have chosen to bracket these phenomena. We are examining the politics of taste, a politics that we need to understand as tied to modes of cultural, social, and political self-representation and images of various "others." Thus, we understand that, in addition to the general opportunities afforded by the study of food, we can understand *taste* as a fundamental node that articulates different modes of structural and power inequality. Taste depends on perception but can also be a tool employed to maintain or transform sociocultural and political distinctions. In this sense, taste/flavor has different meanings that supplement each other: it is our ability to perceive edible and inedible foods, to distinguish the foods of different groups, to support a hierarchy of groups on the base of taste perceptions, to articulate senses of belonging and exclusion, and, of course, to symbolically, culturally, economically, and politically place some social groups above others.

Importantly, to recognize the political significance of taste, we have to position ourselves inside the field of social, cultural, historical studies of the senses. Profiting from the contributions of colleagues within the field, we can now look at how different bodily, but also socially meaningful senses are put in action to produce and reproduce the taste of a food, or the elements that constitute a culinary or gastronomic grammar that founds local, ethnic, regional, national, or cosmopolitan identities. At the same time, by analyzing the political importance of food taste, we take into account the aesthetic value of meals, ingredients, food production, and consumption. There is a sensual aspect to the production of a meal. Cooking something "right" implies achieving colors, aromas, flavors, textures, and sounds that invoke an everyday aesthetics of the meal.

But a meal is never just a meal. The right taste (as in perceiving the sensual and sensorial attributes of food) and recognizing good taste (as in manners and social distinction) invokes feelings of belonging and exclusion into differently scaled groups: being Italian from the south means that to cook seafood right you do not use milk, butter, or cheese, and adding any of them onto you food means that you do not know how to cook or eat something, marking you as an outsider, a non-Italian. This can be followed down to small localities where small differences in taste preference matter to distinguish between someone who is from the village, or from outside. Nationalisms, regionalisms, localisms, and ethnic and religious identities often base their uniqueness in the ingredients chosen, or the techniques and technologies used to prepare a meal, or the terroir that imparts flavor on meats and vegetable products, but also in the final taste that the cook achieves—which, in addition, corresponds or not with that expected from the subject's memories of previous meals. In these instances, gender, age, ethnicity, and religion can be mobilized to intensify the political importance to food choices and culinary practices that lead to certain tastes. While sometimes this level of identification can be used to justify claims to have one's food and food taste institutionally recognized as heritage, this is not always the case. Often, regardless of level of state or UNESCO's recognition, what local people seek is the recognition from among those who consume their food, that it is unique, and that the taste of their food is tied to their values as a group, and that in this recognition they also found their politics of identity. In all cases, cooking and consuming a meal are profoundly political acts, full of meaning as much as they are full of taste. It is by analyzing these political dimensions that we all, in this volume, hope to contribute to this conversation.

References

Ackerman, D. (1990), *A Natural History of the Senses*, New York: Vintage.

Adorno, T. (1973 [1966]), *Negative Dialectics*, London: Routledge and Kegan Paul.

Agamben, G. (2017), *Taste*, trans. C. Francis, London: Seagull Books.

Appadurai, A. (1981), "Gastropolitics in Hindu South Asia," *American Ethnologist* 8(3): 494–511.

Avieli, N. (2012), *Rice Talks: Food and Community in a Vietnamese Town*, Bloomington: Indiana University Press.

Ayora-Diaz, S. I. (2015), "Food in Anthropology," in J. D. Wright (ed.), *International Encyclopedia of the Social and Behavioral Sciences*, Second edition, vol. 9, pp. 290–5, Oxford: Elsevier.

Ayora-Diaz, S. I. (2019a), "Postfacio: Las ambivalencias del patrimonio culinario y alimentario," in S. Bak-Geller Corona, R. Matta, and C.-E. de Sureiman (eds.), *Patrimonios alimentarios. Entre consensos y tensiones*, pp. 207–19, San Luis Potosí: El Colegio de San Luis – IRD Editions.

Ayora-Diaz, S. I., ed. (2019b), *Taste, Politics, and Identities in Mexican Food*, London: Bloomsbury Academic.

Ayora-Diaz, S. I., G. Vargas Cetina, and F. Fernández Repetto (2016), *Cocina, Música y Comunicación. Tecnologías y estética en el Yucatán contemporáneo*, Merida: Ediciones de la Universidad Autónoma de Yucatán.

Bak-Geller Corona, S., R. Matta, and C.-E. de Sureiman, eds. (2019), *Patrimonios alimentarios. Entre consensos y tensiones*, San Luis Potosí: El Colegio de San Luis – IRD Editions.

Banerjee-Dube, I., ed. (2016), *Cooking Cultures: Convergent Histories of Food and Cooking*, Cambridge: Cambridge University Press.

Berliner, D. (2020), *Losing Culture. Nostalgia, Heritage, and Our Accelerated Times*, trans. D. Horsfall, New Brunswick: Rutgers University Press.

Bourdieu, P. (1984), *Distinction: A Social Critique of the Judgment of Taste*, trans. R. Nice, Cambridge, MA: Harvard University Press.

Brulotte, R. and M. A. Di Giovine (2014), *Edible Identities: Food as Cultural Heritage*, Surrey: Ashgate.

Brumann, C. and D. Berliner, eds. (2016), *World Heritage on the Ground: Ethnographic Perspectives*, New York: Berghahn.

Capatti, A. and M. Montanari (2000), *La cucina italiana. Storia di una cultura*, Bari: Laterza.

Classen, C. (1993), *Worlds of Sense: Exploring the Senses in History and Across Cultures*, London: Routledge.

Classen, C. (2012), *The Deepest Sense: A Cultural History of Touch*, Urbana: University of Illinois Press.

Coleman, L., ed. (2011), *Food: Ethnographic Encounters*, London: Bloomsbury Academic.

Comaroff, J. L. and J. Comaroff (2009), *Ethnicity Inc.*, Chicago: University of Chicago Press.

Counihan, C. (1999), *The Anthropology of Food and the Body: Gender, Meaning, and Power*, New York: Routledge.

Counihan, C. (2004), *Around the Tuscan Table: Food, Family, and Gender in Twentieth Century Florence*, London: Routledge.

Counihan, C. (2018), *Italian Food Activism in Urban Sardinia: Place, Taste, and Community*, London: Bloomsbury Academic.

Counihan, C. M. and S. L. Kaplan, eds. (1998), *Food and Gender: Identity and Power*, Amsterdam: Harwood Academic Publishers.

Counihan, C. M. and P. Van Esterik, eds. (2013), *Food and Culture: A Reader*, New York: Routledge.

Cwiertka, K. J. (2006), *Modern Japanese Cuisine: Food, Power and National Identity*, London: Reaktion Books.

Cwiertka, K. J. (2012), *Cuisine, Colonialism and Cold War: Food in Twentieth Century Korea*, London: Reaktion Books.

Cwiertka, K. J. (2020), *Branding Japanese Food: From Meibutsu to Washoku*, Honolulu: University of Hawaii Press.

Denker, J. (2003), *The World on a Plate. A Tour through the History of America's Ethnic Cuisines*, Boulder: Westview Press.

Farquhar, J. (2002), *Appetites: Food and Sex in Post-Socialist China*, Durham: Duke University Press.

Featherstone, M. (1991), *Consumer Culture and Postmodernism*, London: Sage.

Feld, S. (2012 [1982]), *Sound and Sentiment: Birds, Weeping, Poetics, and Song in Kaluli Expressions*, Third edition, Durham: Duke University Press.

Ferguson, P. P. (2004), *Accounting for Taste: The Triumph of French Cuisine*, Chicago: University of Chicago Press.

Finn, S. M. (2017), *Discriminating Taste: How Class Anxiety Created the American Food Revolution*, New Brunswick: Rutgers University Press.

Flandrin, J.-L. and M. Montanari, eds. (1999), *Food: A Culinary History*, New York: Columbia University Press.

Gabaccia, D. R. (1998), *We Are What We Eat: Ethnic Food and the Making of Americans*, Cambridge, MA: Harvard University Press.

Garcia, M., E. M. Dupuis, and D. Mitchell, eds. (2017), *Food Across Borders*, New Brunswick: Rutgers University Press.

Grasseni, C. (2017), *The Heritage Arena: Reinventing Cheese in the Italian Alps*, New York: Berghahn.

Gronow, J. (1997), *The Sociology of Taste*, London: Routledge.

Habermas, J. (1973), *Theory and Praxis*, Boston: Beacon Press.

Harris, D. (2000), *Cute, Quaint, Hungry and Romantic: The Aesthetics of Consumerism*, Lexington: Da Capo Press.

Heldke, L. (2003), *Exotic Appetites: Ruminations of a Food Adventurer*, London: Routledge.

Heller, A. (1984 [1970]), *Everyday Life*, London: Routledge and Kegan Paul.

Hennion, A. (2005), "Pragmatics of Taste," in M. D. Jacobs and N. W. Hanrahan (eds.), *The Blackwell Companion to the Sociology of Culture*, pp. 131–44, Oxford: Blackwell.

Hisano, A. (2019), *Visualizing Taste: How Business Changed the Look of What You Eat*, Cambridge, MA: Harvard University Press.

Hjalager, A.-M. and G. Richards, eds. (2002), *Gastronomy and Tourism*, London: Routledge.

Holtzman, J. (2006), "Food and Memory," *Annual Review of Anthropology* 35: 361–78.

Holtzman, J. (2009), *Uncertain Tastes. Memory, Ambivalence, and the Politics of Eating in Samburu, Northern Kenya*, Berkeley: University of California Press.

Howes, D. (2005a), "HYPERESTHESIA, or the Sensual logic of Late Capitalism," in D. Howes (ed.), *Empire of the Senses: The Sensual Culture Reader*, pp. 281–303, Oxford: Berg.

Howes, D., ed. (2005b), *Empire of the Senses: The Sensual Culture Reader*, Oxford: Berg.

Howes, D. and C. Classen (2014), *Ways of Sensing: Understanding the Senses in Society*, London: Routledge.

Ichijo, A. and R. Ranta, eds. (2016), *Food, National Identity and Nationalism: From Everyday to Global Politics*, New York: Palgrave-Macmillan.

Ichijo, A., V. Johannes, and R. Ranta, eds. (2019), *The Emergence of National Food. The Dynamics of Food and Nationalism*, London: Bloomsbury Academic.

Issenberg, S. (2007), *The Sushi Economy: Globalization and the Making of a Modern Delicacy*, New York: Penguin.

Jütte, R. (2005), *The History of the Senses: From Antiquity to Cyberspace*, Cambridge: Polity Press.

Karpik, L. (2010), *Valuing the Unique: The Economics of Singularities*, Princeton: Princeton University Press.

Kirshemblatt-Gimblett, B. (1999), "Playing to the Senses: Food as a Performance Medium," *Performance Research* 4(1): 1–30.

Klein, J. A. and J. L. Watson, eds. (2016), *The Handbook of Food and Anthropology*, London: Bloomsbury Academic.

Korsmeyer, C. (1999), *Making Sense of Taste: Food and Philosophy*, Ithaca: Cornell University Press.

Korsmeyer, C. and D. Sutton (2011), "The Sensory Experience of Food," *Theory, Culture and Society* 14(4): 461–75.

La Cecla, F. (2007), *Pasta and Pizza*, Chicago: Prickly Paradigm Press.

Lane, C. (2014), *The Cultivation of Taste: Chefs and the Organization of Fine Dining*, Oxford: Oxford University Press.

Lebesco, K. and P. Naccarato, eds. (2018), *The Bloomsbury Handbook of Food and Popular Culture*, London: Bloomsbury Academic.

Le Breton, D. (2017 [2006]), *Sensing the World: An Anthropology of the Senses*, London: Bloomsbury Academic.

Leddy, T. (2012), *The Extraordinary and the Ordinary: The Aesthetics of Everyday Life*, Toronto: Broadview Press.

Leschziner, V. (2015), *At the Chef's Table: Culinary Creativity in Elite Restaurants*, Stanford: Stanford University Press.

Levenstein, H. (1988), *Revolution at the Table: The Transformation of the American Diet*, Oxford: Oxford University Press.

Long, L., ed. (2010), *Culinary Tourism*, Lexington: University of Kentucky Press.

Lowenthal, D. (1998), *The Heritage Crusade and the Spoils of History*, Cambridge: Cambridge University Press.

Macpherson, F. (2011), "Introduction: Individuating the Senses," in F. Macpherson (ed.), *The Senses: Classic and Contemporary Philosophical Perspectives*, pp. 3–43, Oxford: Oxford University Press.

Medina, F. X. (2005), *Food Culture in Spain*, Westport: Greenwood Press.

Medina, F. X. (2017), "Reflexiones sobre el patrimonio y la alimentación desde las perspectivas cultural y turística," *Anales de Antropología* 51: 106–13.

Mennell, S. (1985), *All Manners of Food: Eating and Taste in England and France from the Middle Ages to the Present*, Oxford: Basil-Blackwell.

Mintz, S. (1985), *Sweetness and Power: The Place of Sugar in Modern History*, New York: Penguin.

Mintz, S. and C. M. Du Bois (2002), "The Anthropology of Food and Eating," *Annual Review of Anthropology* 31: 99–119.

Moro, E. (2014), *La dieta mediterranea. Mito e storia di uno stile di vita*, Bologna: Il Mulino.

Ngai, S. (2012), *Our Aesthetic Categories: Zany, Cute, Interesting*, Cambridge, MA: Harvard University Press.

Ohnuki-Tierney, E. (1994), *Rice as Self: Japanese Identities through Time*, Princeton: Princeton University Press.

Padoongpatt, M. (2017), *Flavors of Empire: Food and the Making of Thai America*, Berkeley: University of California Press.

Paolini, D. (2005), *Enciclopedia dei Prodotti tipici d'Italia*, Milan: Garzanti Libri.

Parasecoli, F. (2014), *Al Dente: A History of Food in Italy*, London: Reaktion Books.

Paterson, M. (2007), *The Senses of Touch: Haptics, Affects and Technologies*, Oxford: Berg.

Pérez, R. (2019), "The Taste of Oaxaca: It's to Die For!" in S. I. Ayora-Diaz (ed.), *Taste, Politics, and Identities in Mexican Food*, pp. 147–60, London: Bloomsbury Academic.

Pettid, M. J. (2008), *Korean Cuisine: An Illustrated History*, London: Reaktion Books.

Phillips, L. (2006), "Food and Globalization," *Annual Review of Anthropology* 35: 37–57.

Pilcher, J. M. (1998), *Que vivan los tamales! Food and the Making of National Identities*, Albuquerque: University of New Mexico Press.

Pilcher, J. M. (2006), *Food in World History*, London: Routledge.

Pilcher, J. M., ed. (2012), *The Oxford Handbook of Food History*, Oxford: Oxford University Press.

Pite, R. E. (2013), *Creating a Common Table in Twentieth Century Argentina: Doña Petrona, Women and Food*, Chapel Hill: University of North Carolina Press.

Poulain, J.-P. (2017 [2002]), *The Sociology of Food: Eating and the Place of Food in Society*, trans. A. Dörr, London: Bloomsbury Academic.

Ray, K. and T. Srinivas, eds. (2012), *Curried Cultures: Globalization, Food, and South Asia*, Berkeley: University of California Press.

Roberts, J. A. G. (2002), *China to Chinatown: Chinese Food in the West*, London: Reaktion Books.

Rousseau, S. (2012), *Food and Social Media: You Are What You Tweet*, Lanham: Altamira Press.

Roy, P. (2010), *Alimentary Tracts: Appetites, Aversions, and the Postcolonial*, Durham: Duke University Press.

Ryang, S. (2015), *Eating Korean in America: Gastronomic Ethnography of Authenticity*, Honolulu: University of Hawaii Press.

Saito, Y. (2007), *Everyday Aesthetics*, Oxford: Oxford University Press.

Samuels, D. W., L. Meintjes, A. M. Ochoa, and T. Porcello (2010), "Soundscapes: Toward a Sounded Anthropology," *Annual Review of Anthropology* 39: 329–45.

Sandstrom (1991), *Corn Is Our Blood: Culture and Ethnic Identity in a Contemporary Aztec Indian Village*, Norman: University of Oklahoma Press.

Sheldon, G. (2004), "Crimes and Punishments: Class and Connotations of Kitschy American Food and Drink," *Studies in Popular Culture* 27(1): 61–72.

Smith, A. W. M. (2016), *Terror and Terroir: The Winegrowers of the Languedoc and Modern France*, Manchester: Manchester University Press.

Spang, R. (2003), *The Invention of the Restaurant: Paris and Modern Gastronomic Culture*, Cambridge, MA: Harvard University Press.

Spencer, C. (2002), *British Food: An Extraordinary Thousand Years of History*, New York: Columbia University Press.

Stoller, P. and C. Olkes (1989), "The Taste of Ethnographic Things," in P. Stoller, *The Taste of Ethnographic Things: The Senses in Anthropology*, pp. 15–34, Philadelphia: University of Pennsylvania Press.

Strong, J., ed. (2011), *Educated Tastes: Food, Drink, and Connoisseur Culture*, Lincoln: Nebraska University Press.

Sturken, M. (2007), *Tourists of History: Memory, Kitsch, and Consumerism from Oklahoma City to Ground Zero*, Durham: Duke University Press.

Sutton, D. E. (2001), *Remembrance of Repasts: An Anthropology of Food and Memory*, Oxford: Berg.

Sutton, D. E. (2010), "Food and the Senses," *Annual Review of Anthropology* 39: 209–23.

Sweeney, K. W. (2018), *The Aesthetics of Food: The Philosophical Debate about What We Eat and Drink*, London: Rowman and Littlefield.

Tell, G. and A. Hennion (2004), "Discovering Quality or Performing Taste? A Sociology of the Amateur," in M. Harvey, A. McMeekin, and A. Warde (eds.), *Qualities of Food*, pp. 19–37, Manchester: Manchester University Press.

Trubek, A. B. (2008), *The Taste of Place: A Cultural Journey into Terroir*, Berkeley: University of California Press.

UNESCO (2020), "Intangible Cultural Heritage," website https://ich.unesco.org/en/lists, last accessed June 23, 2020.

Vercelloni, L. (2016 [2005]), *The Invention of Taste: A Cultural Account of Desire, Delight, and Disgust in Fashion, Food and Art*, London: Bloomsbury.

Wu, D. Y. H. and S. C. H. Cheung, eds. (2002), *The Globalization of Chinese Food*, Honolulu: University of Hawaii Press.

2

Centralization and Standardization of Taste

Dashi in Japan

Yoshimi Osawa

In 2017, the Japanese Ministry of Education, Culture, Sports, Science and Technology (MEXT) announced the revised National Curriculum Standards for kindergarten, elementary, and lower secondary schools. This revision stipulates new provisions in the field of home economics in elementary schools, one of which is to teach the intrinsic role of *dashi* (i.e., broth) in Japanese cuisine (*washoku*). Current home economics courses in elementary schools include miso soup preparation, and children only learn how to make dashi in the process of learning how to cook miso soup. The new guidelines aim for a more in-depth study of dashi that involves not only learning how it is made but also its role as a foundation of Japanese cuisine. Several media outlets reacted to this revision. For example, *Asahi*, a national newspaper, reported that the new guidelines strongly reflected the Abe administration's emphasis on respecting Japanese tradition and culture (Asahi Shinbun 2017). On the other hand, *Yomiuri*, another newspaper, wrote that significant descriptions have been enhanced following the registration of *washoku* in the UNESCO list of intangible cultural heritage (Yomiuri Shinbun 2017).

In this chapter, I focus on dashi, Japanese soup stock. As described in the revised Curriculum Standards, dashi is often considered an essential element of Japanese food, playing a role as the basis of taste and flavors of Japanese dishes. Dashi is the end result of the extraction of tastes and flavors from various ingredients through soaking or boiling them in water. Japanese dashi is an ingredient used in many dishes, such as miso soup, simmered meals, hotpot dishes, and soup for noodles, to name a few. While being considered a basic ingredient for Japanese food, dashi exhibits great regional diversity in terms of the ingredients used, ways of cooking, use, and, therefore, taste. This chapter aims to elucidate the social, cultural, and political process of how dashi became the basis of Japanese food by tracing the history and transformations of food practices related to the use of dashi in Japanese society. My fieldwork in the kitchens of Japanese households started in 2007 in the Kanto region, including Tokyo. One of the objectives of this study was to understand the ways in which umami-rich foods, including dashi, are treated. The first part of this chapter is primarily based on the analysis of historical documents, cookbooks in particular, and the latter part is based on data obtained from my fieldwork.

Dashi and its Taste Diversity

There are many cooking practices all over the world that are similar to those involved in making of dashi, such as the preparation of the French *fond*, and bouillon, English-speaking stock and broth, and Chinese *tan*. Vegetables, meat, or seafood including bones are usually boiled in water to make a soup or sauce that is next used as a base for flavor. These stocks are sometimes regarded not only as the simple outcome of a cooking technique or process but also as something like a seasoning that adds meaningful taste and flavor to everyday meals. These stocks commonly produce the taste called umami, and some explain that Japanese dashi carries a more pronounced umami flavor because its ingredients do not contain as many fats, oils, and spices as compared with stocks from other cultures (e.g. Yamaguchi and Ninomiya 2000). In 1908, a Japanese chemist discovered the umami flavor in dashi made from kombu kelp and found glutamic acid as the source of umami taste. Since this discovery, the presence of other substances that provoke the perception of umami, such as inosinic acid and guanylic acid, have been discovered by Japanese researchers in other dashi ingredients such as dried bonito (*katsuobushi*) and shiitake mushrooms (Yamaguchi and Ninomiya 1998). Umami, in particular, has been recognized as the universal fifth taste since the discoveries of the umami taste receptors in the first half of the twentieth century (Chaudhari, Landin and Roper 2000).

Within Japanese society there is a strong sentiment attached to umami, which is described as the proudest discovery of Japan or the proudest taste of Japan. Therein lies a logic that umami was discovered by the Japanese in a specific Japanese food, dashi, and that it has become recognized as a fifth taste within the frame of universal Western science (Osawa 2018). For instance, the website of the National Diet Library of Japan has a special page titled "Japanese Dashi Culture and the Discovery of Umami." It states that

> when people think of Japanese food, many people probably think of typical Japanese dishes such as sushi, tempura, and miso soup, but there is one thing that is a step away from these, that is dashi, which is inseparable from Japanese food. . . . The "deliciousness" represented by "dashi" has been named "umami" and has been presented as the fifth taste, which is different from sweet, sour, salty or bitter, and today umami has established its position as "UMAMI" not only in Japan but also worldwide. (National Diet Library, Japan, 2013)

In this website, Japanese dashi culture and the deep relationship between dashi and umami, including the discovery of umami from dashi, are presented in a narrative style along with historical documents and materials.

At the same time, the emphasis on the relationship between umami and dashi at the national level can be seen from a sociopolitical perspective. In Japan, there has been an increase in political and economic efforts to popularize "correct" and "authentic" Japanese food practices in response to the rise in global of popularity of Japanese food and to preserve the traditional Japanese diet in response to the decline in domestic consumption of Japanese food and ingredients such as rice (Assmann 2017; Sakamoto and Allen 2011). For example, on the political front, there was the enactment of the basic law on *Shokuiku* (food education) in Japan in 2005, as well as the 2013 inclusion of Japanese food (*washoku*) in the UNESCO list of intangible cultural heritage.[1] In these contexts, umami often appears as a taste, but also as a source of national pride. For example, the concept of umami is often used to define Japanese food in the UNESCO's registration. The Ministry of Agriculture, Forestry and Fisheries' pamphlet on Japanese food states that the characteristic of Japanese food as "by using umami well, achieves low-animal-fat diets, thus contributing to long life expectancy and prevention of obesity among the Japanese" (the Ministry of Agriculture, Forestry and Fisheries, n.d.). But what does umami actually taste like, and how can we explain the sense of umami as a taste? Even in Japan, umami is a relatively new concept. For instance, Yoshida, who conducted a research on Japanese taste vocabulary, argued in 1998 that it has been claimed that there is a taste called umami in Japan; however, it is not generalized, nor is it recognized as an independent taste term (Yoshida 1998: 386). In this case, dashi is used as a tool to embody the umami taste of Japanese food, that is, the taste of Japanese food.

I had an opportunity to attend a dashi event at Kasetsart University in Bangkok, Thailand, organized by the Japanese Culinary Academy (JCA) on January 2016.[2] The event, organized jointly with Ryukoku University in Kyoto, was joined by Thai university students who study Japanese, agriculture, and food science, as well as faculty members and chefs. According to the JCA, the event aimed to provide an opportunity for the participants to experience dashi as the foundation of Japanese cuisine. Lectures by chefs and professors from Japanese universities about umami and traditional Japanese cuisine emphasized the importance of umami in Asia and Thailand and used examples of umami-rich foods in Thai culture. The lectures were then followed by a cooking demonstration by four Kyoto *kaiseki* chefs.[3] After they demonstrated the method to make dashi using bonito flakes and kombu kelp, the participants joined in a tasting of dashi and clear soup made with the dashi and other ingredients such as prawns from Thailand, and yuzu (*Citrus junus*) for its aroma. Thai students and chefs who were tasting dashi for the first time expressed their admiration for the taste and commented on how delicious it was. The four chefs who took part in the event also emphasized their amazement at how they could create different tastes of dashi, even when using the same basic ingredients.

Activities aimed at promoting traditional Japanese food culture using dashi have taken place overseas, but also in Japan. The JCA, in cooperation with Kyoto City, has been holding food education classes at elementary schools in Kyoto since 2005. A series of classes, titled "The Secret of Dashi and Umami," have been delivered by the *Ajinomoto* company since 2006, and there have also been "Japanese food and dashi hands-on classes" delivered by the Osaka Gas Company, and "Japanese Food Day tasting through dashi" by the Washoku Association of Japan (supported by the Ministry of Agriculture, Forestry and Fisheries), to name a few. These activities have one thing in common: they are part of a food education program that deals with dashi. The Osaka Gas project, for example, has the endorsement of the Ministry of Agriculture, Forestry and Fisheries in its efforts to promote the experience of taste of Japanese food among children, who are in the process of developing food preferences and taste. Thus, food education activities using dashi have been conducted regardless of the type of entity such as the government or companies.

There are three reasons why dashi is considered an important theme in food education: first, it is instrumental to convey the umami flavor and to experience dashi as the "Japanese" taste; secondly, sponsors seek to emphasize the health benefits derived from using dashi in cooking, specifically to support the claim that using dashi allows one to cut down on fats and salt, a celebrated advantage of Japanese food that is often claimed, for example, in the definition of washoku it its UNESCO's registration. And last but not least, the making and the use of dashi is foregrounded as an important part of traditional Japanese food culture.

The Cabinet Office's basic plan for promoting food education also calls for food-related companies to be actively involved in promoting education as one of the main drivers. In this way, government agencies, from national ministries to local governments and the private sector, mainly food-related industries, collaborate in centralized food education activities on the subject of dashi. It is no coincidence that the food education activities using dashi by these different organizations have become events that fit well with the national educational guidelines for schools. In this sense, dashi is clearly used as a culinary tool to materially demonstrate the taste of Japan and traditional Japanese food habits within the broad political preoccupation with protecting "correct" Japanese food practices and taste, at least partly in response to the globalization of Japanese food overseas, as well as with the aim of preserving "traditional" food habits in response to dietary changes within Japan.

The Generalization of High Cuisine and Standardization of Taste

As an icon of Japanese cuisine, dashi is an ingredient that embodies umami flavor, but in fact it displays regional variability. For instance, there is a strong preference for bonito dashi in the Kanto region[4] and for kombu dashi in the Kansai region.[5] Yet, the ingredients for dashi are not restricted to dried bonito and kelp. Furthermore, different regions of Japan have their own local dashi culture and use local ingredients available to them. For example, from Tohoku (northeast Japan) to Kyushu on the coast of the Sea of Japan, communities are known for using dashi made from flying fish (*ago dashi*) locally obtained. In the inland areas, which are far from the coast, communities traditionally use roasted and dried river fish to make dashi. The regional dashi characteristics and preferences in various parts of Japan were developed on the basis of various conditions such as the source of and access to ingredients, the local and regional histories of trade, and local food culture.

In the revision of the curriculum, mentioned at the beginning of this chapter, the authors only stated that "dashi is the basis of Japanese cuisine, and the acquisition of dashi from various ingredients such as dried bonito, kelp, and dried sardines (*niboshi*) is to be taught," providing no specific instructions or explanations about what the ingredients of dashi are, nor instructions on how to cook it during the home economics class. From an interview I conducted with an elementary school teacher in Saitama Prefecture in Kanto region, in 2019, it became clear that it was the teachers of each school who decide how to handle dashi in practice, how to make it, and what ingredients to use—and understood that they generally use dried bonito or dried sardines. She also added that she thinks that the field of school education is too busy to dwell into the specific details of home economics.

The word "dashi" is a contraction of *nidashi-jiru* (boiled broth), and as its name suggests, it is made from boiling a variety of ingredients such as dried or salted seafood, mushrooms, and vegetables to extract the tastes and flavors of these ingredients into the hot water. Moreover, modern dashi preparation is now more detailed and meticulous than just boiling the ingredients. For example, *ichiban dashi* (first dashi) requires the painstaking process of slowly heating the kelp previously soaked in water, removing it just before the water boils, reheating, adding the bonito flakes, heating it again for a short time, and taking the bonito flakes out.[6]

The earliest description of dashi appears in a sixteenth-century cookbook, *Okusadono yori soden no kikigaki* (n.d.). In a recipe for swan, the book directs that one must first prepare two dried bonitos, scrape off the bad parts from their surface and place only the good parts in a cloth bag, boil them in water, and thoroughly strain them. This is believed to be the earliest blueprint for present-day dashi. This type of dashi was originally used in *honzen* cuisine, that is, dishes served to the shoguns and other guests of honor.[7]

In general, dashi made from two ingredients, such as kelp and dried bonito flakes, called *awase dashi* (combined dashi), is often seen as the basic form of dashi. According to Matsumoto (2018: 243), "it was only in the 1900s that bonito and kelp dashi, which is respected as a taste that has nurtured the Japanese taste buds, came to be considered simply *dashi* [among various dashi]." With so many different types of soup stock available across the different regions in Japan, why is dashi made from dried bonito and kelp considered as the most basic form of *dashi*? To understand this requires examining the process whereby *dashi*, a combination of dried bonito and kelp, became the standard dashi in Japan during the 1900s.

A cookbook published in 1919 to teach practical cooking at home describes dashi as an essential part of Japanese cuisine (Kajiyama 1919). What is noteworthy about this book is that it touches on the differences in how to make dashi according to the social classes. It says, "when cooking at home, lower to middle-class households often add bonito flakes, sugar, soy sauce, etc. all at once, but this causes the bonito flakes to stick (to other ingredients), which is not ideal. On the contrary, middle to upper-class households often make something called dashi in advance" (Kajiyama 1919: 5–6). The cookbook also explains in detail how to make dashi (e.g., for the best dashi, it instructs, put dried bonito flakes in the water when it comes to a boil, cover it with a lid, boil it two to three times, leave it for around five minutes, and then strain it). In other words, we can see that dashi varies depending on the different cooking methods (i.e., only boiled or lightly boiled and strained), and that this difference also depends on the social class. The more complex and time-consuming the cooking process, the more refined the taste is. Furthermore, the hierarchical structure of dashi is manifested not only in the preparation process but also in the ingredients used. A cookbook published in 1893 stated that bonito flake dashi is used to make regular clear soup, and that it can be used together with kelp dashi to make "premium" soup (Hananoya 1893:10). After this time period, there were more references to kelp as a superior ingredient, in addition to its deliciousness. Kombu kelp was originally introduced to Honshu (the main island of Japan) as a tribute or trade item from Hokkaido, where it was produced. With the development of vegetarian cuisine, it was later used as an ingredient in cooking and confectionery. During the middle of the Edo period, large quantities of kelp were transported from Hokkaido to Osaka and Kyoto on Kitamae ships via the Seto Inland Sea, and the use of kelp dashi was said to have spread to the Kansai region, especially Kyoto.[8]

In the 1933 magazine *Hoshioka*, written by renowned artist and gourmand Kitaoji Rosanjin (1883–1959),[9] it is mentioned that only the best restaurants in Tokyo knew enough about kombu dashi. He considered that this was so probably because for a long time it was not customary to use kombu in Tokyo, and added that the dashi made of kelp is very good especially for fish dishes, while in contrast, in bonito soup stock the two tastes of fish overlap, so one cannot help but feel unwell (Kitaoji [1933] 2008). This might seem to be a typical description by Rosanjin, who was born in Kyoto and later settled in Tokyo. It seems that the kelp, which was used in the Kansai region, especially in Osaka and Kyoto, came to Tokyo in the form of high-quality dashi by way of first-class restaurants.[10]

In the late nineteenth and early twentieth centuries, Japan underwent major societal changes such as the opening of the country, modernization, and the Industrial Revolution. From the viewpoint of dietary history, it was during this period that elements of Western food began to spread for the first time, and the category of home cooking emerged as Japanese society and family changed their shape. With the birth of the "housewife" as a middle-class phenomenon, and an increasing number of women going into girls' schools, social expectations grew for women to know more about "home cooking." According to Ehara and Higashiyotsuyanagi (2008), the term *katei ryori* (home cooking, or home-cooked food) first appeared in 1903. Prior to this year, the upper classes in Japan had servants who did the cooking, while, in contrast, the common people did not have the time nor the resources for such home cooking. In addition, this was a period in which the number of cookbooks targeting these middle-class women grew, and many women's magazines were launched. The ideology of home cooking circulated on to literate and educated middle- and upper-class women via these cookbooks and magazines. With the popularization of such media contents, descriptions abounded of many aspects of cooking—including explanations about the use of utensils and on how to handle different ingredients, as well as instructions on how to cut, boil, bake, steam, and so on and how to cook rice—provided recipes for specific dishes, and contributed to standardize the knowledge of health and nutrition according to centralized policies. Among these abundant and diverse pieces of information, these cookbooks and magazines also included detailed instructions on how to prepare dashi.

Among the authors of these books, there were chefs from recognized fine Japanese restaurants as well as teachers and culinary educators from different women's or cooking schools. They taught the upper-middle-class housewives about high cuisine.

Mirroring Jack Goody (1996)'s view on how this knowledge is transmitted, this meant that the dashi recipe most probably came from an upper-class restaurant such as *Kappo* or *Ryotei*. It should also be noted that, at that time, there was a disparity in the dietary habits between urban and rural areas, as well as among the social groups of workers, laborers, and peasants.

It was not until the latter half of the twentieth century that the combined dashi of kelp and dried bonito, which had been considered as an upper-class ingredient, became popular. A magazine issued in 1956 ran a six-page feature on dashi (Eiyo to Ryori 1956). This special feature taught readers how to make dashi using (and defining) its key ingredients—bonito flakes, kelp, and dried sardines—and also described the characteristics and grades of each ingredient as well as suggestions on how to choose and buy them. Dried bonito was described in greatest detail, followed by kelp. This magazine article illustrates the situation at that time, when Japanese society was gradually recovering from a stage of postwar confusion and it was possible to turn one's attention to various interests, such as the actual preparation of daily food.

According to Kubo (2020), who has conducted research on the transformation of Japanese home cooking, from the 1950s to the 1960s, talk of "Japanese food" as a general category, rather than the description of local dishes rooted in each region's landscape, became popular throughout various media. In addition to conventional cooking magazines and cookbooks, new media such as television cooking programs emerged and contributed to establish and generalize the ranking of dashi made from different ingredients (thus, it was agreed that the best dashi is made from kelp and bonito flakes, while *niboshi* dashi is inexpensive and suitable for everyday cooking). In sum, during the first half of the twentieth century, dashi, which was initially used in "upper-class" Japanese cuisine, quickly spread to the upper middle class, and then to the "common" people in the latter half of the century. This was encouraged by the centralized creation of a unified "Japanese cuisine" in Japanese society and, thus, through the standardization of what had been high cuisine, which was then established as proper Japanese cuisine. Since then, the taste of dashi was refined through the adoption of more detailed and advanced cooking methods, such as the practice of straining, the strict control of cooking temperature and time and, at the same time, the selection and amalgamation of ingredients, specifically the combination of two sources of umami, vegetable- and animal-based, such as kelp and bonito flakes.[11]

Another Standardization of Taste

Now, let us return to the emphasis on dashi in modern school education mentioned earlier in this chapter. The MEXT's commentary on the revised curriculum guidelines states that cooking rice, dashi, and miso soup is representative of the "traditional" Japanese diet. In the minutes of the Curriculum Division's Working Group on Technology and Home Economics which discussed this revision, a member said that, at home, customs that used to be commonplace in the past, such as making udon noodles, making clothes with a sewing machine, and preparing dashi, are disappearing (the Ministry of Education, Culture, Sports, Science and Technology 2015).

During my own research on the use of dashi in ordinary households, I found that only a few households regularly make dashi from scratch. However, it was used daily in some dish, especially in miso soup. The most common way of eating dashi was to use Japanese flavor seasonings. Flavor seasonings are commonly known by their trade names: *Dashinomoto* or *Hondashi*. They are mainly based on amino acids such as monosodium glutamate, with flavoring ingredients that include sugar and salt and exclude spices. As an edible commodity, they are usually found in the form of dried, powdered, or granulated substances that must be added into food to enhance the aroma and taste when cooked. By using flavor seasonings in granular or powdered form, dashi can be "made" instantly by simply dissolving the powder in water. In other words, it is possible to "use" dashi without "making" it.

The history of flavor seasonings is recent, and it was first introduced through the release of "Shimaya Dashi-no-moto" in 1964 by the Shimaya Corporation. Subsequently, several other food companies joined in the production of flavored seasonings, and their household consumption rapidly expanded during the 1970s and the early 1980s. At the same time, the use of flavor seasonings in the food of schools, hospitals, and cafeterias was also expanding. Production increased tenfold in twenty years—from 4,821 tons in 1970 to 47,800 tons in 1989 (Nikkankeizaitsushinsha 2007). On the other hand, the amount of dashi ingredients (e.g., bonito, kelp, dried shiitake mushrooms, and dried sardines) purchased by ordinary households was on a downward trend since 1963 (Osawa 2012). With the advent of flavor seasonings, the custom of cooking changed from making dashi to using or buying it. In political terms, this translates into the disappearance of "traditional" food culture, and, on the other hand, it contributes to a nationwide standardization of dashi taste as standardized products emerge and are distributed across Japan.

Dashi's Rationality

The generalization of high-grade, sophisticated dashi made from kelp and dried bonito described so far, and the advent of instant dashi, seems to have contributed to standardize and homogenized the taste of dashi in accordance to centralized national politics. Here, however, I would like to argue that there was (and still there is) a strong association between taste and flavor preferences for dashi that is tied to their regional characteristics. During my research in ordinary households, I observed that people make dashi in a variety of ways ranging from using instant stock (flavor seasonings) to making it from scratch with various ingredients. I also found new products such as paper packets with powdered dashi ingredients called dashi packs, or in liquid mixtures of already-made dashi. In other words, the means for attaining dashi were diversified, and there was no consistency even within a single household, using sometimes one presentation, sometimes another. Out of these various choices, within each household, cooks explained their choice of dashi for reasons such as economy, time, health, and its deliciousness. In terms of economy and time, the convenience and economy of using instant dashi is overwhelmingly high. On the other hand, when it comes to health, many people believe that dashi made from scratch is better than using instant stocks that contain different chemical seasonings and food additives.

As for the taste of dashi, I found that there were two factors involved in the people's taste preferences of dashi: ranking according to the type of dashi and their regional characteristics. With regard to the ranking of dashi, the dashi made from kelp and dried bonito is often perceived as having an extraordinary quality and as superior to other types. For example, this is the dashi of preference when hosts must entertain guests, or when cooking good-quality soba noodles. In terms of taste, dashi made from kelp and bonito is considered to be better and tastier than instant dashi. It can be said that school education and various media for delivering cooking recipes have played an important role in conveying the meaning of "good" dashi and generalized it, which in turn has led to its recognition as a delicious food item.

At the same time, the regionality of dashi is manifest in everyday eating habits. For example, a woman in her fifties, originally from the Fukushima prefecture, remembers that in her hometown, Fukushima, and in Ibaraki, where she currently lives, *niboshi* (dried sardines) are the most frequently used ingredient for making dashi, but when she learned how to make dashi in her school's home economics class as a child, she learned how to make dashi not with *niboshi*, but with dried bonito, and she was surprised by the difference in taste. What we can learn from her story is that she was capable of noticing the differences in taste between the two and preserved this difference as a long-term memory. I have found more stories on the regional differences of dashi: Another woman in her thirties began using *ago* (flying fish) dashi for the first time after she married. She comes from the Kanto region and did not know what *ago* dashi was, but her husband, from Osaka, prefers *ago* dashi, so she started making it. Another woman, in her twenties, was surprised to learn that her husband's family in the Saga Prefecture in Kyushu uses chicken and yellowtail as ingredients for dashi. In this way, subtle differences in people's daily food habits, such as dashi preferences, can become apparent in the process of highlighting regional differences.

Despite the widespread use of standardized dashi recipes and instant dashi, it is clear that a preference for dashi based on individual household preferences has been constructed, to some extent, on the basis of regional differences. In particular, when it comes to the importance of the regional characteristics of dashi, people tended to emphasize the differences between their hometowns and their current place of residence or talk about the deliciousness of dashi in their hometowns with a keen sense of nostalgia. In recent years, there has also been a market diversification of food products onto which different regional dashi "flavors" have been added. These are edible commodities that cannot be attributed a regional origin, such as potato chips and instant noodles. Producers add onto them regionally distinctive dashi flavors such as when they advertise potato chips with Kansai dashi flavor. Stores and companies that specialize in regional dashi products have also recently emerged. For example, in 2010, *Kaya-no-Ya*, a company based in Fukuoka, opened a branch store in central Tokyo privileging products made with *ago* dashi, the favorite taste of the Fukuoka region. This shop has become popular nationwide, expanding its business to multiple cities across the country and even overseas into Hong Kong.

The process of homogenization and standardization of dashi in accordance with a centralized view of Japanese taste did not erase regional preferences for dashi and its taste, but rather created an opportunity to promote the uniqueness of regional taste and brought more attention to the diversity of dashi. The taste of dashi, which historically has been deeply rooted in local regions, has transcended geographic boundaries while still maintaining the context of local taste. In this chapter, I have focused on dashi, which has been attracting attention as a vehicle to showcase the umami taste of Japan, taking advantage of contemporary political tendencies surrounding the national and global imagination of Japanese cuisine. I have argued that dashi is important as a tool that embodies a taste and that, with the aid of scientific narratives, has been added onto the somewhat narrowly defined category of "physiological taste." On the other hand, in examining its history, it is clear that there is a homogenized cultural construction of the taste of dashi in Japan based on the condensation of recipes and the standardization of taste fostered by the advent of instant cooking. Here, I have examined the process whereby taste was socially and collectively constructed. Even though the basic taste foundation of dashi is umami, there is a diversity of flavors inscribed in it, highlighting the transformation and modernization of food in Japan in a global context. Thus, the relationship between dashi and taste provides us with an opportunity to reconsider the difference between collective and individual tastes, physiologically conditioned tastes, and cultural and socially constructed tastes, as well as their relationship to individual, regional, and national political histories.

Notes

1 With regard to food education, the nationalistic nature of food education has been criticized in Japan. For instance, Nakamura (2012) argued that the various policy objectives of the relevant ministries and agencies, from improving health status and food self-sufficiency to preserving traditional food culture, were integrated into the symbol "food education," and Assmann (2019) critically examined the relationship between the introduction of food education at the national level and in regional areas. Also, much research has been already done on the registration of Japanese food as an intangible cultural heritage by UNESCO. See, for example, Bestor (2018), who discussed how *washoku* became a brand for political and economic purposes.

2 The JCA is an organization dedicated to education, cultural, and technical research and to the promotion of Japanese cuisine, organized mainly by Kyoto's *kaiseki* chefs. They are also involved in promoting Japanese cuisine to the world. See de St. Maurice (2018) for further information on their activities.

3 *Kaiseki* cuisine is a type of Japanese food that originates in food served for tea ceremony.

4 The region includes the Greater Tokyo Area and encompasses seven prefectures.

5 The region is located in the western-central region of Japan's main island. It encompasses seven prefectures including Kyoto and Osaka.

6 *Ichiban dashi* is first cooked with kelp and bonito flakes, and second, dashi is boiled again with the leftover ingredients from making the first dashi. There are many other instructions on how to prepare dashi, such as how long the kelp should be soaked,

when to add the bonito flakes, how long the bonito should be heated, and so on. This is a drastic change from the dashi's origins simply as a boiled broth.

7 *Honzen* cuisine is one of three basic styles of Japanese cuisine that has its origins in food prepared for samurai families.

8 It has been pointed out that the reason why kelp dashi spread in the Kansai region is because the water was so soft that it was suitable for making kelp dashi, and it was also compatible with the type of light soy sauce used in the region.

9 As a gourmand, Kitaoji Rosanjin ran a restaurant and was influential in the financial world as well. His popularity continues to this day. Also, *Hoshioka* was the phantom magazine of a Tea House, a members-only restaurant run by Rosanjin. It has since been reprinted in various formats.

10 A few cookbooks also claim that kelp is more economical than dried bonito. For instance, a cookbook from 1918 states that the dashi from bonito is used for fine dishes, and bonito flakes and kelp dashi are more economical and delicious than bonito flakes alone (Nakano 1918). Another cookbook refers that the combination of bonito flakes and kelp can help the cook to save on bonito flakes, in addition to being delicious (Ochi 1925).

11 The synergistic effect of the different umami substances of kelp and dried bonito was scientifically explained later on (Kuninaka 1964; Yamaguchi and Ninomiya 1998).

References

Assmann, S. (2017), "Global Recognition and Domestic Containment: Culinary Soft Power in Japan," in A. Niehaus and T. Walravens (eds.), *Feeding Japan*, pp. 113–37, Cham: Palgrave Macmillan.

Assmann S. (2019), "Mediating National Identity, Practicing Life Politics: Visual Representations of a Food Education Campaign in Japan," in J. Dürrschmidt and Y. Kautt (eds.), *Globalized Eating Cultures*, pp. 53–68, Cham: Palgrave Macmillan.

Bestor, T. (2018), "Washoku, Far and Near: UNESCO, Gastrodiplomacy, and the Cultural Politics of Traditional Japanese Cuisine," in N. Stalker (ed.), *Devouring Japan: Global Perspectives on Japanese Culinary Identity*, pp. 99–117, Oxford: Oxford University Press.

Chaudhari, N., A. Landin, and S. Roper (2000), "A Metabotropic Glutamate Receptor Variant Functions as a Taste Receptor," *Nature Neuroscience* 3(2): 113–19.

de St. Maurice, G. (2018), "Making the Multi-Dimensional Taste of Japanese Cuisine Public," in C. Counihan and S. Højlund (eds.), *Making Taste Public: Ethnographies of Food and the Senses*, pp. 113–25, London: Bloomsbury.

Ehara, A. and S. Higashiyotsuyanagi (2008), *Kindai rydrisho no sekai*, Tokyo: Domes Shuppan.

Eiyo to Ryori (1956), "Dashi ni Tsuite," *Eiyo to Ryori* 22(4): 112–17.

Goody, J. (1996), *Cooking, Cuisine and Class: A Study in Comparative Sociology*, Cambridge: Cambridge University Press.

Hananoya, K. (1893), *Nenchu Sozai no Shikata: Shiroto Ryori*, Nagoya: Seikando.

Kajiyama, A. (1919), *Jissen Ryoriho*, Tokyo: Seirindo.

Kitaoji, R. (2008 [1933]), *Hoshioka*, reprinted in M. Hirano (ed.), *Rosanjin no bishoku techo*, Tokyo: Kadokawa Haruki Jimusho.

Kubo, A. (2020), *Kateiryori Toiu Senjyo: Kurashi wa Dezain Dekiruka*, Tokyo: Kotonisha.

Kuninaka, A. (1964), "The Nucleotides, a Rationale of Research on Flavor Potentiation," in *Proceedings of the Symposium on Flavor Potentiation*, pp. 4–9, Cambridge: Arthur D. Little

Matsumoto, N. (2018), *Nihonshoku to Dashi*, Tokyo: Yuzankaku.

Ministry of Agriculture, Forestry and Fisheries (n.d.), "Washoku," Ministry of Agriculture, Forestry and Fisheries. Available online: https://www.maff.go.jp/j/keikaku/syokubunka /ich/pdf/leaflet_jjpg.pdf, last accessed April 10, 2020.

Ministry of Education, Culture, Sports, Science and Technology (2015), *Kyoikukatei Bukai Katei, Gijyutu-Katei*, Working Group Daiikkai Gijiroku, Ministry of Education, Culture, Sports, Science and Technology. Available online: https://www.mext.go.jp/b_ menu/shingi/chukyo/chukyo3/065/siryo/1382040.htm, last accessed April 10, 2020.

Nakamura, M. (2012), *Shinboru kozo to shugo koi o meguru dainamikusu: Shokuiku to suro fudo undo JA no shokuno kyoiku kara*, Tokyo: Sairyusha.

Nakano T. (1918), *Kappo Kyokasho*, Yamaguchi: Yamaguchi Kappo Koshujyo.

National Diet Library, Japan (2013), "Daijyunanakai Nihon no dashi bunka to umami no hakken," National Diet Library, Japan. Available online: https://www.ndl.go.jp/kaleido/ entry/17/, last accessed April 10, 2020.

Nikkankeizaitsushinsha (2007), *Shurui shokuhin sangyo no seisan hanbai shiea*, Tokyo: Nikkan Keizai Tsushin Sha.

Ochi, K. (1925), *Katei Eiyo Nihon Ryori*, Kyoto: Hoshino shoten.

"Okusadono yori sodden no kikigaki" (1959 [n.d.]), in H. Hanawa (ed.), *Gunsho Ruiju Vol 367*, Tokyo: Zoku Gunsho Ruiju Kanseikai.

Osawa, Y. (2012), "Glutamate Perception, Soup Stock and the Concept of Umami: The Ethnography, Food Ecology and History of Dashi in Japan," *Ecology of Food and Nutrition* 51: 329–45.

Osawa, Y. (2018), "'We Can Taste but Others Cannot': Umami as an Exclusively Japanese Concept," in N. Stalker (ed.), *Devouring Japan: Global Perspectives on Japanese Culinary Identity*, pp. 118–32, Oxford: Oxford University Press.

Sakamoto, R. and M. Allen (2011), "There's Something Fishy about That Sushi: How Japan Interprets the Global Sushi Boom," *Japan Forum* 23(1): 99–12.

"Shin! Gakushushidoyoryo" (2017), *Asahi Shinbun*, March 31: 27.

"Shingakushushidoyoryoan" (2017), *Tokyo Yomiuri Shinbun*, February 15: 30.

Yamaguchi, S. and K. Ninomiya (1998), "What Is Umami?" *Food Reviews International* 14(2–3): 123–38.

Yamaguchi, S. and K. Ninomiya (2000), "Umami and Food Palatability," *The Journal of Nutrition* 130(4): 921S–926S.

Yoshida, S. (1998), "Aji no ninshiki to choumi no ruikei" (Perception of Taste and Types of Seasoning), in S. Yoshida (ed.), *Jinrui no shoku bunka*, pp. 369–407, Tokyo: Ajinomoto shoku no bunka centre.

3

Heritagization of Fermented Taste in Southwestern Fukui, Japan

Shingo Hamada

Introduction: *Kyodoshoku*

Kyodoshoku is a Japanese term, concept, and practice, which translates literally into English as *hometown dish* and is generally interpreted to mean "vernacular heritage dish." It first emerged in the 1920s and resurged again when the commoditization of local specialties and cuisine developed in the early 1980s, as the migration from rural to urban areas accelerated (Rath 2015). *Kyodoshoku* used to be crafted and consumed at the household, but shifted to industrial methods of production, distribution, and marketing. Along with this change, the time and place of passing on culinary knowledge and skills of *kyodoshoku* were externalized from home kitchens to school meal programs and local cooking events and lessons.

Heritage dishes are passed down regionally from one generation to the next, preserving the food system while negotiating its authenticity and authorship with revised recipes within shifting historical and social contexts. The taste of *kyodoshoku* is now taught and studied in various settings, such as food education programs and special promotions. A heritage dish is both practice and concept. Just as nationalization and localization of food and cuisines emerge paradoxically in the process of globalization (e.g., Wilk 1999), anthropologists capture the heritagization of local dishes in the negotiation with state power, modernization, and rural-urban geopolitics (Brulotte and Di Giovine 2014; Klein 2018; Mak 2014). Heritage dishes operate as a symbol of local and regional identities, which are reproduced in relations with others, including nonlocal tourists, as well as neighboring communities and towns (Ardren 2018; Hashimoto and Telfer 2008). The heritagization of food is a process of materially and ideologically creating and placing food and taste through human-human and human-environment relations.

The reevaluation of *kyodoshoku* is related to contemporary food movements which criticize conventional industrial food systems and attempt to revitalize close relationships between production and consumption sites, and producers and consumers. The foods whose origins of production are clearly identified, which are hand and/or homemade, and which are made from organic ingredients are considered more genuine than industrially manufactured products. The authenticity of food is also enhanced when its cultural values are framed as a part of local and regional folklores and histories. In contemporary market-based consumer society, authenticity based on taste and cooking methods that have been handed down the generations draw attention as an added value for local specialty food products. However, authenticity does not exist inherently within the materiality of food. Rather, authenticity is created, negotiated, and cultivated in the discourse of food producers and consumers. Handler (1986) suggests that authenticity is a socially constructed product in the West and that it is deeply related to the concept of the individual vis-à-vis a particular social group. However, authenticity that questions whether or not a given material or event is genuine does not only originate in the West. There is a potential for authenticity to also emerge and be negotiated anytime and anywhere there is cultural contact and friction, and wherever and whenever local foods and tastes are made public (Counihan and Højlund 2018).

This chapter presents an ethnographic case study of how Japanese heritage dishes (*kyodoshoku*) are formed, with reference to an ethnographic case study of fermented mackerel sushi (*heshiko-narezushi*) in the Uchitomi Bay region of Fukui, Japan.[1] Touching on the discourse of taste, the regional history of purse seine mackerel fishing, and the subsistence and exchange economy, this chapter demonstrates how the acceptance and rejection of changing recipes are profoundly related to inter- and intra-regional identity politics. Fermented food is alive with microbial activity, and local households as well as coastal communities create a variety of tastes using a minimum of ingredients, such as salt, rice koji (fermented rice, *Aspergillus oryzae*), and rice vinegar. In the meantime, artisanal producers focus on consumers' tastes while preserving their recipe and making it distinct from industrially manufactured products. Some artisanal producers use rice vinegar as a sweetening agent, while others criticize the addition of *alien* ingredients to *their* collective food heritage, as though it taints the identity and taste of their collective memory (Holtzman 2006; Sutton 2001). On the other hand, salt, which is necessary for safe and successful preservation, is shunned by health-conscious urban consumers seeking to avoid high levels of salinity.

Based on ethnographic research that I conducted in 2015 and 2016 in Tagarasu and neighboring communities, this chapter demonstrates how the changing recipes of collective food heritage and concerns over its future direction generate friction over the authorship and authenticity of heritage dishes. This chapter also highlights that it is this friction that sustains the diversity and resilience of regional identity. Taste and tasting are practices of both internalization and externalization. While tasting is a subjective experience, it is also expressed externally through the description of taste in both verbal and nonverbal communications. The experience of taste and tasting at both individual and communal levels influences the social production of identity through food practices and politics. The question of authenticity and the degree of acceptable change in taste arises among artisanal and household producers and is manifested in the dilemma between preserving the *right* taste for reproducing regional identity and commoditizing local heritage food for younger and urban consumers in postindustrial Japan.

Fermented Seafood

Terroir greatly matters when it comes to locally crafted fermented food. Local fermented food develops and produces a unique taste due to fungi, which in turn is greatly influenced by the regional climate, topography, and seasonality. As the terroir differs locally and regionally, homemade fermented food often requires local culinary and environmental knowledge which has been developed and handed down the generations. Fermentation contributes to the edibility, preservability, and gourmetization of food. It is a culinary technique used to preserve and store vegetables, fish, and shellfish that are harvested in a great quantity in a short period of time, especially for winter times when food production activities are limited. By using fermentation to preserve, maintain, or even enhance nutritional values of food, while at the same time preventing them from spoilage, food becomes available even in times and places where food production is challenging. In addition to these functional aspects, fermentation also enhances the flavor and taste of food. Fermenting techniques are used not only for long-term food preservation but also for enriching the taste. Therefore, gaining an understanding of fermented food requires the examination of cultural values, as well as nutritional and economic values.

Narezushi is a fermented food made in many places in East and Southeast Asia with lactic acids and steamed rice. The commonly known sushi is categorized as "fast sushi" (*hayazushi*) as it uses a plant-based vinegar, unlike "aged sushi" (*narezushi*) which utilizes natural lactic acids in its fermentation process. *Narezushi* has a much longer history than *hayazushi*, and it has been studied and documented by Shinoda (2002) and Ruddle and Ishige (2010). Fermented food like *narezushi*, using fish and rice, is seen as a local food in the Asia Monsoon area, which is characterized by high temperatures and humidity. Fermented rich-fish products, including fish sauce, are associated with wet rice agriculture. It is traditional local food adapted to the regional environment (Ishige 2011; Nakao 2012: 131; Ruddle and Ishige 2010; Sato 2008).

Tagarasu and the *Satouri* Foodscape

Tagarasu is a small coastal community situated in the Uchitomi Bay of Western Fukui, with a population of 404 people living in a total of 108 households. It is known as the first place where the purse seine fishing method was used for mackerel in the Sea of Japan area. The community organized local cooperatives for purse seine mackerel fishing, so they received the monetary and fish dividends. As they were unable to consume all the fresh fish at once, they dried and fermented mackerels for preservation, as well as for food exchange with inland farming communities. When mackerel was yielded in large quantities, it was sent to markets, but also distributed to local residents. Purse seine mackerel fishery flourished between 1947 and 1951, but it dwindled as mackerel became scarce in the late 1970s and 1980s, and it ended in 1987 (Obama City History Compilation Committee 1998). As the coastal fishery declined, the local economy shifted to tourism based on traditional-style inns with seawater baths. However, the development of infrastructure, including highway networks, enabled tourists to make daytrips and avoid an overnight stay. At present, only a few households still run their inns. Most fishermen and women retired from fishery, and some residents now buy fish at local wholesale markets and sell home-processed seafood such as dried fish and seaweed.

Coastal communities like Tagarasu in the Uchitomi Bay area had access to rich aquatic resources, but the land for agriculture was very limited as they were surrounded by mountains. Because rice production was not enough to provide for all households, coastal fishing communities engaged in an exchange economy with nearby farming communities on the other side of the mountains. Fishing communities provided seafood, such as dried and fermented fish products, to inland farmers. Farmers paid for the seafood with their rice and other agricultural products. The people of Tagarasu and other coastal communities called this practice *satouri* (lit. trans. village business). *Satouri* was a locally developed food system by which farming and fishing households interdependently enhanced their food securities all year long. Fishers had a different business route and economic opportunity to sell their products in Kyoto for cash income. However, *satouri* was and still is practiced between particular fishing households and farming households, rather than individually, and the *satouri* relationship is a long-term engagement, rather than short-term business opportunity.

Only a few still continue their village business with farming partners today, but *satouri* is still alive in terms of social memory, and fermented sea products played a key role in it. For farming communities, access to locally produced seafood specialties shifted from *satouri* to today's local co-op stores. Though consumer groups may have changed, *heshiko-narezushi* (fermented mackerel sushi) made locally by coastal households is also sold at a local farmer's market in early winter, especially in the run-up to the New Year's holiday. According to a saleswoman, there is still a healthy demand for *heshiko-narezushi* in neighboring farming communities. Most buyers are senior women living nearby, and local seafood artisans never fail to mention the *satouri* system when talking about their *heshiko* and *heshiko-narezushi*. However, this transition of marketing has also meant a change in intercommunal producer-consumer relations; while both producers and consumers knew each other under the *satouri* system, now local fermented food and other sea products are being sold to unidentified consumers, who may or may not be local residents.

Heshiko, Narezushi, and *Heshiko-Narezushi*

Heshiko and *narezushi* are mostly produced in the Hokuriku and Chugoku regions facing the Sea of Japan. *Heshiko* is a fermented food made with salt, rice bran, and a variety of locally yielded fish. *Narezushi* is also a local and regional food using lactic acid fermentation, which is made with rice, fish, and rice koji. *Narezushi* is one of the most well-known fermented foods using rice and fish in the Asia Monsoon region. Spatially, Japan is situated in the northernmost and easternmost part of this hot and humid monsoon zone, in which lactic-fermented fish and rice is produced and consumed.

Homemade *heshiko* is prepared at home but fermented for a period of several months in a designated hut. The hut is privately owned and the source of *heshiko's* unique flavor and taste, as each hut has differing amounts and varieties of bacteria on the casks, shelves, and roof. Bacteria are one of the major components for enabling preservation and enriching the flavor (Kozaki 1986). Traditionally, cedar-made casks were used to store and ferment the mackerel, but most local artisans use plastic casks these days as they are cheap and readily available. However, Mr. M, one of the local crafters, told me that *heshiko* tastes better when fermented in the wooden casks. Numerous microbes live within the wooden casks, and in order to keep microbes alive he prevents the casks from drying out by occasionally wetting them with water (including the ones not currently in use). Due to the high volume of microbes, the fermenting process is quicker, the color of the end product is nicer, and the taste is diverse and profound when using wooden rather than plastic casks. Plastic casks are inexpensive, but wooden casks can be used for a longer time if cared for properly. Still, the use of plastic casks is widespread because of their usability and low price. Unlike wooden casks, plastic casks can be washed with chemical detergents, ensuring hygiene and safety.

Before putting the mackerel into the cask, all of the intestines, gills, blood, and blood clots are removed, and the body is cleaned in water. Salt is then put in the gutted stomach of the fish, and they are placed into casks. The salted mackerel are later taken out of the casks and rinsed with water to desalinate them. The mackerel are then put back into casks again, this time covered and stuffed with rice bran, along with some red chili peppers to prevent worms from breeding. Three to four weighing stones of approximately 20 kilograms each are placed on the casks. The mackerel ages in the cask with the rice bran. Locals call this process "aging" (*nareru*) rather than "fermenting" (*hakkousuru*). The process of aging takes place over the summer, and the umami is enriched as a result.

The recipe of *saba-narezushi* (mackerel and pickles) in Tagarasu is unique, though it is crafted and consumed in Fukui and other parts of Japan. While salted mackerel is used for making *narezushi* in other regions, people in Tagarasu and neighboring villages use *heshiko*-mackerel for crafting *narezushi*. They state that by using *heshiko*-mackerel, rather than salted mackerel, their *narezushi* does not smell so fishy, so even those who dislike *narezushi* crafted in other areas can eat Tagarasu's *narezushi*.

Heshiko-narezushi using mackerel is a special dish served at seasonal ceremonies, including the spring gathering at local shrines. In Tagarasu, the *heshiko-narezushi* was a necessary item for locals to practice the autumn festival, which was held on September 25 after the rice harvest. However, there was a major fire on the day of the festival in the mid-1960s and locals suffered from a flood disaster in the same year (Kurumizawa 1995). From that point onward, the largest local festival, which used to be held after rice harvest in September, was moved to May 25. As the local residents' ways of life diversified, the date of the festival became more flexible. It is now usually the Sunday before May 25, because more locals can participate in the festival if it is held on the weekend rather than the exact date of May 25. However, this change of festival date conflicted with the serving of *heshiko-narezushi*; the process for making *heshiko* takes place over the summertime as the heat of the summer months is required for fermentation. As a result, *heshiko-narezushi* stopped being served at the spring festival until advances in freezing technology allowed locals to store the *heshiko-narezushi* in the freezer until May. This has meant that *heshiko-narezushi* has gradually lost its seasonality. Locals are now able to serve it at the important local festival, as well as attract tourists by serving local variations of *heshiko-narezushi* all year round.

The major ingredients for making *heshiko-narezushi* mackerel are *heshiko*-mackerel, rice, and rice koji. In some areas and/or households of the Uchitomi Bay region, rice vinegar and rice wine are also used in the making of *heshiko-narezushi*. The people of Tagarasu use *heshiko*-mackerel, which have been fermented in casks for a minimum of one year, spanning at least one summer, and they start making *heshiko-narezushi* at the end of November. They take the *heshiko*-mackerel out of the casks, remove the rice bran and desalt the fish by rinsing it in a river or under a tap overnight. The thin skin is then peeled off the fish, and steamed rice with rice koji is stuffed into the opened bodies of the *heshiko*-mackerel. The purpose of this step, however, is not to promote the process of fermentation. According to artisans, stuffing rice with rice koji into the fish bodies means that "umami infuses into the fish bodies." The *heshiko*-mackerel stuffed with rice and rice koji is placed back into the cask, and rice koji is sprinkled over the top layer of mackerel, before wrapping it up in a plastic bag.

Saba-heshiko-narezushi is only made in winter, and fermentation proceeds slowly in the cold temperatures. It only takes two days to two weeks to ferment the *heshiko-narezushi* in casks. During these two weeks, the rice koji helps further enhance the *heshiko*-mackerel's umami, with a delicate balance of sweetness and sourness. The duration of fermenting for *heshiko*-narezushi differs in places, eras, and households. What is considered to constitute a "good taste" also differs from one area to another and from one household to another, as judging the maturity of taste in casks requires experience-based knowledge. All local *heshiko-narezushi* crafters I interviewed agreed on one thing: the best *heshiko-narezushi* is the one made at their own home.

Core Ingredients

Local residents used to have access to locally yielded mackerel, but after the collapse of the local fishery they started purchasing mackerel through locally organized fishing cooperatives. The season for making *heshiko*-mackerel starts when the local mackerel fishing season begins and continues from October to March. Winter mackerel tends to have a higher fat content, but according to local artisans, as of recently this is not always so. Local fishers still catch mackerel in May and beyond, but these post-winter mackerel are not as fatty as winter mackerel. Fat content is important for the quality of *heshiko*, and locals stress the importance of starting to put mackerel in casks while it is cold and have them ferment over the summer. They therefore need to finish the preparation of *heshiko*-mackerel by April or early May. Local residents are careful about choosing the right mackerel for their local fermented heritage dish. They avoid small-sized mackerel as they tend to have less fat content, but they also avoid large-sized mackerel because the umami flavors from the rice and rice koji will not infuse sufficiently into the bodies of the fish if they are too large. Therefore, their preference is to use mackerel with a body weight of 650–700 grams. They also prefer to use foraging mackerel, rather than spawning mackerel to ensure a suitable level of fat content.

The difference in the quality of mackerel influences the taste of homemade *heshiko* and *heshiko-narezushi*. In recent years, locals have been able to purchase Norwegian mackerel easily throughout the year. Artisans in Tagarasu use mackerel domestically caught in other parts of Japan, as well as mackerel imported from Norway. They are biologically categorized in different subspecies: the Japanese mackerels is *Scomber japonicaus*, and the Norwegian mackerels is *Scomber scombrus*. Local artisans of Tagarasu use both domestic and Norwegian mackerel for making *heshiko*, but they only use the domestically captured mackerel for *heshiko-narezushi*. Norwegian mackerels have a high fat content, which make them good ingredients for making *heshiko*, and they cost approximately one-fifth of domestic mackerel. However, local crafters also state that the fat content of Norwegian mackerel is too high to make *heshiko-narezushi*. If domestic mackerels are used, the color of the rice put in the casks together with them turns a pure white after fermentation. However, in the case of Norwegian mackerel, the rice turns a yellowish color due to the high fat content. The whiteness of food matters in the Japanese cultural context, especially if the food is used for ceremonies and holds important symbolic meanings in local communities (Ohnuki-Tierney 1993). Therefore, local artisans emphasize the importance of using domestic mackerel in making *heshiko-narezushi*, although this is not the case when it comes to making *heshiko*.

Unlike mackerel, where domestic varieties are preferred, local artisans show little preference as to the type or brand of salt they use for making *heshiko*. Most local crafters purchase bags of standard salt (*namishio*) through the local fishing cooperatives. Salt is a necessary ingredient for the fermentation process, and it is also a major factor for the taste and appearance of fermented mackerel. Artisans are able to turn the color of the mackerel to the nice brick red color they strive for just by using the right amount of salt. If less than the required amount of salt is used, the color of the fermented mackerel will be paler. In order to prevent the fish rotting during the long period of pickling time, the amount of salt used to make *heshiko* is approximately 15–20 percent of the weight of mackerel. However, as far as I observed, many artisans do not measure the exact weight of salt; rather, they made a rough visual estimation. This indicates how *heshiko* and *heshiko-narezushi* crafted in the Uchitomi Bay region maintains its vernacular taste, unique to each household, rather than experiencing the standardization and scientization of taste through the formulation and inscription of measurements in recipes. The characteristics of heritage dishes reflect tradition and terroir—the accumulation of knowledge and techniques by each household and community, conditioned by local and regional environments and climates.

The amount of salt used for heritage food represents something of a dilemma: it is required for production yet avoided by consumers, who for health reasons generally prefer to reduce or abstain altogether from food with a high sodium content. The crafters say that if they use less salt when making *heshiko* fish, it does not achieve the same taste. Large-scale manufacturers that produce *heshiko* in greater quantities for tourists design and sell low-sodium *heshiko* by using fermented seasoning materials to shorten the fermentation period. To meet the demand of consumers for low-sodium, convenient food products, while using less salt, producers create and balance the taste by artificially flavoring rather than by the natural process of fermentation.

As the material environment has changed over time, the cultural and practical values of heritage preserved food have also changed. Due to the development of infrastructure and home storage appliances and technologies, the availability of food in terms of spatial and financial accessibility is very high in contemporary Japan—even in rural areas like Tagarasu. Locals do not need to store the bulk of preserved food prior to winter, because they can now go to grocery stores in family-owned vehicles. The functional necessity of traditional heritage food, its preservability made possible by fermentation with salt, has undoubtedly declined with the common use of refrigerators and freezers at home. The use of rice koji (*Aspergillus oryzae*) is prevalent in colder environments, where koji molt helps to promote the fermentation process. Koji dies in environments of over 40 degrees Celsius and becomes inactive under 0 degrees Celsius. Though all crafters I interviewed now use rice koji to make the *heshiko-narezushi*, rice koji was not originally used. Until the 1950s, only steamed rice and *heshiko*-mackerel were used for making *heshiko-narezushi* (Shimonaka and Ichiya 2016). Contemporary local artisans are unsure when the use of rice koji became common in this area. A female informant in her seventies told me that she and her mother began using rice koji as an ingredient in the 1960s, while a couple in their sixties said they started using it for their homemade *heshiko-narezushi* only about a decade or so ago.

What made local crafters in Tagarasu and the neighboring coastal communities use rice koji in the making of *heshiko-narezushi*? The first reason is the enhancement of flavor. Several household crafters mentioned that their *narezushi* tastes better by adding rice koji to the steamed rice. When only steamed rice is used in the fermenting process, it can produce a sour flavor. Using rice koji, however, adds a sweet, sake-like flavor and makes the overall taste milder. Secondly, the addition of rice koji enhances production efficiency by promoting the fermentation process during the cold winter. However, the process of slow aging (*nareru*) is considered important in the production of *heshiko-narezushi* in winter. It is unnecessary to add koji to speed up the fermentation process of the fish. Given that household *heshiko-narezushi* crafters make their homemade *narezushi* on a small scale, and do so mostly for personal consumption, giving to relatives, and in *satouri* exchange, rather than using it for commercial purposes, there is no real need for them to add rice koji to produce more *narezushi* stimulating the fermenting process. It is therefore likely that local artisans accepted rice koji as a new key ingredient of their heritage dish in order to give the taste broader appeal and make the taste of their salty heritage dish known to the general public, including nonlocal consumers.

I was not able to establish exactly when rice koji became one of the key ingredients for *heshiko-narezushi*, but the localization of rice koji usage is notable. Using rice koji is now common practice in Tagarasu and the neighboring communities. Local crafters try to adjust the sweetness of *heshiko-narezushi* by changing the amount of rice koji, making the inter- and intra-household and communal taste of the heritage dish yet more diverse. This process of localization of new ingredients accompanied by a simultaneous diversification of local taste can be conceptualized as a cultural practice in which local heritage dish artisans construct and negotiate their regional identities through food in postindustrial society.

Taste

While locals agree that *saba-heshiko-narezushi* is the symbol of their shared heritage food culture in the Uchitomi Bay area and potentially a cultural resource for community revitalization, there is no agreement on the genuine taste of *saba-heshiko-narezushi*. Some residents of Tagarasu and the neighboring communities continue to make *heshiko-narezushi* (although their numbers are declining); however, the recipes of *heshiko-narezushi* differ by household and community. In the discourse surrounding the taste and authenticity of *heshiko-narezushi*, household crafters place emphasis on their home recipes and they aim to preserve the recipe and taste their ancestors have passed down the generations. To be loyal to their tradition, I often hear them stating, "I do not add unnecessary things (*yokei na mono wo ireteinai*)." That is, using what their ancestors did not use for making this heritage dish is like introducing a contaminant to the sacred domain of the heritage recipe (Douglas 2012). The symbolic pollution and material change in taste of the *heshiko-narezushi* is a matter of great importance in the social production of local food tradition and identity.

Authenticity holds a nonmaterial value enacted in the representation and discourse of heterogeneous actors, and the standard of authenticity is not fixed but rather continuously negotiated among them (Appadurai 1996). The "right" taste and the "authenticity" of taste also emerge through cultural and political frictions. Household crafters criticize the commoditization of heritage *heshiko-narezushi* by nonlocal food companies. However, they are ambivalent about the effort of maintaining culinary knowledge and techniques by training other local residents, part of which involves both nonprofit and for-profit commercialization of locally crafted *heshiko-narezushi* for building reputation and securing operational income.

Vinegar, Rice Wine, and Other Seasonings

The regional acceptance of new ingredients emerges in the discourse of authenticity among local crafters. Recipes of *heshiko-narezushi* have developed and been passed down by each fishing household. Local artisans state that all *heshiko-narezushi* tastes different each year. The texture and color of the fermented mackerel and mildness of the taste differ from one cask to another and from one household to another. For example, most people of Tagarasu use the seven ingredients for making *heshiko-narezushi*: mackerel (*heshiko*), salt, rice bran, red pepper, rice, rice koji, and rice vinegar. Using any other material is considered tantamount to an act of polluting the heritage recipe beyond the household level. If anyone uses materials other than those seven ingredients, their *heshiko-narezushi* will be rumored to be "not real" or "fake," and he or she will become subject to criticism for promoting "inauthentic" and "unsafe" *heshiko-narezushi* outside their communities.

The tension between communities over the authorship of an authentic *heshiko-narezushi* exists. The people of Tagarasu dip the cleaned *heshiko*-mackerel in rice vinegar before stuffing their bodies with rice and rice koji. However, artisans in neighboring communities state that this only happens in Tagarasu. *Heshiko-narezushi* is a kind of *narezushi* (aged sushi), which generates sourness with natural lactic acid fermentation by using rice and rice koji. In theory, it does not require the addition of plant-based vinegar to create a sour flavor or for the purpose of sanitization, as with *hayazushi* (fresh sushi). The addition of rice vinegar might be for balancing the flavor, for enhancing food safety, or due to an undocumented hybridization of the regional heritage aged sushi method and the globally accepted fresh sushi preparation method.

It is safe to say that heritage dishes like *saba-heshiko-narezushi* have changed their ingredients and tastes over time. In Mihama town, which is known for its *heshiko* production, rice wine and soy sauce are often added to rice bran and salt in the production process in order to sweeten it and adapt it to the palate of contemporary consumers. Meanwhile, *heshiko* crafted in Tagarasu and other Uchitomi Bay coastal communities is made only from mackerel, rice bran, salt, and red pepper. Because the sweetness derived from rice wine and sugar is different from that which rice bran generates through fermentation, local artisans in Tagarasu and other neighboring coastal communities argue that this kind of seasoning process makes it inauthentic.

The sweetening of heritage dishes is also seen in the production of *heshiko-narezushi*. For example, a female crafter in her sixties adds rice wine when making *heshiko-narezushi* in order to sweeten it. By doing so, she argues that *heshiko-narezushi* becomes more assessable in terms of taste—her grandchildren and other people of younger generations find it a more familiar taste and closer to food they consume on a daily basis. While she recognizes that people in her own as well as neighboring communities do not use rice wine in order to maintain and pass on the taste that has been inherited from their ancestors, she simply hopes that more people will be able to enjoy and appreciate the taste of their heritage dish; otherwise, she believes that it will be difficult to maintain *heshiko-narezushi* as a heritage dish and preserve its cultural significance and cooking practices in the future.

Heritage Dish as a Boundary Object

Local artisans recognize that it takes time to make *heshiko-narezushi* and that labor and time are required for the proper aging and taste of their heritage dish. It takes a minimum of around one year to make *heshiko*-mackerel, and it takes an additional ten days to two weeks to complete the second fermentation process for *heshiko-narezushi*, if artisans hope to make it with a less fishy smell but without using salted mackerel. They hope that this process of aging, the slow fermenting cooking method, adds the value for commercializing the product outside of their communities. Meanwhile, local artisans are critical of the industrialization of *heshiko-narezushi* production targeting nonlocal tourists. In order to maintain *heshiko-narezushi* as a heritage dish for future generations, some local crafters emphasize the importance of the number of present and potential consumers. The commoditization of *heshiko-narezushi* targeting urban foodies may help develop their consumer base beyond their kinship and *satouri* exchange networks. However, others believe that large-scale production of *heshiko-narezushi* is unrealistic because the *real heshiko-narezushi* is produced at a household or a community level. While they welcome the promotion and widening recognition of their heritage dish outside of the local communities, they are concerned that industrially produced *heshiko-narezushi* manufactured with food additives might give nonlocal tourists and potential new consumers a bad impression based on its inauthentic taste, as opposed to the *real* taste of their handcrafted produce.

Defining the right recipe is difficult in terms of time and space. There may be as many variations of the "real" taste of *heshiko-narezushi* as there are household crafters. It is challenging to define the "old, authentic taste" and regulate the quality of *heshiko-narezushi* beyond households and communities. Each household has a unique microbial environment, or unique terroir. Thus, each household creates the traditional taste of *heshiko* and *heshiko-narezushi*. Should Norwegian mackerel be used as its fattiness is suitable for contemporary taste preferences? Should rice koji be accepted as a traditional ingredient? How about rice vinegar? The distinction between real and fake becomes complex as the definition of "old times" is very blurry. However, it is this blurriness that heritage food can operate as a boundary object (Star 2010) to reproduce regional identity. Local artisans can claim the authenticity of their recipe because each of them can translate the reality of *heshiko-narezushi* from their experience and perspective (Satsuka 2015). Translations of food heritage and taste draw together local *narezushi* artisans and maintain their identity as gatekeepers of right recipe in opposition to industrial manufacturers, without compromising the cultural value of their unique double-fermented *kyodoshoku*, yet simultaneously enabling locals to distinguish their authorship from others and creating the intracommunal food diversity.

Conclusion

Heshiko-narezushi plays multiple social roles in the identity construction and negotiation in rural fishing communities in postindustrial Japan. It is mobilized as a regional cultural resource that supports local community revitalization and reproduces regional identity through various social food activities. Recently, a group of veteran crafters have been teaching their knowledge and techniques to other local residents, and they work together to organize food education events for local elementary schools by offering free *narezushi* workshops. They have also established a small-scale, communal facility to produce and sell *heshiko-narezushi* to nonlocal, urban consumers, which secures the funds for running the free workshops. However, the scale of production is limited, and their operation is still nonprofit by nature. Demand for *heshiko-narezushi* remains strong locally, but not so much from nonlocal consumers. Local revitalization based on this heritage dish may help to maintain inter- and intracommunal networks and reproduce regional identity, but *heshiko-narezushi* has not yet received as much attention and reputation beyond the local region as local crafters would like, and they have yet to see the hoped-for increase in tourists and new residents moving to their areas.

Acknowledgments

This research was undertaken as part of *the Fukui Satoyama Culture Project* (PI: Ryo Nakamura) at the Fukui Satoyama-Satoumi Institute (2014–17). It was also funded by the Japan Society for the Promotion of Science Kakenhi C (JP17K03303).

Note

1 This chapter is based on a Japanese article that the author published in the *Bulletin of the National Museum of Ethnology*, Japan (Hamada 2019). Parts of this chapter were also presented at a workshop "Living Food: Foodways, Heritage, Health, and the Environment," held at Ecole des Hautes Etudes en Sciences Socials, Paris, France, in February 22–23, 2018.

References

Appadurai, A. (1996), *Modernity at Large: Cultural Dimensions of Globalization*, Minneapolis: University of Minnesota Press.
Ardren, T. (2018), "Now Serving Maya Heritage: Culinary Tourism in Yaxunah, Yucatan, Mexico," *Food and Foodways* 26(4): 290–312.
Brulotte, R. L. and M. A. Di Giovine, eds. (2014), *Edible Identities: Food as Cultural Heritage*, Burlington: Ashgate.
Counihan, C. and S. Højlund, eds. (2018), *Making Taste Public: Ethnographies of Food and the Senses*, London: Bloomsbury.
Douglas, M. (2012), *Purity and Danger*, New York and London: Routledge.
Hamada, S. (2019), "Changing Authenticity of Heritage Food: A Case Study of Fermented Mackerel Sushi in Coastal Southern Fukui," *Bulletin of the National Museum of Ethnology* 44(2): 291–322 (in Japanese).
Handler, R. (1986), "Authenticity," *Anthropology Today* 2(1): 2–4.
Hashimoto, A. and D. J. Telfer (2008), "From Saké to Sea Urchin: Food and Drink Festivals and Regional Identity in Japan," in C. M. Hall and Liz Sharples (eds.), *Food and Wine Festivals and Events around the World*, pp. 249–78, Amsterdam: Butterworth-Heinemann.
Holtzman, J. D. (2006), "Food and Memory," *Annual Review of Anthropology* 35: 361–78.
Ishige, N. (2011), *History of Japanese Food*, London and New York: Routledge.
Klein, J. A. (2018), "Heritagizing Local Cheese in China: Opportunities, Challenges, and Inequalities," *Food and Foodways* 26(1): 63–83.
Kozaki, M. (1986), "Microbes and Food (*Biseibutsu to Shokumotsu*)," in M. Kozaki and N. Ishige (eds.), *Fermentation and Food Culture (hakko to shoku no bunka)*, pp. 13–27, Tokyo: Domes Shuppan (in Japanese).
Kurumizawa, K. (1995), "The Starting Point of the Mackerel Route: The Heritage of Fish Distribution in Wakasa (*sabakaido no shiten - wakasa no sakana ryutsu densho*)," *Folkloric Culture* 7: 69–117 (in Japanese).
Mak, S.-W. (2014), "The Revival of Traditional Water Buffalo Cheese Consumption: Class, Heritage and Modernity in Contemporary China," *Food and Foodways* 22(4): 322–47.

Nakao, S. (2012), *Origin of Cuisines (Ryori no Kigen)*, Tokyo: Yoshikawa-Kobundo (in Japanese).

Obama City History Compilation Committee (1998), *The Municipal History of Obama*, vol. 2, Obama: Ohama City History Compilation Committee.

Ohnuki-Tierney, E. (1993), *Rice as Self: Japanese Identity through Time*, Princeton: Princeton University Press.

Rath, E. (2015), "The Invention of Local Food," in J. Farrer (ed.), *The Globalization of Asian Cuisines: Transnational Networks and Culinary Contact Zones*, pp. 145–64, New York: Palgrave MacMillan.

Ruddle, K. and N. Ishige (2010), "On the Origins, Diffusion and Cultural Context of Fermented Fish Products in Southeast Asia," in J. Farrer (ed.), *Globalization, Food and Social Identities in the Asia Pacific Region*, Tokyo: Sophia University Institute of Comparative Culture. URL: http://icc.fla.sophia.ac.jp/global%20food%20papers/html/ruddle _ishige.html, last accessed April 14, 2020.

Sato, Y. (2008), *Rice and Fish (kome to sakana)*, Tokyo: Domes Shuppan.

Satsuka, S. (2015), *Nature in Translation: Japanese Tourism Encounters the Canadian Rockies*, Durham: Duke University Press.

Shimonaka, T. and N. Ichiya (2016), "Traditional Events and Mackerel in Wakasa Obama (*Wakasa obama no dentogyoji to saba*)," in Wakasa Obama Food Culture Museum (ed.), *Traditional Event and Food in Obama City (Obamashi no dentogyoji to shoku)*, pp. 211–19, Obama: Wakasajibunka Kenkyukai (in Japanese).

Shinoda, T. (2002), *A Book of Sushi*, Tokyo: Iwanami Shoten (in Japanese).

Star, S. L. (2010), "This Is Not a Boundary Object: Reflections on the Origin of a Concept," *Science, Technology, & Human Values* 35(5): 601–17.

Sutton, D. E. (2001), *Remembrance of Repasts: An Anthropology of Food and Memory*, Oxford and New York: Berg.

Wilk, R. R. (1999), "'Real Belizean Food': Building Local Identity in the Transnational Caribbean," *American Anthropologist* 101(2): 244–55.

4

Tides High and Low

The Changing Landscapes of *Gongfu Cha* Tea Culture in Contemporary China

Lanlan Kuang

Introduction: *Gongfu Cha* as Heritage

One of my fondest memories of visiting my grandparents in Chaozhou, the "city of tides,"[1] is of drinking endless rounds of strongly brewed, highly fragrant, and boiling-hot *gongfu cha* in their lake-front courtyard house. Served in a set of three small, shallow porcelain cups,[2] the clear, caramel-colored oolong tea, poured from a hand-sized clay teapot in the shape of a persimmon, had an airy, aromatic scent, a robust flavor, and a long-lingering sweetness, after initially a slight bitterness. The tangible preparation of *gongfu cha* started with fetching water fresh from the well in the courtyard and continued with boiling water in a clay kettle over burning smokeless olive-pit charcoal on a small red clay stove, made in a local style. Customarily prepared by the head of the family, the processes of making and drinking *gongfu cha* was not to be rushed. Served throughout the day from the moment one woke in the morning until one retired at night, for the Chaozhouese people, *gongfu cha* was and remains an intangible cultural heritage,[3] which defines people's sense of time, space, taste, and identity (see Lefevbre 1991).

In this chapter, I start reviewing the philosophical implications of the name of *gongfu cha* itself—a name rooted deeply in Confucian[4] ethos and neo-Confucian practice, long part of Chaozhou's local history and folk tradition under the influence of Tang dynasty statesmen like Han Yu (768–824 CE; in all dates I am using the Gregorian, and not the Chinese calendar). I argue that the conscious revival of *gongfu cha* as an instance of Chaozhouese cultural heritage, led by elite connoisseurs and intellectuals in present-day China, evokes nostalgia for a philosophical landscape of traditional Chinese aesthetics far beyond tea drinking. This landscape, embodied in Chaozhou *gongfu cha*, is generally overlooked in studies that focus on the role of Chaozhou *gongfu cha* as an inspiration for the modern invention of *chayi*, the Chinese tea art (Kim and Zhang 2012; Zhang 2016), or on its role as an everyday practice in contemporary Chaozhou (d'Abbs 2019). I propose that it is through this shared, philosophically rooted, aesthetically defined taste that a uniquely Chaozhouese identity is formed in a reterritorializing process—locally, regionally, nationally, and internationally. For the Chaozhouese people, *gongfu cha* became what Krishnendu Ray called "a place-making practice" (2004: 5). This shared taste and the reterritorializing process must nevertheless be understood within the dialogues among Chaozhouese culture, its diaspora communities, and Confucian tradition—dynamic processes that emerge from and embody the performative processes of *gongfu cha* heritage in the concomitant trends of modernization and globalization. As Ayora-Diaz pointed out, cooking and food create a (social) sense of taste that inspires "a set of aesthetic values and worldviews that are furthered as the ontological property of the hegemonic group of a society, and are used to draw cultural boundaries that separate it from other social groups" (2012b: 58). In this case, a shared aesthetic taste for *gongfu cha* heritage transcends territorial and socioeconomic differences and reflects the traditional Chaozhou ideals of harmonious social bonds.

Combining historical analysis of the origin and transmission of Chaozhou *gongfu cha* with multisite ethnographic fieldwork in Chaozhou and Jingdezhen, this chapter investigates the landscape of *gongfu cha* tea culture, among both the local and diaspora Chaozhouese communities in contemporary China. It highlights the tangible and intangible elements of Chaozhou *gongfu cha* tea culture against the backdrop of contemporary China's economic growth and sustainable consumption, such as branding porcelain tea wares and capitalizing ancient tea tree cultivation.

Gongfu in the Chinese Cosmos

Tea and the highly cultivated art of tea drinking epitomize Chinese philosophy, yet most scholarship on *gongfu cha* seldom addresses the philosophical and aesthetic suggestions behind its name. Without exploring performatively its naming process as taxonomic, *gongfu* tea has thus been removed from the history of philosophical ideas that should have provided aesthetic substance and cultural context for an understanding of *gongfu cha* as a living, changing, and dynamic intangible heritage characteristic of the city Chaozhou.

In this chapter's section, Chaozhou *gongfu cha* is discussed first in relation to *gongfu*, the philosophical concept used by the Song-Ming neo-Confucians as a general term for their Confucian learning. Second, I introduce the arrival and long-lasting influence of Tang dynasty statesman Han Yu, a forerunner of the later neo-Confucian school, who "reversed the tide of Confucian decline" (Chan 1963: 450) as a part of Chaozhou's local history and folk tradition. The history of *gongfu cha* as an intangible cultural heritage in Chaozhou concludes this section and lays the foundation for the next one, on *gongfu cha*'s tangible form, aesthetic essence, and gendered landscape. The final section investigates the transmission and development of *gongfu cha* in Jingdezhen in Jiangxi Province in contemporary times while highlighting a uniquely Chaozhouese identity, discursively formed locally, regionally, nationally, and internationally through sharing a philosophically rooted, aesthetically defined taste for Chaozhou *gongfu cha*.

My goal is to establish a philosophical foundation for explaining the shared aesthetic taste that contributes to the creation of a Chaozhouese identity through what Ayora-Diaz (2010, 2012a) called *territorialization*, a process which encompasses a complex of historical transformations that explain how a specific set of gustatory preferences has become coextensive with the territory and the culinary culture of a particular region.

In Confucianism, the highest aim is to become a sage, and "the ultimate purpose of Neo-Confucianism is to teach men how to achieve Confucian Sage-hood" (Fung 1991: 489). To the Song-Ming neo-Confucians, especially Wang Yangming (1472–1529 CE), the term *gongfu* encompasses the effort, method, aim, and achievements for Confucian learning. *Gongfu* methods aim at achieving excellence in ability, whereas moral norms are standards for regulating people's behavior at an acceptable level. The use of this term shows that cultivation is not merely a matter of conforming to a set of moral norms, but more broadly a matter of mastering the art of living. *Gongfu* is hence understood as an art that allows a person to attain a virtuous state far beyond the mere restoration of a normal condition.

Neo-Confucianism was a reaction to the challenge of Daoism and Buddhism during the Sui and Tang dynasties, when Han Yu, Li Ao, and other scholars were calling upon China's intellectual elite to rebuke Buddhism as a form of superstition, but the term *gongfu* nevertheless developed into "a locus from which a cluster of meanings emerged and used broadly for all the arts of life that require cultivated abilities and effective skills" (Ni 2016: xii). The Daoists and Buddhists unequivocally spoke of their learning as *gongfu*. This was paired with *Benti* for replacing the original pair of opposites *Yong* and *Ti* in Wang Bi's (226–49 CE) commentary on the fourth chapter of Daoist canon, *Lao Zi*, and these terms refer to paired cosmic states: the latent and the manifest. The unconscious bearing of Buddhist elements in the mind of the neo-Confucians led to attempts to synthesize the ethnically humanistic realism and the highly religious mysticism of Chan Buddhism. In the Tiantai School of Buddhism, the fountainhead of Chan Buddhism, the Absolute is regarded as *Ti* and its manifestations as *Yong*, following the teaching of Seng-Chao, the fourth-century Buddhist who continued to view the cosmos in terms of *Xin* (mind), which refers to *Ti*, the "latent" and *Yong*, its manifestations. Wang Yangming then argued for a different philosophical interpretation and cultivation of the *xin* (Mind-Heart).

Song-Ming neo-Confucianism revived multiple strands of Confucian philosophy and political culture, beginning in the middle of the ninth century and reaching new levels of intellectual and social creativity in the eleventh century in the Northern Song dynasty. The first phase of the revival of the Confucian tradition, completed by the philosopher Zhu Xi (1130–1200 CE), became the benchmark for all future Confucian intellectual discourse and social theory. Opposing the escapism and nihilism of Daoism and Buddhism and promoting activity and stability in an unstable society, the humanistic concepts in the teaching of neo-Confucianism were initially welcomed by realistically minded Chinese. The argument, prominently made by Mencius (370–290 BCE), that humans by nature are fundamentally good, became an assertion that morality could be pursued through an engagement in human affairs. By the fourteenth century, Zhu's version of Confucian thought, known as *dao xue* (the Teaching of the

Way) or *li xue* (the Teaching of Principle), had become the standard curriculum for imperial civil service examinations until the whole system was abolished in 1905.

Gongfu in Chaozhou

Located on the far east of the Guangdong province on a plain of approximately 10,000 square kilometers in the coastal area in southern China, Chaozhou is known as "the seaside homeland of Mencius and Confucius" with many unique cultural attributes. Cultural development began flourishing in the region as early as the end of Eastern Han (221–316 CE). Chaozhouese dialect is considered one of the oldest Chinese dialects and has a special position in the study of Chinese linguistics. While most Chaozhouese can communicate with any subgroup of the Min, a group of Chinese dialects spoken mainly in southeast China and the peninsular territory, the local Chaozhouese dialect differs entirely in phonetic structure from Cantonese spoken in the Pearl River Delta to its west and from Hakka spoken in the mountainous areas to its north. For instance, the Chinese character for tea is pronounced *cha* or *ch'a* in both the Cantonese dialect spoken by China's southern coastal population and the Mandarin dialect spoken by the northern Chinese, but in Chaozhouese dialect, tea is pronounced *dê* or *tê*.[5]

Chaozhou was under the influence of the official ideology based on Confucianism during China's imperial times, like other regions of Guangdong. Han Yu's arrival in Chaozhou as prefectural governor in 819 was a key factor in the city's celebration of Confucian tradition. Known for bringing the Zhou Lu Traditions,[6] Han Yu, minister of justice during the reign of the Tang emperor Xianzong (778–820 CE) was sent to Chaozhou because of his admonition against the emperor's decision to welcome Buddhist relics. During his time as governor of Chaozhou prefecture, Han focused on education and advocated Confucianism, in which items of heritage are handed down from generation to generation. Confucianism has therefore infused into Chaozhouese lives. For instance, local people call Chaozhou music and Chaozhou opera "Confucianism music" and "Confucianism opera." Confucius emphasized social harmony and ethics. Music was considered both an art to be revered and, more importantly, part of the rite to bring harmony to oneself, to society, then to the country, and ultimately to the cosmic order.

After the Tang's collapse and the unrest of the Five Dynasties (907–60 CE), China's central government and cultural center was moving southward. Gazetteers therefore explicitly referred to Chaozhou's flourishing cultural treasures and gradual association with the Central Plains. Specifically, the *Chaozhou Provincial Gazetteer* in the Jiajing era (1522–66 CE) recorded the influence that Confucianism was having on local customs of the time:

> The rise of the Ming dynasty brought massive cultural development. As scholars-*literati* became acquainted with Neo-Confucianism, customs changed dramatically. Rites for capping,[7] marriage, death and sacrifices were largely guided by the rules in Zhu Xi's *Family Rites* and people regarded the area as the "seaside homeland of

Confucius and Mencius." . . . In all families, people read the *Book of Songs* and the *Book of History*, and the sound of their recitation and singing echoed throughout the land. (Chen 2018: 236)

As a result of the revival of Confucianism in China since the Reform and Opening in the 1980s, Chaozhou studies (*Chao xue*), dedicated to addressing the Confucian literati's representations of Chaozhou in classical literature, was created as an academic discipline in the 1990s. Pertinent scholarship was initially funded by merchants of Chaozhou origin in Hong Kong, one of the homes of the global Chaozhou diaspora community.

"Chaozhou *Gongfu Cha*" Tea Culture

In ethnographic disciplines, special attention has been directed to analyzing the discursive aspects and the narrative characters of cultural representation. Naming is explored here as a form in the gastro-rhetorical strategy, specifically, Chaozhou *gongfu cha* tea culture, *chayi* "tea art," and *chadao* "the way of tea."

In 2008, when *Chaozhou gongfu cha* was named one of China's national intangible heritages, *chayi* (tea art) was added at the end of the term, possibly for categorization purposes. *Chaozhou gongfu chayi* was listed in the "Folk Custom" category. While "Chaozhou," the regional specification, highlights the cultural-geographic aspects of *gongfu cha* as an intangible heritage within the rhetoric of the Chinese nation, stating the administrative power over the region and its cultural policies, categorizing the Chaozhou *gongfu cha* as a "tea art" highlights the reinvented and modernized nature of the heritage under current sociopolitical and economic influences.

The differences among Chaozhou *gongfu cha* (as a tea culture), *chayi* (tea art), and *chadao* (the way of tea) are notable. In Chaozhou and among the Chaozhouese diaspora communities, *gongfu cha* is almost never referred as a "tea art" but as a performative tea culture that enacts the region's philosophical way (the *gongfu* [Way]) of *being* in the world (Kuang 2019a). According to Kim and Zhang (2012), who traced the modern application of the word *chayi* to Feng Shiye's *The Art of Drinking Tea* (1971), *chayi* (tea art) is but a modern Chinese tea practice emerged from *gongfu cha* under the influence of Taiwan and Japan. *Chayi* was then transmitted from Hong Kong to, and flourished during the 1970s in, postcolonial Taiwan (from its Japanese occupation between 1895 and 1945) as a reaction to China's Cultural Revolution[8] and Taiwan's economic growth after the Second World War.[9] For these reasons, Zhang (2016: 53) argued:

Gongfucha has been transformed from a regional practice to one with a national identity, and is increasingly talked of as a Chinese way of tea, rather than simply as a Chaozhouese method of brewing tea. . . . Not only does this new form of tea brewing, named *chayi* (tea arts) by its proponents, owe its form to Chaozhouese tea practice, but it also borrows aesthetic and philosophical underpinnings from the Japanese tea tradition.

The Jiajing era was also a time that witnessed a growing interest in covenants (*xiangyue*), a concept of subcounty organization that emphasized the harmonizing of social relations and moral education, but with ultimate individual responsibility for one's self-cultivation. The covenant of the Wang Yangming school stressed *gongfu*, the constant work of moral effort to extend one's innate moral knowledge, and covenants were implemented in Chaozhou as early as 1404. The neo-Confucian formula of covenants created a form of [local] public sphere which continues into modern time as various forms of "societies" (*hui*), including chambers of commerce (Rankin 1990; Woodside 2006).

When discussing the development of *chayi* under the Japanese occupation of Taiwan, or as a part of China's national rhetoric, it is critical to consider the prominence of Chaozhouese diaspora communities and their culinary heritages in Taiwan from a historical perspective. In a study on the spatial distribution pattern of the prominent family in Taizhong, a special municipality in central Taiwan, Huang (2018) shows that more than half of the families migrated from the southern part of Chaozhou prefecture during the Qing Dynasty (1644–1912 CE). Such a diasporic community in present-day Taizhong city "marks a close and continuous connections between the island and Chaozhou due to their existing phonetic relations and geographical relations" (Huang 2018: ii). In Tseng's (2015) research on Taiwan's "*sha-cha* sauce," a popular culinary culture that originated in Southeast Asia, he highlights the role Chaozhouese immigrants play as cultural agents in transforming the culture of *satay* into *sha-cha*, which then made its way to Taiwan with the Chaozhouese diaspora after the Second World War. Many Chaozhouese people moved to Taiwan's port city of Gaoxiong as part of the Chinese Nationalist Party's exodus from Mainland China. Many of them settled in the present-day Southern Gushan (Hamashin) District, which had been the most important business and administration district in Gaoxiong during the Japanese colonial period of Taiwan. These Chaozhouese immigrants introduced *sha-cha* sauce to Gaoxiong, both by establishing a factory to produce it and by serving cuisine based on it in local restaurants to outsiders who would come to Gaoxiong to pursue commercial opportunities.

Unlike the controversial word *chayi*, which is "a neologism without historical background" (Zhang 2016: 55), the term *chadao*, "the Way of tea," has a historical reference going back to Jiaoran (730–99 CE), a prominent Tang dynasty poet-monk and a close friend of Lu Yu (733–804 CE), author of the earliest extant treatise on tea, the *Classic of Tea*. In "Floating Alone on West Stream," Jiaoran wrote:

> The first drink dissolves torpor and sleepiness.
> A radiant feeling fills heaven and earth.
> The second drink purifies my spirit,
> As a sudden shower washes away the light dust.
> With the third drink I immediately attain the *dao*.
> Why labor so hard with the mind to destroy the afflictions?

The term *dao* (the Way) has a philosophical status in ancient Chinese thought similar to that of "Truth" in Western philosophy. In Confucian contexts, the Way is typically the principle of moral behavior manifested through human acts, such as the virtuous act of benevolence, or music and other arts expressed through rites (Kuang 2019a). Instead of a form of *chayi*, Chaozhou *gongfu cha* was described historically as "a way of brewing generated from Lu Yu's *Classic of Tea* by Yu Jiao, a scholar who visited Chaozhou during the late eighteenth century." In *Chao-jia fengyue ji*, a book in which he recorded various customs and practices in Chaozhou at the time, Yu used the term *gongfu cha* for the first time: "Gongfu cha, the way of brewing originated from Lu Yu's *Classic of Tea*, except the tea wares are even more exquisite" (Yu 1994: 750). Scholars therefore came to believe that contemporary Chaoshan *gongfu cha* is a modern manifestation of the methods for preparing and drinking tea in the Tang dynasty (Chen and Chen 2004). Given the Confucian origin and application of the term *gongfu*, Chaozhou *gongfu cha* may therefore be best approached as a tea culture which enacts the Way of tea in a performative manner.

Chaozhou *Gongfu Cha*: Form, Essence, and Gendered Landscape

In the previous section, the nature of *gongfu* in Song-Ming neo-Confucian philosophical context is defined as a way that allows a person to attain a virtuous state for obtaining sagehood. In this section, Chaozhou *gongfu cha* is further explored as a conceptual time frame that emerged from within the embodied aesthetic experience of *chadao*, "the Way of tea."

In a tangible form, Chaozhou *gongfu cha* involves meeting three conditions ("three gains taste") and having four so-called treasures. The three conditions are people who (co-)exist and embody a harmonious space for enjoying tea, suitable water from natural spring or flowing river, and high-grade tea, preferably Fenghuang Dancong (Phoenix Dancong). The four treasures include a set of three Ruoshen porcelain teacups, a Mengchen clay teapot, a Yushu clay kettle, and a Chaoshan-style red clay stove.

Three Gains Taste

From the Confucian perspective, striving for harmony necessarily encompasses self-cultivation so that he may realize the Way (*dao*). To follow the Way means to follow one's human nature and demonstrate benevolence (reciprocity) (*ren*) to other people. For this reason, the concept "One gains spirit, two gains rhyme, three gains taste" gives more than the ideal number of people for sharing Chaozhou *gongfu cha* at one setting. It provides context for understanding Chaozhou *gongfu cha* as a philosophically rooted heritage performance.

In Chinese philosophy, especially aesthetic theories, *shen* (spirit) refers to the moment when the artist's mind and body become perfectly attuned, resonating with the creative source of the cosmos. *Shen* is also known and sometimes translated as *qi*, the vital principle or natural energy of all nature—animate and inanimate—not just of living beings. When one enjoys Chaozhou *gongfu cha* alone, one's mind and body are synchronized through a series of mindful, conscious action. Tea making is thus a creative process through interaction between animated human agency and unanimated objects, such as tea wares, and the surrounding space. Alone, one is to perform the act of self-cultivation for obtaining sagehood through prescribed rituals.

There are "occasions in which the change/transformation of qi is so extraordinary, subtle and mysterious that it transcends our grasp" (Henry 2008: 2). At such moments, *qi* becomes *yun*, as in the phrase "*qi yun*," often translated as "spirit consonance," suggesting agreement or harmony, and the translation "spirit resonance" suggests an amplification produced by a sympathetic vibration. When two people enjoy Chaozhou *gongfu cha* together, their bodily presence and coordinated interactions creates *yun*. The Chinese character for "taste" or "appreciate" is *pin* 品, an iconographic image of three mouths sharing food in one occasion. Three *gongfu cha* teacups form the character 品 visually. If there are more than three people, then the emptied teacups are rinsed with boiled hot water before they are rotated to the other drinkers. The number *three* in the Chinese cosmos looms large, as it applies to heaven, earth, and human, a triad that, when realized in one setting, creates harmony. This view of number correspondences as embodying numinous significance has been recorded in early Chinese philosophical texts, such as the *Huainanzi*:

> Thus it is said, "The Dao begins with one." One (alone), however, does not give birth. Therefore, it divided into *yin* and *yang*. From the harmonious union of *yin* and *yang*, the myriad things were produced. Thus it is said, "One produced two, two produced three, three produced the myriad things," and Heaven and Earth. (Major 1994: 125–6)

Four Treasures

Unlike modernized *chayi*, for which the tea set must include numerous items, traditional Chaozhou *gongfu cha* requires only the "four treasures": a set of two to three small, shallow porcelain cups, known as Ruoshen cups (若琛瓯); a hand-sized, persimmon-shaped Mengchen clay teapot (孟臣罐) from Yixing; a Yushu clay kettle (玉书煨); and a small, Chaoshan-style red clay stove (潮汕炉). High-grade olive-pit charcoal, which produces almost no smoke, is preferred for boiling water. Among these, the teapot is the most important, and the purple-sand teapot produced in Yixin, Jiangsu Province, is the best choice. Ruoshen cups refer to its maker, Li Ruochen 李若琛, a famous potter in Jindezhen, present-day Jiangxi Province, during the Qing Dynasty.

The selection and use of each set of highly specialized, fine porcelain tea wares together create a landscape that connects nature and culture, the individual and society, utility and beauty. The aesthetic ideal emerging from these relations is the philosophical idea of "*Tian ren he ye*," or "Heaven Human United in One." This has been one of the most prominent aesthetic ideals or principles founded in traditional Chinese arts since ancient times. It is more than a principle dominating the philosophy of beauty, but a philosophical idea that has penetrated and governed various fields in the Chinese society—social, cultural, political, and economic.

Aesthetic Essence: Time, Space, Taste

Time

Time, which stands at the core of Chaozhou *gongfu cha*, is approached both philosophically and in relation to its tangible form for understanding the essence of a shared taste cultivated though the complex process. Preparing *gongfu cha* is a time-consuming task. Scholars have broken the whole process from eight to twenty-one steps that starts with utensil preparation using the "four treasures." In a passage describing the process of experiencing *gongfu cha*, the Qing Dynasty gastronome Yuan Mei (1716–97 CE) wrote in *The Menu of the Sui Garden*, a book on food: "Holding the cup to the mouth, you must not swallow in haste, but first smell its fragrance, and then taste and contemplate it." In light of globalization and commercialization, the lifestyle in Chaozhou remains relatively slow in comparison to metropolitan cities like Beijing, Shanghai, and Guangzhou. Stephanie Assmann (2010) has investigated how the members of Japan's "Slow Food Movement" advocate an overall slower pace of life that "invites people to connect with their local food heritage and re-think their conventional eating habits and living patterns while emphasizing the pleasures of (sharing) food" (Assmann 2010: 7). Instead of arguing that Chaozhouese people are consciously keeping a slow-paced lifestyle through promoting its intangible heritage like *gongfu cha*, I argue that through *gongfu cha* the Chaozhouese people creates a conceptual time frame in a performative manner. It is common for the Chaozhouese people to communicate and plan events in *gongfu cha* tea time: "come visit, we are about to have tea," "we are having [number rounds of] tea now," or "you are late, we already finished [rounds] of tea." It is also common for people to enjoy *gongfu* tea when they are at work or alone. Chaozhou *gongfu cha* is not bounded by business hours (as in a teahouse) nor by daily routine (as in a specified, set time scheduled to be enforced). Instead, it defines time for the Chaozhouese people, thereby creating a conceptual time frame that contributed to the discursive formation of a Chaozhouese identity.

Space

Spaces created through tangible objects are measured in various forms: the size and thus volume of *gongfu cha* tea wares and the spatial arrangement of a Chaozhou *gongfu cha* session. As Yuan Mei observed in the same passage on *gongfu cha* quoted earlier: "The cups are small as walnuts, the pot as small as a fragrant lemon. No more than one *liang* (ounce) is poured at a time." The size and volume of the teapot and the teacups sets restrictions over time that produce the taste uniquely tied to Chaozhou *gongfu cha*. The pot and cups restrict the amount of tea leaves and water to be used for each round of tea being served, thereby determining the taste and consistency of each round of the tea being served and the temperature of tea for each round.

The spatial arrangement for Chaozhou *gongfu cha* distinguishes it from most commercialized *chayi* (tea art) in most tea shops and teahouses. For Chaozhou *gongfu cha*, the three teacups are always placed on a circular-shaped tea dish (thereby forming the Chinese character for "taste") as the host and the guests sit around the table in a circle. Traditionally, tables in Chaozhou are more likely to be square or round for facilitating access to all the dishes, in this case to the *gongfu cha* tea set. Modernized *chayi* most frequently uses an elongated table for demonstrating the tea master's skill and for providing access to a larger group of guests. The physical space created by the different table shape creates different conceptual space. A space of circular design is highly preferred in the Chinese tradition as it enhances the circulation of *qi* (see last section), connecting one body to another and creating resonance in a balanced manner. This kind of space also facilitates the Confucian communitarianism, a social and political thought that highlights social-harmonizing civilities. In comparison, the rectangular, elongated table creates a hierarchy based on the distance from the host (tea master). The demonstrative nature of *chayi* also created a space of exhibition, thereby changing the speed and the nature of interactivities among the performative cultural agents. In this sense, one could argue that the spatial arrangement of traditional Chaozhou *gongfu cha* tea culture is also a critical, embodied element in the creation of a regional identity during its reterritorializing process.

Taste

The notion of taste has been widely explored by philosophers and food scholars (Bourdieu 1984; Ayora-Diaz 2010, 2012a, b). In the realm of Chinese aesthetics, the human body is an integral part in the discussion of taste as the parochial bodily experience, the social-political practices, and philosophical understanding. Cognitively, a person who has practical understanding is said to be aware of the "self-so" or "self-disclosing" nature of the natural world while language provides conceptual metaphors representing the mind-body dichotomy (Kuang 2019a). In the Confucian context, especially according to Mencius *ku*, the taste of bitterness, is associated with physical and mental exercise that prepares one for advancement in life, while *gan*, the taste of sweetness, resembles the hard-earned reward after a Trial in life. To obtain the taste of *gan* means to have experienced and acquired a combined understanding of all the Five-Flavors (referring to sourness, bitterness, sweetness, piquancy, and saltiness) and the delicious taste of each of the Five-Flavors is called sweetness (*gan*).

In the case of Chaozhou *gongfu cha* tea culture, two seemly contrasting notions: *ku* 苦 (the taste of bitterness) and *gan* 甘 (the taste of sweetness) complement each other in both a physic-psychological and a socio-philosophical manner. *Huigan* 回甘 (turns from bitterness to sweetness) refers to the highly aestheticized taste experience characteristics of Chaozhou *gongfu cha*. Highly aromatic, "even more elegant than chewing plum blossoms," as Yuan Mei described, Chaozhou *gongfu cha* is a strongly intense brew to be appreciated in a contemplative manner. The appreciation for *huigan* and a cultivated, refined taste manifests Confucius's "self-discipline," as it is based on human desires for pleasure and a correct "Way" to sagehood. The inquiry into Chaozhou *gongfu cha*'s philosophical root are as essential to gastronomic commentary as to the refined appreciations of the shared, aestheticized taste. In *Mencius*, the sharing of taste in food and other bodily senses (the biological and the factual) lead to a shared taste in "heart" (the moral and the normative) as aspects of the human nature.

Gendered Landscape

Gender specification was a common social phenomenon in premodern China under the influence of Confucian ethos. Chaozhou was no exception. Unlike *chayi*, Chaozhou *gongfu cha* is served in a private, noncommercial setting, among families and friends. Women may be present, not for demonstrating their skills as a *chayishi* (tea master), nor for entertaining business clients in a commercialized tea shop setting. According to Confucian ethics, it was improper for a man and a woman to touch each other's hands when handing objects to one another. The *Li Ji* (Record of Rites) states that the distinction between men and women must be observed and preserved for the good of all: "If no distinction were observed between males and females, disorder would arise and grow" (Dawson 1915: 32). Such a rule of separation permits exchange in a Platonic sense but forbids physical contact: "The Master said, 'According to the rules, male and female do not give the cup, one to the other, except at sacrifice. This was intended to guard the people'" (Dawson 1915: 35). Taiwan's Ten Ren Group, a tea shop franchiser invested heavily throughout China and a main facilitator of the invented *chayi* was nevertheless known for its tea shops' female tea master-hosted sessions (Kim and Zhang 2012; Liu 2009).

In a study of gender and the needlework industry in eighteenth-century Chaozhou, Ellen Cai (2018: 85) highlights *fugong*, the female virtue of being diligent and good at weaving and sewing: "The image of an ideal wife was measured against this traditional yardstick."[10] *Fugong* signifies the Confucian ethic that a woman should tend household affairs from within, physically and metaphorically, whereas a man should handle affairs concerning the outside world. For this reason, in Chaozhou the head of the family, usually a senior male member, would prepare and serve *gongfu cha*. Adult male members are expected to shoulder most responsibilities of the family, just as it was the host's responsibility to handle everything during a *gongfu cha* session. Chaozhou men are assigned the task of overseeing family gatherings and hosting guests. Today, while such a gender pattern is still going strong in Chaozhou prefecture, Chaozhou women, especially those who live outside Chaozhou region but identify themselves as members of a diaspora community, provide an alternative to this tradition by taking up the role of host and serving friends and family *gongfu cha* in their own home.

In 2019, I interviewed two younger women who had moved from Chaozhou to Jingdezhen. Their comments shed light on both the changing and the unchanged patterns in Chaozhou *gongfu cha*'s gendered landscape. What remains the same is still the direct association between being the head of the household and the host of the *gongfu cha* session. As the younger generations of Chaozhou women become financially and socially independent, they gain the ability to afford their own housing and become the head of their own household without relying on a male companion.

Interviewee A is a single, career-driven, economically secure professional porcelain artist in her late thirties, who holds a lecturer position at Jingdezhen Ceramic University. She hosts *gongfu cha* sessions with her colleagues and students at her home almost daily. Her guests bring tea for sharing, and her students assist with fetching water and cleaning the tea wares, but she is always the one who serves the guests. When her father comes to visit, however, she is his assistant because "he is more skillful than I am" (Kuang 2019b).

Interviewee B works as a successful independent ceramic artist in Jingdezhen. Although she is married, she is the designated host of *gongfu cha* sessions in her family because her husband is "not from Chaozhou." Her responses showed superior knowledge and skill regarding *gongfu cha* sessions. She confessed that she had "never thought about this matter [gender patterns] regarding *gongfu cha*" (Kuang 2019b). When I asked if other female members in her family, such as her mother, are also the designated host of *gongfu cha* at her parents' household, she found the question fascinating and said, "yes, but my mother is an exceptional case [in comparison to most Chaozhou family units]. She [her mother] is a businesswoman and has a very strong, outgoing personality. She therefore serves her clients *gongfu cha* when they visit her at home" (Kuang 2019b).

Whereas female tea masters dominate the world of *gongfu chayi* tea art with increasing influences from China's market-oriented economy, in Chaozhou *gongfu cha* is still a male-dominated landscape. My study indicates that gender patterns should be considered a key factor for understanding the changing landscape of Chaozhou *gongfu cha* in contemporary time and for revealing the complexity and delicacy of the process of power negotiation within the Confucian framework of omnipresent patriarchy.

Tides Near and Far: Transmission and Development of Chaozhou *Gongfu Cha*

Chaozhou is known for its diaspora communities throughout China and around the globe. In Singapore, Chaozhouese make up about 20 percent of the Chinese resident population. Many prominent business tycoons and past and present cabinet ministers of Singapore are of Chaozhou origin, including its key architect, Lee Kuan Yew. Outside Asia, the Chaozhouese represent France's largest Chinese group. Tightly structured and culturally hegemonic, they dominate the Chinese economy in France (Benton and Gomez 2008: 164–5).

In the late 1980s, and after Deng Xiaoping's southern visit in 1992, people from Chaozhou started to migrate to booming inland cities or domestic metropolises in China and introduced the distinctive Chaozhouese culture through their network and within its diaspora communities. As Cheng (1997: 110) states: "Chaozhou émigrés brought this ritual to many overseas countries. It is safe to say that where there is Chaozhou people, there is Gongfu tea."

Chaozhou diasporas and gongfu cha in Jingdezhen, Jiangxi Province

The city of Chaozhou and Chaozhou *gongfu cha* are connected to Jingdezhen in more than one way. While Jingdezhen is the historically known "porcelain capital" of China,[11] in 2004 the China state government awarded the title of porcelain capital to Chaozhou, stripping Jingdezhen of the designation (Gillette 2016: 95–6). The Chaozhouese porcelains are famous for their fine quality, exquisite style, and colorful paintings. Ceramic artists from Chaozhou are trained first and formally as painters of traditional Chinese art before they start incorporating their skills and designs onto ceramic creations. Many porcelain merchants come to Jingdezhen from Chaozhou to establish business connections and make investments, but a handful of ceramic artists have moved to Jingdezhen. My ethnographic fieldwork in Jingdezhen since 2016 has been focusing on the diaspora community who made Jingdezhen its second home.

During my study of Chaozhou *gongfu* tea in Jingdezhen, I interviewed two groups of ceramic artists: local porcelain producers and merchants from Jingdezhen and Chaozhou porcelain producers and merchants who form a diaspora community in the city. While *chayi* has made its way throughout China and landed in Jingdezhen with investors from Taiwan and Hong Kong, Chaozhou *gongfu cha* was brought to Jingdezhen mainly through the Chaozhou diaspora community. Unlike the more popular *chayi*, which dominates the city's commercialized teahouses as a marketing strategy, Chaozhou *gongfu cha* is shared mostly within the Chaozhou diaspora community or its extended network affiliations. There are several reasons for Chaozhou *gongfu cha* to have taken root in Jingdezhen. Some Jingdezhen locals have acquired the competence and thus the reputation of "understanding the [*gongfu cha*] tea" by the Chaozhouese diaspora communities, as seen in Interviewee X's case (Kuang 2019b).

Representing Jingdezhen locals who "understand [*gongfu cha*] tea [culture]," Interviewee X and I met in his workshop over rounds of *gongfu cha*. In comparison to the fine porcelain tea ware and the high-grade Dancong oolong tea used for our *gongfu cha* session, X and his workshop appear plain and modest. During our interviews, X would make fresh rounds of *gongfu cha* on a small round table without interrupting our conversation. The design of the physical space in his workshop and the fluidity in his bodily movements during the tea session create the time-space unique to *gongfu cha* that I identified in the previous section.

In his study on the transmission of *sushi* in America, Kasulis (1995) identified four metrics needed for people and society to accept a foreign culture. These metrics are availability, positive image or respect of the host culture, internal need, and the acquiring of a taste. The first three must all be combined for the fourth metric to be met. Before Chaozhou *gongfu cha* started to take root in Jingdezhen, Interviewee X had been working with various Chaozhouese diaspora communities in China's metropolitan cities as their designated suppliers of fine porcelain tea sets. With a global network of chambers of commerce, Chaozhouese merchants have a powerful economic presence. X's clients are Chaozhou merchants who hold business meetings in their membership-only clubs, where only *gongfu cha* is served. "To meet my clients' need, I must first understand their need," said X, who worked as a librarian at the local ceramic institute before quitting to become a full-time ceramic merchant who designs and produces sample pieces.

According to Interviewee X, although Jingdezhen is known for producing some of the best-quality and best-known ceramic tea wares, including the Ruoshen cups in the "four treasures" for making *gongfu tea*, Jingdezhen's local tea culture is far from refined. According to Bourdieu, the food habits of working-class people were fundamentally different from middle-class food culture (1984: 179–201). Workers' food habits emphasized being and doing in the here and now, whereas the bourgeoisie escaped into forms, appearances, and better futures, as they did in other aesthetic areas. Unlike Chaozhou, Jingdezhen consists of generations of immigrant workers who come for purely economic reasons. The way the workshops in Jingdezhen are set up was highly specialized—meaning, each workshop would take on only one part of the production process. Such an assembly line guarantees speedy turnovers, but workers are trained as technicians who do one task their entire life. Even today, most of Jingdezhen's population consists of highly skilled technical workers. They consume tea to stay awake, in a less refined manner. Low-grade loose-leaf tea is prepared directly in a tall ceramic teacup with boiling water, often without a tea-leaf filter. Interviewee X's understanding of Chaozhou *gongfu cha* comes from his contact with the Chaozhouese diaspora communities (availability), his respect of the clients (positive image), and his desire to produce porcelain wares that meet the clients' aesthetics (internal need). Interviewee X therefore arrived at the final metric—taste—through his conscious cultivation of Chaozhou *gongfu cha* tea culture in Jingdezhen.

Conclusion

As I have argued in my study on the globalizing process of China's culinary heritage, the landscape of food in China has been transformed dramatically since ancient times. Mark Swislocki (2009), Jakob Klein (2006, 2013), and other scholars have presented extensive research on such transformations in China's culinary history, paying special attention to the resurgence of regional food culture in Shanghai as a form of "culinary nostalgia," and on diversity and foreign fare in China's gastronomic writings during Deng Xiaoping's "opening and reform" period, starting in the early 1980s. Growing local awareness and global recognition of traditional food as an intangible heritage accelerated these transformations (Kuang 2017). Chaozhou *gongfu cha* tea remains an exemplary cornerstone of a regional and local culinary identity while it also contributes through the global Chaozhouese diaspora communities to the design of a modern, reinvented Chinese identity. In this chapter, I have further argued that process of "manufacturing" Confucianism by reinventing it to suit the needs of their times—a process that commands both attention and admiration because it involved the virtual creation of a universal civilization that incorporates healthy elements from both Chinese and Western civilizations.

Notes

1 Folk etymology translates *Chaozhou* as "a place of rising and falling tides."
2 Each of these tools for making Chaozhou *gongfu cha*, collectively known as the "four essential treasures," is explained in detail in the following text.
3 In 2008, Chaozhou *gongfu cha* was officially listed as one of China's national intangible heritages.

4 Confucius was a political philosopher who lived *c.* 551–479 BCE and founded
   Confucianism, one of China's three teachings, of which the others are Daoism and
   Buddhism.

5 From a structural linguistic point of view, tea is considered a cultural item
   unconsciously adopted by individuals who exist within a given physical and social
   space through a set of language and grammatical rules.

6 "Zhou Lu Tradition" (Zhou Lu *zhi feng*) refers to the teachings from Zhou and Lu,
   the birthplaces of Mencius and Confucius, respectively. It first appeared in the Tiandi
   chapter of *Zhuangzi*, "Zhou Lu" is now an adjective term for praising a place for being
   highly civilized and cultured.

7 Chen's translation of "capping" refers to *guanli* and *jili*, the Confucius coming-of-age
   ceremony for men and women, respectively.

8 During the Cultural Revolution, from 1966 to 1976, traditional values were criticized
   and objects destroyed on a massive scale, leading to the revival of traditional
   culture known as the *guoxue* 国学 (national learning) movement, which started in
   postrevolutionary China in the 1980s.

9 Trade relations between Taiwan and the Chinese mainland were historically close and
   remained highly active, even during the Japanese occupation in the 1930s (Ash and
   Kueh 1993).

10 Weaving has been used metaphorically for describing women's virtuous work to cover
   even statecraft, the very apparatus with which Confucian scholars ensured.

11 Jingdezhen was the home of China's imperial kilns and a center for porcelain exports
   in the late Ming Dynasty (1368–1644).

References

Ash, R. and Y. Kueh (1993), "Economic Integration within Greater China: Trade and
    Investment Flows between China, Hong Kong and Taiwan," *The China Quarterly* 136:
    711–45.

Assmann, S. (2010), "Food Action Nippon and Slow Food Japan: The Role of Two Citizen
    Movements in the Rediscovery of Local Foodways," in J. Farrer (ed.), *Globalization,
    Food and Social Identities in the Asia Pacific Region*, pp. 1–14, Tokyo: Sophia University
    Institute of Comparative Culture.

Ayora-Díaz, S. I. (2010), "Regionalism and the Institution of the Yucatecan Gastronomic
    Field," *Food, Culture & Society* 13(3): 397–420.

Ayora-Díaz, S. I. (2012a), *Foodscapes, Foodfields, and Identities in Yucatán*, New York:
    Berghahn Books.

Ayora Díaz, S. I. (2012b), "Gastronomic Inventions and the Aesthetics of Regional Food:
    The Naturalization of Yucatecan Taste," *Etnofoor* 24(2): 57–76.

Benton, G. and E. Gomez (2008), *The Chinese In Britain, 1800–Present: Economy,
    Transnationalism, Identity*, New York: Palgrave Macmillan.

Bourdieu, P. (1984), *Distinction: A Social Critique of the Judgement of Taste*, trans. R. Nice,
    Cambridge, MA: Harvard University Press.

Cai, E. (2018), "Christianity and Needlework Industry in Chaoshan," in J. Lee (ed.),
    Christianizing South China: Mission, Development, and Identity in Modern Chaoshan,
    pp. 81–101, London: Palgrave Macmillan.

Chan, W. (1963), *A Source Book in Chinese Philosophy*, Princeton: Princeton University
    Press.

Chen, B. (2018), "Rites Bridging the Ancient and Modern: The Revival of Offerings at Urban Ancestral Temples," in *Rites Bridging the Ancient and Modern: The Revival of Offerings at Urban Ancestral Temples*, pp. 235–61, Leiden: Brill.

Chen, X. (1997), *Chouzhou gongfucha gailun* (Theories of Chaozhou *gongfucha*), Shantou: Shantou daxue chubanshe.

Chen, X. and Z. Chen (2004), *Gongfucha yu Chaozhou zhuni hu* (*Gongfucha* and vermillion clay pots of Chaozhou), Shantou: Shantou daxue chubanshe.

Cheng, C. (1997), "Chaozhou People and Chaozhou Culture," *American Journal of Chinese Studies* 4(1): 101–20.

d'Abbs, P. (2019), "Tea Art as Everyday Practice: *Gongfu* Tea in Chaoshan, Guangdong, Today," *The Asia Pacific Journal of Anthropology* 20(3): 213–31.

Dawson, M. M. (1915), *The Ethics of Confucius, The Sayings of the Master and His Disciples Upon The Conduct Of The "Superior Man,"* New York: G.P. Putnam's Sons.

Fung, Y. (1991), *Selected Philosophical Writings of Fung Yu-Lan*, Beijing: Foreign Language Press.

Gillette, M. (2016), *China's Porcelain Capital: The Rise, Fall and Reinvention of Ceramics in Jingdezhen*, London: Bloomsbury Academic.

Henry, S. (2008), "Grace Bakst Wapner's Scholar's Garden: An East-West Aesthetic Dialogue," *Hyperion: On the Future of Aesthetics* 3(4): 29–38.

Huang, M. (2018), "Study of Spatial Distribution and Meaning for the Hakka and Southern Min Ethnic Groups in Shigang District, Taizhong City," MA diss., National Taichung University of Education.

Kasulis, T. (1995), "Sushi, Science, and Spirituality: Modern Japanese Philosophy and Its Views of Western Science," *Philosophy East and West* 45(2): 227–48.

Kim, L. and L. Zhang (2012), "A Quintessential Invention Genesis of a Cultural Orthodoxy in East Asian Tea Appreciation," *China Heritage Quarterly*. Available online: http://www.chinaheritagequarterly.org/features.php?searchterm=029_kim.inc&issue=029, last accessed March 30, 2020.

Klein, J. (2006), "Changing Tastes in Guangzhou: Restaurant Writings in the Late 1990s," in K. Latham, S. Thompson, and J. Klein (eds.), *Consuming China*, pp. 104–20, New York and London: Routledge.

Klein, J. (2013), "Everyday Approaches to Food Safety in Kunming," *The China Quarterly* 376–93.

Kuang, L. (2017), "China's Emerging Food Media: Promoting Culinary Heritage in the Global Age," *Gastronomica: The Journal of Critical Food Studies* 17(3): 68–81.

Kuang, L. (2019a), "(Un) consciousness? – Music in the Daoist Context of Nonbeing (*wuwei*)," in R. Herbert, D. Clarke, and E. Clarke (eds), *Music and Consciousness 2: Worlds, Practices, Modalities*, pp. 306–24, Oxford: Oxford University Press.

Kuang, L. (2019b), Ethnographic Interviews in Chaozhou, Guangdong Province and Jingdezhen, Jiangxi Province.

Lefevbre, H. (1991), *The Production of Space*, trans. D. Nicholson-Smith, Oxford: Blackwell.

Liu, A. (2009), "Taiwan Enterprises Sow Opportunity in Fujian," *China Central Television .com*. Available at: http://www.cctv.com/program/chinatoday/20090628/101641.shtml, last accessed March 30, 2020.

Major, J. S. (1994), "Celestial Cycles and Mathematical Harmonics in the 'Huainanzi,'" *Extrême-Orient, Extrême-Occident* 16: 121–34.

Ni, P. (2016), *Confucius: The Man and the Way of Gongfu*, Lanham: Rowman & Littlefield Publishers.

Rankin, M. (1990), "The Origins of a Chinese Public Sphere. Local Elites and Community Affairs in the Late Imperial Period," *Études Chinoises* 9(2): 13–60.

Ray, K. (2004), *The Migrants Table: Meals and Memories in Bengali-American Households*, Philadelphia: Temple University Press.

Ray, K. (2016), *The Ethnic Restaurateur*, London: Bloomsbury Academic.

Swislocki, M. (2009), *Culinary Nostalgia: Regional Food Culture and the Urban Experience in Shanghai*, Stanford: Stanford University Press.

Tseng, L. (2015), "Migration and Food: The Chaozhou–Shantou Migration to Kaohsiung after WWII and Sha-cha Beef Hot Pot," *Bulletin of Taiwan Historical Research* NTNU 8: 93–128.

Woodside, A. (2006), *Lost Modernities: China, Vietnam, Korea, and the Hazards of World History*, Cambridge, MA: Harvard University Press.

Yu, J. (1994), *Chao-jia fengyue ji* (The world of the Chaozhou and Jiazhou courtesans), Shanghai: Shanghai Shu Dian.

Zhang, L. (2016), "A Foreign Infusion: The Forgotten Legacy of Japanese Chadō on Modern Chinese Tea Arts," *Gastronomica: The Journal for Food Studies* 16(1): 53–62.

5

Italian Cheese in the Global Heritage Arena

Cristina Grasseni

The Heritage of Transhumance

This chapter offers cultural anthropological insights into a longitudinal ethnographic investigation of the making of a heritage cheese. Cheese is here the chosen pivot of broader epistemologies of heritage that are acted on the ground, mediating personal, local, and scalar levels of agency. The story in brief: in order to achieve a Protected Designation of Origin (PDO) for their mountain cheese *Strachitunt*, a number of stakeholders from a tiny alpine valley, Val Taleggio in Lombardy, mobilized the concept of *tipicità*. The discourse and performance of *tipicità* forms the back- and front-stage of what I call the heritage arena. *Tipicità* is a complex, often tacit semantic cloud that synergizes with other concepts: *patrimonio* ("patrimony"/heritage) but also singularity, and *eccellenza* (excellence). Heritage cheese, as I will show, becomes a dynamic process of meaning making as a marker of distinction through taste, as a normative sedimentation of specific traditional practices, and as a political conduit to the politics of food, for the stakeholders involved.

In my book *The Heritage Arena* (2017), I compared the cases of significant neighbors of Val Taleggio's Strachitunt: Bitto, Branzi, and Formai de Mut—partly or entirely produced in the Bergamasque uplands, and the transhumant cheeses Taleggio and stracchino—nowadays associated with the Lombard lowlands. Their divergent histories and uneven prestige and commercial fortunes place the story of Strachitunt in perspective. We should imagine these upland and lowland cheeses as complementing Strachitunt in a geography of opposites: the cooked and the raw, so to speak. All of them originate from a tradition of transhumant cheesemaking straddling peaks and plains, summers and winters, fresh grass and hay, craft and industry.

Made in the high-altitude summer pastures at the head of the Bergamasque valleys, Bitto, Formai de Mut, and Branzi triangulate different versions of one ideal type of upland cheese: cooked, fat, round-shaped, matured, high-prestige, yellowish 10-kilo wheels with a brushed-hardened crust similar to that of Parmesan or Grana. On the other hand, Taleggio and stracchino are, respectively, the PDO and non-PDO evolution of fresh, uncooked, square, whitish, soft, flowery-crust slabs of 2 kilos at most, made for common consumption and cheap markets. *Alpage*, or upland cheese, is for the discerning and the affluent. Lowland cheese by contrast is the unassuming by-product of transhumance.

The soft, white square cheese stracchino (called *strachì* in Bergamasque dialect) originates in the historical context of transhumant dairy farming, which was documented among others in the second half of the nineteenth century by the first national survey of Italian agriculture after the unification of the kingdom (Jacini 1882). This production technique, covering a very broad area though pivoting around seasonal return trips to the alpine valleys, eventually achieved the distinction of the PDO as "Taleggio." Unfortunately, Taleggio cheese failed its valley of origin—Val Taleggio—at least in the eyes of its residents and entrepreneurs, because it favored lowland large dairy producers who conclusively transferred the dairy craft to the lowlands, kept production abundant, and prices cheap.

In Italian food politics, geographic indications—and especially PDO—play a key role in supporting local and broader food economies. An unexploited "patrimony," a lost "typicity," Taleggio cheese looms large in the resentment of the people of Val Taleggio, a dwindling community of about 800 people who feel forgotten by history and marginalized by the dairy economy. Caught in the chasm between the "quantity economy" of cheap lowland cheeses and the "quality economy" of exclusive upland cheeses, the cheesemakers of Val Taleggio tried renaming the valley's cheese as "Taleggio of Val Taleggio" or "stracchino of Val Taleggio"—but they were legally cautioned and effectively prevented from further qualifying the already-"protected" designation of Taleggio. They then turned to reinventing Strachitunt as the valley's own cheese and claimed a PDO for their valley alone. A consortium of dairy farmers and cheese refiners was established in Val Taleggio in October 2002 to request a PDO for Strachitunt. It took them more than eleven years to obtain it, mostly due to appeals and conflicts with other producers in the neighboring lowlands, but it was eventually registered as an EU-wide PDO trademark in March 2014. But what was actually gained, and what was lost?

Strachitunt PDO can be considered a post-transhumant reinvention of a cheesemaking tradition that historically connected the alpine pastures and lowlands of northern Italy. In 1882, Stefano Jacini, in his parliamentary investigation on "the state of the art of Italian agriculture and the conditions of the rural class," states that "the word *stracchino* derives from the small soft cheeses produced during the journey from the mountain to the lowland and vice versa. These *malghesi* make it swiftly in their resting stations, with milk from tired cows after their long journey" (Jacini 1882: 27). Transhumant herders were necessarily also skilled cheesemakers, as they would transform their milk in their seasonal stations, taking their herds from the upper pastures in the Lombard Alps for the summer grazing season to their lower reaches along the rivers Ticino and Adda. *Strac* means "tired" in Bergamasque dialect, hence *strachì* as a name for the cheese, the Bergamasque word for stracchino. Taleggio was nothing other than a stracchino cheese "of Val Taleggio." What we know about the origins of strachì in all its forms is that it was cheese made by transhumant mountain peasants who could not even afford to heat their cows' milk and would curdle it at milking temperature, hastily (*all'infretta*), in their makeshift abodes, on the trail of available grass.

Technically, like the stracchino of origins, Strachitunt is a raw milk cheese, namely an uncooked cheese made with unpasteurized milk. This is worked *a munta calda*, namely while still "warm from the milked cow." It is furthermore a double-paste cheese, obtained from layering cold curd from the night before with warm curd that has been freshly renneted. It is manipulated in such a way as to allow natural molds to penetrate and nest in the fault lines between the two curds. As a result, Strachitunt is a blue cheese (*formaggio erborinato*), namely it develops molds inside the paste, which give it specific aromas and sometimes a sharp taste. Dry-salted and aged for seventy-five days, it is pierced twice during maturation, twenty days after casting and again after a fortnight. This allows the development of blue molds without inoculation, but solely as a result of interaction with the maturing environment. As a raw strachì, Strachitunt would belong to the family of lowland cheeses like Taleggio or stracchino. But as an aged, cylindrical, and heavy wheel it positions itself among nobler upland cousins. Matured even longer than Bitto PDO (at least seventy-five days vs. the seventy days of Bitto), Strachitunt is however produced all year round and not just in alpeggio. Its PDO protocol prescribes that it can only be produced in the four municipalities of Val Taleggio, a mid-mountain environment. Triangulating Taleggio and strachì, it adds a modern zest for uniqueness to the tectonic of the raw and the cooked, and combines it with the European obsession with pedigree: claimed as an upland, aristocratic precursor of Gorgonzola itself (just as strachì of Val Taleggio is claimed to be the precursor of Taleggio), it is the rawest of the raw: *a natural blue cheese*.

Calibrating the Raw

Calibrating this raw cheese to a "global hierarchy of value" (Herzfeld 2004) means negotiating and enforcing protocols of production. One of the most contested issues about geographic denominations regards their area of origin, namely the geographical boundaries within which protocols should be enforced. While there is substantial literature on this question (Brulotte and Di Giovine 2014; del Marmol, Morell and Chalcraft 2015; Fournier et al. 2012; Roigé and Frigolé 2012) I wish to go in depth here on how this is actually intrinsic to another fundamental but apparently different matter in cheesemaking, namely milk: its treatment, quality, and provenance. According to it PDO protocol, Strachitunt is *and must remain* a raw milk cheese, not only because of the consortium stakeholder celebrate its superior organoleptic qualities but also as a sure means to limit the range at which milk can travel within the boundaries of the PDO territory. Raw milk for Strachitunt is curdled *a munta calda*, namely while still warm from the milked cows. The procedural imperative to make cheese with warm milk without reheating it determines per se the very short distances it can travel. It can move from a shed to a creamery next door, or even from a borough to another within the same valley, but it cannot travel afar. In the present conditions of compliance with strict regulations about the hygiene of the creameries, raw milk cheese is sedentary by definition—an ironic result, considering that stracchino is originally a transhumant cheese.

Alpeggio, or *alpage*, is connected to—though not identical with—cattle transhumance. Still in the nineteenth century, transhumant trails could extend over hundreds of kilometers and be used in a seasonal cycle (Corti 2004). Transhumance has evolved over time and it is now virtually extinct in northern Italy—at least in the form described by historian Fernand Braudel in his *The Mediterranean at the Age of Philip II*. Nowadays only very few herders move all the way from peaks to lowlands and these tend to be mostly sheep flocks. Transhumance was only one of often highly professionalized forms of seasonal migration that could integrate the income of alpine families: for example, winter migration would be based on exercising salaried professions in urban areas, including the development of guilds of carpenters, lumberjacks, smithies, builders, decorators, stonemasons, and carriers (Viazzo 1989).

In a paradoxical symbolic inversion of the politics of (food) identity, practices that were historically a ticket for the world are currently a powerful symbolic device for marketing *locality*. Of Val Taleggio, which in the sixteenth century was a remote mountain backwater of the vast Republic of Venice bordering with the Dukedom of Milan, Governor Antonio da Lezze desolately observed how

> [T]hese valleys don't enjoy revenue of any sort. . . . They do not reap wheat nor corn, but most of these people travel the world, to Italy, mostly to Rome and Venice, keeping themselves busy trading goods, working in inns, or as coppersmiths, tinkers etc. They do not return to their homeland but once every two or three years, staying only for six months. (da Lezze [1596] 1988: 508)

Among such itinerant crafts were metal-working, logging, and carpentry, which made their bearers professional seasonal migrants. Cheesemaking and dairy farming were residual, subsistence activities unless mobilized for transhumance. Connecting with outside the valley, for example in the form of transhumant farming, was part of the local repertoire. Only the clueless stayed behind, firmly rooted in their turf, as the normative imaginary of geographical indications currently prescribes. So goes da Lezze: "Those who stay in the village are poor people, and tend their own cattle, the richest having up to 25 cows. These, at winter, descend to the Milanese plains. . . . In Taleggio there are 500 cattle, 100 among horses and mules, 200 sheep" (da Lezze [1596] 1988: 510, 512). Now that local cattle are even fewer, there is no need to descend to the Milanese plains to feed them—and hay and grass can in any case easily be imported by truck.

By contrast, *alpeggio*—the summer grazing season spent by cattle (and occasionally goat) herds on the high pastures, which are otherwise covered by snow during the harsh mountain winters—is heavily praised as a traditional tastemaker of local cheeses. Often the word "transhumant," referring to cattle, is used for the alpeggio, even though this generates confusion, as cow breeders take only short summer trips to the closest higher pastures. Notably, alpeggio entails more limited cattle movement than original transhumance trails—which took place practically all year round, following fixed routes and visiting well-stocked stations. Nowadays the *alpeggiatori* are mostly mountain farmers who drive herds from the village stables to the upper pastures, while they make hay in the meadows around the village to stock up for winter. Or by converse, they can be breeders from far away, attracted to the high summer pastures more by the EU subsidies to incentive this traditional grazing practice, than by considerations of ecological continuity. While nowadays the high pastures are either private properties or municipal land, pastures in the high grounds could be "commons" in the past—the shared regulated and inalienable usufruct of a community, with formal covenants regulating access and obligations to maintenance work. Some of these regulations—*statuti* or *regole*—would be granted to individual communities by a higher authority, for instance a duke or other feudal sovereign. Even when the high pastureland was held as a "common," access to it was historically highly regulated, as land and grass are key economic and ecological resources (McNetting 1981: 89). Crucially, with long-distance dairy transhumance gone, the families of cheesemakers eventually settled down in the richer plains, investing in large-scale dairy creameries, leaving the bothersome business of making upland cheese during the alpeggio to the (other) mountain people.

This contextualizes Val Taleggio within a complex historical and geographical scenario of competing and partly overlapping cheese productions, each claiming distinction for their tradition, and the urgency of survival for their communities of producers. Alpeggio is often claimed as the common heritage of the dairy breeders of the Bergamasque valleys and proudly celebrated by local historians and scholars. This calls for a timescape of "structural nostalgia" (Herzfeld 2005: 147): a lost time of plenty of which successive generations reminisce. While we do not have evidence here that the previous generation in turn had been reminiscent of a more wholesome era before themselves (à la Herzfeld), modern entrepreneurs collectively perform as present witnesses to the relics of pristine times, and competitively claim to be true heirs to those. This is precisely the cultural work of heritage, namely harnessing history (in this particular case, a nostalgic perception of history as natural repository of lost values) as a form of value addition.

So, for example, tourist brochures systematically present transhumant cattle herders as authentic specimens of timeless tradition. Less benignly, agricultural consultants also argue that family-run dairy farming businesses with just a few cows and goats are remnants of preindustrial times and should be encouraged to die out. And they routinely are, either through unsustainable requests for audit paperwork and structural requirements, or by monetary incentives to cull small herds and pack up business: a practice infamously known as *abbattimento*—culling—as productive livestock are sent to the abattoir because their husbandry is uneconomical or simply uncompetitive.

John Agnew has noted how in a geopolitics of uneven socioeconomic power distribution, certain geographical areas become associated with essential attributes of time, relative to other geographical "blocks": thus "modernity, confused by some with the United States, becomes a social model to which other 'less developed' societies can aspire" (1998: 46). Within a stereotypically "backward" Italy, hence, Alpine dairy farmers would appear even more exotic and "primitive." Marginal cheesemakers and family farmers feel that they are indeed the survivors of an era: prematurely culled, persuaded into bankruptcy, or cornered into foreclosure. Naturally then, their economic plight assumes also broader significance in a politics of identity for which heritage food is the main conduit.

The Politics of Identity through *Tipicità*

The public audition for the establishment of a PDO production protocol for Strachitunt cheese, held in Val Taleggio in October 2010, was a heightened collective event that showed how economic and political actors compete and sometimes converge to define heritage food in the contemporary market. As I witnessed the succession of "witnesses" called up to speak out for or against the PDO as in a public trial, chaired by an envoy of the national Ministry of Agriculture, it became apparent how each was speaking at once to national and European regulators, as well as to very local competitors. Cast as distant and inscrutable, European normative agencies in fact had become very real magnifying glasses for very local but very real animosities.

For local cheesemakers it was important to determine the pedigree of their cheeses, including which Bergamasque valley produced which cheese back in the sixteenth century. *Tipicità* had become their language of food heritage. By making Strachitunt, tasting it, naming it, selling it, eating it, and celebrating it, the entrepreneurs, farmers, and administrators of Val Taleggio had found a distinctive way of talking about their valley as a community, and to lay claim to cheese denominations as a form of cultural property. *Tipicità* is therefore here eminently a political conduit. But it is also of course much more than that, as the politics of identity reaches deep.

Hygiene regulations and the nitty-gritty of animal husbandry form the normative and environmental substratum of cheesemaking as a heritage enterprise. The "war of the cheeses" that unfolded around Strachitunt was certainly opportunistic and strategic like all wars, but, as any drama, displayed powerful symbolic moments both individual and choral—such as the public reading of the PDO protocol, but also at a number of moments over the years leading up to this milestone. Each time, the drama was inevitably at once orchestrated and heartfelt by all involved, and the language of *tipicità* came to the fore:

> What is a consortium? It is a group of entrepreneurs that represent the entire value and supply chain of one product. These entrepreneurs have realized that they own a product, which has been handed down to them from previous generations and that they can make. They consider this product unique, and in danger of being imitated. A consortium is an institution that preserves something that can be *reinvented*. Those who make this product somewhere else, in a different guise, under different conditions, *invent* it. This is a fundamental distinction. We can do a few things to make our product in slightly updated ways, with new tools and everything that innovation has offered us in the latest decades. But we are not *inventing* anything. We are *reinventing* something that already existed, maybe dwindling, but continuously. We give it a new image, new clothes, and a typicity [*una tipicita*]. *If* we'll be able to do so, we'll make it *consistent,* and we'll put it back on the market. (Sagra dello Strachitunt, Pizzino di Val Taleggio; October 20, 2006, audio-recorded public speech by the president of the Consortium Strachitunt)

Tipicità is not a synonym of terroir, as it designates both environmental and specific historical circumstances for local and regional craft productions that are intrinsically dynamic. To make sense of it, I use two metaphors, one of drama and one of war, conflated in one conceptual image, that of the arena. The war metaphor underlines how the reinvention of cheese as a heritage item is a process to which many competing actors concur: key local producers, influential food activism groups, local and regional decision-makers, and media figures. The drama metaphor highlights how the power relations and the strategic interactions among them are played out as political and cultural performances, often very public, which allows them to claim moral representation and political responsibility for an entire community. The concept of the arena indicates "either a battleground or a stage or theatre" (Buijtin, van Ophem and Casimir 2013: 16). The trope of the drama allows me to linger on the linguistic and symbolic practices of *tipicità* that turn a "community of practice'" of cheesemakers, cheesemongers, and cheese eaters into an "imagined community," or as Nicolas Adell, Chiara Bortolotto, and Regina Bendix indicate, the subject and cultural owner of heritage cheese as a patrimony (Adell et al. 2015). In fact, Adell and coauthors underline the transition, in the language and practice of the heritage complex, from an expectation of communities "bearing" cultural heritage to one of "participating" in it (Adell et al. 2015: 8).

Precisely because of its intrinsically strategic character, however, the reinvention of cheese as heritage is an ongoing and dynamic process: it is constantly repitched and reperformed in relation to the actors' reciprocal repositioning. Pierre Bourdieu, talking about "the space of literary or artistic position-takings," explains "that the structure of the field, i.e. of the space of positions, is nothing other than the structure of the distribution of the capital of specific properties which governs success in the field and the winning of the external or specific profits (such as literary prestige) which are at stake in the field." Di Giovine adapts this analysis of "positions and position-takings" (Bourdieu 1993: 30) to "the heritage-scape's field of production" (Di Giovine 2009: 14). Referring to UNESCO World Heritage sites, Di Giovine looks at the "protracted negotiations that exist in UNESCO's designating process, management procedures, and tourism" (p. 8). In our case, this "field of heritage production" juggles the social production of recognition (such as food prestige) with the very serious business of making a living for the socioeconomic actors involved, such as cheesemakers, merchants, journalists, middle-men and brokers.

Arjun Appadurai has taught that the politics of authenticity and the politics of connoisseurship are but some of the forms that "politics," understood as "the link between regimes of value and specific flows of commodities," can take (1986: 57). His use of the word "arena" pertains specifically to how "large-scale exchanges" interact with "more humble flows of things": "in the politics of reputation, gains in the larger arena have implications for the smaller ones" (Appadurai 1986: 20). Similarly, the production of heritage value for Strachitunt cheese in Val Taleggio was a pivotal albeit extended process that brought politics to the fore aligning social actors in relevant ways to obtain a PDO for their valley. This extended moment is only one step in a longer history, during which Val Taleggio lost "cultural ownership" of the Taleggio cheese that bears the valley's own name, subsequently fought for a cheese of its own by another name, rediscovered strachì—a humble transhumant cheese—and won for its Strachitunt a PDO (a protected regime of geographical indication for a sedentarized strachì).

The discourse and practices that turned Strachitunt into a piece of heritage include key interpretations and performances of cheese as patrimony (patrimonio) and as a bearer of *tipicità*, and only worked as a result of active and continuous intervention and positioning, including commercial tactics, symbolic politics and the pervasive performance of a culture of gastronomic discernment (gustatory, sensorial, historical, genealogical, geographic, agronomic, and culinary) on which I wish to dwell on next.

Sweet and Sour: Normalizing Taste

The sensorium linked to the taste of cheese provides the backdrop to the performance of locality and the rhetoric for its consumption. In tourist venues, professional fairs, and open-air festivals, the cheesemakers of Val Taleggio perform the cultural meaning of cheese, showcasing relevant activities such as hand milking, or milk curdling, or cheese tasting. Performance is fundamental to the reinvention of cheese both in closed-door negotiations and in strategies for public communication, as the performance of authenticity is elicited and extracted from cheesemakers, refiners, and dairy farmers. I investigated this ethnographically over time, through my own apprenticeship as a cheese-taster alongside the valley's cheesemakers in 2007, as well as attending the performance of street theater and interactive video installations that were organized by the Ecomuseum Valtaleggio in 2008–9 and 2013. The Ecomuseum participated also in the Turin's Slow Food Salon as part of its effort to boost tourism and the cheesemaking industry in the valley. The most recent instance of this choral and longitudinal effort to place Val Taleggio on the map of the world cheese heritage was a three-day festival in the mountains of Bergamo reflecting on Strachitunt's success and future challenges in February 2020. This performance of locality around Strachitunt as a marker of identity for Val Taleggio was a three-day event that included a very well-attended conference, workshops, and visits to the production sites in the valley (dairy farms, creamery, and cheese refines).[1] At Turin's Slow Food Salon or in educational workshops, at festivals, and at conferences, this performance is ambivalent and prescriptive for all involved performing food heritage to urbanite consumers, tourists, and connoisseurs.

The taste of heritage is indeed bittersweet. In the case of Strachitunt, both the actual cheese and the long-drawn sagas of their makers are double-layered, and sweet and sour at once. This reinvention is only one, possibly *the* most successful and hard-fought, of many other attempts to achieve the ever-elusive goal of using local cheese to leverage systemic issues of paramount importance: market branding, rural development, and ultimately economic and social survival. Heralded as the dairy "excellence" of Val Taleggio by a number of paladins (initially Slow Food, then the valley's own Ecomuseum) who celebrated its gustatory and moral suasion, Strachitunt delivered its PDO in 2014, eleven years perhaps too late, leaving the unsurpassed protagonists of its reinvention as veritable kings of a ghost valley (Grasseni 2017).

Crafting and marketing Strachitunt's traditional taste in an innovative and unique canon played a paramount role in the way traditional producers were corralled to reposition themselves within Bourdieusian "fields of forces." Within the field of force of heritage foods, pivoting on the identity of singular products, the taste of Strachitunt played a subtle and ambivalent role, because cheese flavor must be recognizably *of one product*. In other dairy industries, this justifies the pressure toward the standardization even of niche productions, and the use of various technologies to "stabilize" cheese, for example with the use of industrial ferments in milk coagulation and during the maturing phase. But in the same breath, the taste of heritage must also be unique and distinctive in order to have "added value." Unique taste can bring surprises, as in the case of raw milk blue cheeses like Strachitunt: its flavor in fact can sometimes be too sharp to be appreciated by the untrained palate. Most importantly, it is impossible to foresee if any slice will taste like another because the cheese has not been inoculated with bacterial cultures. Its molds grow naturally, which means they might not grow at all. So Strachitunt can have the mild, lactose sweetness of Taleggio *and* the piquant sharpness of a gorgonzola mold, *or either of them*.

It is at the heart of this paradox between distinction and standardization that the so-called middlemen such as the National Associations for Cheese Tasting (ONAF) and Slow Food play a significant social, cultural, and political role, namely training the taste and educating consumers to articulate the "added value" of heritage cheese. Through my own apprenticeship as a cheese-taster alongside the valley's cheesemakers, I could appreciate how laborious it was for some of them to equip themselves with an apt vocabulary to market the cheese they could *make*, but not describe and extol. Those who could, had a cutting-edge advantage. Attending the local Ecomuseum and participating and observing commercial fairs such as the World Cheese Awards (2019) or Turin's Slow Food Salon (2010), and a number of educational presentations of Strachitunt offered to perspective buyers in the period in between, I could appreciate the ambivalent and prescriptive nature of the roles of those involved: tourists, valley residents, and cheesemakers alike are involved in the community conundrum of performing and co-performing a calibration of local cheese to largely projected expectations: those of the European legislator, those of the urbanite consumers, and those of the hoped-for tourist and connoisseurs.

In my previous work on the transformation of animal husbandry in the Alps, *Developing Skill, Developing Vision* (2009), I maintained that, among the dairy smallholders of the Lombard mountains, skill and "practices of locality" are mutually co-constitutive. I described how their skilled practice of animal husbandry is not ahistorical but rather intimately connected with a regime of agricultural counselling, hence with both local and translocal politics of food, prescribing and enacting certain ways of looking at cattle—"skilled visions" (Grasseni 2007a). Following the cows, and their milk, I turned to investigate the transformation of cheesemaking—particularly its spaces and timescapes of production and consumption. During several years of observation, I witnessed how upland cheesemaking was driven from high-pasture domestic mountain huts to Hazard Analysis Critical Control Point (HACCP)-run creameries. The introduction of HACCP production protocols was but one of the many ways in which artisan cheese was being repositioned within the global forces of a "field of production" (Bourdieu 1993). This entailed a powerful incept of "audit cultures" (Strathern 2000), which had momentous effects on high-pasture cheesemaking. I began to observe its effects at the end of the 1990s, and I referred to the consequent adjustments of local cheesemaking as a process of *calibration* (Grasseni 2007b: 61–90).

Reinventing cheese meant calibrating its "ecology of production," an apt phrase which I adopt from Heather Paxson (2012), to the increasing pressures to standardize procedures, environments, and operations. But it further entailed a symbolic calibration, namely its transformation from a perceived "traditional" yet everyday foodstuff to a distinctive item of food heritage (Grasseni 2011). It meant that production systems must be *calibrated* to normative and commercial expectations that have purchase both on international economic circuits and on very local arrangements. This does not mean that the alpine cheeses I am talking about have suddenly begun to sell on international markets—though some of them do and have done for some time. Rather, it means that they have to be entirely refashioned *as if* such potentiality was at hand. The arena they choose as audience, although in practice very local, is symbolically, rhetorically, and normatively global.

Moreover, the expectation that tradition has unexploited commercial potential, that it is a resource deserving of "valorization," calls for added value to be made evident and relevant not only to consumers, but to "communities" at large. Anthropology offers an ethnographic long take of the sometimes-conflicting voices and agendas that contributed to determine which strategies of reinvention and icons of locality became in turn viable: supportive local administrations, well-established entrepreneurs, food activists, international buyers, local historians, and social workers with political ambitions. The overall result is a skillful and precarious reinvention of the everyday, often dependent on selling ambivalent notions, including the very concept of community. Within a "food heritage" framework, some ambitious local administrators and entrepreneurs, far from solving local conflicts, have succeeded in using the language of dairy "excellence" as a springboard, hopefully for the valley and certainly for their own political careers and economic viability. However, reading the Strachitunt PDO story as a mere social construction of a geographical indication would be diminutive of the "ecologies of sentiment" (Paxson 2012) that underwrote this epic.

Conclusion

Claiming control of a cheese as patrimony falls nothing short of advocating sovereignty over it. In the cultural mobilization of food as heritage, the aspects of guardianship and reinvention are conjoined. Economic rivalries, moral maneuvering, and political alliances populate the intertwined histories of neighboring mountain communities whose entrepreneurs and administrators choose divergent paths to "valorize" their cheeses. Small and fiercely territorial PDO geographic indications coexist with other forms of self-safeguarding of other niche productions in the same area: some opt for the distinction of hard-core authenticity, with marketing support of associations such as Slow Food. Others make use of more malleable quality certifications such as the commercial trademarks bestowed by local chambers of commerce. Others linger between quantity and quality, caught in the chasm. Each agenda is pursued by local politicians, entrepreneurs, and activists who skillfully trade in the most viable currency of the moment (whether European PDOs, Slow Food Presidia, or production protocols of the chambers of commerce).

Entire localities are thus called into play in the moral labor of identifying with, and properly exploiting, one's heritage (*patrimonio*). In Italian this process goes under the name of *patrimonializzazione* (roughly translatable as "heritagization"). Patrimonializing alpine cheese entails that a number of social actors (not only dairy farmers, cheesemakers, and refiners but also public administrators, consumer associations, and tourist entrepreneurs, for instance) cooperate to identify, describe, study, safeguard, extol, reproduce, and market specific items of tangible and intangible heritage. Patrimonio is often described as a commonwealth—a patrimony in fact, which is handed down (patrilinearly, presumably) from generation to generation.

It thus pertains to autochthonous residents or at least to a community that identifies itself as largely unchanged over time. To the risky rhetoric of autochthony (Geschiere 2011; Kalb 2004), patrimonialization adds a "metaphysics of sedentarism" (Malkki 1992) that, even in a realm that is not usually considered political, introduces some serious frictions and dilemmas. Which cheeses are authentically "mountain cheese"? Is it important to produce "traditionally" with raw milk? These are not naïve questions and the ingenious answers that each producer gives is in itself an act of economic and political strategy. Rethinking the economy through calibrating protocols of production for raw milk cheese in the Italian mountains today is not just a question of marketing but of political imagination. The politics of food designations is neither an invention of tradition nor a tradition of invention (Paxson 2014), but a reinvention of food within a specific field of production that includes heritage and place-based names as major force fields. These articulate and shape both the marketability and political capacity of food to mobilize resources and passions, to foster conflict and suggest alliances. Their outcome, in the marginal rural areas of the northern Italian Alps, may determine the very serious business of economic viability and even demographic survival for a whole mountain community. For the few hundred people involved, the cause of obtaining a Europe-wide protected denomination for Strachitunt was believed to make the difference between becoming a dying valley or following in the footprints of other niche producers, such as the "Bitto rebels" (Corti 2012), namely heritage cheesemakers who had fought bitterly, and commercially won, against larger consortia. This was a veritable war, a war of the cheeses, and each economic actor involved fought for their livelihoods with the resentment that only history's losers can have.

Acknowledgment

The project "Food citizens? Collective food procurement in European cities: Solidarity and diversity, skills and scale" has received funding from the European Research Council (ERC) under the European Union's Horizon 2020 research and innovation program (Grant agreement No. 724151).

Note

1   See https://www.strachitunt.it/strachitunt-da-risorsa-per-la-famiglia-a-valore-per-il-territorio-convegno/.

References

Adell, N., R. Bendix, C. Bortolotto, and M. Tauschek, eds. (2015), *Between Imagined Communities and Communities of Practice*, Göttingen: Universitätsverlag Göttingen.

Agnew, J. (1998), *Geopolitics: Re-visioning World Politics*, 2nd edn, London and New York: Routledge.

Appadurai, A. (1986), "Commodities and the Politics of Value," in A. Appadurai (ed.), *The Social Life of Things: Commodities in Cultural Perspective*, pp. 3–63, Cambridge: Cambridge University Press.

Bourdieu, P. (1993), *The Field of Cultural Production*, New York: Columbia University Press.

Braudel, F. (1995 [1949]), *The Mediterranean at the Age of Philip II*, Berkeley: University of California Press.

Brulotte, R. and M. DiGiovine, eds. (2014), *Edible Identities: Food as Cultural Heritage*, Dorchester: Ashgate.

Buijtin, C., J. van Ophem, and G. Casimir, eds. (2013), *The Arena of Everyday Life*, Wageningen: Wageningen Academic Publishers.

Corti, M. (2004), "*Sussura de l'aalp*. Il sistema dell'alpeggio nelle Alpi lombarde," *Annali di San Michele* 17: 31–155.

Corti, M. (2012), *I Ribelli del Bitto: Quando una tradizione casearia diventa eversiva*, Turin: Slow Food Editore.

Da Lezze, G. (1596), *Descrizione di Bergamo e del suo territorio*, reprint 1988, Bergamo: Provincia di Bergamo/Lucchetti Editore.

Del Marmol, C., M. Morell, and J. Chalcraft, eds. (2015), *The Making of Heritage: Seduction and Disenchantment*, London: Routledge.

Di Giovine, M. A. (2009), *The Heritage-Scape: UNESCO, World Heritage, and Tourism*, Lanham: Lexington Books.

Di Giovine, M. A. (2014), "The Everyday as Extraordinary: Revitalization, Religion, and the Elevation of *Cucina Casareccia* to Heritage Cuisine in Pietrelcina Italy," in R. Brulotte and M. A. Di Giovine (eds.), *Edible Identities: Food as Cultural Heritage*, pp. 77–92, Surrey: Ashgate.

Fournier, L., D. Crozat, C. Bernié-Boissard, and C. Chastagner, eds. (2012), *Patrimoine et desirs d'identité*, Paris: Editions L'Harmattan.

Geschiere, P. (2011), *The Perils of Belonging: Autochthony, Citizenship, and Exclusion in Africa and Europe*, Chicago: University of Chicago Press.

Grasseni, C., ed. (2007a), *Skilled Visions: Between Apprenticeship and Standards*, Oxford: Berghahn.

Grasseni, C. (2007b), *La reinvenzione del Cibo: Culture del gusto fra tradizione e globalizzazione ai piedi delle Alpi*, Verona: Qui Edit.

Grasseni, C. (2009), *Developing Skill, Developing Vision: Practices of Locality at the Foot of the Alps*, Oxford: Berghahn.

Grasseni, C. (2011), "Re-Inventing Food: Alpine Cheese in the Age of Global Heritage," *Anthropology of Food*, n. 8. http://aof.revues.org/index6819.html; https://doi.org/10.4000/aof.6819

Grasseni C. (2017), *The Heritage Arena: Reinventing Cheese in the Italian Alps*, New York: Berghahn Books.

Herzfeld, M. (2004), *The Body Impolitic: Artisans and Artifice in the Global Hierarchy of Value*, Chicago: University of Chicago Press.

Herzfeld, M. (2005), *Cultural Intimacy: Social Poetics in the Nation-State*, 2nd edn, New York: Routledge.

Jacini, S. (1882), *Atti della Giunta per la Inchiesta Agraria e sulle condizioni della classe agricola. Volume VI, Tomo I, Fasc. I. Relazione del Commissario Conte Stefano Jacini, Senatore del Regno, sulla DECIMA CIRCOSCRIZIONE (provincie di Pavia – meno i circondari di Voghera e Bobbio – Milano, Cremona, Mantova, Como, Sondrio, Bergamo e Brescia)*, Rome: Forzani e C., Tipografi del Senato.

Kalb, D. (2004), "Editorial: Danse Macabre," *Focaal* 44: v–vii.

Malkki, L. (1992), "National Geographic: The Rooting of Peoples and the Territorialization of National Identity among Scholars and Refugees," *Cultural Anthropology* 7(1): 24–44.

McNetting, R. (1981), *Balancing on an Alp: Ecological Change and Continuity in a Swiss Mountain Community*, Cambridge: Cambridge University Press.

Paxson, H. (2012), *The Life of Cheese: Crafting Food and Value in America*, Berkeley: University of California Press.

Paxson, H. (2014), "Re-Inventing a Tradition of Invention: Entrepreneurialism as Heritage in American Artisan Cheesemaking," in R. Brulotte and M. Di Giovine (eds.), *Edible Identities: Food as Cultural Heritage*, pp. 29–38, Dorchester: Ashgate.

Roigé, X. and J. Frigolé, eds. (2012), *Constructing Cultural and Natural Heritage: Parks, Museums and Rural Heritage*, Barcelona: Documenta.

Strathern, M., ed. (2000), *Audit Cultures*, London: Routledge.

Viazzo, P. P. (1989), *Upland Communities: Environment, Population, and Social Structure in the Alps since the Sixteenth Century*, Cambridge: Cambridge University Press.

6

The Gastronomic Capital of the World

Food, Politics, and Identity in Lyon

Rachel E. Black

Introduction: Becoming a Gastronomic Capital

Lively markets, "authentic" neighborhood restaurants, and a wide constellation of Michelin-starred fine dining establishments are the main draw for many visitors to Lyon. For nearly a hundred years, this city has been considered the gastronomic capital of France, and this claim to fame has shaped the Lyon's economy and identity. This chapter will consider the ways in which culinary excellence as a critical element of local identity has been closely connected with local and national politics, from the rise of the regionalist movement in the 1930s to the current attempts to attract tourist euros in an ever-changing French economy and culinary landscape. In particular, this chapter looks at the ways in which forms of *cuisine bourgeoise* and *cuisine gastronomique* incorporated peasant and working-class cuisines and became the dominant form of national culinary representation. In the process, women's contributions and those of the lower classes were supplanted.

What makes a city a gastronomic capital? Who gives out this title and what does a city have to do to keep it? Trying to trace Lyon's claim to gastronomic fame is more complicated than it first appears. Like most origin stories, this one is a little murky. Historian Julia Csergo (2008) has carefully examined the publications that note Lyon's culinary reputation, and she found that it was not until the 1920s that Lyon became frequently mentioned as a place where locals and visitors eat well. Most notably, in 1925, Curnonsky, "the Prince of Gastronomes," declared Lyon the "Gastronomic Capital of the World." This declaration came at an opportune time when the city was seeking to reinvent itself after a period of economic decline at the end of the nineteenth century and the start of the twentieth century.

The second largest city in France at the time, Lyon was famous for silk production and later for synthetic textiles and pharmaceuticals. It was also a center for insurance companies, banking, and commercial trade. All of these industries meant that Lyon not only had a large working class but also an affluent bourgeois population. For some time, the bourgeoisie lived in close proximity with the working classes and often rubbed shoulders in eating and drinking establishments. This was particularly true of the small restaurants called *bouchons* that served both the silk workers, known as *canuts*, and the *commerçants* (businesspeople and textile traders) (Rouèche 2018). This intermingling of the classes influenced the local cuisine—both working-class and middle-class cultures marked the development of Lyon and its cuisine.

In the late 1920s and early 1930s, Lyon started to recover economically in the wake of the First World War. With the textile industry still reeling from the decline of silk production, political and industry leaders in Lyon explored new possibilities for the city's economy. Situated at the crossroads between the North and the South of France and at the confluence of two important waterways, Lyon had always been an important place for trade, and the city's *foire* (fair) had remained popular since the fifteenth century. However, in 1916, leaders of the chamber of commerce decided to revive and expand the *Foire de Lyon* as an opportunity to highlight the city's industries and its role as a center for international trade (Rouèche 2018).

It is this history of trade and its location that helped Lyon's cuisine flourish: access to excellent ingredients as well as a steady stream of business travelers in need of meals meant the development of many quality restaurants catering to a middle-class clientele. Along with the promotion of the *foire*, came the promotion of Lyonnais cuisine in the form of guidebooks, gastronomic literature, and gastronomic clubs. The rise of automobile tourism also meant the beginning of culinary tourism; in this case, travelers were exploring the cuisine of other regions rather than the exotic far-off lands that are evoked in Long's definition of culinary tourism (2004: 2). Culinary and automobile tourism were relatively new forms of travel that were open to mainly middle-class travelers who were finding new ways to explore their country at the start of the twentieth century (Harp 2001). Travelers who wanted to eat at the best tables could learn all the local secrets through the numerous tracts of gastronomic literature, a growing genre of travel literature in the interwar period.

Guidebooks and Gastronomes

Nineteenth-century food critics, such as Grimod de la Reynière and Jean Anthelme Brillat-Savarin, acted as mediators between two worlds for the French bourgeoisie who had recently come to power but still strove to find legitimacy (Poulain 2005). These early food writers, often from noble families, told the bourgeoisie what to eat, where to eat, and how to eat—they were constructing a cultural field that would serve as an important marker of cultural capital for the new ruling class (Ferguson 2004). Moving into the twentieth century, the role of the food critic began to change. Now that the bourgeoisie had established their place at the top of the political and economic hierarchy, food writing found a new project in amalgamating culinary forms that could possibly compete with the dominant cultural forms of the bourgeoisie, which were, in this case, *cuisine bourgeoise* and haute cuisine. This was part of a larger project to valorize regional differences and create a unified French nation that celebrated regional diversity. While there were regional differences, it was a broader bourgeois culture that became synonymous with normative French culture. Similar movements, where dominant bourgeois culture incorporated or displaced regional cultural forms, could also be seen in architecture and crafts (Peer 1998; Whalen 2007). Gastronomic literature and guidebooks were the forces that moved French cuisine toward a bourgeois cuisine that encompassed regional variation.

The advent of the guidebook was central for making Lyon a tourist destination for fine dining. Guidebooks originally developed in conjunction with the spread of train lines and then the extensive use of the automobile and the improvement of roads in France (Harp 2001). Thanks to the growing market for cars and the consequent development of automobile-oriented tourism, the *Guide Michelin*—first published in 1900—quickly became one of the most prominent guidebooks. Initially, it was a technical guide that explained to drivers how to change a flat tire, where to go for assistance, and it indicated itineraries and destinations that could not be reached by train. According to Lucien Karpik (2000), the *Guide Michelin* encouraged the French to free themselves of the limits of train travel; it encouraged them to personalize their itineraries and trips. Above all else, this new guide, which was initially distributed for free by the Michelin Tire Company, encouraged motorists to drive their cars (with the aim of having them wear out their tires).

In 1923, the *Michelin Guide* stated: "In a certain number of big cities, in which a tourist might stop simply to have a meal, we have indicated the restaurants that have been pointed out as having good cuisine" (Michelin 1923). However, not all restaurants being equal, it quickly became apparent to the *Michelin Guide* publishers that it was necessary to develop a more precise indication of the quality of the food and the locale of the restaurants indicated in the guide. It took several years for the guide to develop its restaurant rating system, and it was not until 1931 that it started using the three-star system and creating a hierarchy of restaurants. For a growing group of gastronomic tourists and gastronomes, this top classification held weight and drew attention to an establishment.

At the turn of the century, the *Guide Michelin* was not the only guidebook in France. There was competition from the *Guide Blue*, Touring Club de France, and Chaix. However, none of the other guides placed as much importance on food. Guidebooks offered an easy entry into the highly codified world of restaurant dining (Spang 2000: 175-177). As much as restaurants themselves were moving toward a middle-class cuisine for middle-class diners, guidebooks played a role in incorporating different regional cuisines into this model. While Paris and its restaurants gathered all of French culinary traditions together into a cosmopolitan culinary culture, it was cities in the provinces that represented their regional cuisines and became important for defining the regional diversity that was at the root of a strong nationalist movement in the first half of the twentieth century (Parker 2015).

In parallel, guidebooks contributed to this project by including lists of local and regional specialties. Once the names of restaurants were included in these books, they also start to name the specialties of specific restaurants. Jean-François Mesplède, former editor of the *Guide Michelin*, explained that the menus in Lyonnais restaurants like La Mère Fillioux and La Mère Brazier rarely changed because diners would arrive expecting to find on offer the specialty of the house as listed in the guidebooks (interview with author, 2013). In 1933, the *Guide Michelin* included the following specialties under the listing for La Mère Brazier: "*Quenelles financière, vollaile demi-deuil 'Mère Brazier', terrine Brazier*," and, for Fillioux: "*Volaille truffé, Quenelles au gratin beurre d'écrivisses, Fonds d'artichauts au foie gras truffé*" (*Guide Michelin* 1933). Both *mères* (mothers, ruling women) faithfully cooked their signature dish, *volaille en demi-deuil*, each evening, for fear of otherwise disappointing clients who came expecting to find these dishes. In this way, tourists and gastronomic guidebooks began to codify regional cuisine: attaching specific dishes to individuals and places. They facilitated consumption and the display of cultural capital (Barabowski and Furlough 2001: 12).

Maurice Edmond Sailland, the most influential gastronomic critic and food writer of the early twentieth century, played an important role in the promotion of regional cuisine in France (Arbellot 1965). In 1921, Curnonsky and Marcel Rouff (1921–8) launched the series *France gastronomique*, which brought together gastronomy and tourism, and was one of the first series to highlight the regional specialties of France. Curnonsky's *Trésor gastronomique de la France* in 1933, which he co-wrote with Austin de Croze, was another work celebrating regional culinary diversity. The aim of this publication was to help: "Gastronomes realize the innumerable joys the French soil has to offer up to their appetite. Tourists will use this book as a daily guide that will allow them to take advantage of the culinary resources of each region" (Curnonsky and de Croze 1933: 10).

Culinary establishments and French middle-class society recognized Curnonsky for the role he played in promoting French cuisine as an important national resource, from both an economic and a cultural perspective. In 1927, 3,000 chefs participated in a referendum organized by *Paris-Soir*, and they elected Curnonsky "Prince de la Gastronomie" (Arbellot 1965). Minister of Education Louis Barthou nominated Curnonsky to the Légion d'honneur in 1929. Curnonsky took on an important public role in shaping the ways in which the French and foreigners perceived French cuisine—as a national treasure that was marked by the diversity of the regions of France. Curnonsky was at the head of a prolific production of gastronomic literature in the 1920s and 1930s. The "Prince des gastronomes" was particularly fond of Lyon and its fine culinary offerings. Some might argue that Curnonsky was responsible for establishing and promoting Lyon's reputation as a gastronomic capital.

In the twentieth-century regionalist movement, secondary cities like Lyon, Dijon, Bourdeaux, and Strasbourg became representative of the terroir of their surrounding rural regions. The regional cuisine presented in these places brought together all the best products of the region, refined them through bourgeois cuisine, and served them up for a middle-class clientele in restaurants. In this way, cities in France beyond Paris became beacons for this celebrated regional diversity but they also tamed it into an aesthetic that was destined for bourgeois lips (Reches 2017). Farmhouse recipes, such as braised chicken from Bresse, were transformed into upwardly mobile dishes through the addition of expensive and sometimes rare ingredients. This is how *poularde en demi-deuil*, braised chicken with truffles under its skin, became one of the signature dishes of Lyonnais restaurants serving dishes based on *cuisine bourgeoise*. This dish is an example of a choice ingredient from the surrounding rural area that is cooked using a refined version of a common domestic culinary and through the addition of prized ingredients becomes a dish accessible only to middle-class diners. These sorts of culinary transformations were common in cities because of the growing number of restaurants and middle-class diners.

The Regionalist Movement and French Cuisine

As gastronomic tourism expanded, so did both good and poor-quality restaurants. Critics shunned establishments that served food that tasted the same no matter where you were in France—lacking in culinary authenticity. Curnonsky and his fellow gastronomic writers were wary of cooking that had little integrity and no sense of place: "It is certainly not in the palaces, nor in the five-franc restaurants that one eats the best. In those places standardized cuisine reigns . . . *false grande cuisine,* which is the worst of all" (Curnonsky in Rouzier 1931: 9). Curnonsky warns his readers against placeless food that all tastes the same. Gastronomes were critical of Parisian cuisine as soulless and lacking in culinary traditions. More generally, the regionalist discourse framed the capital as morally corrupt and lacking authenticity (Reches 2017: 148). Bourgeois food writers and consumers were celebrating the particularities of regional cuisines as the heart of French cuisine. As Koshar argues (1998: 339), guidebooks attempt to "visualize an authenticity that could provide meaning beyond the marketplace": they played a role in defining the nation that the tourist was consuming. The rise of automobile tourism in France also coincides with the regionalist movement, which used food as a way to showcase regional diversity while constructing a strong sense of French nationalism (Theisse 1997).

To counter the spread of a homogenized form of French cuisine that was ever present in hotels and large restaurants, the gastronome and discerning bourgeois tourist sought out small eateries, local dishes, and wines. Homogeneity was seen as a cultural threat, and it was synonymous with the threat of Paris' dominance over the rest of France, both politically and culturally. In search of gastronomic authenticity, the tourist was attempting to create a cultural heritage or social identity built on national identity that celebrated regional diversity (MacCannell 1989; Gohen 1988). This trend can be seen in the ways that gastronomes celebrated regional cuisine in their writings. Count Austin de Croze, the leader of the Académie des Gastronomes Régionalistes, wrote *Les plats régionaux de France* (French Regional Dishes, 1928) in which he celebrates French diversity through a series of regional dishes. This work also has the effect of codifying which dishes should represent which regions. de Croze praises French cuisine while expressing the uniqueness of each region's contributions to a national cuisine (Reches 2017: 63). In 1931, Édouard Rouzier edited the *Livre d'or de la gastronomie française* (Golden Book of French Gastronomy) on the occasion of the Salon d'Autonme—an annual art exhibition held in Paris since 1903. Here Rouzier lays out the culinary riches of various regions of France. It is telling that this was the first time the Salon had featured the gastronomic arts among other art forms and crafts. In addition to numerous advertisements for food-related businesses and articles about fine dining, this book is a celebration of culinary diversity and regional cuisine in France (Wright 2003: 10).

Regionalism in France is highly political. Starting with the French Revolution, Jacobin leaders did their best to undo regional allegiances in the late eighteenth and early nineteenth centuries: they saw these divisions as a challenge to nation building and the centralization of power. In the late nineteenth and early twentieth centuries, right-wing interests in the deployment of regionalism have often overshadowed this growing political, intellectual and cultural movement. Historians have largely cast-off regionalism due to its association with the politics of Vichy, viewing the interwar regionalist movement and accompanying folklorist research as a regressive and nostalgic movement that encouraged a return to the soil as a form of anti-urbanization (Wright 2003: 10). Anne Marie Thiesse (1991) and Julian Wright's (2003) research has aimed to show that the regionalist movement, which developed during the Belle Époque and between the two wars, should not be discarded because of its associations with Pétanism. Regionalism was a much more diverse movement beyond its right-leaning expressions. Historian Thomas Parker explains France's regionalist movement of the 1930s as: "Instead of considering itself a melting pot where flavors come together to add seamless dimension to the 'plate' as a whole, France has historically found its unifying aspect in diversity, characterized by starkly different, sometimes contrasting ingredients" (2015: 3). The regionalism that emerged at the end of the nineteenth century and which flourished after the First World War portrayed French national identity as pluralistic and harmonious. In her study of the 1937 Paris World's Fair, Shanny Peer shows how the French state sought to showcase the diversity of regional traditions and culture while presenting a strong unified France.[1] Regionalism became a pervasive idea in the interwar years. It was reflected in architecture, design, and crafts as well as in gastronomic discourses and culinary trends.

In the nineteenth century, cookbooks and gastronomic literature codified and raised middle-class French awareness about distinctive regional cooking styles. Cookbooks such as Edmond Richardin's *La cuisine française du XIVe au XXe siècle: L'art du bien manger* (1913) and Marthe Daudet's (Pampille) *Les Bons plat de France: Cuisine régionale* (1913) are forms of culinary republicanism: they offer a tour of provinces, showcasing the diversity of produce and recipes. Parkhurst Ferguson argues that "Culinary works turned readers into practitioners, natives into cosmopolitans, and most important, provincials into French" (2004: 131). The regionalist culinary movement was also a way for bourgeois cuisine to incorporate rural, regional cuisines into its own traditions, making bourgeois cuisine into the dominant form of French cuisine.

Gastronomes, Guidebooks, and *Les Mères*

At the center of Curnonsky's accolades for Lyonnais cuisine were a number of female cooks who he saw as guardians of "true" Lyonnais cuisine. Curnonsky played a central role in the popularization of the *cuisine des mères lyonnaises*. This was the cuisine of women who had cooked professionally in bourgeois households and then gone on to work in restaurants after the economic downturn at the end of the nineteenth century. This cuisine had its foundations in *la cuisine bourgeoise*, the rich food that was served in the homes of well-to-do middle-class families, but it was also elaborated upon and refined when it moved to the context of the restaurant. Expensive ingredients, such as truffles and foie gras, family-style service, and perfect execution were all distinguishing markers of this cuisine. Unlike the more homogenized food served in the big hotel restaurants to international travelers, regional dishes were the hallmark of *la cuisine des mères*. Some of these dishes included *volaille en demi-deuil*, *quenelles de brochet*, and *fonds d'artichaut avec foie gras*. These are dishes that use high-quality local ingredients such as the famous Bresse chicken and pike from the Saône River but also high-status ingredients from other areas such as foie gras from the Périgord. The focus in the *cuisine des mères* became less about seasonal variation and more about the perfect execution of specific dishes that could be made year round. Guidebooks mentioned the specialties of each restaurant and this led to the further canonization of the dishes that dinners expected to find on the menu. Although it is difficult to consider the *cuisine des mères* as a coherent movement per se, Curnonsky brought together in his guidebooks some of its best-known practitioners—most notably *la mère* Brazier and *la mère* Fillioux. This is one way in which middle-class diners recognized women's important role in defining Lyonnais cuisine in the first half of the twentieth century. This was quite remarkable given that the previous dominance of the international style of French cuisine that was served in the *grande palace* (big hotel dining rooms), which professional male chefs produced almost exclusively.

It was women who were often responsible for bridging the worlds of the domestic and the public. This was the case as cuisine bourgeois moved from the bourgeois home to the restaurant dining room. The *mères lyonnaises* represent this trend well: they were women, usually from the countryside, who cooked in bourgeois homes but lost their domestic employment in the economic downturn of the 1890s. Many of them opened their own small restaurants and dining establishments with help of male partners, husbands, or other male family members. These women were largely responsible for bringing bourgeois cuisine into the semipublic sphere of the restaurant, where critics could evaluate it and where a broader audience could enjoy it.

Les mères lyonnaises' recipes were deeply tied to regional products and preparations that generations of cooks had developed in Lyon and the surrounding areas. The cuisine in Lyon reflected the abundance of the produce that was available from the areas surrounding the city, the affluence of the Lyonnais people, and influences from Italy that had seeped into the culinary repertoire over the years. Historically, Lyon has been an important intersection for trade. Its location at the confluence of the Rhône and the Saône rivers made Lyon a key river port. As the construction of train lines expanded throughout the nineteenth century, Lyon became a central railway hub. Goods, including foodstuffs, from other regions were increasingly accessible and began to show up on restaurant menus. Cooks incorporated these new ingredients, making them Lyonnais. This process of adaptation and authorship is not atypical in the history of the circulation of food (Gabaccia 2004). However, during times of scarcity, local ingredients once more became the focus for Lyonnais cuisine. *Les mères lyonnaises* were masters at preparing sumptuous meals that had the underpinnings of domestic frugality but also the showy affluence of a recently arrived ruling class.

Many of the women who Rouff, Curnonsky, and de Croze lauded as the guardians of "true" French cuisine and who were seen as the keepers of regional traditions, trained men in their kitchens. The most notable cook-apprentice relationship was between the *mère* Brazier and Paul Bocuse. This relationship perhaps most symbolizes the shift in power that was about to occur after this moment of regional celebration. While a few female cooks who were central to the regionalist culinary movement were celebrated as culinary masters and upholders of authentic regional cuisine, men largely supplanted women in the professional kitchen across France.

After the Second World War, the state increasingly regulated most trades and the training that was needed in order to practice them. In the culinary arts, the government certified culinary training program, in addition to apprenticeship. New culinary schools excluded women. It was not until after the Second World War that culinary schools began to admit women, and it would take several more decades before women were a regularly admitted to these institutions (Marie 2014: 174–5). This was one of the reasons for which men became the central creative, cultural figures in this field.

Paul Bocuse: A Lyonnais Culinary Juggernaut

After the Second World War, Lyon reasserted its place as a gastronomic capital. As explained earlier, in the interwar years, women's local peasant food was transformed into a more refined local cuisine that became deeply rooted in the *cuisine bourgeoise* and then transformed into haute cuisine. However, after the war, a new culinary movement drew into question the heaviness this cuisine and the right-wing politics that it symbolized. This was the rise of nouvelle cuisine. Lyonnais chef Paul Bocuse was one of the leading figures to popularize this new lighter, seasonal way of cooking. Bocuse's rise to fame and his long-standing position at the top of French culinary world played a big part in reaffirming Lyon's position as the gastronomic capital of France.

Paul Bocuse was born in 1926 in Collonges-au-Mont-d'Or, where his family ran a small hotel. Bocuse was destined for a culinary life and early on he apprenticed with some of the best chefs in France, including the legendary *mère* Eugénie Brazier. Bocuse learned from the masters of *cuisine bourgeoise*, and he affirmed his craftsmanship when he was granted the *Meilleur Ouvrier de France* diploma in 1961. However, it was not long before Bocuse broke with tradition: he became a central actor in the nouvelle cuisine movement of the late 1970s and early 1980s. Bocuse was one of the champions and front-runners of this new way of cooking, which avoided heavy sauces, placed an emphasis on the freshness of ingredients and paid close attention to the artful presentation of the scaled-down portions of this food. Historian Patrick Rambourg (2005: 293) explains that "chefs wanted to renew their image to be more aligned with the evolution of society, their arguments were even stronger because they were amplified by the media." In the late 1970s and 1980s, French cuisine changed to reflect social and political realities: the decadence and richness of the Gaullist past and the economic prosperity of the "thirty glorious years" was thrown off to embrace a more ecological, simple, and approachable way of eating, which was also a reflection of the rise of François Mitterrand's socialist government. Through this movement, Paul Bocuse also became a protagonist of the dining room, the media and popular culture.

Previously, cooks and chefs largely remained behind closed doors and the food and the diners were the center of attention at the restaurant. Through the second half of the twentieth century, the social status of the chef was on the rise. Paul Bocuse's charismatic, macho personality made him a perfect candidate for the spotlight—not only was he a master of his craft, he was also an innovator and a star ready to perform the role of the hypermasculine chef for the cameras and reporters. Paul Bocuse may have been the first modern superstar chef and his rising stardom was tied to Lyon. In 1987, Bocuse created the Bocuse d'Or, an international culinary competition that takes places in Lyon every two years—an event that is often dubbed "the culinary Olympics." Teams from around the world come to compete for prestigious medals. Hosting such a prestigious competition draws a large crowd of international culinary professionals and spectators; this event has helped solidify Lyon's reputation as a place of culinary excellence.

In 1990, the École des Arts Culinaires et de l'Hôtellerie in Ecully, just outside of Lyon, was renamed the Institut Paul Bocuse. This institution draws talented young culinary students from all over the world, who are hoping to break into the big leagues of the culinary world. Some of the school's alumni have gone on to compete in Top Chef France, and open successful restaurants in Lyon and other areas of France and the world. Lyon and its surrounding areas are also home to a number of trade schools that have excellent culinary programs. It is both Bocuse's name and the culinary elitism that it stands for that brings students to the institute and to many of the other culinary training programs in the Lyon area. As a hub of culinary training, Lyon has a deep bench of upcoming culinary talent.

Paul Bocuse was perhaps France's best-known chef of the twentieth century and his name has become synonymous with Lyon. His memory lives on strongly in the restaurant empire he left behind, the culinary competition he founded and through the many chefs that trained in his kitchens. Paul Bocuse's name and image are indelibly part of the gastronomic and physical landscape of the city from the covered market La Halle Paul Bocuse to the chef's image in painted murals throughout the city. Even after his death in 2018, Paul Bocuse remains a symbol of Lyon's gastronomic dominance and his legacy continues to draw people to the city.

La Nouvelle Cuisine Lyonnaise: When the International Becomes Local

While doing my research in Lyon, I befriended a group of young chefs cooking creative food that they call "nouvelle cuisine lyonnaise." Tabata and Ludovic Mey from *Les Apothicaires*, Connie Zagora and Laurent Ozan from the *Kitchen Café*, Hubert Vergoin from *Substrat*, and Arnaud Laverdin, Thomas Pezeril, and Stephen Theibaut-Pellegrino from *la Bijouterie* are at the core of this group. They hang out together, share ideas and push each other's thinking about food and cooking. I have been fortunate enough to eat in these restaurants, and they all place locally sourced, seasonal products at the center of their cooking. Their techniques range from classic French braising and poaching to Asian-inspired steaming and raw meat and Scandinavian fish preparations. The flavors are eclectic with herbs such as thyme or tarragon that are familiar to French cuisine but also ingredients from further afield such as miso and jalapeños. The portions are dainty, and the presentation of the dishes is artistic but not overdone. There is a creative touch in much of this cuisine, with an attention to presentation of the dishes that does not obscure the ingredients. When you finish eating a meal, you feel good—it does not leave you feeling overfed or with your senses saturated. These restaurants have a relaxed atmosphere, and they all eschew tablecloths as stuffy and "environmentally unfriendly."

In 2015, Hubert Vergoin, the chef from Substrat, Gaëtan Gentil, the chef at *PRaiRiaL*, the blogger Julien Le Forestier, and communications expert Romain Bombail formed the association "Bande de Gourmand." Their motivation was to promote a new type of cuisine in Lyon: a cuisine that "sees the pertinence of culinary fusion that is open to the world, that defends local products and provisions using a short supply chain" (Le Progrès 2016). The central goal of the association was to bring like-minded chefs, writers, and producers together to push back against the dominating cuisine with a capital C to show that there is another cuisine that is representative of Lyon at this time. Although the association site is no longer active and their Twitter feed has slowed down, the spirit of this group is alive and well in a growing number of kitchens in Lyon.

This group of chefs includes foreigners and French people set on exploring the techniques and flavors of the world. They are pushing the boundaries of Lyonnais cuisine and claiming their place as the new trendsetters outside of the Michelin-starred sphere. This group is part of a broader "bistronomie" movement in France: restaurants that do not have linen table cloths, where the menus tend to have a limited number of seasonal items, and the food is meticulously prepared using fresh local products. An article in *Forbes* magazine defines "bistronomie" as "a combination of simplicity and the best traditions in French cooking" (Rodriguez 2017). Estérelle Payany declares that the traditional, upscale restaurant will disappear in 2020, which is good news in her opinion. Payany was in no way predicting the devastating effects of the Covid-19 pandemic on the restaurant industry, but rather a waning interest in expensive, upscale eateries.

Often when Parisians or French people from other regions think of Lyonnais cuisine, they claim it is classic French food with heavy sauces and traditional dishes like *blanquette de veau* (veal in white sauce), *poulet au vinaigre* (vinegar chicken), tripe dishes, and cooked sausages served with Beaujolais sauce and a side of lentils. This is still the sort of food that is served to tourists in the *bouchons* (a typical Lyonnais dining establishment) that line rue Mercière and the cobblestone pedestrian streets of Vieux Lyon. However, this is not the only cuisine that Lyon is known for. Increasingly, tourists come to Lyon looking for accessible fine dining experiences that are on the cutting edge of French cuisine. Lyon expresses a more diverse French cuisine that is still grounded in regional products and flavors, but which has an openness to incorporating techniques and ingredients from other parts of the world.

With the turn of the twenty-first century, France came to recognize its colonial heritage and cultural diversity, but not without a great deal of resistance and xenophobia. At the same time, French cuisine has become increasingly less of a monoculture. At a popular level, the kebab is one of France's most ubiquitous forms of fast food. For some this has been the cause of an identity crisis (Sage 2014). However, at the level of the bistro and fine dining, this new openness to cultural diversity has meant an opportunity to incorporate ingredients and techniques from around the world—cultural diversity has brought incredible innovation to Lyonnais kitchen.

The group of young chefs who identify with the "nouvelle cuisine lyonnaise" includes many foreigners and women. The numerous culinary schools, in particular the Institut Paul Bocuse, which attracts many non-French students, have been drivers in making Lyon one of the centers for this culinary development (Cheshes 2018). Tabata Mey of *Les Apothicaires* and Ruijun Sun from the *Table de Wei* are both graduates of the Institut Paul Bocuse, and they demonstrate a grounding in classic French techniques with strong influences from their own cultures and an openness to experiment. At the same time, their food respects and showcases the seasonality of local products. I would argue that this is what makes their food truly Lyonnais.

There is a deep bench of students of local culinary schools who have flocked to the city, but there are also aspiring chefs from the world over who come to apprentice with notable Lyonnais chefs. Often this young talent stays because it is less expensive to open a restaurant in Lyon than somewhere like Paris, and there tends to be an openness to novelty in Lyon. In particular, there are numerous Japanese chefs, such as the Michelin-starred Takao Takano and Tsuyoshi Arai, who cook French food with a strong Japanese influence. There is a strong dialogue between many of these chefs and they are building a sense of a movement. In a recent article in *GQ*, Tabata Mey talked about the "Bande des Gourmands": "We are really close. We share recipes, we share producers. There are no secrets, like there were in the old days" (Martin 2018). The locals and discerning tourists are gravitating toward lighter fare, and tourists are drawn to Lyon to indulge in the classics but also to experience the future of French cuisine.

Conclusion

The economic crisis of the 1920s plus the failure of the silk industry were catalysts for Lyon to reinvent itself as a gastronomic capital—food would become the city's new calling card. Cuisine was one way in which France and Lyon could regain some of their prestige after the devastation of war. Tourism and gastronomy are often mobilized during times of economic and urban repositioning because of their attraction that is based on notions of identity and ability to knit together social ties and create regional cohesion around local traditions (Csergo 2008). Regional cooking thus showcased French diversity, quality, and good taste.[2] The dining room table offered the perfect place to embrace French diversity while taking refuge from the troubled national climate (Peer 1998: 72). At the same time, Lyon as the gastronomic capital of France further propelled bourgeois culture to become the dominant cultural form in a wide range of cuisines related to working-class and agrarian cultures.

The ebb and flow of political power has been reflected in French cuisine from the cuisine of the French court to haute cuisine that was then mixed with *cuisine bourgeoise* to create a *cuisine gastronomique* that imposed bourgeois cultural forms of cooking and dining as a national norm. Even at a regional level, as we can see from the case of Lyon, the local rural, working-class and domestic form of cuisine that mark the regional differences are subsumed into a highbrow form that is showcased in restaurants to tourists and middle-class diners. It is this cuisine, ranking high on the *Michelin Guide* echelon, which has become representative of not only the city of Lyon but also its connections with the surrounding farmlands and also its history of rebellious silk workers. Lyon initially seized on a moment when there was a strong movement to define France through its regions. This was partly motivated by politicians and powerful cultural brokers, such as gastronomic writers, who wanted to decenter Paris. The sophisticated, untethered cuisine that was prominent in fin de siècle Paris became the foil for "honest" and "authentic" regional cuisine. A group of women known as the *mères lyonnaises* were unlikely protagonists in stealing this culinary title from the nation's capital.

At the turn of the twenty-first century, it was once again women who are central to reinvigorating Lyon's culinary reputation. This time the even more unlikely protagonists are not only females but also foreigners. The city has remained a gastronomic capital because of its rich tradition of culinary excellence and innovation. Lyon is still on the map as the gastronomic capital of France largely due to the influx of new talent that has mixed with the homegrown base of culinary knowledge. Lyon remains a place where the local and the imported and the new and the old mix to create something original, delicious, and deeply Lyonnais taste.

Notes

1   The regionalist *Félibrige* literary movement attracted centrist, Catholic conservatives, monarchists, and left-leaning republicans. On the right, Charles Maurras and Maurice Barrès' work promoted decentralized monarchy and a return to the land, respectively, as solutions to France's social and morals ills. In contrast, Jean Charles-Brun's *Fédération régionaliste française*, founded in 1900, was a very inclusive movement that gathered followers from the entire political spectrum.
2   Thiesse (1997) attributes the growth of regionalism in the interwar period to diminished international prestige and loss of confidence in the state.

References

Arbellot, S. (1965), *Curnonsky, prince des gastronomes*, Paris: Les Productions de Paris.

Barabowski, S. and E. Furlough, eds. (2001), *Being Elsewhere: Tourism, Consumer Culture, and Identity in Modern Europe and North America*, Ann Arbor: University of Michigan Press.

Cheshes, J. (2018), "The Most Innovative Chefs in Lyon, France's Gastronomic Capital," *Wall Street Journal*, July 24. https://www.wsj.com/articles/the-4-most-innovative-rest aurants-in-lyon-frances-gastronomic-capital-1532459914, last accessed February 29, 2020.

Csergo, J. (2008), "Lyon, première 'capitale mondiale de la gastronomie' 1925–1935," in J. Csergo (ed.), *Voyages en gastronomies: L'invention des capitales et des régions gourmands*, pp. 33–49, Paris: Autrement.

Curnonsky and A. de Croze (1933), *Trésor gastronomique de la France: répertoire complet des spécialités gourmandes des trente-deux provinces françaises*, Paris: Librarie Delagrave.

Curnonsky and M. Rouff (1921–28), *La France Gastronomique: Guides des merveilles culinaires et des bonnes auberges françaises*, 13 vols, Paris: F. Rouff.

de Croze, A. (1928), *Les plats régionaux de France, 1400 succulentes recettes traditionnelles de toutes les provinces françaises*, Imp Ramlot, 1928, reprint Paris: Morcrette, 1977.

Ferguson, P. (2004), *Accounting for Taste: The Triumph of French Cuisine*, Chicago: University of Chicago Press.

Gabaccia, D. (2004), "Food, Mobility, and World History," in *The Oxford Handbook of Food History*, pp. 305–23, Oxford: Oxford University Press.

Gohen, E. (1988), "Authenticity and Commoditization in Tourism," *Annals of Tourism Research* 15: 371–86.

Harp, S. (2001), *Marketing Michelin: Advertising and Cultural Identity in Twentieth-Century France*, Baltimore: Johns Hopkins University Press.

Karpik, L. (2000), "Le guide rouge Michelin," *Sociologie du travail* 42(3): 371–2.

Koshar, R. (1998), "'What Ought to Be Seen': Tourists' Guidebooks and National Identities in Modern Germany and Europe," *Journal of Contemporary History* 3(3): 323–40.

Long, L., ed. (2004), *Culinary Tourism*, Lexington: University Press of Kentucky.

MacCannell, D. (1989), *The Tourist: A New Theory of the Leisure Class*, New York: Schocken Books.

Marie, P. (2014), *Hommes et femmes dans l'Apprentissage et la transmission de "l'art culinaire,"* Paris: L'Harmattan.

Martin, B. (2018), "Make a Pilgrimage to the Real Capital of French Food," *GQ*. https://ww w.gq.com/story/lyon-french-food-travel-guide, last accessed January 9, 2020.

Michelin (1923), *Le Guide Rouge*, Paris: Michelin.

Parker, T. (2015), *Tasting French Terroir: The History of an Idea*, Oakland: University of California Press.

Peer, S. (1998), *France on Display: Peasants, Provincials, and Folklore in the 1937 Paris World's Fair*, Albany: SUNY Press.

Poulain, J. P. (2005), "French Gastronomy, French Gastronomies. Culinary Cultures of Europe: Identity, Diversity and Dialogue," in D. Goldstein and K. Merkle (eds.), *Culinary Cultures of Europe: Identity, Diversity and Dialogue*, pp. 157–70, Strasbourg: Council of Europe Publishing.

Rambourg, P. (2005), *De la cuisine à la gastronomie: histoire de la table française*, Paris: Louis Audibert.

Reche, L. (2017), "Region, Nation and Gastronomy: Regionalism and Gastronomic Texts in of the (1900–1939) Early Twentieth Century," Phd diss., The Graduate Center, The City University of New York.

Reynaud, C. (2016), "Bande de gourmands, des potes au service d'une cuisine en liberté," *Le Progrès*. https://www.leprogres.fr/lyon/2016/02/05/bande-de-gourmands-des-potes-au-service-d-une-cuisine-en-liberte, accessed November 6, 2020.

Rodriguez, C. (2017), "Top 100 Bistros in Paris: New Gastronomic Stars at Affordable Prices," *Forbes*, April 29. https://www.forbes.com/sites/ceciliarodriguez/2017/04/29/top-100-bistros-in-paris-the-new-gastronomic-stars-at-affordable-prices/#a0950d7370b9, accessed March 2, 2020.

Rouèche, Y. (2018), *Histoire(s) de la gastronomie lyonnaise*, Lyon: Libel.

Rouzier, E., ed. (1931), *Livre d'or de la gastronomie française*, Paris: Jacquet & L'Hopital.

Sage, A. (2014), "Kebabs are Causing an Identity Crisis in France," *Business Insider*. https://www.businessinsider.com/r-in-france-kebabs-get-wrapped-up-in-identity-politics-2014-10, last accessed September 24, 2019.

Spang, R. (2000), *The Invention of the Restaurant: Paris and Modern Gastronomic Culture*, Cambridge, MA: Harvard University Press.

Thiesse, A. M. (1991), *Ecrire la France. Le mouvement littéraire de la langue française entre la belle époque et la libération*, Paris: Presse Universtaire de France.

Thiesse, A. M. (1997), *Ils apprenaient la France: l'exaltation des régions dans le discours patriotique*, Paris: Les Editions de la MSH.

Whalen, P. (2007), "Burgundian Regionalism and French Republican Commercial Culture at the 1937 Paris International Exposition," *Cultural Analysis* 6: 31–69.

Wright, J. (2003), *The Regionalist Movement in France, 1890–1914: Jean Charles-Brun and French Political Thought*, Oxford: Clarendon.

Part II

Translocal and Transnational Politics of Taste and Identity

7

Fetid Flesh and Fragrant Fare

Food, Scandal, and Identity in Contemporary Bengal

Ishita Banerjee-Dube

One of the wheels of a taxi falls "in a deep pothole" in the Budge Budge area of the South 24 Parganas district, about 28 kilometers from Kolkata, the capital of the state of West Bengal in Eastern India. The cab driver and his aide, a casual laborer, unable to lift the cab, ask local residents for help. "When the vehicle did not budge after much pushing," the local residents decide to clear out the trunk of the cab. To their surprise and horror, they discover parts of dead animals and animal skin there. Suspecting that the shocking contents of the "luggage compartment" had come from a dump yard nearby, the residents lodge a complaint with the local police, asserting that carcass meat was regularly supplied to restaurants and food stalls. This happens on April 19, 2018.

This "accidental" discovery, which in itself was the result of a mini-accident, started not just a chain of enquiries, raids, interrogation, and apprehension by the police, the Central Investigation Department, and the Kolkata Municipal Corporation (KMC), and assaults by the Congress Party and the Union government of the Bharatiya Janata Party (BJP) on the current Trinamool Congress government of Mamata Banerjee in West Bengal, but also a chain of serious and suggestive, perky and witty exchanges on WhatsApp and Facebook and other forms of social media. The news of the rumor and the scandal was first reported in the *Hindustan Times (HT)* ("Two held in Bengal for selling skin and meat . . ."), a national English-language newspaper on April 21, 2018. Soon it made headlines in other national dailies as well as in English- and Bengali-language newspapers with wide circulation in West Bengal and outside, all also available online. It was also picked up for a short while by television news channels. Such sensational reportage conferred on a scandal that temporarily shocked and scared most middle-class Bengali meat-eaters, an enduring and enigmatic life with diverse reverberations.

Taking a slightly off-beat path, and making use of the author's position of a trespasser as a historian among anthropologists, this chapter will examine this apparently short-lived yet significant scandal to probe its multiple facets and implications that enable acute understandings of food and eating as activities laden with immense social meaning and value. Starting off from important assertions of anthropologists about the "semiotic virtuosity" of food consequent upon its perishable nature that makes the need for food constant and indispensable, and the fact that food has the capacity to generate powerful emotions (Appadurai 1981: 494), this chapter will play on the diverse manifestations of the perishability of food—including its ties with life and death in Hindu thought—that can suddenly transform an attractive palate into an abhorred one and produce conflicting emotions.

It will also attempt to open up and extend anthropological analyses of food—often viewed as a closed cultural system that carry and convey particular meanings for specific groups—by placing food and cooking in the context of actual sociopolitical and economic processes, and by paying serious attention to the increasingly potent presence of the virtual world of social media, and the traditional print media as important points of entry into worlds of taste, flavor, health, and dietary practices that in turn are expressive of emotions, moral values, and sensibilities that go beyond preference for food and the lure of consumption. Drawing inspiration from Ramanujan's suggestion of taking the cultural system of food as a language of poetics that aptly addresses metaphors and breeds many more (1992: 221–2), and his explorations of such metaphoric meanings in proverbs and sayings in South India, this chapter will savor the flavor of wit, jokes, fear, and sarcasm concocted as reactions to a shocking rumor and scandal over fetid flesh and its consumption literally and figuratively in order to "make sense of taste" (Korsmeyer 1999). It will try and untangle the multifarious, metaphoric, and contradictory meanings of the reactions and their rippling effects that traverse worlds of taste, flavor, diet, morality, and sensibility to tread into those of identity, belonging, and politics. This exploration hopes to contribute to an understanding of the "gastro-politics" tied to beliefs around food in South Asia as a set of important social and moral propositions that can serve diametrically opposed semiotic functions by creating homogeneity and heterogeneity among those who transact in it (Appadurai 1981: 507–8), and comment on wider sociopolitical and cultural processes inflected by metaphoric allusions.

Food, Morality, Sensibility

India, particularly Hindu India, has been known for its elaborate and intricate distinction and classification of food and edible ingredients in accordance with their qualities, the values attached to them, and the effect they have on human bodies. Such elaborate distinctions rest on the fact that Hindu classical thought has conceptualized food as a moral system, a "life-guiding presence" that conjoins this-worldly with the otherworldly, life and death, matter and spirit, the gross and the subtle, the individual and the collective, essence and aesthetics, and experience and emotion, making food conducive to *gastrosemantics*, an extraordinarily loaded system of symbolization and communication (Khare 1992: 1, 27–8). Such conceptual and cosmological primacy of food—from the selection of edible ingredients through the process of its preparation to the effect it has on the one who eats it (Khare 1976) —also confers on food great significance and value as a media of contact between human beings (Appadurai 1981; Marriott 1968). Norms and taxonomy have carefully tried to regulate interpersonal and group contact, as well as relations of kinship that rest on transactions of different categories of food among different groups and individuals. In general, the givers of food are held to be higher than the receivers in social and caste ranking, and raw food has less potential of polluting than cooked food. Cooked food, again, is distinguished on the basis of the sequence of culinary steps and cooking media (Khare 1976: 4) into *kaccha* (boiled, sometimes considered inferior but not necessarily so) and *pakka* (fried, superior, prepared with ghee). While there is an enormous variation and heterogeneity in the norms of particular regions that undergo constant transformation, the overall ideas of *pakka*, *kaccha*, and raw, as well as their exchange, often tied to the offering of services, appear to loosely hold true in rural areas, particularly of the North (Khare 1976; Marriott 1968). For our purposes, we will briefly examine some broad and general ideas and norms that uphold the Hindu gastronomic system and continue to have some relevance.

The cosmological and conceptual distinctions and gradations of different kinds of food and edible ingredients together with an emphasis on eating as a moral act links, in Khare's opinion, the three concerns of the gastronomic triangle: the self, food, and body (Khare 1992: 28). Such concerns in turn bond qualities of food with innate qualities/strands/dispositions (*gunas*) of individuals (and groups). The Bhagavad Gita has a classic passage that relates food to temperament and the taste for food as expressive of the character of the person (Ramanujan 1992: 228). The three strands/ qualities are *sattvik* (derived from *sattva*, good and constructive), *rajasik* (derived from *rajas*, passion and confusion), and *tamasik* (derived from *tamas*, dark and destructive/ chaotic). *Sattvik* food promotes life, virtue, strength, vitality, health, happiness, and satisfaction; it is savory, smooth, firm, and pleasant to the stomach, and is held dear by *sattvik* individuals (Ramanujan 1992: 229; Sargeant 2009: 641). *Rajasik* food, on the other hand, causes pain, misery, and sickness; it is bitter, sour, salty, stinging hot, pungent, dry, and burning, and is held dear by the man of passion (Ramanujan 1992: 229; Sargeant 2009: 642). Stale, tasteless, putrid, rotten, and refuse, as well as the impure, is the food dear to the *tamasik*, the man of darkness (Ramanujan 1992: 229; Sargeant 2009: 643). Interestingly, in common perception, the temperamental and sensory bond between *rajasik* food and the man of passion identifies *rajasik* food with food of the raja, king, and hence with richness and extravagance: an association that allures rather than dissuades. Moreover, for the growing cosmopolitan middle classes of urban India moved by multiple desires of consumption, the linking of eating and morality, of this world and the next, are matters of mirth. But they can acquire discrete significance in moments of vulnerability as we will see later. In common practice, *sattvik* individuals can and do get attracted to *rajasik* (and even *tamasik* food) without overtly worrying about the moral and physical effect of such food on them. This is probably because the moral-cosmological-gastronomic system of "Hindu" India did not pay adequate attention to the discrepancies between the normative-prescriptive and their perceptions and appropriations in practices, as well as the factors that made the construction of the moral-normative system necessary.

The modern Hindu's discourse on food, remarks Khare, is based on another anomaly: the superiority it ascribes to vegetarianism counters the rituals of Vedic Indians of sacrificing animals and consuming the flesh of such animals (Khare 1992:

9; see also Achaya 1994). Even more significant is the fact that this exclusive focus on Hindu gastro-politics leaves out the long presence and intrinsic influence of various groups and cuisines from outside India: the Persian-Islamic, European, Anglo-Indian, Southeastern, for instance—in the highly developed and discerned cuisine of India. An awareness of the composite processes that shaped Indian (Hindu) cuisine and taste (Banerjee-Dube 2016: 2) would allow an understanding of why many upper-caste, upper-class persons across India who try and stick to *sattvik*, vegetarian food, have no qualms in ingesting garlic and onion, considered to be hot and impure. They are impure because they generate sluggishness, spiritual disquiet, and immoral thoughts (Khare 1992: 42) and are meant to be shunned by people who wish to preserve their corporeal, mental, and moral equanimity.

Indeed, a large part of Hindu India has appetite and attraction for fish and meat, consumed in accordance with the economic resources of families and individuals. Climate, topography, and the easy availability of different ingredients together with economic, ecological, cultural, and political factors have aided the development of a shared yet differentiated collective taste in food (Ayora-Diaz 2019), as has the evolution of food and cuisine through intermingling with distinct peoples and cultures. Keeping these important facts in mind, let us return to the story of the "scandal."

Shocked Sensibilities and Shuffled Palate

The April 21 report of the *HT*, it bears mention, stated that despite the arrest of the casual worker and the taxi driver and several raids in the street markets of the Sealdah-Rajabajar area of central Kolkata, no evidence had yet been found of carcass meat being supplied to food stalls and restaurants, and no one had been reported sick. Almost as a counterpoint to this last statement of the *HT* report by its Kolkata correspondent, the headline of a feature in the *Ananda Bazar Patrika* (a Bengali newspaper with a vast readership) of April 26, 2018 (updated on 1 May), by Suma Mukhopadhyay, referred to a "specialist" to warn its many readers of the acutely dangerous consequences of the consumption of *bhagad* (dump yard) meat. The feature carried a photo of the anatomy of the human body on the left corner superimposed on that of bountiful quantities of meat with a part of the meat under microscope on the upper-right corner. Quoting a medical doctor, it carried a list of diseases that could result from eating the meat of dead and decaying animals. And that included not just the expected stomach cramps and diarrhea, blood in feces and severe headaches, but also the unsuspected ones of septicemia and the lethal neurocysticercosis in which "bacteria" from the rotten meat spreads all over the food while it is being cooked, and the egg of a dangerous worm, immune to the heat of cooking, transforms into a larva later and reaches the brain via the nervous system. The feature asserted that the people caught in the raids have admitted to the fact of a mix of rotten and fresh meat being supplied on a large scale to roadside eateries and tiny restaurants.

The *Times of India* (another national daily) reported on April 27 that following the accidental discovery of April 19, a nightlong raid in an ice factory in the Rajabajar area conducted by the Kolkata police had yielded twenty tons of carcass meat, packed and ready to be distributed (Ghosh 2018a). This detailed report revealed that that the use of carcass meat was not a one-time affair but a well-organized business racket in operation for five years and that, in addition to Budge Budge, Kalyani and Sonarpur dump yards in the close surroundings of Kolkata were major pick-up centers. It detailed the modus operandi of this shocking trade, commented on how the rotten meat was processed, and confirmed that mixed with fresh meat, it was packaged, labeled, and distributed for use in the making of sausage, meat balls, ham, and salami sold across the city, and hinted that it probably reached big restaurants as well. This report confirmed the arrest of nine persons till then, including the "alleged" kingpin Sunny Malik from Bihar.

The headlines of a second report the following day in the same newspaper ran thus, "Stick to fresh meat: Experts." It stated that the news of suspected carcass meat being supplied to eateries had caused panic and that medical practitioners were being flooded with phone calls and messages that queried whether people should avoid eating meat altogether in order to stay healthy. While doctors felt that the fear was exaggerated, they did ask people to stick to fresh meat and to avoid buying packaged meat, particularly salami, sausage, and bacon that could not be cooked at the minimum temperature of 60 degrees Celsius required to kill disease-causing bacteria. Eating dump yard meat could cause "organ malfunction," especially of the liver and the pancreas, in the long run.

A *HT* report of May 1 indicated a considerable dip in the sale of raw, packaged, and cooked meat (Chatterjee 2018). Restaurants, fast-food joints, and even confectioners that sell meat products witnessed "a significant drop in footfall over the weekend" (of April 29–30). This is because police investigation had indicated that carcass meat of animals ranging from cows to cats was being mixed with fresh meat and supplied to several restaurants and eateries in Kolkata. The report mentioned a public interest litigation that had been filed by Citizens for Justice, a nongovernmental organization, in the Kolkata High Court, and the instruction issued by Indian Railways and Tourism Development Corporation to its suppliers of not storing frozen meat as a precautionary measure. It referred to the thousands of messages in the social media that named restaurants and eateries, and the precaution taken by customers of raw meat by checking the live chicken before having it killed. "Dog meat fear halves the sale of non-veg food in Kolkata eateries," reported the *Times of India* on May 1 (Mitra and Bandyopadhyay 2018).

A *Firstpost* report of May 2 based on that of the Press Trust of India (PTI) affirmed that the scandal over the sale of rotten meat had left restaurants cautious and made foodies turn to fish and *even* vegetarian options. It quoted the president of Hotel and Restaurant Managers' Association of Eastern India to assert that although there was no significant drop in people coming to eat in restaurants, they were desisting from ordering meat or chicken dishes ("Chaos over rotten meat sale in Kolkata leaves restaurants cautious; foodies turn to fish, vegetarian options," *Firstpost*, May 2, 2018). At the same time, the dip of almost 60 percent in orders of mutton (goat meat in Bengal instead of sheep) and chicken that member restaurants of the association were facing was being made up by the hike in orders of fish, prawn, and shrimp delicacies. The report also referred to the comment of the owner of "two iconic restaurants in Kolkata" that chefs had become more alert to the quality of raw supplies. But since fresh meat for his restaurants was acquired from highly accredited places and since his restaurants had been serving food of very high quality for years, he was confident that his clients were not going to be scared off by the scandal (*Firstpost* May 2, 2018).

The May 3 report in the *Telegraph*, the English daily of the *Ananda Bazaar* group, echoed the *Firstpost* in claiming that the "meat scam" had led to a "surge in fish sales across Calcutta" ("Meat scam leads to surge in fish sales across Calcutta" 2018). Quoting the general manager of the State Fisheries Development Corporation, it confirmed that while meat sales had plummeted over the past few days, sale of fish had received a boost of 30 to 40 percent. It further mentioned that a spokesperson of the association of meat traders had admitted a slump of 20 to 25 percent in the sale of the flesh of chicken, goat, cow, and pig resulting from the carcass meat controversy, and had attributed the slump primarily to a fall in demand from restaurants and eateries. The general secretary of Bengal Poultry Association was reported to have said that the sale of live birds killed before the consumer had not dropped while that of frozen chicken had.

The *Scroll.in*, a part of "Free press," reported on May 5 that raids across the city in restaurants and meat markets by a special investigation team set up by the Trinamool Congress government had yielded further "harrowing results." On April 27, a wholesale chicken outlet in the New Town area of suburban Kolkata was found to house sick birds along with five freezers full of rotten chicken and that a few restaurant owners had admitted buying chicken from that outlet. A raid led by the KMC in the New Market area on May 3 found and destroyed 100 kilograms of rotten meat.

These reports were accompanied by posts in the social media that indicted various well-known restaurants in Kolkata. The *Scroll.in* of May 5 confirmed that WhatsApp messages and other posts in the social media were adding to the "stink" of the panic created by the rotten-meat scandal ("Ghosh 2018b"). It pointed to the circulation of innumerable messages containing a long list of Kolkata restaurants that served rotten meat on WhatsApp from the end of April that had made a well-known advertising professional and many others stay away from the restaurants listed for the time being, although there had yet been no evidence that the restaurants were guilty of serving meat gone foul. The advertising professional, moreover, had started eating only fresh chicken prepared at home and was staying away from sausages and minced meat anywhere.

A large number of posts on Facebook shared photos of rotten meat and gave names of specific restaurants where the photos had been taken. The reverberating effect of the panic generated by the meat scandal and extended by the social media forced the owner of *Shiraz Golden*, an old and renowned restaurant serving "Mughlai food" (food of the Mughals), to take legal action against people who were "disseminating false information to taint our brand" and "destroy our goodwill" (*Firstpost*, May 2, 2018). We do not know what came of that legal action, but it is true that for a couple of weeks the *bhagad* (dump yard) meat scandal together with its accompanying ripples "dulled" the city's appetite for kebabs, rolls, and biryani (*Firstpost*, May 2, 2018). The report of *Scroll.in* referred to the statement of a well-known food blogger that the "trust" on which the restaurant business is based had been broken and it will take some time for that to be "re-established" (*Firstpost*, May 2, 2018).

Robust Recovery and Piquant Tastes

Kolkatans (and Bengalis), who take pride in their wit and delectable sense of humor, did not take long to recover from the scare and the shock. On April 28, I received two WhatsApp messages from an older cousin. The first of these had a photo of a vulture looming large with two short texts on the upper-left corner and the lower-right corner, almost in the manner of the report in the *Ananda Bazar Patrika* of April 26. The text on the upper-left corner affirmed: "Now we know the reason for the disappearance of vultures from Bengal." The one on the lower right sardonically admonished "Selfish human beings" who "have now started preying on the food of the vulture in the *bhagad*" (dump yard).

The second message was even more playful. It had Lalmohan Babu, the immortal character created by the celebrated film director Satyajit Ray in his detective series Phelu'da, on a red poster (as if of a Ray film) with the iconic words of Lalmohan Ganguly in *Sonar Kella* (Golden Fort), the first Pheula'da story made into a feature film by Ray: "Highly suspicious! Can't fathom how Bengalis have managed to completely digest bhagad meat."

The third one, of May 1, was short and witty. It ran: "Such audacity! A dog went past me singing 'I will get transformed into mutton when I die.'" This was a playful take on the song of a popular Bangla film *Bonpalasir Padabali* of the 1980s sung by the superhero Uttam Kumar, an allusion which the younger generation is unlikely to catch. More importantly, dogs and pigs are considered to be dirty animals because they eat leftover food and refuse. Hence the play with dog being transformed into the flesh of goat after death.

There were others that flippantly indicated that while real mutton started being used in the rolls (circular flour flat-bread rolled with meat, chicken, vegetable, and cheese) sold in roadside stalls as a result of the scandal, consumers got suspicious because they had come to savor the taste of dog meat in them. And there were many, many more that derided the shocking disclosure and made light of the matter in a variety of ways. This led the writer of a feature on the changing dietary practices of Bengalis that was published in the wake of the *bhagad* meat affair in *Ananda Bazar Patrika* to comment: "*Bipake podle Bangalir buddhi khole, raser ban dake*" (Bengalis rise to their wittiest best in moments of crisis when a tide of humor sweeps over; *Ananda Bazar Patrika*, June 3, 2018).

As opposed to this, a person who runs an organization dedicated to the preservation of communal amity in his neighborhood raised a few troubling questions in his Facebook post of April 27 around the *bhagad* meat affair. How many tons of meat was required by Kolkata restaurants and how many tons of rotten meat of dead dogs, cats, and pigs was available in the dump yards? Why was attention being directed toward Rajabajar, a predominantly Muslim area of Kolkata? Weren't the Muslims, many of whom were butchers by profession, the soft targets? He also indicated a more devious connection between the closing of tiny shops and stalls and the entry of Reliance Fresh, a large corporate chain of grocery stores, as well as a push toward vegetarianism on the part of the Hindu right among the notoriously nonvegetarian Bengali middle classes, urging his friends and acquaintances to seriously consider the implications.

Such complementary and contradictory reports and responses aroused my appetite for a deeper relishing of the matter. I was intrigued and amused and wanted to enquire if this scare was to have an enduring effect on the dietary practices of the primarily Hindu middle-class Bengalis. And whether it told us anything about the ways people relate to the consumption of "flesh" and the changing configurations of taste. To such purpose, I sent out an informal questionnaire to a host of friends, colleagues, and relatives with differing academic training and professional careers, based in Kolkata and other parts of India. I sought answers to a few core questions and some different ones. My queries were sent out at the end of May 2018 and most of the responses came in the first half of June. In addition, I gathered information from focused and informal conversations in Kolkata with friends, colleagues, and relatives in the winter of 2018. I offer and deploy the responses, Facebook posts, and WhatsApp messages as a living archive that captures the myriad meanings generated around the pleasures and pangs of eating with their intimate links with selfhood, community, and identity at moments of vulnerability.

Eating In and Eating Out

Did the rumor and reports of the carcass meat racket generate a scare powerful enough to have a lasting impact on eating patterns of middle-class Bengalis? Most of my respondents sounded skeptical within a month and a half of the first exposé. This was because after the raid in the Rajabajar ice factory mentioned in the *Times of India* news report, raids in restaurants did not yield much except for some stored moldy flesh in refrigerators of a few, which were sent for lab tests by the KMC. Apart from the fact that the reports of such tests took some time to come, newspapers did not give them the pride of place that the initial reporting of the scam got. Indeed, as one of my friends, an entrepreneur and journalist, affirmed: "no agency, investigator, or media investigation managed to (or bothered to) buy samples and get them tested" in order to conclusively prove that anything that was being sold at a consumer consumption or sale point was contaminated. In addition, he wondered how much meat could actually be got from the cadavers of dogs and cats that had most likely died of starvation. Scare or concern over adulterated food moreover, he pointed out, was nothing new in Bengal and elsewhere in India. On July 10, the same friend drew my attention to a follow-up report in the *Times of India* that stated that most samples of raw and cooked meat collected by the health department of the KMC during the carcass meat scare were "safe" ("Samples collected during carcass scare safe: KMC").

A friend who writes on food but was in Delhi at the time news reports started coming out, felt, on the other hand, that the consumption of meat had definitely gone down in Kolkata in May (and early June) and that people were turning back to fish. But she did not feel that the scare will have any lasting impact since Bengalis love to "wine and dine." A friend, a high-level government employee, who lives in Mumbai but visited Kolkata toward the end of June informed me that people were still desisting from eating meat in restaurants. Another friend, also based in Delhi and a veteran journalist, stated that people in Kolkata were staying away from eating meat outside.

She affirmed that the dump yard meat "racket" had drawn serious media attention and that national English-language newspapers such as the *Times of India* and the *HT* had carried more than one report on the matter. This friend, therefore, was not certain in early June as to whether the unearthing of a carcass meat "racket" would have a lasting effect. Informal conversations with friends and relatives in December that year revealed that hosts stopped serving mutton and chicken dishes for wedding and other feasts for a short while.

A Kolkata-based singer, a cousin of mine whose husband is a medical doctor was skeptical about the scare from the beginning. The source of such reports, she stated, was dubious and the matter of *bhagad* meat was something to laugh about rather than worry about. She and her family were so unaffected by the matter that they had not bothered to follow the newspaper reports with care. While she did eat out at regular intervals, the meat at home was always got fresh from the market and prepared by her. An acquaintance made through a shared interest in culinary cultures seconded my cousin. He and many of his friends were surprised rather than outraged by initial reports of the *bhagad* meat scandal. And that surprise, he stated, soon changed to jests and ingenious rhymes and limericks on social media. His eating pattern, including eating out during the height of the scare did not change, and to the best of his knowledge, only a few small eateries in Kolkata took mutton off their menu for a few days. Even though newspaper reports affirmed that restaurant goers had turned to fish, he had not seen any extra rush to the fish vendors to replace fish with meat at home.

Contemplation of these comments and responses allow access to patterns of eating as well as different attitudes and sensibilities to the savoring of taste and perceptions of pleasure. Most of my respondents, it bears mention, consider themselves to be "foodies" in the sense that they like to try out a variety of foods and cuisines, have the economic resources for it, and pride themselves for possessing discerning taste, and some also as accomplished cooks. In other words, they are *rajasik* in terms of their eating patterns and experience of taste, although they may not indicate this consciously. Unsurprisingly, therefore, they made a distinction between eating out and eating at home. Eating at home had the great advantage of ensuring the quality and freshness of ingredients, in particular of raw meat and fish. Eating out, although with the lure of offering a fare distinct from that at home, was a little dicier in the context of the scandal since one was not sure of the "source or quality" of meat and chicken. Hence, the ones who ate out during these few weeks of uncertainty turned to fish and shrimp—considered riverine Bengal's very own—in order not to put their health in jeopardy. At home, however, they continued to have goat meat and chicken, making sure that the live bird was butchered in front of their eyes and the carcass of a recently killed and cleaned goat was hanging in the butcher's stall. This practice, it bears mention, is still common among many despite the proliferation of supermarkets and food chains that sell packaged chicken. Newspaper reports confirmed my respondents in stating that the ordering of fish dishes had peaked and those of meat and chicken plummeted in restaurants and eateries. In addition, at weddings and other collective feasts of the time, the serving of meat and chicken was avoided, but was made up for by the offering of a greater variety of fish dishes.

Fresh and Fetid: Variant Indulgence

Let us pause to carefully consider the insistence on freshness of the flesh got for home consumption. What does it tell us about the ways people relate to the perishability of food, to health and disease, and life and death in relation to eating? It may not be out of place here to draw upon Piero Camporesi's challenging exploration of the lives of peasants and artisans in medieval Italy that prompted him to present hunger as a moving force of history, as a "gut" drive arising out of fear that led to fantasy, rebellion, and utopia (Camporesi 1989). His formidable imagination had pushed us to reflect on the ways people related to eating meat, the pleasures and expectations associated with the consumption of the flesh of certain animals, the taboos with regard to others, and the revulsion and fascination that surrounded the notion of eating human flesh. The fear of hunger and starvation and fancies of their satisfaction prompted the poor not just to indulge in food binges during carnivals, that included the consumption of moldy and rotten meat, but also to use herbs, seeds, and vegetables with narcotic qualities in their bread that generated toxic delusions and staved off the feeling of hunger.

The scandal around a melding of rotten and fresh meat in twenty-first-century Kolkata appears to be a far cry from the vicarious satiation of the medieval poor. Only members of the amorphous middle classes of differing economic and social status can afford to eat meat in restaurants, eateries, and roadside stalls. Besides, their consumption is guided not by deprivation but by excess. We will not be able to explore the implications of this explosion of appetite here; but we will try and tease out a few meanings around the aspirations that guide taste and pleasure among privileged groups and their blends with selfhood and identity.

The meat that has been popular in Bengal for a long time is mutton (goat flesh, as indicated earlier, and in all likelihood connected to the ritual sacrifice of a goat offered to the goddess Kali), with fowl becoming popular since the 1970s and gaining a greater preference among the younger generation. The disposition to consume goat flesh was bolstered by the long presence of Islamic rule in Bengal and the influence of the imperial Mughals reflected in a wide range of kebabs and biryani (a preparation of rice, meat, and aromatic spices cooked in ghee) in the palate of the Bengali upper- and middle classes (along with the roast, stew, and "curry" of colonial India). Biryani in particular, prepared now with mutton and chicken, has witnessed a remarkable surge as a favorite among the youth from the turn of the twenty-first century. Such craze has gone hand in hand with the mushrooming of innumerable roadside eateries and restaurants serving it, so much so that for many eating out is often equated with having biryani, and having biryani forms part of celebrations of special days such as Valentine's Day but, more intriguingly, with that of the adoration of the goddess Durga in autumn. It is also the most common takeaway dish for young IT professionals with long and changing hours of work. Biryani is widely considered to be of Islamic origin even though Sanskrit has a compound noun for it: *palanna, pal misrita anna* (rice mixed with meat), and references to *palanna* are found in the Hindu epics and other texts (Hajra 2018). The biryani in Kolkata, in particular, was further embellished by the arrival of Nawab Wajid Ali Shah—the gourmand but impoverished Shia nawab of Awadh deposed by the English East India Company—to Kolkata in 1856, who is taken to have introduced the Awadhi biryani, which includes potato in addition to meat (and egg). Biryani is a sumptuous dish and constitutes a full meal (Dasgupta 2017). Its association with (Muslim) royal kitchens and its use of rich and expensive ingredients, such as ghee, nutmeg, and saffron (probably not used in its preparation in most of the humble eateries), evoke the aroma and ambience of regal indulgence, now made accessible and hence remarkably appetizing.

Did the rotten-meat scandal affect these innumerable biryani places that have sprung up over the last decade and a half? Some of my respondents felt that their sales had gone down while others commented that such drop was temporary, and they were speaking of the established and better-known places. The *Firstpost* report of May 2 mentioned that according to the cashier at Arsalan, "the biryani major" of Kolkata, the scare over rotten meat was not going to have any "cascading effect" on the sale of biryani because their customers were confident about high standard of their restaurants. The owner of another renowned restaurant chain assured his consumers that they had nothing to worry, at least in his restaurants. The dip in sales of a few mutton items, he stated further, were just for a few days.

At the same time, in a situation of uncertainty over the quality and freshness of meat served in restaurants, taste and health got inextricably bound in practices of eating to result in an avoidance of meat dishes in restaurants and an insistence on the freshness of chicken and goat meat procured for home consumption. Fish, a normal part of the midday meal in most upper-middle-class Bengali homes, did not get any added value; it substituted the desire for mutton and chicken of the notoriously nonvegetarian Bengalis in restaurants. While fish continued to be purchased for home consumption, great premium was placed on the source and freshness of the fish purchased. If this reveals the "semantic virtuosity" of food linked to its perishability that makes fresh food acquire remarkable significance at particular moments, it also upholds Camporesi's insights about the close connection and quirky relation between food—the most organic sustainer and staff of life—with the laws of growth decay and putrefaction, and with death, the once living cutoff for human consumption. A robust appetite and the expectations of the fragrant flavor of the cooked flesh of a live bird or an animal killed exclusively for home consumption overcome and surpass the shock that must certainly result from witnessing a live bird or animal being killed. Alongside, this expectation verging on gluttony is replaced by repugnance for fetid flesh.

What was so shocking about carcass meat? The visualization of dead animals rotting in the lurid filth of dump yards, the idea of putrefied flesh as a potent carrier of worms and bacteria, and disease and death, or just a revulsion to the notion of not knowing what we are eating? Did the idea of *tamasik* food, of the rotten and impure, get transposed onto the *rajasik*, which is classically meant to be the source of misery and sickness (of the body and mind) for its excess? Without making a direct connection, my respondents indicated that full knowledge of what they were eating was vital, and the idea of freshness was closely linked to that of unprocessed food: from the market to the table of the live as opposed to the meat of animals that died in unknown circumstances and surreptitiously end up on the table.

At the same time, the quirky relation between humans and their patterns of eating animal flesh produced strange fantasies about humans preying on the food of vultures in dump yards and occasioning the death of vultures on account of starvation. Did the WhatsApp droll exchanges, which spoke of a dog being reborn as mutton or the fact that the consumers of a favorite roll eatery got suspicious when real mutton instead of dog meat started being used after the scandal, spell appeal for flesh that is not normally consumed? Can easy satiation of appetite and access to a variety of food create fancies about that which is not meant to be eaten?

There are no clear answers, but the divergent perceptions of the scandal push us to take up Camporesi's insights about food as the principal driving force of human history and of Ramanujan's suggestive statement about the cultural system of food as a language of poetics that offer precious whiffs of social lives and worlds. Did fantasies about putrefied meat of the starving medieval poor resurface in imaginings of famished vultures in satiated fancies of twenty-first-century middle-class Bengalis, so much so that they were be able to stomach and digest live or decomposed, dog or cat flesh, with mirth? What does this tell us about cultures of eating and constructions of identity around food? Do they have any bearing on politics?

Aftertaste?

By the end of 2018, the "scandal" had almost died down. Between May and December 2018, there were probes into the quality of milk being supplied by the dairies, a newspaper report on adulterated milk being supplied to government schools, and mild warnings against the consumption of a particular variety of fish, all illustrative of a certain awareness and alertness on the part of the authorities and the consumers. The *bhagad* meat scandal has left its impression on the minds of the middle-class Bengalis in their concern over the quality and source of what they consume. There was a sudden resurgence in early December 2018 when people of the North 24 Parganas district of West Bengal spotted a truck carrying meat, stopped it, and reported it to the police, which resulted in some arrests. Although there has been no further news related to rotten meat since then, the vigilance of the KMC was disclosed in unannounced visits made by the deputy mayor and other health officers to well-known bakeries of Kolkata a week before Christmas to check the conditions under which cakes were being baked. Such visits brought famous and favorite bakeries under the cloud.

But there was more to the matter. And to understand that we need to move back to the Facebook posts that wondered whether Muslims were the soft targets of the rotten-meat scandal and whether the scare was a ploy to push the entry of Reliance chain into Kolkata. My colleagues and friends were not totally convinced that Muslims, many of whom are butchers by profession, were the soft targets of the scandal. They did, however, mention that the Hindu right-wing government at the center and its supporters, particularly of the Hindi-speaking North, were making use of the scandal and scare to emphasize the superiority of vegetarianism in terms of nutrition and morality, and belittling the moral uprightness and physical strength of the flesh-eating Bengalis. The variety of satirical and self-deprecating jokes that Bengalis produced about their dietary practices was probably a way of dealing with such pressure from a self-righteous Hindu right.

In September 2018, a WhatsApp message expressing serious concern at the sudden surge in the use of Hindi in Kolkata started circulating. In addition to urging Bengalis to hold their own and speak Bangla, their *own* language in their *own* city, it brought up the *bhagad* meat scandal as illustrative of the insults and insinuations Bengalis are made to undergo continually in their *own* place. Bengalis, the message asserted, even accepted the implied accusation that they were capable of having rotten flesh from dump yards without demur. Instead of vigorously and vocally responding to such unfounded and unjust accusations in the wake of the scandal, Bengalis chose the mellowed "mew, mew" of the cat, because they weren't sure if they had eaten the flesh of dead cats unknowingly. The message commanded the Bengalis to order food in Bangla in restaurants and online.

A curious message with jumbled metaphors. The totally unexpected insertion of the scandal in a call to Bengalis to save their language against the onslaught of Hindi offered an unusual insight into precarious constructions of Bengaliness that in turn was evocative of attitudes to politics. If we place the message in the context of the virulent onslaught of the BJP and the Hindu right in Bengal, their active promotion of Hindi and vegetarianism, and their barely concealed scorn at the flesh-eating Bengalis, the linking of the accusation of having rotten meat and of speaking Bangla in public spaces acquires a different piquancy. Nonvegetarianism and the use of Bangla in restaurants and other public spaces get jumbled to add a new spice of Bengaliness and uphold an anti-fundamentalist and anti-rigid stance. It also gets coupled with a longing to reclaim Kolkata as Bengali.

It is beyond the scope of this chapter to trace the gradual evolution of Hindu elite and middle-class food practices in Bengal. It is, however, vital to underscore the evolution of Hindu-Bengali food practices in conjunction with the presence and influence of Islamic, Portuguese, Armenian, English, and other European cultures in Bengal, the reciprocal borrowings from Southeast Asian cuisine coupled with factors such as the abundance of rivers and the proximity to the sea. This rich flux and meld have conferred on Bengalis a loose sense of identity as connoisseurs of food and as discerning lovers of fish and mutton.

The *bhagad* meat scare suddenly confronted this almost-unstated and yet widely acknowledged consensus; it also cast aspersions on their pronounced nonvegetarianism that was related to their politics. The Facebook posts that expressed concern at Muslims being targeted or the Reliance chain being granted easy access may have overstated the case. But the fact that they got tied to a message that spoke of the menace posed by Hindi and Hindi culture to Bangla and *bangaliana* (Bengaliness) exhibits a kind of gastro-politics where social and moral propositions linked to food serve contrasting semiotic functions, and food habits and eating patterns combine to forge and sustain rival and competing community identities at particular moments of stress.

It is difficult to gauge the reach of the September 2018 message and its impact on the recipients. The fact remains that it was widely circulated and some of my WhatsApp contacts mentioned that they were, indeed, trying to induce their nonchalant and aggressive Hindi-speaking colleagues to try and follow Bangla, and address cab drivers and waiters in restaurants in their own language without referring directly to the carcass meat affair. This was to challenge not just Hindi and the broadly left Bengali perceptions of Hindi culture, but to take a nonconformist stance to the intolerant practices of a belligerent Hindu nationalist state. In curious ways, the mix inherent in Bengali cuisine and the vast cultural reach of its semantic system centered on food contributed to the construction of a fragile (and possibly fleeting) Bengali identity where language and place conjured a sense of belonging and aroused aspirations of reclaiming that place as one's own—pure and unsullied—not governed by the dictates of an assertive and blinkered culture of language and politics, and of being in the world.

Acknowledgments

I wish to thank Steffan Igor Ayora-Diaz for the invitation to contribute to this volume and his comments on an earlier draft of the chapter. My thanks extend to a host of colleagues, friends, and relatives who helped with their comments, suggestions, and references to newspaper articles and media posts, in particular: Sarvani and Pradeep Gooptu, Sushweta Ghosh, Nilajan Hajra, Gautam Bhadra, Rajat kanti Sur, Kuhu Ganguli, Paramita Banerjee, Indrani Maitra, and Moushumi and Sayanti Mukherjee.

References

Achaya, K. T. (1994), *Indian Food: A Historical Companion*, Oxford: Oxford University Press.
Appadurai, A. (1981), "Gastro-politics in Hindu South Asia," *American Ethnologist* 8(3): 494–511.
Ayora-Díaz, S. I. (2019), "Introduction: Matters of Taste: The Politics of Food and Identity in Mexican Cuisines," in Steffan I. Ayora-Díaz (ed.), *Taste, Politics, and Identities in Mexican Food*, pp. 1–18, London: Bloomsbury Academic.
Banerjee-Dube, I. (2016), "Introduction: Culinary Cultures and Convergent Histories," in I. Banerjee-Dube (ed.), *Cooking Cultures: Convergent Histories of Food and Feeling*, pp. 1–17, Cambridge: Cambridge University Press.
Camporesi, P. (1989), *Bread of Dreams: Food and Fantasy in Early Modern Europe*, trans. D. Gentilcore, Chicago: University of Chicago Press.
Hajra, N. (2018), "The History of Biryani. Kolkata Biryani: Culture, Identity, and Politics," *Sahapedia*, August 14. Available online: https://www.sahapedia.org/the-history-of-biry ani, last accessed March 16, 2020.
Khare, R. S. (1976), *The Hindu Hearth and Home*, New Delhi: Vikas.
Khare, R. S. (1992), "Introduction, and Food with Saints: An Aspect of Hindu Gatronomics," in R. S. Khare (ed.), *The Eternal Food: Gastronomic Ideas and Experiences of Hindus and Buddhists*, Albany: State University of New York Press.
Korsmeyer, C. (1999), *Making Sense of Taste: Food and Philosophy*, Ithaca: Cornell University Press.
Marriott, M. (1968), "Caste Ranking and Food Transactions: A Matrix Analysis," in M. B. Singer and B. S. Cohn (eds.), *Structure and Change in Indian Society*, pp. 133–72, Chicago: Aldine Publishing Company.
Ramanujan, A. K. (1992), "Food for Thought: Towards and Anthology of Food Images," in R. S. Khare (ed.), *The Eternal Food: Gastronomic Ideas and Experiences of Hindus and Buddhists*, pp. 221–51, Albany: State University of New York Press.

The Bhagavad Gītā (2009), trans. Winthrop Sargeant, ed. Christopher Key Chapple, foreword by Huston Smith, Albany: State University of New York Press.

Media Reports

"Chaos over Rotten Meat Sale in Kolkata Leaves Restaurants Cautious; Foodies Turn to Fish, Vegetarian Options" (2018), *Firstpost*, May 2. Available online: https://www.fir stpost.com/india/chaos-over-rotten-meat-sale-in-kolkata-leaves-restaurants-cautious-f oodies-turn-to-fish-vegetarian-options-4453719.html, last accessed March 16, 2020.

Chatterjee, T. (2018), "Carcass Meat Probe: Citizens Shun Eateries, Stores in Kolkata; NGO to File PIL," *Hindustan Times*, May 1. Available online: https://www.hindusta ntimes.com/kolkata/carcass-meat-probe-citizens-shun-eateries-stores-in-kolkata-ngo -to-file-pil/story-IHqUiqgR99zRVhIHvDlHmL.html, last accessed March 16, 2020.

Dasgupta, S. (2017), "Here's How Wajid Ali Shah made the Kolkata Biryani," *The Times of India*, May 11. Available online: https://timesofindia.indiatimes.com/city/kolkata/ heres-how-wajid-ali-shah-made-the-kolkata-biryani/articleshow/58622647.cms, last accessed March 16, 2020.

Ghosh, D. (2018a), "20 Tonnes of Carcass Meat Found in Kolkata Factory, Could be of Dogs & Cats," *The Times of India*, April 27. Available online: https://timesofindia.indi atimes.com/city/kolkata/20-tonnes-of-carcass-meat-found-in-rajabazar-factory-pac ked-ready-to-be-sold/articleshow/63932532.cms, last accessed March 16, 2020.

Ghosh, D. (2018b), "As Kolkata Rotten Meat Scandal Creates Panic WhatsApp Messages Add to the Stink," *Scroll.in*, May 5. Available online: https://scroll.in/article/877770/as -kolkata-rotten-meat-scandal-creates-panic-whatsapp-messages-add-to-the-stink, last accessed March 16, 2020.

"Meat Scam Leads to Surge in Fish Sales across Calcutta" (2018), *The Telegraph*, May 5. Available online: https://www.telegraphindia.com/states/west-bengal/meat-scam-leads -to-surge-in-fish-sales-across-calcutta-nbsp/cid/1416069, last accessed March 16, 2020.

Mitra, P. and K. Bandyopadhyay (2018), "Dog Meat Fear Halves the Sale of Non-veg Food in Kolkata Eateries," *The Times of India*, May 1. Available online: https://timesofindia .indiatimes.com/india/dog-meat-fear-halves-sale-of-non-veg-food-in-kolkata-eateries/ articleshow/63979908.cms, last accessed March 16, 2020.

"Samples Collected during Carcass Scare Safe: KMC" (2018), *The Times of India, City*, July 10. Available online: https://timesofindia.indiatimes.com/city/kolkata/samples-collecte d-during-carcass-scare-safe-kmc/articleshow/64929063.cms, last accessed March 16, 2020.

"Stick to Fresh Meat: Experts" (2018), *The Times of India*, April 28. Available online: https:/ /timesofindia.indiatimes.com/kolkata/stick-to-fresh-meat-experts/articleshow/639468 97.cms, last accessed March 16, 2020.

"Two Held in Bengal for Selling Skin and Meat of Dead Animals Dumped in Kolkata Outskirts" (2018), *Hindustan Times*, April 21. Available online: https://www.hindusta ntimes.com/kolkata/two-held-in-bengal-for-selling-skin-and-meat-of-dead-animals- dumped-in-kolkata-outskirts/story-fA2f2vKiCD0eRXIe4rHPfJ.html, last accessed March 16, 2020.

8

Tasting "Innovation"

The Politics of Taste in Contemporary Restaurant Food in Seville, Spain

Steffan Igor Ayora-Diaz and Gabriela Vargas-Cetina

Tasting Authenticity and Innovation in Seville, Spain

In April of 2019, we were at a downtown medium-scale tapas restaurant at lunch time in Seville, Spain. Sitting next to our table, a man accompanying a woman interrogated the waiter about how the *Solomillo al whiskey* was prepared. The waiter explained that the pieces of pork tenderloin are marinated in whiskey and herbs and then roasted. The man, in his fifties, asked whether the pork was from Seville, and the waiter replied that it is brought from the south of Andalusia, and when asked about the origin of the whiskey, the waiter replied that it is imported. The customer ridiculed the waiter asking how they can claim to serve Seville tapas if neither the pork nor the whiskey were produced in Seville. He then asked similar questions about another dish listed as Andalusian on the menu, obtaining the same sort of responses and then repeating his mockery of the restaurant. He then asked for a beer and some cheap tapas, probably satisfied with his own petulant performance. Notwithstanding this troublemaker's routine, for an outsider the question remains: What is Seville's food and how does its taste? How do we recognize it? What should one expect when looking for local cuisine?

We have frequently received two contrasting answers to our questions among local friends, restaurant owners, and chefs: On the one hand, some say that the "traditional" food of the city is based on fish, encompassing different recipes for *merluza* (hake), tuna, and sardines, as well as on other sea products such as *ortiguilla* (sea nettle, a type of anemone), shrimps, crayfish, *carabineros* (*Aristaeopsis edwardsiana*), *navajas* (*Ensis arcuatus*), as well as *boquerones* (*Engraulis encrasicolus*) by themselves or in different combinations, such as with fried calamari rings, pickled anchovies, or steamed carabineros. On the other hand, others define "traditional" Sevillian food as "ladle food" (*comida de cucharón*), that is, rich stews in which cooks combine meats such as pork, *chorizo* sausages, ham, bacon, potatoes, and seasonal vegetables along with garbanzos, lentils, or broad beans. The owner of an *abacería*[1] told us that his menu also includes hare stews and meat dishes cooked with potatoes, tomatoes, onions, and garlic.

Arriving in Seville in 2019 during the week prior to Holy Week, and with many local people avoiding meat because of Lent, we found that spinach with chickpeas had become a common feature on restaurant menus. However, since local people eat fish and seafood as part of the everyday diet, two chefs at different restaurants explained that they don't really need to change their restaurants' menus. They said that since their traditional diet gives Sevillians the choice between either fish and seafood or meat stews, they normally include on their menu dishes sought by those respecting Lenten food avoidances (especially of red meats). Restaurants advertised as "traditional" listed spinach and chickpeas on their regular menus, but some restaurateurs, seeking recognition as agents of innovation and creativity, were offering meals based on fish and seafood as alternatives to "traditional" meat recipes.

Within the Seville restaurant scene, in addition to restaurants with a "traditional" emphasis, a number of young restaurateurs and chefs seek to position their restaurants as "creative" and "innovative" (much in the style described by Rachel Black in Chapter 6). Their number is growing, and some of their establishments feature fusion-style cuisine, blending oriental and local flavors—occasionally mediated by Peruvian-Japanese sauces such as the so-called *tiger's milk*, made with lime juice and pureed cooked seafood.[2] Other chefs adopt nouveau cuisine aesthetic forms for food plating; and still others blend local and French influences. Those who can afford it may introduce new technologies in their kitchens to prepare ingredients and cook recipes under the aesthetic influence of restaurants such as Ferran Adrià's *elBulli*, of molecular cuisine fame.

In this gastronomic context, one Sunday evening we sat at the bar of one of the reputedly best local restaurants, recognized for its chef's creativity. To get a table at this restaurant, one usually has to reserve well in advance, but we just happened to be very hungry from the long trip from home (in Yucatan, Mexico) and entered their restaurant, as it was the first one open that we found, and were quickly seated at their bar (no tables available). Because they use fresh, local produce, their menu changes all the time, so instead of printing it, they handwrite on a chalkboard that the maître d' carries from table to table. We started dinner with foie gras, presented as two large slices in an X-shape, decorated with grapes and thyme sprigs and accompanied by two large pieces of *regañá*, a local cracker-style bread. As main course, we had *merluza* (hake) served on a bed of broad beans and wild venison with herbs, sesame seeds, and asparagus. A wild berries sorbetto completed our dinner. Like us, most people took pictures of the food they were served at their tables. This restaurant caters to clients looking for high-quality local products and flavors blended with techniques and the aesthetics of new Spanish high cuisine. Eating at restaurants promoted as either "traditional" or "modern" highlights their differences and similarities. While the "traditional" restaurants seek to recreate the established aesthetics and flavors of meals, "modern" ones seek to bring new flavors and aesthetic experiences. However, in contemporary Spanish culinary discourse, both *traditional* and *modern* menus aim at emphasizing the quality of local produce: vegetables, meats, fish and seafood, and wine. Hence, local taste has become an important sign value in all of them.

In this chapter, we examine the different ways in which "tradition," "creativity," and "innovation" are deployed by restaurant owners and chefs in Seville. Differences in the taste of food become the defining features that chefs and cooks seek to highlight in their menus. It is in this context that individual chefs and emerging groups of young entrepreneurs must negotiate the meaning of "good food," and of their reasons for respecting or departing from established local recipes. The contemporary foodscape is an arena where one can find that differences and similarities between Spanish, Andalusian, and Seville food are instituted and are accepted or frowned upon by both chefs and customers. In the following section, we will discuss some of the strategies that different entrepreneurs devise to secure their survival in this highly competitive business. Here we illustrate how the taste of Seville food is negotiated in restaurants, between restaurant chefs, and with their customers. To explain this diversity, in the following section we describe the translocal process that decanted as the recognizable foods of Seville and Andalusia. As we demonstrate, this has been a long historical process in which recent events have resignified iconic dishes, and cookbooks have become instrumental in configuring regional and urban cuisine. Finally, we discuss how innovation and creativity are deployed to add sign value to restaurant meals.

The Taste of Seville

When we arrived in Seville for the first time in 2016, we were excited by the large number of places to eat, from tapas bars to upscale restaurants, some claiming to uphold traditional recipes, others highlighting their novelty. Local friends recommended some restaurants but warned us that without advanced reservation it could be difficult to get a table—Alas! That was the case. The next year, during Holy Week in 2017, we found dramatically restricted the number of tables available at well-reviewed restaurants, whether *traditional* or *innovative*. Long waiting lines were the norm not only at these but also at practically all restaurants. Our friends recommended different places and took us to taste tapas at different "classic" bars, where we sometimes ate fried *boquerones* and sardines, fried calamari, steamed shrimps, and crayfish. At other bars, we tasted *pringá*, a fried dish that, when made at home, is prepared with *cocido* (stew) leftovers; Iberian hams of different qualities, including *Jabugo* and *liston* (ribbon) hams; meat in tomato/wine sauces (usually *carrillada*, i.e., beef or pork cheeks, and *rabo de toro*, i.e., ox tail); Spanish tortillas; and very seldom, paella. In contrast to our previous experiences in Madrid, Cordoba, Malaga, Cadiz, and Granada, where tapas were usually free of charge, bars in Seville charged for the tapas.[3] In fact, menus listed regular orders that could be served as small portion tapas at a cheaper rate.

When we asked our friends and new acquaintances which ones are the meals that characterized Seville, some sided with meats and stews, while others clearly favored fish and seafood. The coexistence of these two types of dishes is reflected by the stalls at popular markets like La Encarnación and La Feria. There, one finds an area with different stalls selling fish and seafood, and in another section stalls offering meat and some specializing in pork, while others sell different beef and veal cuts, and at some one finds sausages, hams, and delicacies such as venison and wild boar preserved in oil.

At other stalls one finds fruits and vegetables, and yet at others Italian pastas. At the La Feria market, which remains open in the evening, some sellers of fish and seafood have stands where customers can buy cooked fish and seafood tapas and drink a *caña* (glass of beer) around tables placed outside between the market and the Palace Marqueses de la Algaba.

Another arena of negotiation was that of "tradition" and "authenticity." Most people we asked confided that they preferred the taste of traditional meals over those sold as "new," "creative," or "innovative." Some said that the new food was fine, but not so good as to warrant the prices they charge. Some even said they have grown tired of finding soy sauce in almost everything at these new places. In contrast, others told us they are open to new flavors and are willing to try new foods. They have not surrendered their predilection for Seville's tastes, but can appreciate and enjoy the culinary experiments proposed at new restaurants. In short, some people show a radical allegiance to local food and others love different modes of culinary eclecticism (Ayora-Diaz 2017). These individuals, as consumers, shape the fortunes of old and new restaurants.

While not all consider themselves foodies,[4] the everyday crowds of customers at bars, *freidurías* (frying fish and seafood places), and restaurants in Seville suggest a knowing appreciation of food and the locales where they eat. One question for us was, how do chefs and restaurant owners decide whether to go "traditional" or "innovative." Tourism in Spain and its regions is not a new phenomenon, as Alfinoguénova (2014) has shown, and it has long-drawn state and private investment. Seville, in addition to its 1929 and 1992 International Expos, has attracted growing number of visitors every year, who come, among other things, to follow and admire the religious processions of *Semana Santa* (Holy Week), to attend the annual Spring Seville fair or/and the Biennial Flamenco Fair, and to visit sites such as the Alcazar—a Moorish building next to the Jewish ghetto—the building of the University of Seville, now occupying the former premises of an old cigar factory, and the many other buildings, museums, and churches such as the majestic cathedral, the Giralda tower, and the Macarena Basilica. The Archivo de Indias, which holds documents pertaining to the Colonial Americas, is a beacon for many Spanish and foreign scholars. Of course, visitors must eat. The resulting growing demand for food has encouraged many local entrepreneurs to launch new businesses to vie for hungry customers.

So, where can local people and visitors eat? In 2012, the *Diario de Sevilla* (Navarro Antolín 2012) reported that there were in the city about 4,000 bars, and close to 10,000 tables (*veladores*) to eat. This is especially true in the downtown area of the city, where a map of these services elaborated by Sevilla's City Hall locates the higher density of restaurants and tapas bars (Sevilla Turismo 2017: 20). We found that, across from the cathedral, the street *Mateos Gago*, bordering the Alcazar, encompasses a row of restaurants ranging from relatively economic tapas bars to upscale restaurants. San Fernando Street, across from the University of Sevilla, hosts within an area of 150 meters some fourteen restaurants and tapas bars, ranging from Starbucks at one end of the street to the upscale Oriza at the other end, including fifth gama restaurants, ice cream parlors, tapas bars, and one restaurant aspiring to become a high-end establishment. Their food offer varies. Some provide Sevillian home-cooking style dishes, comprising either seafood and fish or a selection of hams, stews, rice dishes, and roasted meats.

Other restaurants promote fusion menus, combining Mediterranean with Asian flavors (some with Peruvian-Asian influences).[5] The upscale restaurants on San Fernando Street highlight the good quality of local produce and modernist aesthetics of meal presentation. Additionally, the downtown area includes tapas bars, which offer paellas, gazpachos, and Spanish *tortillas*, and *abacerías* for stews and meats, as well as fast-food chains, ethnic restaurants (Indian, Turkish, North African, Mexican, Peruvian), coffee shops, and restaurants announcing menus based on the Mediterranean Diet. All of them are seeking to secure their niche in the local urban foodscape.

What is new and what is traditional in a restaurant? Some restaurants such as Barbiana, La Moneda, Enrique Becerra, and El Rinconcillo are models for "traditional" Seville food—among these El Rinconcillo boasts continuous service since 1670, and Enrique Becerra, a gastronomic reference, closed in 2020 after forty years of service in the context of the economic crisis triggered by the SARS-CoV-2 pandemic. There are also tapas bars which Sevillanos recommend as local hangouts: among many, Bar Plata, El Vizcaíno, La bodega de la Alfalfa, Bodeguita Antonio Romero, Garlochí, and Abacería San Lorenzo. These places are appreciated for their fried and steamed fish and seafood, their *pringá*, and other traditional tapas. In interview with the owner of an *abacería*, he confided that, in the past, he experimented with soy sauce and other oriental flavors, but he got tired from it: "Tiger's milk here and there, tiger's milk everywhere! I could not have it anymore." He decided to reclaim local, "authentic" flavors. He told us he was drawing from oral tradition to select and execute recipes, and that he has used recipes from people in rural villages. For example, he served us hare stew, the recipe of which he said he learned from one of his wine suppliers. Other traditional restaurateurs have found it safe to stick to well-established Seville recipes. At El Rinconcillo, we had their garbanzos with spinach, and also *merluza* (hake) and baked piglet, on different occasions. Their dishes were unpretentious and were served with the conviction that this is the way real Seville food is prepared and eaten.

In contrast, new restaurants have to struggle to establish new taste fashions. Fusion cuisine is now well established, and many restaurants continue serving Asian-inspired flavors. As we were writing this chapter, one restaurant announced (Oriza) on its Facebook page that they were serving local tuna with a sauce of "*pack* [*sic. pak*] *choi*" and pine nuts (March 3, 2020). Tuna tartare frequently made with soy sauce, and tiger's milk is now a usual sauce in fusion restaurants not particularly marked as "Peruvian." The chef and sous chef of a trendy restaurant explained that their locale has been expanding, and in one of their wings, where the décor is more sober, they serve traditional foods in the portions expected by local people. The section they have designated as a tapas bar has, in contrast, a "modern" décor: high shelves lining up wine bottles, dim lights, high tables, and small portions of familiar meals, served with nouveau cuisine aesthetics. They said that most local patrons wish to stick to traditional taste, and it is mostly visitors who wish to be surprised. This seems to be so at trendy restaurants such as Petite Comité, Slavia, La Azotea, and Lobo López, to mention just a few of the new fashionable restaurants and tapas bars (from 2016 to 2019), where one finds a contemporary ambience and experiments with flavors and cooking techniques, but still attempting to invoke local flavors. As another chef explained, he has been playing with Asian flavors but also with some unusual flavor pairings (i.e., unusual in

Seville). For example, his version of *huevos rotos* (fried eggs on top of fried potatoes) includes shaved black truffles and truffle oil. At his and other emerging restaurants responding to new fashions, they aspire, in the future, to have open kitchens. This is a desirable addition in the fashionable spectacularization of cooking and eating that customers enjoy. None of the chefs we have spoken to have introduced the taste effects derived from molecular gastronomy. One of them explained: the technology is too expensive to even think about it—and another one suggested that it is now quickly becoming old-fashioned. Today the aesthetics of plating, we can observe, seems to be more influenced by the minimalistic "new Nordic cuisine" of NOMA and other Scandinavian restaurants (Nordic Cooperation 2004).

Translocal Transformations

In 2020, a restaurant menu in Seville can invoke the flavors of both sea and land. Other than some small *freidurías* (eateries specialized in fried fish and seafood), most restaurants, whether serving tapas or upscale food, can bring together in their menus, tuna, hake, octopus, anchovies, *boquerones*, calamari, shrimp, crayfish, oysters, and other seafood, along with pork, beef, goat kids, and lamb, often including offal (kidneys, sweetbreads, liver). This is a strategic representation that highlights and responds to the wide range of local taste. As such, it glosses over the historic process during which the ingredients, cooking techniques, recipes, and cooking technologies have been gradually adopted, displaced, and, in some cases, replaced—and more recently, how some are reclaimed, recuperated, and turned into indexical evidence of either the "authenticity" of the meals, or references to "local" flavors in "new" meals served at different restaurants. To understand how the taste of Seville and Andalusia have coalesced into the array of recipes and interpretations we find in the contemporary urban foodscape, we need to first to trace their transformations over time so as to discern how flavors have become sedimented in regional and local history, and thus have naturalized the taste of the city and region (Ayora-Diaz 2012b).

Translocal Relations through Time

The history of Seville stretches for several centuries. Consequently, here we provide just a brief outline. It is important to remember that the region has been inhabited since at least 2000 BCE. In addition to the original inhabitants (Celtiberians and Tartessians), what today is Andalusia has been colonized by Phoenicians, Carthaginians, Romans, Visigoths, and Arabs. The latter were expelled from the peninsula, along with Jews, at the end of the fifteenth century, concluding the *Reconquista* of the Iberian territories by the Catholic monarchy and coinciding with the "discovery" of the New World (de Mena 1975). Some groups dominated Andalusia and Seville for longer periods than others, and the Arabs remained in Seville from the beginning of the eight until the end of the fifteenth century (de Mena 1975). Descendants of these multiple cultural groups overlapped and intermarried over time, gradually merging their predilections for ingredients and flavors, historically rooting cooking and eating dispositions. The expulsion of Arabs and Jews elevated pork to prominence, as in addition to its culinary virtues it was politically used to identify false converts who struggled to include pork in their diet (Montanari 1999: 190).

Seville underwent dramatic economic changes during the sixteenth century when the city reaped the fruits of the conquest of America. In 1503, Seville was granted total administrative and customs control of commercial traffic with the new continent (*Casa de Contratación y Consulado del Mar*, Transactions House and Sea Consulate). Even though some 90 kilometers separate Seville from Sanlúcar de Barrameda, the linking with the sea through the Guadalquivir river made the city a key post for the development of maritime connections (Trueba 1990). However, economically and politically, Seville experienced a gradual decline with the transference of the Casa de Contratación y Consulado del Mar to Cadiz, in the southern coast of Andalusia (de Mena 1975: 268; Morales Padrón 2009: 42). The end of the nineteenth and first seven decades of the twentieth century encompassed sometimes violent confrontations and negotiations between the monarchy, the Catholic Church, and republicans of different persuasions. These negotiations led to two attempts to install a democratic republic, and later to Francisco Franco's dictatorship, that ended in 1975 with his death. It was probably on account of unsuccessful economic and agricultural policies that Spaniards suffered the Years of Hunger (*los años del hambre*), 1940–6, following the end of the civil war (Radcliff 2017).

The Spanish Civil War was particularly brutal for the people of Seville and of Andalusia. In 1936, the Franco forces marching from North Africa toward Madrid murdered some 8,000 people in Seville and some further 10,000 in Cordoba (Radcliff 2017: 190). In addition, as Andalusia had become an agricultural region that privileged cotton and olives up to the end of the 1930s, it particularly suffered the effects of failed development projects leading to the Years of Hunger, and the despair of rural people, as some of the women with whom we spoke reminisced during our conversations (see also de Mena 1975: 369). The end of Francisco Franco's dictatorship and the return to democratic institutions progressively improved the economic conditions in Spain in general, and Andalusia in particular. The Seville Expo of 1992 showcased the regional culture, including the food, music, and dance (see expo92.es). Each of the different Spanish regions built its own pavilion to display its culture and industry, including its foods. In a newspaper interview, anthropologist Isabel González Turmo (2013b) suggested that food nationalism and regionalism were effects of Franco's dictatorship, as the Feminine Section of the *Falange* (the fascist wing of the government) was charged with the elaboration of a map of Spanish regional cuisines.[6] It is possible, however, that the *Sección Femenina* just profited from previous undertakings.

During the 1920s, for example, Dionisio Pérez (1929) was praising the culinary virtues of each Spanish region, echoing previous concerns from other Spanish writers to the effect that the cuisine of Spain should not be judged through foreign standards of national cuisines elsewhere (see also Anderson 2013). In fact, even though opposing the rather centralist position upheld by Thebussem, Pérez's praise of regional cuisines corresponded and coincided with state efforts to create a manageable culinary identity for each region for the promotion of tourism in Spain (Afinoguénova 2014). Despite some setbacks during the twentieth century, the foodscape of Seville and Andalusia began a radical expansion during the 1990s, partly triggered by the International Expo of 1992. This now shows on the diversity of foods one can find in Seville and other Andalusian cities.

Translocal Ingredients

To understand the contemporary foodscape, it is important to examine some of the important elements contributed by different groups to the diet of contemporary Spaniards, Andalusians, and Sevillians. Many culinary ingredients that came long ago from different regions of the Mediterranean and beyond have today become defining parts of the taste of everyday meals and the food at restaurants. Carthaginians introduced garbanzos and lentils into Iberian agriculture (Luján and Perucho 2003: 109), and while there seem to have existed olive trees in the region, the Greek imported new varieties and changed olive production methods. They also introduced wine and had an impact on the increased consumption of grains and meats, including wheat, barley, and millet as well as lamb, goat, and pork (Medina 2005: 4). The Romans introduced *garum* and *hellax*, condiments today forgotten, but also peaches, apricots, melons, lemons (Medina 2005: 7), and garlic (Pérez 1929: 13), which are still widely consumed. Later, the Arabs introduced artichokes, eggplants, beans (*alubias*), pomegranates, and dried nuts (Medina 2005: 9–10). The Arabs also introduced rice in the area of today's Valencia (Crist 1957). Dionisio Pérez (1929: 15–39) adds saffron, sugar, nutmeg, and black pepper to the list of Arab contributions to Spanish and Andalusian cooking. In turn, Ramón-Laca (2003) enlarges the list of Arab contributions to include lemons, limes, zamboas (*Citrus medica*), and bitter oranges (today known as Seville oranges) and points out that mandarins and sweet (Valencia) oranges were introduced by the Portuguese between the fifteenth and nineteenth centuries.

The conquest of America led to the "Columbian Exchange" (Crosby 1973). While Crosby's analysis focuses on maize and chili peppers, more widely accepted in Eastern Europe than in the Iberian Peninsula, at the end of the sixteenth century, potatoes, tomatoes, and some other varieties of pimentos became slowly integrated into the Spanish diet (Andrews 1993; Hawkes and Francisco-Ortega 1992). Gradually, along with gold and American natives, ships brought back to Seville and Spain new spices and fruits, vegetables and fowl, adding novel ingredients to the tables of the well-to-do: cocoa and turkeys joined chickens, quail, ducks, veal, pork, rabbits, lamb and goats, fish, olives, oil, wine, and eggs in Andalusian recipes (Núñez Roldán 2004: 198–201).

Following the move of the Casa de Contratación and Consulado del Mar to Cadiz, the economy of Seville and Andalusia shifted, in general, toward agriculture and fishing. Agriculture in the region, as already noted, privileged cotton and olives over horticulture. Because of their poor, peasant cuisine, Andalusian and Spanish people became infamous for their unexciting cuisines. During the twentieth century, small differences were found between the diet of the rich and the poor (González Turmo 1993). In her study of western rural Andalusia, González Turmo (1993) found that the diet consisted mainly of chickpeas, pork, sausages, bacon, fish, and seafood. Potatoes and tomatoes had become part of the regional diet, and most meals consisted of stews and other broths (*caldos*) cooked with seasonal vegetables. The main difference between the diets of the poor and the rich, she argued, consisted in the quality of the ingredients to which each group had access. The middle class had access to better-quality ingredients, and it was only the few very rich landlords who lived mostly in urban centers and spent only short seasons in the villages, who introduced, in their diets, different types of meals that reflected the influence and taste acquired in their cities of residence. The Years of Hunger accentuated the image of a poor and unexciting food. During that period, de Mena (1975: 370 [our translation]) writes:

> Each person was legally allotted 100 grams of bread daily, one kilogram of garbanzos and one of lentils every ten days, and one eight of oil per week. When potatoes were available each person received two kilograms per ten days, vegetables were not rationed but [people] may not have been able to find them for several days. People went [from Seville] to villages to bring, concealed, some bacon or meat. During those winters, many people ate, instead of beans: *yeros* [*Vicia ervilia*], lupin seeds, peas, *arvejones* [*Lathyrus sativus*], *muelas caballunas* [another type of pulse that Álvarez Arias, 2006, places under *Lathyrus sativus*], and instead of rice, they cooked wheat soup.

Following a period of stagnation, Seville nominated itself in the 1970s for hosting the International Expo. Once accepted, the city began preparations for the expo of 1992. De Mena suggests that, in general, this expo failed to bring Seville entrepreneurs what they had imagined, but it did not lead to a regional catastrophe like the 1929 Seville Expo when the economic failure pushed some entrepreneurs to suicide. Still, the regional government of Andalusia, the Spanish government, and private entrepreneurs combined their efforts changing urban features, connecting Madrid and Seville via rapid train, and attracting immigrants with different cultural backgrounds. Some foods were made internationally recognizable icons of Seville and Andalusia. Gazpacho, with an existence that long predated the expo of 1992, became paradigmatic of the city's cuisine. Today, one can find in the urban foodscape, in addition to Seville "traditional" and "new" cuisines, restaurants specialized in Indian, Turkish, Arab, Chinese, Japanese, Mexican, Peruvian, Italian, and French cuisines, among others.

Cookbooks and the Seville Identity of Andalusian Taste

The identity of Spanish food has been tied to the global hegemony of French cooking. In contrast to French, Spanish cuisine was widely recognized in Europe in negative terms. It was thought of as peasant, poor food, and tourists and other travelers complained of the abundant use of garlic and fried foods. During the nineteenth century, the Royal Court favored, in their daily and ceremonial occasions, the consumption of French or French-influenced dishes. Suggestively, in Guichot y Parody 1882's visitors' guidebook to Seville (reissued as a facsimile edition in 2007), other than describing local ruins and other archeological remains, he made no suggestions of what or where to eat while visiting—in fact, he completely sidestepped the subject of food.

In 1888, the published epistolary exchange between Dr. Thebussem and His Majesty's cook constitutes a conversation on the virtues and defects of French and Spanish food. Thebussem firmly argued for the revaluation, in positive terms, of Spanish cuisine, a cuisine that he initially conceived as one: all of Spanish cooking was to be recognized by its *cocido* (stew). He marveled at the almost infinite variations of *cocidos*, which in each Spanish region took different ingredients and flavors, but still underscored the unity of Spaniards around the *cocido* stewpot (Thebussem 1997; see also Anderson 2013). Dionisio Pérez, also known as Post-Thebussem (1929), praised Spanish cuisine over the French one, and, in fact, he accused French cooks of stealing many Spanish recipes from different monasteries during the Napoleonic occupation of Spain. Hence, in his view, it was false that Spanish cuisine was unsophisticated. Then, he proceeded to describe the cuisine of what he recognized as the main Spanish regions (Extremadura, Andalusia with separate sections for Seville and Huelva, Cadiz, Malaga and Granada, and Cordoba, Jaen, and Almeria; Levante, Catalonia, Aragon, and Navarre; Basque and Santander; Leon, Asturias, Galicia, Castilla, Madrid, La Mancha, and, finally, the Baleares and Canary islands). In each section, he praised the local produce, recounted anecdotes, and provided a few recipes. Yet, the tension between a unified Spanish cuisine around the *cocido* and its regional diversity persisted for a long time. In 1970, the travelogue-culinary guide *El libro de la cocina española* (Luján and Perucho 2003) continued to praise *cocidos*, while seeking to highlight regional differences and regional recipes for which each region could be recognized.

Dionisio Pérez's book was not a cookbook, but a guide to the food of different Spanish regions that included some recipes. In describing the food of Seville, he noted that as a capital city of the region they were in the position to concentrate the edible resources of, and recipes from all of the Andalusian villages. Thus, Seville's cuisine was not a collection of recipes locally created by the city's cooks, but an assemblage of regional recipes encompassed by the city's name. In praising the sophistication of Seville's food, he emphasized that one could find a large array of imported edibles in the city stores, while at the same time he recognized that many small rural communities, inland and along the Mediterranean shores, contributed their agricultural and maritime resources to the enrichment of the city's diet (Pérez 1929: 71–3). González Turmo (1996), in turn, has reviewed the transformation of eating in Seville through restaurant menus. She demonstrates that food practices changed with the political and economic context, shaping the success of restaurants and their menus. Tapas, she suggests, were the product of food scarcity during the 1940s (González Turmo 1996: 127). In her view, the 1992 Expo only brought disillusion among restaurateurs, as those of renown remained outside the expo grounds, and once the masses of tourists left, the number of customers at restaurants declined and once more money became scarce to pay restaurant bills (González Turmo 1996: 175).

Anthropologists and other scholars have shown the importance of cookbooks for the reproduction of culinary knowledge, but, most importantly, for the construction of ethnic, gender, local, regional, and national identities (Appadurai 1988; Ayora-Diaz 2012a; Bower 1997; González Turmo 2013a). Anderson (2013) has argued that Emilia Pardo Bazán, a leading twentieth-century intellectual, was ambivalent regarding Spanish cuisine. She published two cookbooks, one on "ancient" Spanish cuisine, and another on "modern" Spanish cuisine (Pardo Bazán 1913, 1918). Pardo Bazán struggled reconciling her nationalist inclination with the recognition of French haute cuisine's "modernity." In fact, in her book on "ancient" Spanish cooking, she did not divide the food by regional provenance—though she identified the local origin of some—for example, *chorizos* from Galicia and Extremadura; blood sausage from Asturias and Catalonia (Pardo Bazán 1913). Mostly, however, she did not make their origin explicit. In her "modern" Spanish cooking, she attempted to locate Spanish food within the universality of international cuisines that, she recognized, was dominated by French cuisine. In this book, she called several dishes "Spanish-style" and made reference to Cuban, "American," Flemish, French, and other national origins (Pardo Bazán 1918). As already mentioned, Thebussem and Pérez sought the recognition of Spanish cuisine, sometimes as a cuisine unified by stews (*cocidos*), but at the same time proposing that Spanish cuisine was a regionally informed one. For Thebussem, it was around the regional variations of the *cocido*, but for Pérez, in addition to the *cocido*, each region had distinctive ingredients and recipes (Afinoguénova 2014; Anderson 2013). The fascist-inspired *Sección Feminista* cookbook listed hundreds of recipes, but only occasionally identified them by place of origin (Sección Femenina de F. E. T. y de las J. O. N. S. 1962), and, in fact, the title makes mention neither of Spain nor of the regions.[7]

A different disposition is found in regional and local cookbooks. For example, in his *Andalusian Cooking* (*La cocina andaluza*), Salcedo Hierro (1980: 11) argues that there is only one Andalusian cuisine, despite some others' claims to the contrary, and he upholds that the region is so large that it could be divided into eight provinces with distinctive culinary "traditions." He defends the culinary unity of the region but recognizes that it encompasses four different ecological niches that provide different produce for Andalusians to eat: the mountains Sierra Morena and the southern tip of the Iberian range are the meat and game area; the Sub-Betis mountain range is the area of wine and oil; the Betis depression is the area for grains, sugar, and oranges; and the Quaternary and Tertiary depressions are the fishing area (pp. 11–12). His cookbook includes 1,089 recipes, and each one is attributed to a city or village of Andalusia. This cookbook contains almost as many recipes for fish and seafood (229) as it does for animal meats (273). In this fashion, we can see that this cookbook contributes to construct the image of an existing culinary region in which all villages and cities equally contribute to the regional taste. A decade later, following the Expo of 1992, the Seville government endorsed a new cookbook in which the food of the city was promoted as an identifiable culinary body of recipes (Reguera Ramírez and Heredia Herrera 1993). This cookbook lists the cooks, female and male, who provided the recipes for the volume, and the village of Seville province where each lived. In total, there are 50 localities, and 126 cooks listed (including 19 men) who provided a total of 238 recipes for meat, fish, and seafood, legumes and stews, plus 68 additional recipes for desserts (306 recipes in total). A more recent cookbook sponsored by the Provincial Corporation of Seville, *Nuevas recetas de cocina sevillana*, offers 370 recipes in the same format as the latter: it is divided into six sections (Entrées and Soups, Sausages and Preserves, First Plates, Fish, Meat, and Desserts; Diputación de Sevilla 2014).

These cookbooks illustrate the translocal connections that make possible claims of culinary regional and local identities. Within the contemporary global foodscape, there is a growing demand for local, ethnic, traditional, and modern innovative cuisines. This is a global context that favors the affirmation of localities which, in turn, are dependent on their relationship with other culinary practices. As we have been showing, the cuisine of Andalusia and Seville is the historical product of the intercrossing and sedimentation of culinary preferences of Celtiberians, Tartessians, Carthaginians, Greeks, Romans, Visigoths, Arabs, New World, and Asian peoples. Yet, regionally and locally, Andalusian and Seville cuisines emerge from the contribution of different forms of edible goods brought from valleys, mountains, rivers, and sea that are cooked in similar and distinct manners. As one of us has argued (Ayora-Diaz 2012a, b), repetition is a key factor in the naturalization of taste. But this is not a repetition of the same, as in each place the same recipe is adapted to local availability of ingredients and seasonality, as well as to the taste preferences of members of any group. Exemplarily, Salcedo Hierro's (1980) cookbook includes thirteen recipes for gazpacho in the Andalusia region, and Reguera Ramírez and Heredia Herrera (1993) include seven gazpacho recipes for the cuisine of Seville (the most recent *Nuevas recetas de cocina sevillana* 2014, includes only three gazpacho recipes). Mikel López Iturriaga (aka *El Comidista*), who writes for the national Spanish newspaper *El País*, in a YouTube short film points out that there is no "true" recipe for gazpacho. Each cook has his or her own, and it is a matter of personal or family taste.[8] Like gazpacho, stew (*cocido*), tripe, and other recipes are repeated, in each place, with a singular twist that marks its locality and, at the same time, contributes to its translocal spirit. In the end, for the people of Seville, meats on the one hand and seafood and fish on the other form an essential part of the city's taste.

Discussion: Food Taste and the Politics of Seville's Culinary Identity

The global condition leads to nonlineal effects. It is through global-local and translocal connections among societies, and through history that we have arrived at today's culinary taste in Seville. The flavors, colors, textures, and aromas of the food of Andalusia and Seville are the outcome of those connections. However, precisely because of the diversity of cultures that converged in the city, and the heterogenous ecological niches of Andalusia, the local food encapsulates a tension between land and sea ingredients. Thus, some identify the taste of the city with stews and meats, while others display a disposition toward seafood and river products—of course, many others seek to come to terms seeing both as part of Seville's culinary tradition. In addition, in a global-local context in which tourism has become a significant economic force, and culinary-gastronomic tourism becomes a more established consumption practice, Sevillanos must also deal and negotiate the meanings of local, authentic, and traditional, with the emergence of new cuisines and tastes, especially with changes that lead to innovation and, hence, the transformation of long-established tastes and gastronomic values.

There is a move toward the modernization of local flavors (that even though they always change over time, during short periods become "naturalized"), sometimes with some homogenizing fashions that, for example, make the fusion of Asian and local flavors likeable and make flavors somewhat indistinguishable from region to region of the world. At the same time, there is a social need to distinguish one's regional culture from that of Madrid, or Barcelona, or the Basque country. Thus, chefs attempt to make the "new" a local invention too. Consequently, the choice of local produce, including wines and olive oil, and the invocation of "traditional" recipes, albeit changed and modernized, seek to turn global tastes into local ones. The expansion of the contemporary global and local foodscapes allows for consumers' culinary choices and for shifting identification with the local, regional, national, Mediterranean, or global scenes, according to context, taste, and personal preferences. In the end, these apparent personal dispositions are tied to their identification of food with the values of "modernity" or "tradition," of Spain or the foreign. At the same time that sharing food preferences identify them as Sevillanos and Spaniards, it seeks to distinguish them from other imported gastronomic dispositions.

Acknowledgments

We conducted this research exclusively with personal funds. Dr. Rocío Cortés Campos, allowed us to adapt our teaching calendars, so we could spend several weeks and even months in Seville. The Department of Anthropology at the Universidad de Sevilla provided us an institutional home as visiting professors for several years in a row. In Seville, our colleague and friend anthropologist Dr. Encarnación Aguilar Criado and her husband Dr. Francisco Javier Florencio Bellido helped us settle in the city, guided us through different cultural events, and introduced us to chefs and cooks. We thank all the chefs, colleagues, musicians, and other Sevillians who have befriended us and helped us learn about Andalusian life and culture.

Notes

1   *Abacerías* are old-fashioned small stores for customers to purchase small quantities of oil, vinegar, dry pulses, salted cod, or wine in bulk. However, the owner of one *abacería* explained to us that during the second half of the twentieth century they changed, first selling tapas to eat at the counter, and presently have a few tables available for sitting customers. We were explained that the beginning of this century, the city restricted permits to open new bars, and he found that the *abacería* was a good choice for selling food without opening a restaurant.

2   According to Lovegren (2005: 420), fusion cuisine first developed during the 1990s in the US west coast, when Japanese-French and Chinese-Italian-French restaurants emerged. Their cooks experimented the blending of flavors that were not associated before and abandoned all claims to "authenticity." Fusion is now used to describe the blending of flavors that belong to different culinary cultures. Since all cuisines are hybrid, fusion is not used as a synonymous of "hybrid" (see also Pearlman 2013: 110–111).

3   On one occasion, at a bar located in the Plaza de la Gavidia, we asked the waiter how was it that, in contrast to other towns and cities, bars in Seville charged for the tapas. He said, "In Seville we have always done it. Surely, in other towns they offer them gratis to attract tourists." This revisionist explanation runs contrary to González Turmo's contention (1996:127, see below), in the sense that tapas were created in Seville during times of scarcity, and they were free of charge. We would suggest that growing numbers of tourists have changed the way food services are charged. As we have shown for the Yucatecan case, *botanas*, small portions of food served like tapas, were also gratis until tourists and newcomers began breaking local rules by demanding *botanas* out of order: with the first beer one used to get a simple snack, and as the customer ordered more beers, he or she got more abundant foods. Tourists demanded expensive *botanas* from the first beer on, and this has led bars to charge for their *botanas* (Ayora-Diaz and Vargas-Cetina 2005).

4   Johnstone and Bauman (2010: 53) borrow from Paul Levy and Ann Bar's *The Official Foodie Handbook* to define a *foodie* as a person highly interested in food and who considers food an art. For Johnstone and Bauman (2010: 53–59), foodies have evolved to encompass a certain tension: those who seek to "democratize" the experience of food and those who consume food as a form of class distinction.

5   Despite our efforts to locate accurate statistical information, we have only found vague references to the numerous places to eat in the city. Government documents and reports provide statistics on people employed in different sectors, and they include no category for eating places. *Veladores* is a category that makes reference to pub-style tables. It is unclear whether the numbers provided make reference to individual pub tables, or rather to businesses that use them. Fifth gama restaurants are chain restaurants where they receive already-prepared and packaged meals, so that when the customer orders the food, the cooks only have to heat up the meal in an oven or stove top.

6   Since its inception, the Feminine Section of the Falange aligned with fascist ideology and advanced and supported the notion that it was necessary to uphold the traditional roles of women. That is, women should support their husbands, procreate, and stay at home. Cooking for the husband and family was one of women's tasks. Also, the Feminine Section rejected divorce laws that had been passed during the 1920s under the First Republic (Richmond 2004).

7   This seems to be a shared issue at the time among newly emerging nation-states. In Italy, Artusi (1970) advanced a national cookbook that integrated regional recipes into a unifying code, while, more recently, Capatti and Montanari (1999) have argued that Italian is a regional cuisine (see Rachel Black's chapter in this volume regarding regionalism in French cuisine). In Mexico, as Pilcher (1998) has shown, despite efforts to promote a single Mexican cuisine, regional cuisines have tended to fragment those claims since the 1950s.

8   https://www.youtube.com/watch?v=o54iEScpVyQ.

References

Afinoguénova, E. (2014), "An Organic Nation: State-Run Tourism, Regionalism, and Food in Spain, 1905–1935," *The Journal of Modern History* 86(4): 743–79.

Álvarez Arias, B. T. (2006), "Nombres vulgares de las plantas en la península ibérica e Islas Baleares," Doctoral Thesis, Madrid, Universidad Autónoma de Madrid.

Anderson, L. (2013), *Cooking Up the Nation: Spanish Culinary Texts and Culinary Nationalization in the Late Nineteenth and Early Twentieth Century*, Woodbridge, Tamesis.

Andrews, J. (1993), "Diffusion of Mesoamerican Food Complex to Southern Europe," *Geographical Review* 83(2): 194–204.

Appadurai, A. (1988), "How to Make a National Cuisine: Cookbooks in Contemporary India," *Comparative Studies in Society and History* 30(1): 3–24.

Artusi, P. (1970 [1891]), *La scienza in cucina e l'arte di mangiare bene*, Torino: Giulio Einaudi Editore.

Ayora-Diaz, S. I. (2012a), *Foodscapes, Foodfields and Identities in Yucatán*, Amsterdam: Cedla – New York: Berghahn.

Ayora-Diaz, S. I. (2012b), "Gastronomic Inventions and the Aesthetics of Regional Food: The Naturalization of Yucatecan Taste," *Etnofoor* 24(2): 57–76.

Ayora-Diaz, S. I. (2017), "Gastro-nomadismo y cultura culinaria: Transformaciones tecnológicas, representaciones y performances afectivos de la identidad yucateca," in A. Guzmán, R. Díaz Cruz, and A. W. Johnson (eds.), *Dilemas de la representación: presencias, performance, poder*, pp. 255–83, Mexico City: UAM-INAH-ENAH-Juan Pablos editores.

Ayora-Diaz, S. I. and G. Vargas Cetina (2005), "Romantic Moods. Food, Beer, Music and the Yucatecan Soul," in T. Wilson (ed.), *Drinking Cultures: Alcohol and Identity*, pp. 156–78, Oxford: Berg.

Bower, S., ed. (1997), *Recipes for Reading: Community Cookbooks, Stories, Histories*, Amherst: University of Massachusetts Press.

Capatti, A. and M. Montanari (1999), *La cucina italiana. Storia di una cultura*, Bari: Laterza.

Crist, R. E. (1957), "Rice Culture in Spain," *The Scientific Monthly* 84(2): 66–74.

Crosby, A. W. Jr. (2003 [1973]), *The Columbian Exchange: Biological and Cultural Consequences of 1492*, 30th Anniversary Edition, Westport: Praeger.

De Mena, J. M. (2014 [1975]), *Historia de Sevilla*, Barcelona: Plaza y Janes.

Diputación de Sevilla (2014), *Nuevas recetas de cocina sevillana*, Seville: Diputación de Sevilla.

Expo92.es (1992), website http://www.expo92.es/laexpo/pabellones.php, last accessed March 1, 2020.

González Turmo, I. (2017 [1993]), *Comida de rico, comida de pobre. Los hábitos alimenticios en el occidente andaluz (Siglo XX)*, Sevilla: Universidad de Sevilla.

González Turmo, I. (1996), *Sevilla. Banquetes, tapas, cartas y menús, 1863–1995*, Sevilla: Ayuntamiento de Sevilla.

González Turmo, I. (2013a), *200 años de cocina. Historia y antropología de la alimentación*, Sevilla: Cultivalibros.

González Turmo, I. (2013b),0 "El nacionalismo culinario es un invento reciente", según la antropóloga Isabel González Turmo, eldiario.es, May 25, 2013, from https://www.eld iario.es/politica/nacionalismo-antropologa-Isabel-Gonzalez-Turmo_0_136136497.htm l, last accessed May 8, 2018.

Guichot y Parody, J. (2007 [1882]), *El cicerone del viajero en Sevilla. Breve noticia histórico-descriptiva de las curiosidades arqueológicas, monumentales y artísticas que encierra la ciudad*, Facsimile edition, Sevilla: Extramuros.

Hawkes, J. G. and J. Francisco-Ortega (1992), "The Potato in Spain during the Late 16th Century," *Economic Botany* 46(1): 86–97.

Johnstone, J. and S. Baumann (2010), *Foodies: Democracy and Distinction in the Gourmet Foodscape*, London and New York: Routledge.

Lovegren, S. (2005 [1995]), *Fashionable Foods: Seven Decades of Food Fads*, Chicago: University of Chicago Press.

Luján, N. and J. Perucho (2003 [1970]), *El libro de la cocina española. Gastronomía e historia*, Barcelona: Tusquets.

Medina, F. X. (2005), *Food Culture in Spain*, Westport and London: Greenwood Press.

Montanari, M. (1999), "Food Models and Cultural Identity," in J.-L. Flandrin and M. Montanari (eds.), *Food: A Culinary History*, pp. 189–93, New York: Columbia University Press.

Morales Padrón, F. (2009), *Sevilla en América, América en Sevilla*, Sevilla: Instituto de la Cultura y las Artes and Ayuntamiento de Sevilla.

Navarro Antolín, C. (2012), "La ciudad de los 4.000 bares," *Diario de Sevilla*, July 25, Internet Version: https://www.diariodesevilla.es/sevilla/ciudad-bares_0_609539570.html, last accessed December 31, 2019.

Nordic Cooperation (2004), "The New Nordic Food Manifesto," website https://www.norden.org/en/information/new-nordic-food-manifesto, last accessed April 11, 2020.

Núñez Roldán, F. (2004), *La vida cotidiana en la Sevilla del Siglo de Oro*, Madrid: Silex.

Pardo Bazán, E. (2012 [1913]), *La cocina española antigua*, Facsimile edition, Valladolid: Maxtor.

Pardo Bazán, E. (2010 [1918]), *La cocina española moderna*, Facsimile edition, Valladolid: Maxtor.

Pearlman, A. (2013), *Smart Casual. The Transformation of Gourmet Restaurant Style in America*, Chicago: University of Chicago Press.

Pérez, D. (2005 [1929]), *Guía del Buen Comer Español. Inventario y loa de la cocina clásica de España y sus regiones*, Facsimile edition, Valladolid: Maxtor.

Pilcher, J. C. (1998), *Que vivan los tamales! Food and the Making of National Identity*, Albuquerque: University of New Mexico Press.

Radcliff, P. B. (2017), *Modern Spain: 1808 to the Present*, Malden: Wiley Blackwell.

Ramón-Laca, L. (2003), "The Introduction of Cultivated Citrus to Europe via Northern Africa and the Iberian Peninsula," *Economic Botany* 57(4): 502–14.

Reguera Ramírez, M. and A. Heredia Herrera (1993), *Recetas de cocina sevillana*, Seville: Fundación Luis Cernuda – Diputación de Sevilla.

Richmond, K. (2004), *Las mujeres en el fascismo español. La Seccion Femenina de la Falange, 1934–1959*, Madrid: Alianza Editorial.

Salcedo Hierro, M. (1980), *La cocina andaluza*, Leon: Nebrija.

Sección Femenina de F.E.T y de las J.O.N.S. (1962), *Manual de cocina (recetario)*, 12th edn, Madrid: Industrias Gráficas Magerit.

Sevilla Turismo (2017), *Plan de Acción 2017*, Sevilla: Ayuntamiento de Sevilla – Sevilla Turismo.

Thebussem, Dr. (1997 [1888]), *La mesa moderna. Cartas sobre el comedor y la cocina cambiadas entre el Doctor Thebussem y un cocinero de S.M.*, Facsimile edition, Barcelona: Parsifal ediciones.

Trueba, E. (1990), *Sevilla marítima, Siglo XVI*, Sevilla: Padilla Libros.

9

Of Corn and Coconuts

Taste and the Cultural Politics of Gastronationalism in Belize

Lyra Spang

Introduction: Kriol Nationalism

Belize, once a small British colonial backwater devoted to timber extraction, is located on the Yucatan Peninsula of Central America, bordered by Guatemala to the south and west, Mexico to the north, and the Caribbean Sea to the east. The only English-speaking country for a thousand miles, Belize brings together the cultures and qualities of the Caribbean and Central America in a small, culturally diverse society of approximately 400,000 people. Three Maya groups (Kekchi, Mopan, and Yucatec) live here alongside Mestizo blends of Maya and Spanish conquerors, including waves of immigrants from Mexico, Guatemala, Honduras, and El Salvador; the Kriol,[1] predominantly a mix of European and African ancestries, were a product of the British colonial enterprise; the Garifuna, original settlers of the Caribbean, are descended from West African and Carib people. These groups rub shoulders with European-descent Mennonites, and descendants of East Indian, Chinese, and North American immigrants who came to Belize within the past 150 years. Belize's cultural identity is a complex one in a young country[2] where many Belizeans claim multicultural heritage, with parents and grandparents from a variety of ethnicities.

How this cultural diversity is represented within national identity, including national cuisine, shapes the flavors that are considered Belizean. In Belize, cultural heterogeneity plays a big role in the expression of "gastronationalism," a term coined by Micheala DeSoucey that explains how culinary heritage is used to express national pride and identity on the international stage (DeSoucey 2010). While the term was invented to describe European contexts, it is a valuable definition of nationalized expression of culinary identity worldwide. The history of Belize, as a country located squarely within Central America yet with strong colonial ties to Jamaica and the rest of the English-speaking Caribbean, also plays a fundamental role in shaping discourse on national culinary identity.

These factors inform how Belizean food is represented internationally. Cultural politics cannot be ignored. Colonial favoritism toward the Kriol ensures the pervasive influence of a model of identity called *hegemonic nationalism*, a form of Creole nationalism which granted Kriol home cooking the power to legitimize ingredients and dishes as being Belizean (Bolland 1987, 1998; Medina 1997). According to hegemonic nationalism, a food, flavor, or dish is fully Belizean when it is prepared and eaten at home by Belizean Kriol people. Most Belizeans consider an ingredient to be truly Belizean only if it has undergone this Kriolization/assimilation process, through use in a Kriol home kitchen and incorporation into Kriol recipes. In order to understand why this is the case, we must examine the competing discourses of national identity present in this tiny country.

Models of Identity

Two divergent models of nationalism shape much discussion of Belizean national identity as it relates to cultural membership (Bolland 1987; Medina 1997). Underlying many Belizeans' subconscious beliefs about Belizean-ness is the model of hegemonic nationalism that orients Belize as an Afro-Caribbean society, predicating "real Belizean" identity on having some form of African heritage, whether cultural and/ or biological (Judd 1989a, b; Shoman 2010). According to the hegemonic model of nationalism, people who do not have any African heritage, especially Maya and Mestizo Belizeans, are considered less fully Belizean than those who do (Medina 1997). Even though this model is not officially recognized or supported by the government nor taught in school, it persists powerfully into the present day. Under hegemonic nationalism, Garifuna people, despite their African heritage, are not given the same status as Kriol people, since they have indigenous ancestry, came to Belize in the early 1800s, and were not directly associated with the British colonial project. Kriol culture, on the other hand, emerged out of the British colonial endeavor as early as the 1600s in the British-controlled logging camps that would one day become Belize. Often problematically[3] described as a mixture of African and European immigrants, in nationalist mythology Belizean Kriol people are often linked to the birth of Belize as a British colony in the heart of Spanish territory (Judd 1989b; Shoman 2010). Ties to other Creole populations and the rest of the British-controlled Caribbean are reflected in the fact that some ancestors of Kriol people were brought to Belize from Jamaica as part of the empire's slave trade (Belize History Association 2015). It is this historic connection to other British-controlled territories in the Caribbean Basin that informs the idea that Belize is culturally a Caribbean society. According to hegemonic nationalism, Belize was invented by the British in the context of colonialism and the Kriol people and culture arose out of that same context; therefore, they must be the legitimate heirs to and representatives of the country. Both discriminated against and favored by the British after the abolishment of slavery in 1834, the Kriol were the dominant group during the British colonial regime, and after independence continued to be the most politically and economically powerful culture in Belize. For most of the history of the colony, they comprised the largest population (Shoman 2010).[4]

Hegemonic nationalism is not the only model of national identity present in Belize, although it is a pervasive and often partially veiled thread in the national identity discourse. The hegemonic model of national identity probably emerged during the colonial era and is likely much older than the official stance of pluralistic nationalism, which has only entered the debate since home rule was achieved in 1964. Pluralistic nationalism is the officially recognized form of national identity, formally adopted since Belize's independence from Great Britain in 1981. This model is taught in the Belizean school system and theoretically embraces all cultures, allowing Belizean citizens to be proud of both their cultural and national identity simultaneously. Following this example of what Richard Wilk calls "domesticated nationalism," Culture Day is celebrated annually in Belizean elementary schools, with children dressing in the cultural clothing of their ancestors and sharing the food of their culture with each other in a school feast (Wilk 1995). A fascinating arena for research would be how multicultural children negotiate this compartmentalized approach to cultural identity. Younger Belizeans, born since independence and often with parents from different cultures, tend to adhere more closely to the pluralistic model of nationalism which allows them to claim multiple cultural affinities, all under the umbrella of Belizean-ness. Followers of the hegemonic vision can be found in all age groups, but the belief that Kriol people are more truly Belizean than other ethnicities is most prevalent among older Belizeans. However, these generational changes are slow to reach the culinary arena. When I asked fifty people of different ages to sort foods into categories of least to most Belizean, all participants showed a clear tendency to identify Belizean Kriol dishes as more Belizean than Belizean Maya, Belizean Mestizo, or Belizean East Indian foods (Spang 2019).

Whose Foods? Whose Flavors?

How do these competing discourses of national identity shape the taste of Belize? What flavor principles have been granted the power to make a dish Belizean? Here arises the ugly question behind all gastronational expression: In a diverse nation, whose foods are given the privilege of representing the country? Ask this question in any nation and from the answer emerges a picture of the internal politics of a country. As Ayora-Diaz argues in the case of Mexican food: "we question its unified construct because it hides, on the one hand, the political tensions and negotiations at work between the ideology of a purported national cuisine . . . and, on the other hand, the actual local, ethnic and regional cuisines in which hybridity thrives" (Ayora-Diaz 2019: 1).

Hegemonic nationalism lumps Maya and Mestizo people together as being "not fully Belizean," ironically so for the three Maya groups who were there long before Belize existed as a country. These cultures are also glossed together through their shared consumption of corn-based foods as a staple. On the other hand, we have the Kriol and Garifuna peoples, connected by their mutual African heritage and the extensive use of coconut as an important flavor component in many dishes. These divisions reflect both the geography of Belize and its historical ties to Jamaica, begging the question: Is Belize Caribbean or Central American? What is "unique" about Belizean flavors in comparison to its Central American neighbors is nothing new for its historical colonial counterparts in the Caribbean. A Guatemalan immigrant may consider coconut milk and oil to be uniquely Belizean flavor principles in comparison to their country of origin, but a Jamaican will be right at home. One could argue that it is simply a geographic/colonial anomaly that makes Belize stand out: its Caribbean-ness in the heart of Central America, and its Central American-ness relative to Caribbean neighbors; Recado paste and corn masa in the midst of coconut milk and oil, both coconut products in the heart of corn country.

How accurately does this imaginary dividing line between Caribbean coconut and Central American corn represent what people eat day to day? Hegemonic nationalism predicates Belize's Caribbean/Creole historical ties and colonial legacy over geographic location, insisting that Belizean Kriol food is the "real Belizean food." Most Belizeans subscribe to this collective memory, even (ambivalently) by young Belizeans who strongly support pluralistic nationalism in other arenas of life. If Kriol food is the "most Belizean," one might expect that a patriotic individual would stick with Kriol dishes and eschew those of other cultures. Not surprisingly, what people claim and what people do are two different things. Most twenty-first-century Belizeans, regardless of background, eat both corn and coconut in some form on a weekly basis, and *dukunu* (a green corn tamale made with coconut milk) combines both ingredients in one dish. In reality, cultural groups and culinary boundaries in Belize are fuzzy sets that interpenetrate each other and often blend to create delicious dishes featuring flavors and ingredients from multiple cultural backgrounds. However, not all of these creations are valued equally Belizean by Belizeans.

While most people eat food from a range of Belizean cultures, and although many Belizean Kriol dishes contain ingredients that do not originate in Belizean Kriol culture, the majority of Belizeans still define "real" Belizean food through what Kriol people cook at home. The Kriol home kitchen has been granted tremendous power to determine the contents of the national culinary category. Flavors and ingredients not utilized by Kriol home cooks are recognized, if they are recognized at all, as "cultural foods" of other groups and typically are not considered fully Belizean, or part of national cuisine. Let us examine some dishes, ingredients, and flavor principles found across Belize and see how, why, and if they have been granted the power to represent Belizean food at a national and an international level.

Staples

Corn or Wheat?

In Belize, as in Mexico, corn and wheat have coexisted side by side as staple grains since the arrival of the first Europeans to the region. As Jeffrey Pilcher noted for Mexico in *Planet Taco*, the choice of staple grain may be revealing of the identity (or desired identity) of the consumer (Pilcher 2012). In Belize, like its Spanish-speaking neighbors, this depended on the nation's European/colonial affiliation. Corn is associated with the Maya and Mestizo peoples, while wheat (typically in the form of white flour) is historically connected to British colonialists for whom the Kriol people worked for centuries. Dating back to the 1600s and the era of slavery and timber production in Belize (then British Honduras), British vessels picking up logwood and mahogany would deliver barrels of flour and salted meat from British farms. For over 200 years, these were used as rations in the logging camps for both slaves and free men alike (Wilk 2006). Thus, the Kriol people inherited a taste for wheat-based breads and pastries from European colonizers in Belize. Living in and around the port of Belize Town, they had much easier access to this cheap imported product than did Maya communities. Maya villages continued their corn-centric diet through the colonial era, while Mestizo households consumed both grains, a nod to their mixed ancestry.

Corn is native to the new world and plays a fundamental role in the diet of the many Maya groups in northern Central America. In Belize, "corn foods" is a catchall term that refers to the many different dishes prepared with corn, particularly corn *masa*. Masa is a wet dough made by boiling mature hard grains of corn in water, with calcium carbonate, in the form of a white powder, added to the pot. This causes the shell of each grain to soften so it can be easily washed off after cooking. This process is called *nixtamal* and it renders the B vitamins in the grain bioavailable for human absorption. The soft deshelled kernels are then ground into masa, which is used to make corn tortillas, tamales, and dozens of other dishes, some found only in rural Maya villages, others sold as fast-food snacks across Belize, neighboring Mexico, and the other countries of Central America.

Some corn foods, such as *tamales, dukunu* and *garnaches*, have been nationalized and recognized as pan-Belizean dishes. In Belize, tamales, a famous corn-based delicacy that originated in the indigenous Maya cultures, are made at home by people of all backgrounds including Belizean Kriol. Belizeans acknowledge that Maya and Mestizo peoples originated the *tamal*, but because some Belizean Kriol people make tamales at their homes, they are also considered integrated into, and assimilated as, a fully Belizean dish on the national stage. Through Kriol adoption and preparation, ingredients, flavors, and dishes initially associated with one or another cultural group migrate, gain new identities, and are legitimized as Belizean or even mixed together to create new dishes.[5] This Kriolization-as-pathway-to-nationalization process is not systematic. Very similar corn dishes that also originated with the Maya peoples and are also steamed in leaves or corn husks, like *poch* (a plain corn masa *tamal* made without filling, usually served with soup) and *shuut* (similar to tamales but made with uncooked masa and refried beans), are exclusively associated with Belizean Maya culture and are unknown to most Belizeans from other backgrounds. Because those dishes are not well known outside of their culture of origin, they are regarded as "cultural foods" pertaining to the Maya peoples. Since Belizean Kriol people do not cook them at home and rarely eat them, *shuut* and *poch* are not considered truly Belizean. Only if Belizean Kriol people begin to eat and prepare these foods in their homes will they become candidates for full Belizean-ness and given a fair chance to represent Belize internationally as part of Belizean cuisine.

This is in part because wheat, an imported grain that cannot grow in the tropics, continues to be a staple and in some households, particularly Kriol and Garifuna, is generally preferred over corn. Wheat is imported by the ton and ground into flour at the Archer Daniels Midland–owned Belize Mills Ltd outside of Belize City, then distributed country wide. Wheat flour in both white and whole grain forms is exempt from the 12.5 percent general sales tax levied on nonstaple food items. In many Belizean households, wheat is ubiquitous in the form of breads such as Creole bread, flour tortillas, fry jacks, pack bread (sliced), Johnny cakes, powder bun, and pastries such as meat pies, coconut and lemon tarts, and bread pudding. Many Belizeans eat white flour in some form every day, and home baking is common. In Kriol homes, children are taught to "stir flour" in the same way that young girls help their mothers bake corn tortillas in rural Maya communities.

Yet today, in Maya villages one finds an increasing consumption of white flour. Growing use of flour, refined sugar, and other imported and processed foods in Belizean Maya communities has caused a nutritional transition and a marked rise in the occurrence of certain diseases such as diabetes, which have long been common in Belizean Kriol populations (Baines 2016). Since independence, there have been real and measurable changes in diet, and not only are Belizean Maya people eating more flour but many Belizean Kriol people also buy and eat common corn masa-based street foods multiple times a week. Fast-foods based on corn masa, like tacos, *salbutes*, tostadas, and *garnaches*, have become increasingly common in all areas of Belize and even in Kriol villages where one can now often find corn tortilla factories churning out tortillas and *garnaches* shells to support this street food industry dominated by entrepreneurs of Mestizo and Maya heritage.

Despite this, cultural identity in Belize is still often determined by whether someone puts a corn (Maya, Mestizo) or flour (Kriol, and to a lesser extent, Garifuna) tortilla on their breakfast plate. Everyone buys tacos on the street, but most believe that it is what is prepared and eaten *at home* that establishes the cultural affinity/ies of a given Belizean. This corn/wheat division is very likely to blur over time, as more and more Belizeans have parents from different cultural backgrounds. Multicultural Belizeans may express these identities through appreciation and consumption of both corn and (wheat) flour-based breads and dishes, not only as already-made street foods but also in their home kitchens.

Rice and Beans

We cannot discuss culinary identity and the taste of Belize without talking about rice and beans. In every country in Central America, rice and beans are two important, cheap, and readily available staples, and Belize is no exception (Wilk 2012; Wilk and Barbosa, eds 2012). The almost daily consumption of red kidney beans (alongside less common but also popular black beans, black eyed beans/peas and pinto beans) across Belize distinguishes it from neighboring countries that use black beans as their default legume. History again plays an important role here, as red kidney beans represent the creolized trading routes of the colonial era, having been brought to Belize Town in the 1800s by ships from New Orleans coming south for loads of British Honduran mahogany. Captains used the beans as ballast and then sold them dirt cheap in the local market (Wilk 2006, 2012).

As in Nicaragua and Costa Rica, where it is called *gallo pinto*, one of the most famous dishes in Belize is rice and beans, a one-pot complete-protein meal made by adding beans to a pot of rice and cooking the whole until dry and fluffy. This dish is almost always served with stewed chicken as part of the unofficial national plate, or some other type of stewed meat or seafood, with the gravy poured over the rice and beans to wet them. Key in the production of this dish in Belize is the use of coconut milk instead of water as the cooking medium. Without the use of coconut, the rice and beans are not "proper." In Kriol and Garifuna households, even plain rice is expected to be cooked in coconut milk (today often made with reconstituted coconut milk powder from the shop). Woe to a cook who leaves out the coconut milk, as they will be accused of producing bland and inferior food. To create a crispy golden nutty crust to rice or rice and beans, Belizean Kriol and Garifuna cooks may even pour coconut oil around the edges of the pot, allowing coconut rice or rice and beans to fry to crunchy, rich perfection. This use of coconut milk sets Belizean rice and beans apart from that of its Central American neighbors, where coconut milk is not utilized in cooking rice or *gallo pinto* except in the aforementioned scattered Creole and Garifuna communities on some Caribbean coasts.

Flavor Principles

Recado Paste

The unofficial Belizean national dish when served with rice and beans and fried plantain, stew(ed) chicken, is a perfect example of Kriol adoption, legitimization, and thus nationalization of non-Kriol ingredients. Featuring chicken introduced from Asia, seasoned with imported British Worcestershire sauce and red *recado* paste adopted from Maya and Mestizo cultures, this dish epitomizes the British-Caribbean-meets-Central America flavors that set Belize apart. Red recado paste is a clay-like seasoning blend made from ground-up annatto or achiote seeds, the fruit of *Bixa Orellana*, a shrub native to Central America. Annatto has been used by indigenous groups of the tropical Americas for hundreds of years. Red recado combines annatto seeds with (introduced) black pepper, onion, garlic, vinegar, and allspice or cloves, all ground together into a vibrantly colored, richly flavored paste that is used to season dishes across southern Mexico, Belize, and Guatemala. Stewed chicken was historically prepared using a freshly killed bird from the yard for a proper Belizean Kriol Sunday Dinner. Eventually, this dish became a popular specialty in the earliest self-proclaimed Belizean restaurants and is now prepared and eaten by Belizeans from all cultural backgrounds (Wilk 1999, 2006). Older Kriol Belizeans are adamant that stewed chicken did not use to contain recado paste as a seasoning element. Color for the stewed chicken was obtained solely through browning of the meat (Spang 2019). Some Kriol cooks initially disdained recado as a mere coloring agent and an inferior substitute for the browning process. Over the past forty years, however, recado as a flavor principle has been adopted into Belizean Kriol kitchens through exposure to Mestizo dishes and cooking techniques. Today, proper Belizean stew(ed) chicken is made by rubbing the meat with herbs and red recado paste diluted in vinegar and Worcestershire sauce, then browning it before braising to fall-off-the-bone tenderness. Not only is red recado an essential flavor principle in Belize's national dish, but it is also seen by some Belizeans as *the* key element that makes our stewed chicken Belizean. As one research participant stated: "other people mek chicken stew but not with di recado and other thing the way we mek it da Belize" ("other people make stew chicken but not with the recado and other things the way we make it in Belize").

According to this and other research participants, the taste of Belize is not found in one particular ingredient or spice, but rather a *combination* of flavor principles that distinguish us as a richly seasoned Central American/Caribbean mash up of a nation. Clearly, red recado paste, which flavors the gravies of all stewed meats and a number of seafood dishes in Belize, is one of those flavor principles that has transcended its culture-specific origins and become representative of a nation, through the legitimizing effect of the Kriol home kitchen.

Chile Peppers

Chile peppers are a good example of a flavor principle that bridges the Caribbean/ Central American division in Belizean cuisine. Originating in the tropical Americas, *chiles* were used by indigenous groups on both the Caribbean islands and the Central and South American mainland for hundreds of years before European and African arrival. Beloved by many in both Mexico and Jamaica, hot peppers are a favorite in Belize as well. For many Belizeans, no meal is complete without a touch of hot pepper. Garifuna, Kriol, East Indian, and all three Maya groups regularly use hot pepper. But specific peppers have different affiliations. The habanero is the national favorite, indubitably the most popular chile pepper in all of Belize. From north to south, east to west, you find habanero-based hot sauces, both homemade and commercially produced, on almost all restaurant and home tables. But head to Toledo District, Belize's southern-most region, and there you will find scores of Mopan and Kekchi Maya villages where another hot pepper is equally important: the tiny but fiery bird pepper. These little brightly colored fruits pack a real punch and grow wild in yards and edges of corn and bean fields, spread by the birds that gave them their name. Belizean Maya villagers collect them by the panful and place them on screens over their wood burning fire hearths, where hot smoke causes the peppers to dry up, at which time they are ground into a fine powder that is used to season everything from a freshly made corn tortilla to soups, tamales, fish, and meats cooked wrapped in leaves.[6]

Because of its universal distribution and consumption, habanero can be claimed as a national flavor, eaten and made into sauces in almost every Belizean household. Bird peppers are not utilized by every ethnicity nor cultivated in all regions of the country; therefore, they remain a cultural ingredient, associated specifically with the Maya villages of southern Belize. The consumption of habanero peppers is not unique to Belize, but anyone describing Belizean food cannot do an accurate job without acknowledging the important place of that particular chile pepper on our national table.

What role did the Kriol kitchen play in nationalizing the habanero? The old-world ancestors of the Belizean Kriol people did not know or use chile peppers. They learned about these fiery fruits when they arrived in the Caribbean Basin and quickly adopted them into their diet over 400 years ago. Unlike with recado, which was added to the Belizean Kriol culinary repertoire within living memory, hot peppers have been part of Creole diets across the Caribbean Basin since European and African peoples were introduced to this enthralling fruit by Carib and Arawak villagers in the 1500s. In Belizean Kriol kitchens today, homemade pepper sauce is regularly prepared by filling a glass jar or bottle with white vinegar, finely chopped onion, habanero, and sometimes sliced carrot and cilantro or a couple allspice seeds. While there are a few Belizeans of all cultural backgrounds who do not like hot pepper, a Kriol kitchen without hot sauce is an anomaly indeed. Rare is the Kriol kitchen, however, that uses smoked ground bird pepper. If this was a daily seasoning in Kriol homes as it is in many Maya kitchens in Belize, it is likely that bird pepper would also be considered a fully Belizean spice.

So far, habanero is the only chile to have achieved that status in Belize. This is the case even in the export market where Belize's famous Marie Sharps habanero hot sauces are shipped to over twenty countries worldwide. To date no one seems to be exporting smoked bird pepper powder. Marie Sharps not only has become a well-known brand outside of Belize, but every year tens of thousands of visitors return to North America and Europe with bottles of her sauces in their luggage. Habanero sauces are popular souvenirs and gifts and, for many, are seen as bringing a taste of Belize to food back home. The fiery orange contents are a potent memory of vacation days, jungle adventures, beach excursions, and sampling Belizean food in local restaurants. For Belizeans living abroad, Marie Sharps brand habanero sauce on the table in a Chicago, New York, or Los Angeles kitchen is a symbol of national identity and belonging and a patriotic statement of Belizean-ness.

Coconut

Coconuts were introduced to Belize. Unlike wheat, which must still be imported, they grow beautifully here, and coconut trees are found in yards across the country. While wheat was the staple grain of choice for European colonialists in the Americas, coconuts represent the tropical old world. Not surprisingly, therefore, the use of coconut in Belize is strongly associated with Belizean Kriol and Garifuna groups, both of whom claim some African ancestry and a long friendship with the palm. In parts of Asia, Africa, and the Pacific islands, coconuts have been cultivated and utilized for a long time. Despite the coconut fruit's ability to float for thousands of miles before sprouting, there is no evidence for pre-Colombian coconuts growing in the Americas (Clement et al. 2013). Maya people were not introduced to it until the 1500s. Similarly, Mestizo culture, with its American indigenous and European Spanish heritage, rarely utilizes the coconut. But in every region where African-descent populations are found across the Caribbean Basin and beyond, coconut is used in the making of sweets, pastries, entrees, side dishes, and drinks (Houston 2005).

In Belize today, people of all cultures are happy to consume dishes containing coconut milk or oil, but even now it is most often in a Kriol or Garifuna household that one will find the tools to process a mature coconut.[7] Husking a coconut and grating its meat is carried out to make coconut milk, a staple ingredient in many Kriol and Garifuna dishes, or, with further processing, the cottage industry production of coconut oil. Coconut meat may be grated for candies and pies or occasionally eaten fresh. But for the most part in Belize, this versatile seed is used in its liquid forms as coconut milk, coconut oil, and coconut water. Coconut milk powder, introduced from Malaysia by a variety of Caribbean importers, is a cheap substitute found in every grocery store that, while often used in home and commercial kitchens, is considered an inferior replacement for fresh milk. Coconut milk is used to make wheat flour-based breads such as Creole bread and Johnny cakes, desserts like potato pound and cassava pudding, meals like *hudut* (Garifuna fried fish in coconut, along with plantain), and Belize's iconic rice and beans.

My research participants view coconut not only as an ingredient in many dishes commonly cooked and eaten in Belize but also as a *key flavor principle* that Belizean- izes whatever it is added to (Spang 2019). The taste of coconut is strongly identified as a "real Belizean flavor." A simple pot of rice is emphatically Belizean when it is made with coconut milk instead of the water or broth of neighboring countries. Beans, similarly, should be cooked with coconut oil added for the "proper" Belizean taste. Fried fish or chicken becomes Belizean by frying it in coconut oil. This is not just an iconic flavor principle; it is a taste that people enjoy. The flavor of coconut is beloved by most Belizeans. I met Belizeans who did not like spicy food and those who did not like fish (in a fishing village!), but regardless of cultural background never once in thirteen months of field data collection did I encounter a Belizean who said they did not like the flavor of coconut. As Ayora-Diaz notes in his introduction to the edited volume *Taste, Politics and Identities in Mexican Food*, taste involves "biological but also, and more fundamentally, social, cultural, ecological, and political contexts that contribute to shape the human experience of food intake and preference" (Ayora-Diaz 2019: 1). This belief prioritizes Belizean Kriol and Garifuna food, with their traditionally heavy use of coconut, over that of other cultures in the selection of a national culinary repertoire.

Unlike recado and chilis, which are also popular in Guatemala and southern Mexico, the use of coconut is seen by Belizeans and immigrants alike as setting the nation apart from its neighbors. In Mexico, coconut products are rarely utilized in local dishes, while in Guatemala, Honduras, Nicaragua, Costa Rica, and Panama the only place where coconut milk and oil are consumed is in tiny pockets of Garifuna and Creole villages located on the Caribbean coasts of these countries. The use of coconut milk by these scattered Afro-descent populations is a strong marker of cultural identity, used to distinguish these communities from the Spanish/Mestizo-dominated national societies within which they persist, tokens of the former extent of British rule, and enslavement of African peoples in the Caribbean Basin.

Across the region most staples are the same: corn, wheat flour, rice, beans, and root crops. Little Belize distinguishes itself in the Central American culinary context by transforming the flavor profile of these base ingredients with the addition of Caribbean coconut. The countrywide consumption of coconut products connects Belize to its historical counterparts in the Caribbean Basin: Jamaica, Trinidad, and Tobago and other former British possessions with large African-descent populations who were well versed in the utilization of this old-world culinary gem. Coconut has been granted the power to Belize-ize food by linking our national culinary traditions to colonial history in the English-speaking Caribbean, whence both the Garifuna and Creole peoples originated.

Conclusion: Nationalist Taste in a Plural Society

David Sutton argued in 2011 that memory should be an important part of what he dubbed a gustemological approach to the study of food. The gustemological approach, Sutton stated, is synesthetic, involving all the bodily senses as well as a polytemporal sense of time, where history and memory play an important, layered role in the experience of food (Sutton 2011). Memory, in the form of collective memory, is a powerful medium for the creation of a sense of identity, be it individual, cultural, or national. A cohesive sense of national identity requires a compelling historical narrative and collective memory that functions to unify a society at the national level (Hobsbawm and Ranger, eds. 1983). In Belize, as in many ethnically diverse former colonies, varied interpretations of our history have generated a plurality of narratives and collective memories leading to divergent conclusions regarding the intersection of cultural, national, and regional identity and the requirements for Belizean-ness. These are clearly seen in the dueling hegemonic versus pluralistic discourses and hegemonic nationalism's exclusive focus on Belize's British colonial-era (Afro/Creole) Caribbean ties.

Culinary heritage is inherently gustemological: the sum of embodied, creatively enacted collective memories of food that are handed down from generation to generation (Brulotte and Di Giovine 2014). These collective, practiced food memories, grounded in the home kitchen, form the foundation for cultural and national culinary identities and gastronational expression on the global stage. Through the lens of food, certain ingredients and flavors are associated with specific cultures, collective memories, and narratives of Belizean history and identity. Coconut is an iconic flavoring agent in Belize that distinguishes the nation from its Spanish-speaking neighbors by linking Belizean Kriol and Garifuna food to the Afro-Caribbean diaspora, narratives of Creole nationalism/hegemonic nationalism, and the slave trading routes of the British Empire (see Houston 2005 for examples of coconut usage across the Caribbean islands). Corn, particularly in the form of corn masa and the multitudes of dishes made from it, ties Belizean Maya and Mestizo food to the broader indigenous history of Mesoamerica, the birthplace of domesticated maize, and resistance to colonial invaders. The flavor of corn evokes one Central American–focused historical narrative, while the taste of coconut expresses another, linked to the Caribbean. Both together make up the beautifully complex story that is Belize. Hegemonic nationalism demands that only one narrative be legitimized. Pluralistic nationalism, on the other hand, offers the opportunity for both historical narratives and all Belizeans, regardless of culture, to be equally respected and represented in our society. To take this model beyond mere lip service and carefully curated Culture Day expression, we must address fundamental problems of inequality and rectify the economic and political marginalization of Kekchi, Mopan and Yucatec Maya, and Garifuna people in Belize.

By asking the question, "what does Belize taste like?" we soon find ourselves picking through the remnants of historical influences and national discourses that have shaped feuding models of nationalism still wrestling for control of the wheel of national identity. Despite Belize's official stance of pluralism, what people consider to be Belizean is often guided by principles of Creole nationalism, a hegemonic model of identity that predicates Belize's colonial ties with Africa and the British-controlled Caribbean over its geographic location or its indigenous history in Central America. At the same time, increasingly Belizeans recognize their multicultural ancestry and many younger Belizeans embrace the official discourse of pluralistic nationalism that theoretically grants all Belizean cultures equal importance within the country. Since independence in 1981 and going forward, there has been an evolution and growing discussion about Belizean identity. What is Belizean? Who is Belizean? And, most importantly for the gastronome, what is Belizean food? Cuisines are often defined by staples and flavor principles. To that end we see certain staples granted the power to represent the nation while other, equally important foods are relegated to the sidelines. The home kitchen functions as a crucible of memory making, generating important narratives of culinary heritage that are the warp and weft of gastronational expression. If we wish to make pluralistic nationalism a reality, it should not matter whether that home kitchen is Kriol, Maya, Garifuna, East Indian, or Mennonite. All Belizeans must be given equal opportunity to contribute to the development of our young nation and emerging national cuisine.

Notes

1   When referring to either the Belizean Kriol language or Belizean Kriol people I use the Kriol orthography recommended by the Belizean Kriol Language Project. I use the word "Kriolization" to refer to the generic "creolization" process *in the specific context of Belize* and to distinguish it from the generic terms "creole" and "creolization."
2   Full independence from Great Britain was achieved only in September 21, 1981.
3   It is problematic because many Belizean Kriol people also have indigenous Maya, Carib, or Miskito ancestry and/or East Indian ancestry, in addition to the predominant African/European progenitors.
4   At one point immediately after the Yucatan caste war in the 1850s, a large influx of Mexican refugees into the northern half of the country tipped the balance in favor of the "Hispanic" or "Spanish" population, but in the later years of the nineteenth century the Kriol regained demographic dominance.
5   Famous Belizean chef Sean Kuylen calls this multicultural fusion "Inspired Belizean Cuisine."
6   This technique of wrapping animal protein in large leaves to be cooked over the fireplace is called *lancha* in Kekchi Maya and steams the meat or fish to perfect tenderness.
7   The small East Indian descent population in Belize arrived mainly from Southern India, and introduced their own coconut processing technology with them, including a specific style of coconut grater. Yet, perhaps because of the small numbers of this cultural group and their large-scale assimilation and blending with Kriol culture, coconut is not strongly associated with them as it is with Kriol and Garifuna food.

References

Ayora-Diaz, S. I. (2019), "Introduction: Matters of Taste: The Politics of Food and Identity in Mexican Cuisines," in S. I. Ayora-Diaz (ed.), *Taste, Politics and Identities in Mexican Food*, pp. 1–18, London: Bloomsbury Academic.

Baines, K. (2016), *Embodying Ecological Heritage in a Maya Community: Health, Happiness and Identity*, Lanham: Lexington Books.

Belize History Association (2015), *A History of Slavery and Emancipation in Belize*. Exhibit by the Institute for Sociocultural Research (ISCR) and the National Institute of Culture and History (NICH).

Bolland, O. N. (1987), "Race, Ethnicity and National Integration in Belize," in Society for the Promotion of Education and Research (ed.), *Belize, Ethnicity and Development*, no page numbers, Belize City: SPEAR Press.

Bolland, O. N. (1998), "Creolisation and Creole Societies: A Cultural Nationalist View of Caribbean Social History," *Caribbean Quarterly* 44(1/2): 1–32.

Brulotte, R. L. and M. A. Di Giovine, eds. (2014), *Edible Identities: Food as Cultural Heritage*, Farnham: Ashgate.

Clement, C. R., Zizumbo-Villarreal, D., Brown, C. H., Ward, R. G., Alves-Pereira, A., Harries, H. C. (2013), "Coconuts in the Americas," *Botanical Review* 79: 342–70.

DeSoucey, M. (2010), "Gastronationalism: Food Traditions and Authenticity Politics in the European Union," *American Sociological Review* 75(3): 432–55.

Hobsbawm, E. J. and T. Ranger, eds. (1983), *The Invention of Tradition*, Cambridge: Cambridge University Press.

Houston, L. M. (2005), *Food Culture in the Caribbean*, Westport: Greenwood Press.

Judd, K. (1989a), "Cultural Synthesis or Ethnic Struggle? Creolization in Belize," *Cimarron* 2(1/2): 103–18.

Judd, K. (1989b), "Who Will Define Us? Creole History and Identity in Belize." Unpublished paper presented at the American Anthropological Association Annual Meeting, Chicago.

Medina, L. K. (1997), "Defining Difference, Forging Unity: The Co-construction of Race, Ethnicity and Nation in Belize," *Ethnic and Racial Studies* 20(4): 757–80.

Pilcher, J. M. (2012), *Planet Taco: A Global History of Mexican Food*, New York: Oxford University Press.

Shoman, A. (2010), *Belize's Independence and Decolonization in Latin America. Guatemala, Britain, and the UN*, New York: Palgrave MacMillan.

Spang, L. (2019), *Bite Yu Finga! Innovating Belizean Cuisine*, Kingston: The University of West Indies Press.

Sutton, D. (2011), "Memory as Sense: A Gustemological Approach," *Food, Culture & Society* 14(4): 468–75.

Wilk, R. (1995), "Learning to Be Local in Belize: Global Systems of Common Difference," in D. Miller (ed.), *Worlds Apart: Modernity Through the Prism of the Local*, pp. 110–33, London: Routledge.

Wilk, R. (1999), "'Real Belizean Food': Building Local Identity in the Transnational Caribbean," *American Anthropologist* 101(2): 244–55.

Wilk, R. (2006), *Home Cooking in the Global Village: Caribbean Food from Buccaneers to Ecotourists*, Oxford and New York: Berg.

Wilk, R. (2012), "Nationalizing the Ordinary Dish: Rice and Beans in Belize," in R. Wilk and L. Barbosa (eds.), *Rice and Beans: A Unique Dish in A Hundred Places*, pp. 203–18, Oxford: Berg.

Wilk, R. and L. Barbosa, eds. (2012), *Rice and Beans: A Unique Dish in A Hundred Places*, Oxford: Berg.

10

Street Food to Restaurant

Politics of Eating and Cultural Heritage in Antigua, Guatemala

Walter E. Little

Introduction: From the Street to Cultural Heritage

Much of Guatemala's distinctive food traditions are practiced in the public spaces of marketplace stalls, *comedores* (inexpensive diners), and on the street by ambulatory food vendors, all of which tend to serve working Guatemalans, not wealthy elites or foreign businesspersons and tourists. In general, Guatemalan cuisine, as defined by particular dishes and flavors, has not been touted as special and worth culinarians' attention. There are no internationally famous chefs like Rick Bayless and Diane Kennedy writing books and hosting cooking shows on Guatemala cuisine. Nor are there homegrown chefs who have risen to global recognition, like Enrique Olvera, the chef and owner of the Mexico City restaurant *Pujol*, and Abigail Mendoza Ruiz, the owner of Restaurante *Tlamanalli* in Teotitlán del Valle, Oaxaca, to mention a couple of prominent Mexican chefs.

Only in the most recent tourism promotions by Instituto Guatemalteco de Turismo (INGUAT[1]), the government's tourism agency is Guatemalan cuisine featured. I will address later how the national government is trying to recalibrate conceptualizations of taste in relationship to Guatemalan food, as an aspect of social distinction and class difference (Bourdieu 1984), within the broader contexts of cultural heritage and tourism. The shift from food perceived of as utilitarian and linked to specific classes of workers to that same food viewed as indexing rather global cosmopolitan sensibilities of taste provides an example of how food and taste are entangled with particular social groups and class. Where French cuisine, for example, not only calls up images of particular kinds of dishes and flavors, it also has strong associations with what the French and others throughout the world conceive of as more broadly French national heritage (Ferguson 2004). Whereas French cuisine brings forth in the minds of most people notions of a particular kind of foodways that deserves attention, even distinction from the rest, Guatemalan cuisine tends to not even get noticed by the outside world.

Not only is Guatemalan food not recognized in international culinary circles, but it also exists in the shadow of Mexico's world-renowned cuisine. The shadow that Mexico casts on Guatemala is so strong that it creates confusion for international tourists visiting the country and a sense of inferiority and anxiety on the parts of those Guatemalans who serve food to tourists. These attitudes are amplified with respect to street food and the place it is granted in the discourses of food and heritage from national and international perspectives. As I have explored elsewhere (Little 2020), locals' and international tourists' fears about Guatemalan street food are palpable, be it preoccupations about health or the social constraints against eating in *comedores* or simply dining on the street, as elites prefer to eat at home and reserve eating out to restaurants that cater to international cosmopolitan flavors rather than local foods. Furthermore, Guatemalan restaurants and their local patrons have a weak tradition of recognizing homegrown dishes, as eating out serves two very different functions. For a celebratory meal out to a nice restaurant, most people do not want to eat food that is commonly associated with home cooking, no matter how much they claim they like and appreciate it. For those workers who eat out for lunch, they tend to eat traditional, homestyle Guatemalan food. Workers in cities rarely pack their lunches. Instead, they frequent local establishments, especially street food, marketplace stands, and *comedores* that only serve basic homestyle Guatemalan dishes. These kinds of places may be frequented by the budget traveler but are largely avoided by both national and international tourists. While the former tends to seek out anything but Guatemalan food, the latter will eat in a very few restaurants that do cater to international tourists' culinary curiosities. In this chapter, I raise the question of street food as cultural heritage by marking these distinctions and the kinds of prejudices that both national and international tourists have, in order to make a case for why Guatemala's street food should, indeed, be considered a form of cultural heritage and national patrimony.

For a country like Guatemala, in contrast to many others (Brulotte and Di Giovine 2014; Haines and Sammells 2010; Man Kong Lum and de Ferrière le Vayer 2016), what is intangible food heritage and, more specifically, how does it play out in a well-known and heavily touristed UNESCO World Heritage site like Antigua? Who, then, eats street food and how do those foods get treated with respect to food heritage?

Enchiladas *Guatemaltecas* I

My first experience with Guatemalan street food was in a small *comedor* in Antigua in 1987, when traveling with a couple of friends, one from Chicago, like myself, and another, his Honduran girlfriend. At the end of a long overland trip from La Ceiba, Honduras, we arrived in Antigua and went in search of comfort food. Near the Central Plaza, we found a rustic little *comedor* with a short menu. Many of the dishes' names were familiar to us—tacos, *caldo de pollo* or *de res*, quesadillas, and enchiladas. None had descriptions. We settled on the enchiladas, imagining a steaming plate of tortillas bathed in a piquant red salsa with chicken and cheese to shake off our cold that rainy evening. After a short wait that we occupied by studying our guidebook and planning the next day, the waiter brought out three plates of enchiladas. Or rather, that is what he told us they were. At first, we thought he and the cook were playing a cruel joke on us, just giving a few tourists a hard time. Despite our skepticism, he earnestly explained this is what we had ordered. As we looked at our plates, disappointed with what we saw, the disconnection between what we imagined we were going to eat and what we were actually served was so great that we could not eat the enchiladas.

We, then, ordered tacos and they, too, were not what we expected. Same name but different from Mexico. The tacos were warm where the enchiladas were not and the tacos, deep-fried rolled tortillas that were stuffed with chicken, were familiar to us as flautas in Mexican cuisine. Our cold enchiladas remained untouched. For foreigner travelers such as us, the problem with enchiladas *guatemaltecas* is that they have nothing in common with Mexican enchiladas, irrespective of regional Mexican styles. The Guatemalan enchilada begins with a whole flat crispy maize tortilla (tostada). A heaping pile of grated beets, mildly seasoned with vinegar and salt, is placed on the tortilla and topped with slices of hardboiled eggs, raw onions, and crumbles of hard white salty cheese. Some versions add ground beef and are drizzled with a mild red sauce but the most commonly sold versions on the street and in some restaurants are simply made with beets and no meat. It took me some time to appreciate Guatemalan enchiladas and, that is, I already liked beets. The dissociation between my taste sensibilities, informed by Mexican versions, and those that I encountered that cold, rainy evening in Antigua all those years ago was a challenge to overcome.

I will revisit enchiladas *guatemaltecas* later in this chapter as I explore the relationships between street food and heritage in Guatemala because they can help us better understand the politics of street food in relation to food as heritage or national and cultural patrimony. Within the contradictory discourses of tourism, heritage, health, and security, the question is how taste is constructed through the quotidian practices of street food sales and consumption in Antigua. Enchiladas *guatemaltecas*, like other Guatemalan street foods, are located in a cultural culinary space that relates to socioeconomic hierarchies, which confuse international tourists. While elites and tourists may avoid street food in Guatemala, it is abundant through the country.

My exploration of Guatemalan food, especially street food, is based on annual visits to Guatemala since 1987. While the majority of my research has been about weavers and handicraft vendors, with major ethnographic and linguistic detours working on Kaqchikel Maya-language pedagogical materials with Kaqchikel teachers, my eating habits were oriented around the ways that my collaborators and informants ate themselves. This meant eating at *comedores* and street food stands with handicraft vendors, as well as eating and, even learning to cook Guatemalan dishes, in the homes of dozens of weavers and teachers. With my Kaqchikel-language work from 1992 to 2012, Kaqchikel teachers and international students often ate together, allowing me to witness students' reactions to Guatemalan food. And because the handicraft vendors sold primarily to international tourists, who would see me eating with the vendors, I got many inquiries about the food and unsolicited comments about it. Over the last four years, I have focused my research more directly on street food sales in Antigua, Guatemala, interviewing the vendors and their consumers, as well as sampling it (Little 2020). This chapter aims to summarize these various threads with an emphasis on the question about the politics of food heritage with respect of typical Guatemala street food. The backdrop is Antigua, Guatemala, an UNESCO World Heritage site that is recognized for its baroque architectural style, rather than intangible Maya cultural heritage or cuisine (Little 2004).

Guatemalan Street Food

Street food serves a pragmatic function in Antigua, as it does almost everywhere. Unlike street food in Mexico City (Hayden 2014) and Bangkok (Isaacs 2014), where it has been elevated to international renown and celebrated by international globe trotters interested in new culinary experiences (Haines and Sammells 2010), it is widely dismissed and viewed as dangerous by many Guatemalans themselves and international visitors. Cedillo Gámez de Barrios (2017) concludes in her study of Antigua street food that the food is unsanitary and served in unsanitary conditions due to the lack of clean water, lack of waste removal, and improper food handling, among other poor health and food preparation practices. The report ultimately was a counter to the municipality's regular missives that street food was dangerous[2] and commonly covered in sensationalistic local media reports that highlighted the food as unhygienic and made of animals like dogs (Patzán 2019; Ramirez 2019; Sicán 2017). Cedillo Gámez de Barrios, by contrast, concluded that the solution is to improve the sanitary conditions and impose new regulations that would help street food vendors sell safe, hygienic food. Embracing such a political policy would align with other studies and policies where street food is conceived as an important intervention to help improve the nutrition of those suffering from food insecurity (Food and Agriculture Organization of the United Nations 2002; Montes de Oca Barrera 2018). Guatemala and Antigua, specifically, have yet to implement progressive food policies.

Irrespective of real or imagined health and safety concerns, street food plays an important role in feeding Antigua's workers, especially, those who commute into the city from other towns. As I mentioned earlier, carrying a lunch prepared from home is rare and, generally, considered odd. The predilection for purchasing lunch, I would argue, indexes cultural and class-based ideologies that are constrained by economic considerations and ethnicity politics. Such convergences of class, economy, culture, and taste are what Bourdieu (1984) challenges us to consider and frame the practices of Guatemalans. Low-level service jobs in Antigua, many serving the tourism industry, have highly restrictive lunch schedules, often no more than a half-hour long. This restriction is enhanced by the fact that the restaurants around the city center are well beyond the financial means of the typical worker, including those employed by the city and those working as bank tellers, store clerks, and indigenous Maya handicraft vendors, among other jobs. Eating in a restaurant, characteristically, costs at least Q70 (US$10) and usually much more, while a meal from a street vendor is a modest Q10 to Q15 (US$1.5 to $2), making it more affordable for workers who earn the minimum hourly wage of Q11.27.[3] Even if a worker or handicraft vendor makes substantially more in wages or earnings, restaurant service is notoriously slow. Having the money to eat in one of Antigua's restaurants in combination with a long slow service is a luxury that only the city's elites and international tourists can afford, except on rare occasions.

Hence, eating in restaurants indicates socioeconomic status. Additionally, what food gets served in these restaurants further contributes to the perception of this status and Guatemalan notions of cosmopolitanism. This is a topic in its own right, that I hope to take up in another essay. Nonetheless, the cost of the restaurant and the time needed to eat in them serve to delineate class and ethnic boundaries in the city.

Workers need to eat and only the poorest skip lunch and the mid-morning and mid-afternoon snacks. Some of the most impoverished may pack a *tamal* or *chuchito* (steamed corn dough with meat or vegetable filling) in their bag but even that marks them as poor. In order to avoid the stigma, I have witnessed many of these workers and vendors go without food. Better to claim you are too busy to eat than to admit to being too poor to eat. Most workers eat street food from vendors who pass by their places of employment or set up temporary stands during snack and lunch times. The food stands may be as simple as vendor women sitting in the Plaza Central or a strategically located street corner with a couple of baskets containing typical meals of the day, such as *pepian* (a mildly piquant sauce made from roasted tomatoes, peppers, and onions and served over rice and chicken or pork), *puliq de pollo* (a thick maize gruel-based stew with chicken), and a variety of cooked greens that are served with handmade maize tortillas. These vendors have a regular clientele and rarely serve strangers. Typically, they sell out within minutes.

Other women street food vendors, often mothers and daughters working together, walking from store to store or offices, sell from smaller baskets carried on their heads. They tend to sell food that can be consumed quickly and is highly portable—like *chuchitos* and tamales that do not require plates and cutlery to be consumed. A third category of street vendor is one that sells hot, or made-to-order, dishes that include Guatemalan versions of tacos, enchiladas, *chiles rellenos* (filled with pork, green beans, and carrot), tostadas (always topped with season avocado or refried black beans that are sprinkled with hard salty cheese, tomato sauce, and parsley), and various *atoles* (maize-based hot beverages), among other foods. These vendors broker deals with the Catholic churches around the city and set up their stands on church-controlled public spaces, notably at the La Merced Church and the San Francisco el Grande Church, both with substantial congregations and in close proximity to many businesses.

Beginning in 1995, all commercial sales on public streets and plazas were banned by municipal regulations (Municipal Code 16-95), which prohibited the use of public thoroughfares, including the Parque Central and national monuments, for all commercial activities, including food vending. The regulations marked the beginning of the city government's multiyear campaign (1995 to 2010) to purge all street vendors from the city (Little 2008). The city was only successful at removing the food vendors who used cooking gas and griddles and fry vats to prepare hot food. Nonetheless, food vendors avoid removal or fines because they occupy a strategic place in the everyday practices of their diners, some of whom are municipal officials and police charged with fining and removing them. Workers, even city workers, needing lunch in a city of expensive restaurants, and local residents' conventions of taste about what constitutes a satisfying meal, serve as a pragmatic confluence of attitudes that allow street food vendors to serve their customers and stay in business because of urban spatial permissiveness (Little 2020). Spatial permissiveness is found in urban public economies where there are gaps between the written regulations, enforcement, and actual street economies. Food vendors work in public places like the Central Plaza and the Calle del Arco (a pedestrian street two days per week) where the symbolic, economic, and political converge for locals, tourists, and vendors. Street food vendors who work securely in these kinds of public places occupy an important niche of serving food to other street vendors and to Antigua's rank and file labor force (Little 2004, 2015). Street food vendors' successes and stability are tied with Antigua food economies of expensive restaurants in relation to wages. They build reliable and loyal customers by providing a needed service, irrespective of the laws, and they often do so by cultivating a range of social identities that make them easily identifiable to Antigua's workers and vendors. The base upon which all this rests is that the quality of their food is consistent, considered tasty, and hygienic. Those vendors who do not serve safe food quickly go out of business and those spend their days looking for random customers are, generally, perceived with suspicion for serving low-quality, unhygienic food.

Spatial permissiveness does not merely play out in pragmatic, functionalist ways. Although safety concerns may dominate official government regulation and media discourse, "tradition" and taste (in both flavor and distinction connotations) are significant themes when food vendors and consumers talk about why they eat what they eat. In all my conversations with vendors, there is almost a universal pride in wanting to eat food that they identify as distinctly Guatemalan. As one police officer commented to me, while eating next to a street food stand that he should have been fined, "This food is satisfying as only a traditional meal can be. If it doesn't taste like the food I grew up on, then, I'll be hungry all day long and not feel satisfied." A vendor explained his reasons for a rather complicated lunch routine, where he ate meals from various different street food vendors on different days, was because of his fondness for *pepian*. His wife would prepare it once a month. By eating lunches from different vendors on different days, he could be relatively sure to be able to eat *pepian* every day of the work week. "I like pepian so much that I can eat it every day for lunch and, then, go home and eat it for dinner." When I mentioned this to his wife, she commented that "he was obsessed with it and claimed it is, really, the true flavor of Guatemala."

Although the street food vendors' customers did not tend to be so singularly fixated on one particular dish, they consistently emphasized that the street food they ate was "traditional Guatemalan food" and that eating it "made them Guatemalan." This is particularly significant because many framed their eating preferences in contrast to those of tourists who visit Antigua but tend to avoid local dishes or get steered away from them by guides, who claim that foreigners' tastes and stomachs are not accustomed to Guatemalan food, making it too dangerous for them to eat. From the perspectives of both vendors and local eaters, there are specific qualities of Guatemalan food that distinguishes it from Mexican food and international visitors' conceptualizations. Here, it is useful to turn to an additional *enchiladas guatemaltecas* story.

Enchiladas *Guatemaltecas* II

It is 1995 and my, then, five-year-old daughter was infatuated with enchiladas *guatemaltecas*. She and one of her Kaqchikel friends would eat them in Antigua and in the girl's hometown of San Juan Comalapa. Aside from the enchiladas' flavor, mildly vinegary and salty, they were inexpensive and allowed them the autonomy to choose what they wanted to eat, when to eat it, and with whom. That summer, the two friends and another Antigüeña girlfriend made it their mission to try as many enchiladas *guatemaltecas* as possible. The international students in the Kaqchikel class noticed their enchilada predilection. Even US tourists raised an eyebrow at them eating food that is rare in the United States. At that young age, she was well aware that most foreigners experienced the kinds of food dissociations that my friends and I experienced when encountering Guatemalan food for the first time in 1987. Unlike me, my daughter cannot remember not eating Guatemalan food, and enchiladas *guatemaltecas* are simply just good food to her. As a game, when we ate with the students, she tried to get them to eat food that she thought would unsettle them—taste odd or too spicy or presented in an unusual way—by eating it in front of them and, then, encouraging them to eat it. She did not expect them to like it but that was not the point; rather, the more revulsed they were, the better it was.

One day, she and her Antigüeña girlfriend, decided to talk the students into eating enchiladas *guatemaltecas* on the street with them. On learning this, her girlfriend's grandmother, Paca, offered to teach them how to make the enchiladas so that they could serve them to the students at lunch. They agreed and the three of them set off to the marketplace to buy the ingredients, prepare the enchiladas, and, then, serve them to four students that regularly ate with us. Paca has a lot of experience boarding and cooking for international students who come to Antigua to learn Spanish or Kaqchikel. She, typically, adjusted her dishes to her guests' tastes. In anticipation of the students not wanting to eat the enchiladas, she also prepared a chicken with rice dish they had eaten before and liked. When lunch was served, the girls insisted on just putting the enchiladas on the table. They announced that "the enchiladas guatemaltecas were served." The students looked at them skeptically. Each of the girls served themselves one. I took one. Paca, too. Her adult son passed through and helped himself. The students were hesitant. Disappointment was mapped across their faces, as they looked at the enchiladas, Paca, and each other. One claimed that she would skip lunch, as she didn't like beets. Another asked hesitantly if these were really enchiladas, since he'd imagined something quite different. The other two tried them—one leaving it after a bite. The other finished it, declaring "it wasn't bad but it's not an enchilada." Paca explained to the students that the enchiladas were just the appetizer and served them the chicken and rice. As we talked, she shared how enchiladas *guatemaltecas* are a typical traditional Guatemalan food and commonly sold on the street and served at social functions. I informed them that we would have small bite-sized versions, along with other kinds of foods sold on the streets and at small marketplace *comedores*, at the Kaqchikel graduation ceremony. When they did not show any enthusiasm about it, I assured them that they would be acculturated to the food by the end of the class, about five weeks later. They weren't.

Guatemala Food as Intangible Heritage

Where the enchiladas *guatemaltecas* examples are meant to highlight the incongruencies between Guatemalans senses of taste and those of foreign tourists and students, as well as delineate the distinctiveness of the enchilada itself from those of Mexico, it is important to acknowledge that Guatemalans are quite proud of their food traditions. However, they have not tended to think of their food as something that non-Guatemalans would want to eat. For most of my ethnographic life in Guatemala I have eaten as a Guatemalan and yet rarely encountered Guatemalans advocating for their food to foreigners. In fact, textile collector–turned–exotic cuisine author (Asimov 2000) Copeland Marks (1985) writes that when he informed people that he was going to write a Guatemalan cookbook, it "was received with utter disbelief that there was a cuisine at all." He concluded, "On the basis of my intuition, I knew that there must be a cuisine, notwithstanding the fact that none of the restaurants serving tourists was presenting the authentic typical foods."

Marks's cookbook, *False Tongues and Sunday Bread*, published in 1985, was the first cookbook aimed at foreign consumers and serves as a template for those that followed (Woodward 1999), like *Amalia's Guatemalan Kitchen: Gourmet Cuisine with a Cultural Flair* (Moreno-Damgaard 2012). These cookbooks highlight Guatemala's diversity, notably calling attention to Maya culture: "Guatemalan cuisine has a strong Mayan influence versus the Aztec," claims the author of *Land of Eternal Spring Wonderfully Exotic Recipes of Guatemala* (Gargus 2018). In the *Taste of Guatemalan Cuisine* (Nikolovski 2017: 4), the author essentially argues that Guatemalan cuisine rests on Maya culture, writing that "Native ingredients that were once cultivated by the Mayan ancient people combine with new items and techniques imported during Spanish colonial rule." By contrast, *El Poyo, la piedra y el nixtamal: Cocina al estilo de Guatemala para neófitos* (Wilson 2017) features straightforward recipes of 280 different Guatemalan dishes without engaging Maya culture tropes.

The publication in the last ten years of several cookbooks for non-Guatemalan consumers, special culinary recommendations in the INGUAT's current promotions, and the emergence of restaurants that offer new takes on Guatemalan food indicate Guatemalans' attitudes about their food and about sharing it are changing. With this relatively recent push to promote Guatemalan cuisine, it is still too early to gauge its success in attracting international interest to its distinctive dishes. Significantly, the employment of Maya trope in Guatemalan cuisine mirrors that found in the tourism industry in Guatemala (Little 2004) and is clearly a marketing ploy seen, as well, in the Yucatán (Castañeda 1996; Taylor 2018). Of course, Maya culture has profoundly influenced Guatemala, but that influence comes with complications, not unlike those described by Ayora-Díaz for Yucatán where gastronomic practices and attitudes "are marked by ambivalent cultural negotiations and are embedded in the unequal structure of national-regional-local power" (2012: 3). In Guatemala, this tension—power relations around food and particular tastes—has played out in the long rejection, by Guatemalans themselves, of promoting their own cuisine to foreigners. Where Maya culture helps Guatemalans and foreigners index Guatemala's distinctiveness for tourists, most food is not conceived of by Guatemalans as necessarily Mayan. My queries of Guatemalans about what is Maya food and what does Maya food taste like tended to draw quizzical looks. No one ever said, "Maya food is this" or that it tastes a specific way, with the exception of one dish, cooked greens (*ichaj* in Kaqchikel and K'ichee' of which there are several different kinds), which was considered distinctly *indigena* and was not eaten by non-Mayans. The rest was just Guatemalan food and much of it considered by all Guatemalans the stuff of home kitchens, marketplace stalls, and street food stands that I described earlier. Their attitude is that it is simply "our food," sustenance that sets them apart from their Mexican neighbors, yet, not worth promoting to outsiders, is now changing.

At the national level, INGUAT's current (2020) promotions include gastronomic tourism.[4] Unlike the foreigners writing cookbooks who highlight Maya culture as influencing the taste profiles of Guatemalan cuisine, the INGUAT descriptions are written with vague platitudes and are ambiguous, fragmented descriptions. For instance, "Why is Guatemalan gastronomy valuable? When you think of Guatemalan cuisine, we can imagine an incredible variety of aromas, combinations, colors, textures, and flavors. Diversity being one of its greatest gastronomic riches." INGUAT gastronomy webpages emphasize cuisines by region that are difficult for visitors to find, outside of eating in the marketplace. The dishes listed for "Sacatepéquez: Tamales colorados, Revolcado de Cabeza de Cerdo, Hilachas, Pepián, Caldo de Gallina, Molletes, Mole y Chiles Rellenos" or "Alta Verapaz: Tamal cobanero, Chirmol y Kak´ik" are common to Guatemalans but not to foreign visitors. Because there is a weak restaurant infrastructure for Guatemalan cuisine, experiencing these foods is a challenge for most tourists. However, these dishes and others are commonly sold by street vendors and small *comedores* to Guatemalan workers.

The INGUAT page concludes with a concrete statement about food as heritage:

> In Guatemala there are three dishes that have been declared Cultural Heritage of the Nation due to their long history of more than four centuries of existence and their fusion between ingredients originating in pre-Columbian Guatemala, mixed with Spanish-Arab products that the Europeans brought to the new world. These dishes are: *Jocón de carne de gallina, El Kaq´ík, El pepián, Plátanos en mole.*
>
> These dishes are linked to a national culinary tradition in a festive, tourist and scientific way, without leaving aside corn, which is the cultural wealth inherited from the Mayan civilization. Also, there are dishes for each tourist region, highlighting spices and unique combinations of the departments.

Unlike the cookbook authors who emphasized the importance of Maya culture on Guatemalan cuisine, the national tourism promotion diminishes it to highlight the fusion of different cultural food histories (Maya-Spanish-Arab), rather than focus on a distinctively Maya culinary tradition with its own pallet of flavors. There are, in fact, no Maya food restaurants in Guatemala. Not even in towns where the local population is mainly Maya. With so few restaurants aimed at attracting consumers looking for new culinary experiences (or converting those in the country to study and volunteer for service and humanitarian organizations), Guatemalan cuisine as heritage does not attract foodies or others seeking to experience Guatemala. Of all the projects related to tangible and intangible cultural heritage that are being developed and promoted by the Guatemalan office of UNESCO,[5] not one is related to gastronomy. Nonetheless, the INGUAT gastronomy pages indicate an awareness that culinary tourism is growing, and Guatemala offers a distinctive cuisine these tourists could experience.

Restaurants' Takes on Guatemalan Food

There are a relatively few restaurants in Antigua that promote food as heritage. Three restaurants of note, however, have taken distinctly different approaches to cultivating interest in Guatemalan cuisine. These restaurants work to make home-cooked meals or common street food palatable and aesthetically pleasing to foreigners' tastes and make Guatemalan cuisine an appealing meal out to Guatemalan diners. Although I would prefer visitors try food from the street vendors and the *comedores*, these restaurants offer eating experiences that are accessible to and without the negative stigmas associated with street food, as described earlier. Rather than list them by name, I label them as the "Traditional Restaurant," the "Aesthetic Restaurant," and the "Experimental Restaurant."

The Traditional Restaurant is nearly forty years old. It has grown and contracted in size with currently three different restaurants, all located near the Plaza Central. Meals are large and meat-heavy to cater to both Guatemalans' and tourists' eating out preferences. This restaurant serves versions of many of the dishes mentioned in the INGUAT gastronomy webpage, emphasizing Antigua versions, specifically. Of the three restaurants, the dishes mirrors most closely what is typically sold by the street vendors on a regular, daily basis. Although it is the main restaurant that tourists guided in groups and individuals may venture into, it primarily draws Guatemalan tourists from elsewhere in the country, neighboring El Salvadoran tourists, and the ever-increasing influx of tourists of Guatemalan origin who return to visit their country of origin. Local Antigüeños do not tend to eat there. The restaurant's menu includes enough alternatives to traditional Guatemalan cuisine, like large platters of grilled meats and large dining halls that can accommodate up to forty people, a typical tour group size. In my conversations with patrons who are Guatemalan tourists or Guatemalan emigrants returning to visit the country, a couple of themes emerge. The dominant one is a particular nostalgia for the food of their parents and grandparents. Emigrants, often, only have stories about this cuisine. Both, however, confess to either not knowing how to make the food or not being able to procure the ingredients to make it. The restaurant offers them a way to experience distinctly Guatemalan flavors.

Where the Traditional Restaurant appeals to Guatemalan food nostalgia and a Spanish colonial aesthetic, the Aesthetic Restaurant, which opened about six years ago, aims for a more cosmopolitan and international clientele. The recipes are not only wider in regional variety but also playful twists on what could be considered the greatest hits of Guatemalan cuisine. Unlike the Traditional Restaurant, which suggests grandmother's cooking and large portions, the Aesthetic Restaurant emphasizes plating and ambience. Small portions are creative combinations with reference to local and regional dishes across the country that index national heritage sentiments and blend colonial aesthetics and Maya culture in pleasing, nonconfrontational ways. For younger Guatemalan elites who are increasingly less likely to cook traditional meals and curious international independent visitors, the restaurant has become an important place to sample Guatemala food. It also makes the most direct nod to street food by offering *elotes asados* (roasted corn), *shuquitos* (hotdogs with guacamole), and various tamales, among other dishes, that are commonly sold by street vendors. Where tourists are hesitant to try food from street vendors and street vendors hesitant to sell it to them, the restaurant provides an accessible way to try these delicacies.

Compared to the other two restaurants, the Experimental Restaurant pushed Guatemalan culinary conventions the most. Although it, too, drew on culinary traditions that, in name, were similar to the other two restaurants and aimed for a similar chic Maya-modern décor scheme as the Aesthetic Restaurant, it closed after only a couple of years, despite its ideal location near the Plaza Central. The chef dispensed with convention and experimentally deconstructed versions of Guatemalan dishes that were plated in ways to give subtle, if any, clues to the original dish. For example, one dish, *tamalitos de viaje*, a tamale that travelers and workers would pack to eat as a snack and sold by women from baskets on the street, resembled nothing anyone would recognize. Interestingly, the food, irrespective of how it was presented, did reference the same flavors as the other restaurants.

What makes these three restaurants unique are the different ways in which they aim to separate traditional Guatemalan food from home kitchens and street food vendors with aesthetic presentations and connections to Guatemalan cultural features, be they related to Spanish colonial heritage, the primary orientation of the Traditional Restaurant, or indigenous Mayas in the décor of the Aesthetic Restaurant. Where street vendors may use identity in strategic ways—sometimes, Maya to signal to Maya consumers they themselves are Mayas and, sometimes, obscuring that same Maya identity when most consumers are not Maya—the restaurants draw on this contemporary culture to serve up food without their diners having to actually interact with Mayas or be challenged by the contradictions and social hierarchies that exist in Guatemalan society that appropriate Maya culture while discriminating against Mayas themselves.

Conclusions

Food, taste, and place converge in ways that illustrate class and ethnic differences and, ultimately, challenge collective notions of cultural culinary heritage. The debates that emerge from the confluence of food, public space, and heritage revolve around the aesthetics and flavors of street food in contrast to that which is considered traditional food served in a few select restaurants that are recognized as promoting food as national and cultural heritage. Street food vendors in Antigua serve a diverse base of workers in Antigua who, while catering to clients with limited budgets and time, are keen to make their food taste as conventionally Guatemalan as possible. These vendors perform a pragmatic function in a city where the typical restaurant is out of the price range of Guatemalans. Furthermore, when spending their hard-earned money on a dinner out with friends and family, Guatemalans have not tended to consider eating in restaurants that promote their own cuisine. Simply, Guatemalan cuisine is the food of home, of the worker's lunch and not, generally, the stuff of dinner out, especially, for wealthier Guatemalans.

Within the broader contours of Guatemalan cuisine attitudes, Guatemalans have an emerging interest to promote their food as heritage. In this context, what can be clearly regarded as culinary heritage and found for sale on the street and in marketplaces throughout the country is disarticulated from international visitors and, even, locals, because of a food politics that frames street food as dangerous—unsanitary and unsavory. Complicating this further is the incongruence between international visitors' expectations of and realities of Guatemalan food. The enchiladas *guatemaltecas* examples serve to highlight this disconnection but other foods could serve the same purpose, like *pepian*, which is quite distinctive from the similarly named dish found in Oaxaca (*pipian*).

While Guatemalan food may still be a hard sell for international visitors to Antigua, most Guatemalans do have affective, emotional connections to their cuisine, as do people throughout the world to their respective food traditions. Food is associated with mothers and grandmothers in the home and, contradictorily, with social class when workers eat street food. While they note that eating this food marks them as distinctively Guatemalan, the public consumption of Guatemalan food takes on class dimensions when eating out by the wealthy and, occasionally, by the middle class and the poor, means not eating Guatemalan food. Local attitudes about Guatemalan cuisine are changing, fortified with the awareness that tourists are interested in new food experiences and, especially, that Guatemalan emigrants want food that serves as memories of home, as well as being distinctly *not Mexican*. This is important, since most live-in ethnic enclaves in the United States are dominated by Mexican immigrants. Within these political and conflicting aesthetic contexts, some restaurants have found a niche to serve and promote Guatemalan cuisine. Ultimately, however, the shift from street to restaurant is as much about the class and social politics of eating out and, specifically, the places where someone eats indexes their socioeconomic class—market and street versus a sit-down restaurant with a menu. It is in this shift—street to fine restaurant—that Guatemalans and international visitors are beginning to recognize Guatemalan cuisine as cultural heritage and rethinking the public consumption of food as an indicator of social class.

Notes

1 https://visitguatemala.com/gastronomia/.
2 http://muniantigua.gob.gt/reglamentos-municipales/.
3 https://www.mintrabajo.gob.gt/index.php/dgt/salario-minimo.
4 https://visitguatemala.com/gastronomia/.
5 http://unescoguatemala.org/visita-nuestra-nueva-pagina/.

References

Asimov, E. (2000), "Copeland Marks, 78, Author of Books on Exotic Cuisine," *New York Times*, January 2.
Ayora-Diaz, S. I. (2012), *Foodscapes, Foodfields, and Identities in Yucatán*, London: Berghahn Books.

Ayora-Diaz, S. I., ed. (2019), *Taste, Politics, and Identities in Mexican Food*, London: Bloomsbury Academic.

Ayuntamiento de La Antigua, http://muniantigua.gob.gt/reglamentos-municipales/, last accessed August 2, 2020.

Bourdieu, P. (1984), *Distinction: A Social Critique of the Judgment of Taste*, trans. R. Nice, Cambridge, MA: Harvard University Press.

Brulotte, R. and M. A. Di Giovine, eds. (2014), *Edible Identities: Food as Cultural Heritage*, Surrey: Ashgate.

Castañeda, Q. (1996), *In the Museum of Maya Culture: Touring Chichén Itzá*, Minneapolis: University of Minneapolis Press.

Cedillo Gámez de Barrios, E. M. (2017), "Caracterización de las condiciones sanitarias de las ventas de alimentos en la vía pública del casco central del municipio de Antigua Guatemala" [Master's thesis], Antigua: Universidad Rafael Landívar, Facultad de Ciencias de la Salud.

Ferguson, P. P. (2004), *Accounting for Taste: The Triumph of French Cuisine*, Chicago: University of Chicago Press.

Food and Agriculture Organization (FAO) of the United Nations (2002), *Comida rápida, económica y también sana*. http://www.fao.org/spanish/newsroom/ac-tion/es_street.h tm, last accessed August 2, 2020.

Gargus, M. (2018), *Land of Eternal Spring Wonderfully Exotic Recipes of Guatemala*, Self-published, Amazon.com Services, LLC.

Haines, H. R. and C. A. Sammells (2010), *Adventures in Eating: Anthropological Experiences in Dining from Around the World*, Boulder: University Press of Colorado.

Hayden, T. B. (2014), "The Taste of Precarity: Language, Legitimacy, and Legality among Mexican Street Food Vendors," in R. De Cassia Vieira Cardoso, M. Companion, and S. R. Marras (eds.), *Street Food: Culture, Economy, Health, and Governance*, pp. 83–97, London: Routledge.

Instituto Guatemalteco de Turismo (INGUAT), https://visitguatemala.com/gastronomia/, last accessed on August 2, 2020.

Isaacs, B. (2014), "The Tastiest Food Is in the Small Steets: The Politics of Flavor and Nostalgia in Bangkok," in R. De Cassia Vieira Cardoso, M. Companion, and S. R. Marras (eds.), *Street Food: Culture, Economy, Health, and Governance*, pp. 83–97, London: Routledge.

Little, W. E. (2004), *Mayas in the Marketplace: Tourism, Globalization, and Cultural Identity*, Austin: University of Texas Press.

Little, W. E. (2008), "Crime, Maya Handicraft Vendors, and the Social Re/Construction of Market Spaces in a Tourism Town," in L. Cliggett and C. A. Pool (eds.), *Economies and the Trans- formation of Landscape*, pp. 267–90, Walnut Creek: Altamira Press.

Little, W. E. (2015), "Urban Economies and Spatial Governmentalities in the World Heritage City of Antigua," *Economic Anthropology* 2(1): 42–62.

Little, W. E. (2020), "Antigua Street Food Vendors," *Revista de CESLA: International Latin American Studies Review* 25: 209–32.

Man Kong Lum C. and M. de Ferrière le Vayer (2016), *Urban Foodways and Communication: Ethnographic Studies in Intangible Cultural Food Heritages Around the World*, Lanham: Rowman & Littlefield.

Marks, C. (1985), *False Tongues and Sunday Brea*, Lanham: Rowman & Littlefield.

Ministro de Trabajo y Previsión Social, Gobierno de Guatemala. https://www.mintrabajo .gob.gt/index.php/dgt/salario-minimo, last accessed August 2, 2020.

Montes de Oca Barrera, L. B. (2018), *Comida chatarra: Entre la gobernanza regulatoria y la simuación*, Mexico City: UNAM.

Moreno-Damgaard, A. (2012), *Amalia's Guatemalan Kitchen: Gourmet Cuisine with a Cultural Flair*, Saint Paul: Beaver's Pond Press.

Nikolovski, G. (2017), *Taste of Guatemalan Cuisine*, Morrisville: Lulu Press, Inc.

Oficina de la UNESCO en Guatemala. http://unescoguatemala.org/visita-nuestra-nueva-pagina/, last accessed August 2, 2020.

Patzán, J. M. (2019, May 3), "Comuna de Antigua Guatemala advierte que dará cumplimiento a acuerdo para evitar ventas ambulantes," *La Prensa Libre*, from https://www.prensalibre.com/ciudades/sacatepequez/comuna-de-antigua-guatemala-advierte-que-dara-cumplimiento-a-acuerdo-para-evitar-ventas-ambulantes/, last accessed May 28, 2019.

Ramirez, M. (2019, March 26), "Autoridades recuerdan que está prohibido la venta de carne de perro," *Canal Antigua*.

Sicán, J. (2017, October 5), "Concejo de Antigua Guatemala autoriza desalojar a vendedores de comida," *La Prensa Libre*, from https://www.prensalibre.com/ciudades/sacatepequez/concejo-de-antigua-guatemala-autoriza-desalojar-a-vendedoras-de-comida/, last accessed May 28, 2019.

Taylor, S. R. (2018), *On Being Maya and Getting By: Heritage Politics and Community Development in Yucatán*, Boulder: University of Colorado Press.

Vásquez-Medina, J. A., M. Bertrán, and F. X. Medina (2016), "Edible Heritage: Tradition, Health, and Ephemeral Consumption Spaces in Mexican Street Food," in C. M. Kong Lum and M. de Ferrière le Vayer (eds.), *Urban Foodways and Communication: Ethnographic Studies in Intangible Cultural Food Heritages Around the World*, pp. 139–53, Lanham: Rowman and Littlefield.

Wilson, C. (2017), *El Poyo, la piedra y el nixtamal: cocina al estilo de Guatemala para neófitos*, Guatemala: Carole Wilson Publisher.

Woodward, L. L. (1999), *Favorite Recipes from Guatemala*, Guatemala: Editorial Laura Lee.

11

Popular Urban Taste and Mass Culture

Chancho and *Terremoto* in Chile

Isabel Aguilera and Alejandra Alvear

Introduction: Food and Popular Culture in Chile

While researching Chilean cuisine, a discourse began to emerge that was full of images and emotions that made reference to the culinary dimension of popular urban culture. This discourse variously refers to (a) a type of place to go to eat and have a good time: *picadas* (joints); (b) certain recipes[1]: *arrollado*, *choripán*, and *terremoto*; and (c) a way of consuming food which is defined by abundant helpings, commensality, and a festive energy surrounding the act of eating. Altogether, it involves a way of enjoying food and drink that is linked to social class.

Picadas are eating establishments that are characterized by four elements: they serve food in large portions and offer quality meals with "homemade taste"; the relationship price/quality/quantity is highly valued; they target working-class people; and are well known largely through word of mouth.[2] These "little corner" shops are usually found in low-income neighborhoods near commercial districts, such as docks, train stations, and public markets. We observed that they have loyal customers, and, according to some informants, they go there to drink in good company, eat in large quantities, and sing along with the local street artists who come in and perform off the streets every day. In these spots, *chancho* (pork and its by-products) and *terremoto* have been institutionalized as iconic items of popular urban cuisine.

However, today *picadas* are no longer sites restricted to popular classes having gained visibility as representative of "authentic" urban working-class culture (Aguilera 2019). Thanks to their visibility and their process of commodification, the food and drink they serve, and related practices of consumption, they have achieved prominence and have become indexical of mass culture. Eaters from other social classes have begun to frequent the *picadas*. Also, *terremoto*—which was practically unheard of ten years ago—has become the most popular drink during national festivities surrounding Independence Day. As a result, a drink that had been previously limited to the space of *picadas* has become a staple at *ramadas*,[3] along with *choripán*, a pork-based recipe— and the two have become inseparable ever since. Currently, *arrollado*, *choripán*, and *terremoto* circulate within three different spheres: those who identify with the popular urban world and claim it as their own; they also appear on television, in newspapers, in internet forums on tourism, as well as in ads as "popular and traditional foods." Lastly, and presently, the *terremoto* occupies a prominent position in the imagination of Chile's national culture.

The aspects that we take into account are part of a popular culture that is broadly defined as a culture that emerges from modern processes of industrialization and urbanization, that is part of a market economy, and that is shared by a large number of people (Storey 2009). Partaking these aspects imply that these goods are part of a mass culture: they are industrially produced, they are promoted through mass media, and, thus, they become widely known. However, at the same time, they encompass aspects that are seen as part of working-class culture and are granted a lower social position and value (Storey 2009: 10). Therefore, here we are concerned with how a particular popular taste is detached from any conception of "purity" and, at the same time, claims for recognition as "authentic."

In this chapter, we argue that *arrollado*, *choripán*, and *terremoto* are mainstays of popular urban taste in Chile. We suggest that these foods can operate as indexical of taste because they are interwoven within the nationalist imagination, they are massively produced and consumed, they trigger shared feelings, and they hold symbolic effectiveness as class identity markers, more so in the case of pork consumption. Finally, we argue that this cultural relationship invites to articulate a critical view of the relationship between the processes of food industrialization and massification, and the consumer demand for "authenticity." This chapter is based on ethnographic fieldwork and the analysis of secondary sources (collections of poems and folkloric documents on Chilean cuisine). We conducted participant observation in *picadas* and *ramadas* during 2014, and intermittently between 2016 and 2018, in the city of Arica in the extreme north of Chile, in the city of Osorno in the south, and in the capital city, Santiago. However, the main focus of our discussion in this chapter will be on Santiago. Our fieldwork in Arica and Osorno will be used only to contextualize some later accounts in this chapter.

Taste and the Flavor of Social Class

Since our observations are focused on the field of restoration and practices of eating out, our conceptual discussion is rooted in the field of cultural consumption (Mato 2009; Wood and Muñoz 2007). The consumption practices we observed are found in a popular urban setting, leading our analysis to focus on the relationship between taste and social class. As we contend that taste, food, and consumption are all related to social status and prestige, the work of Pierre Bourdieu becomes one of our main points of reference (Bourdieu 1984; see also Cappeliez and Johnston 2013; Maxwell and DeSoucey 2016; Oleschuk 2017; Ward, Martens, and Olson 1999). We find this approach useful on three accounts: First, it systematically links the individual to the sociocultural sphere and, at the same time, calls for a nondeterminist approach. Secondly, it pays close attention to the relation between taste and the distribution and accumulation of capital. Thirdly, it sheds light on the demand for cultural goods from the perspective of taste (Gutiérrez 2002: 58).

In examining and discussing taste, Bourdieu demonstrates the tension existing between "structure" and "agency." For Bourdieu, taste can be considered a "manifested preference [that is] the affirmation of an inevitable difference" (1984: 56), as well as the ability to discern and to differentiate (Bourdieu 2010). Taste can also be defined as the ability to appropriate particular types of objects that express the subjects' class habitus (1984). Taste is never on either of the two ends of the spectrum. It is not subjective, it is not individual, it is not an automatic process, nor the agent is an automaton blindly obeying social forces. Tastes change and may, as in the case we examine, be appropriated by a variety of people and still be representative of a particular social class' preferences.

As Sutton points out (2010: 211), Bourdieu's work on taste seldom refers to the senses. However, his work supplements anthropological studies of the senses, precisely because it tends to consider taste as a phenomenon that is both social and individual. Moreover, according to Le Breton (2007: 268), taste is a "product of history, especially of the way in which human beings place themselves within the symbolic frame of culture." However, at the same time, it is an intimate and individual sense, a "sense of differentiation" (2007: 268) that encompasses knowledge (empirical and sensory), as well as affection, and that implies the appropriation of the world through the mouth. This means that eating—as a total sensory act—allows transcending the imagined boundaries of identity and alterity. Furthermore, Le Breton (2007: 286) argues that "taste is the sense of perception of flavors, but responds to a particular sensitivity that is marked by social and cultural belonging, and by the way a single individual adjusts, depending on the person's own knowledge of his or her own history"—and we may also add, by the knowledge and social imaginaries that emerge within his or her social class.

Taste is a systematic and long-lasting disposition. In other words, the members of a class demonstrate consistent preference for specific things. As we know, this disposition is shaped by the accumulation of different types of capital (cultural, social, symbolic, economic), and not by the price of things, a fact worth highlighting as we discuss the taste of the working classes in Santiago. The foods we are discussing are popular, but not cheap. Eating *arrollado* is not cheaper than eating other popular foods such as hotdogs and barbecued meats or foods at fast-food chains. A cup of *terremoto* costs the same as a pint of beer and a little less than a glass of Reserve red wine. The *choripán* is different, because some versions are definitely cheaper than others—although, as we suggest, taste preferences are far from determined by the price of the food, nor by its association with other popular cultural practices. In brief, *arrollado*, *choripán*, and *terremoto* are generally perceived as part of a popular urban universe, and taste preference for them is associated with working-class values establishing their position in the hierarchical structure of "cultural" items. This position, however, does not restrict its consumption to the working class. We have found that neither the definition of these foods as "popular," nor the labeling of others as "foreign" lineally determine their consumption and preference.

As *picadas* gained popularity, they turned into tourist attractions. According to some interviewees, this meant that *cuicos*[4] were coming to their "exclusive" spots, sometimes by themselves, but also frequently along with tourists (a practice now called "slum tourism"; see Dürr and Jaffe 2012). We observed that within groups of tourists, hosts describe the food and drinks as "exotic," in other words, as foods that do not belong to their own social class, but rather, they are foods of the other. We asked them straightforwardly why they take tourists to a *picada*. One of the responses they gave was that it is "fun," and these foods are also a novelty for them. That is, the hosts also become tourists when they venture out into low-income neighborhoods (Heldke 2003). Therefore, the ability to appreciate and consume foods that belong to the popular urban world is not exclusive to the working classes, and the meaning of those foods change. Once they become part of mass culture, they are available to be appropriated by other groups, as *cuicos* and tourists do.

Individuals with consumption practices that unsettle the established class habitus/ food preferences can be called "cultural omnivores." We find it useful to understand cases in which the agent's class does not coincide with what theoretically "should be" his or her cultural consumption preferences, and his or her taste explores otherness and the exotic. According to Cappeliez and Johnston (2013), this omnivore inclination reveals a form of cultural consumption that appropriates both the "high" and the "low," high and popular culture. The omnivore thesis proposes that to demonstrate high-status people are no longer exclusively driven toward goods that are considered to belong to "high culture," but they can demonstrate their ability and disposition to appreciate and recognize the significance of a wide range of types of food in which "authenticity" is particularly cherished. The omnivore tendency explains the transgressive appreciation and consumption of *arrollado*, *choripán*, and *terremoto*, as well as other meals recognized as part of mass culture (Ward, Martens, and Olsen 1999).

Terremoto, Sweet Homeland

The *terremoto* is a fresh, sweet beverage[5] made of white *pipeño* wine, pineapple sorbet and a touch of grenadine cocktail syrup, fernet or pisco. It is served in 400 milliliter plastic cups or glasses, and drunk through a straw. Although there is a scoop of sorbet in it, a spoon is not necessary because the aim is to allow the sorbet to melt into the wine a few minutes after stirring them. Given that the *terremoto* has gained recognition, and has become a central part of national festivities, sellers have created a nonalcoholic version of the drink, the "*Terremotín*," which is a combination of fruit juice and pineapple sorbet aiming to initiate boys and girls into this drink.

The name of this drink, which means earthquake, evidently refers to the earth's movements and, as we mention ahead, to the sensation of being drunk. Some claim today that it was created in the context of the 1985 earthquake, but others suggest that the drink was created farther in the past as Chile has been historically shaken by many earthquakes.[6] It is not an overstatement to say that earthquakes have destroyed and built Chile, both materially and symbolically. This history of earthquakes and their consequences has shaped the need for safety and the design of building and urban development plans, thus the ways in which buildings and neighborhoods are constructed, and the manners in which people use spaces to create social and community life (Lawner 2011). From this perspective, *terremoto* drinks implicitly embrace a national theme that has fostered its commercial success and its role as marker of identity.

It's Not Wine, It's Pipeño

In 2015, September 4 was declared National Wine Day. An unexpected controversy emerged from this celebratory day regarding which drink truly represents national identity. While acknowledging the important role that wine plays in national culture, searching for legitimacy, some emphasized the historical relevance of pisco consumption, and others called attention to the pre-Hispanic origins of *chicha*.[7] At the same time, we have observed during fieldwork that wine was good to drink, but not good to think. Patrons at the *picadas* confirmed that they drink red wine but did not talk about it. Their narratives focused on the *terremoto*. They said that typicality, traditionality, and national identity would be embodied by the *terremoto* and would therefore also entered the battle for recognition as the national drink.[8] However, in contrast to arguments that, on the basis of precedence and consumption, opposed wine to other drinks, the disputes that we witnessed at the *picadas* associated wine consumption with social class. They perceived National Wine Day as a *cuico* celebration, and they considered the possession of wine knowledge as snobbish.[9] In contrast, despite the fact that *terremoto* is made with wine, *picada* attendees claim that it is "more Chilean than Chile's own chicha." For them, it is, in fact, a popular, traditional, authentic drink. As a client at the *picada* stated: "It's not wine, it's pipeño."

Pipeño dates back to the eighteenth century and its name is derived from the barrels in which it was stored: the *pipa*. *Pipeño* was made from *País* grapes or *Criollas*,[10] "which were treaded by the feet of men, fermented in open wineries and preserved in *pipas* made of Chilean oak" (Lacoste et al. 2015: 91). During the nineteenth century, Chile had undergone the process of adopting and replacing local varieties of grapes with those imported from France. This process had an impact on the methods of wine production, as well as on purchasing cost. According to Lacoste et al. (2015), *pipeño* had survived this tremendous transformation because it was considered to be marginal, "typically consumed by peasants and the poor" and, due to that, ruling groups in Chile developed no interest in it. It was never produced for the elite, but rather its production remained geared toward working-class people, and its consumption remained linked to expressions of popular social life, "of parties and celebrations that peasant farmers enjoy having [. . .] an atmosphere of socializing, of romantic love encounters, points of contact and divergence, of dramas and memorable events" (Lacoste et al. 2015: 93).

Pipeño is an unfiltered and unclarified wine, considered to be rustic and unsophisticated, which does not share the same reputation as wine from imported grapes. Thus, in erasing it from the hegemonic history of Chilean wine, *pipeño* has remained confined to a social imaginary and history of mass popular culture. Hence, it remains attached to the imagination of "popular" culture and subordinated as the Other's wine (Cervasco 2014). At the same time, however, its history reveals the resistance of the subjects' popular culture to hegemonic constructions of taste preferences. At the beginning of the twenty-first century, *pipeño* reappeared as an icon of national identity, this time in *terremoto*, a drink in which meanings that were previously associated to *pipeño* converge: a strong connection to the working class, a festive mode of consumption, and a strong identification with the "rustic." However, significant changes can be observed. *Terremoto* makes no reference to rural life, and none of its ingredients is particularly valued for either method or place of production. On the contrary, the popular claim is that it can be made with any *pipeño*. Notably, at *ramadas* they use unidentified pipeños bottled in 5 liter plastic jugs with no label; and the same lack of value of origin is given to the pineapple sorbet used to fix the drink.

The Sweetness of Misfortune

According to the website of a well-known *picada* called *El Hoyo*, terremoto was created by accident. Right after the 1985 earthquake hit Santiago, a group of foreign journalists came to the *picada*. It was hot out and "our classic *Pipeño* was served, and they asked for pineapple sorbet to be added to their drinks [. . .] when they tried it one of them exclaimed, 'This is what I call an Earthquake!'"[11] Another origin story was found on TripAdvisor: "apparently some *gringos* asked for *Pipeño* and because they were boiling hot, they asked for pineapple sorbet, and that is how the base of this Chilean drink came to be."[12] In the different origin stories of this beverage that we have collected, two aspects are repeated: the time frame and the foreigners represented as "gringos," that is, white North Americans or Europeans who are not fluent in Spanish, nor have a grasp on the cultural codes and could, therefore, easily run into social misunderstandings.

The presence of these characters takes us to a stage in which tragedy, impersonated by the earthquake, takes on layers of a comedy in which the chance meeting of different people leads to cultural misunderstanding and the creation of something unique. People laugh as the narrator tells this story highlighting and apprizing the idiosyncrasy of popular cultural responses: to laugh at one's own misfortune, to be quick-witted and creative, and to respond humorously to the needs of others. The original story of the *terremoto*, as well as the way it is told, illustrates a bittersweet way of experiencing the world. On the one hand, the name evokes the shaking movements of the earth and its severe consequences; on the other hand, it denotes the effects the drink has on the body: it is devastating and "makes people shaky." According to a *picada* customer, the *terremoto* is famous for "being able to shake the foundations of even the most experienced drinker," and for provoking undesired drunkenness. They claim that the sweetness of the drink is to blame. Because it is sweet, the drinker barely notices the alcohol, which encourages further fast drinking. In other words, it is the pineapple sorbet that is to blame.[13]

The *terremoto* can be bought and consumed all year long, although it is more frequently consumed in the spring and summer, especially in September at the *ramadas* that are set up during national Independence Day festivities. The names of the *ramadas* change year after year, and they tend to use wordplay and puns based on mass culture to convey some sort of amusing anecdotal summary of the events of the year, for example: "Terremotón Go . . . catch your terremoto," which refers to a popular online game (Pokemon GO); "The Terremoto Master" invokes a Columbian soap opera that a few years earlier was a big hit; "Terremotos that Spea" summons a locally well-known television program. In less than a decade, national Independence Day celebration became linked to *terremoto* and, in consequence, to Chilean identity. This resulted in restricting the consumption of *terremoto* to a specific date, place, and social context. However, this restriction was promptly contested by the *picadas*: the phrase "Here! Terremoto all year long!!" could be read on signs hanging outside them, along with the day's specials that were proposed to passers-by, underlining the difference in meanings between something that constitutes a fad and something that is part of a way of life and stands the test of time.

We observed how *terremoto* was consumed in different ways. Customers might go to *picadas* just to have a terremoto, on its own, without a meal. During warmer months, it is usually drunk as an aperitif at the beginning of the meal. During autumn and winter, people drink it as a dessert, to complete meal. At the *ramadas*, people tend to drink it while standing or walking around, not integrated into a sequence of meal courses.

Chancho: *Choripán* and *Arrollado*

The *arrollado*, which is described by Pereira Salas as "cooked pork, in pieces, mixed with egg and rolled in *Malaya* or pig skin" (2007: 230), is considered to have a rural origin[14] and has always been present at workers' celebrations. It refers to a nineteenth-century social imaginary, to times of migration from the countryside to the cities, and to urban poverty represented as a bittersweet life, where most of life's sweet moments are found in festivities and food. This discourse coincides with the history of Chilean cuisine that seems to have permeated into common knowledge. Nevertheless, some consumers argue that this food is connected to sentiments: they consider the *arrollado* eaten at *picadas* to be "home cooked," "prepared with loving hands," and "filling"; it is ideal for sharing with friends after work, or during celebrations with extended family members. The *arrollado* comes in two forms, both characterized by abundance; it can be served whole as the main dish with a side portion of boiled potatoes, or it can be served as an appetizer cut into slices.

In turn, *choripán* is a sort of hotdog made with a barbecued chorizo served in a bun. At the *ramadas*, it fits under the category of "fast-food"; in other words, it is seen as part of group of foods—which includes the *terremoto*—that are consumed as snacks. However, its cultural value is not tied to the *ramadas*, nor to a particular history, as is the case of the *arrollado*. Instead, it is associated with collective forms and moments of consumption filled with sentiments and nostalgia: family feasts on weekends, birthday celebrations, Chile's national soccer team games, events that bring people together, where the act of warmhearted and festive commensality comes first. *Choripán* consumption is a new "tradition," but it is widespread and crosses all social classes: as our friend John puts it: "Absolutely everyone eats barbecue and choripán is a staple at barbecues."

Since *choripán* is consumed by all social classes, there is no single recipe to cook it. Some say that "there are chorizos and [then some] chorizos," which means that as consumers they make the distinction—especially in the south of Chile—between industrial chorizos, "typically consumed by the people from Santiago," and artisanal chorizos. This distinction reveals the appreciation of the sausage quality, which affirms regional differences, and yet, at the same time, highlights differences regarding access to foods. While industrial chorizo is sold in large packages (by kilogram), artisanal sausages are found in packages of two to six pieces which are more expensive than the industrial ones. We shall now take a look at the part pork holds in popular consumption and take its symbolic role into account.

Notes on Producing and Consuming Pork in Chile

Pork is one of the three types of meat that is most consumed in Chile. Since the 1970s, there has been a significant increase in pork consumption hitting its peak in 2008, surpassing beef consumption. In 2010, the annual amount of pork consumed per person reached 24.4 kilograms, and in 2011 it reached its highest point at 25.6 kilograms per inhabitant.[15] The Association of Pork Producers of Chile states that during 2018 pork consumption reached 314,000 tons, the equivalent to 21 percent of the total consumption of meats.[16]

Pork consumption varies depending on by-products and time of the year. According to the National Association of Industrial Cured Meats, during the second half of the year, the consumption of pork sausage and chorizos rises, "reaching four thousand tons more than during the first six months, [and] this is due to the high level of consumption of these products during the celebrations, of the National Independence Day festivities."[17] Unfortunately, we lack data that cross-references consumption, the type of product and time of the year, but some information we found may help to visualize where chorizos and *arrollados* are positioned. According to a survey conducted by the Chile government, regarding the first semester of 2018, pork by-products that were primarily manufactured were wieners (31.86 percent), followed by mortadella and cold cuts (12.12 percent) and, in third place, sausages such as *longanizas*, chorizos, and *choricillos* (baby sausages) (11.05 percent). *Arrollado* production is about 3.34 percent of the national production, occupying eighth place.[18] This data confirms the widespread growth in pork consumption, and particularly the consumption of cold meats in Chile. Moreover, the significant increase in consumption during the second semester of each year coincides with its location at the heart of the national Independence Day festivities.

Chancho as a Symbol

As already mentioned, the foods that we are discussing are massively consumed and, at the same time, highly meaningful. Their meaning depends on the symbolic framework in which they are set in the form of recipes and where they are highlighted as products derived from pork—an animal that incorporates multiple meanings. The Spaniards brought pigs to Chile around 1541, and, according to Pereira Salas (2007), they were present in the origin of national gastronomic history. Legend has it that two small pigs were "saved" by Inés de Suarez, the wife of the conqueror Pedro de Valdivia in the middle of a great battle fought between Spaniards and Mapuche[19] in the city of Santiago. That heroic act also managed to preserve some wheat and a few chickens, which would later become the foundation of our Mestizo cuisine (Montecino 2015). Indeed, the taste for pigs crossed all racial borders and was adopted by the Mapuche during the colonial period. According to Gustave Verinoy' memoires, a man who worked on the expansion of the railway into Mapuche territory toward the end of the nineteenth century, pork was widely consumed by indigenous people (Pereira Salas 2007).

The *arrollado* appears as a typical dish in the history of Chilean cuisine during the republican period (Pereira Salas 2007), and Plath provides a description of *ramadas* in mid-nineteenth century: "there were pieces of pork on display on flat baskets, it was well-seasoned and wrapped; in large casseroles huge colored arrollados; fragrant *malayas*; spiced up pig's feet" (2015: 64). *Arrollado* and chorizo also appear in compilations of popular poetry; for example, in the "Pig Keeper's Toast," *arrollado* is mentioned and, surprisingly, the chorizo is associated with upper classes' taste: "The chorizo is distinguished and fancied by the rich. By those towns and valleys" (Lenz 1894: 617).

In addition to their mention and description in multiple narratives about Chilean cuisine, pork and its by-products trigger and support various popular social imaginaries. Its consumption is associated with ritual festivities and celebrations, such as San Juan and with other saint's days, which turns it into a symbol of extravagance; that is, of profusion and excessive spending; of abundance (prosperity and well-being), and food security (Montecino 2014). The connection between pork, abundance and excess is such that it is included in colloquial language as an adjective: "*pasarla chancho*," loosely translated to "having a pork time," which, in turn, means having a great time; "*comer como chancho*," translates as "eating like a pig," and it means to eat in excess. Popular, colloquial language contains many different uses of the term *chancho*.

In addition, in the rural social imaginary, pigs are identified as feminine. For instance, through the figure of the piggy bank: that which is capable of saving and accumulating. According to some folk tales, the pig may be a good ally to humans, precisely because it is considered a provider. This is the case of the legend of the "amazing pig": while performing the activities of a horse, the pig was able to carry out tests asked for by a father as a condition to give his daughter's hand away in matrimony, leading to the joy and wealth of a young man who had been loathed by his own parents as a child (Pino 1960). This story brings together a few positive connotations that pigs have in the Chilean social imaginary: it is a sign of good fortune and denotes treasures. However, this animal is also seen as having a dark side, and some see it as a diabolic figure with the power to cast spells and turn a human's head into that of a pig (Montecino 2015).

Finally, we cannot overlook the association between pig and fat. According to Poulain (2012), the logic behind fat tends to fall under three categories: the first is linked to those who have suffered hunger and who see a form of "social revenge" in eating fat, which is perceived as beneficial; the second is related to the fear of fat, given its modern dietary consequences; and the third poses that people adjust their fat consumption according to different social situations. In Chile, the consumption of pork fat occurs under the first and third categories. This is because pork consumption is linked with abundance and spending, but also because it's peak is related with a particular social context: the national Independence Day festivities, in which sociability demands its consumption to reaffirm the social identity of the person who consumes it.

Conclusion: Popular Culture and the Politics of Authenticity

The *chancho* and the *terremoto* comprise a stable and meaningful duo in popular taste, although both elements are not always together, nor do they need each other to exist and to be valued. Their co-occurrence is justified by interweaving factors: preference, availability, and price. *Terremoto, arrollado,* and *choripán* are mostly available at *picadas* and *ramadas*. Consumers eat "whatever is offered" in places where they choose to go, and they frequent these places because they like their culinary offer; additionally, because they enjoy the "atmosphere" and what it implies: direct contact with popular urban culture and with national identity.

The three meals discussed have different origins in space and time. *Arrollado* is the only one that dates far back to colonial times, while the *choripán's* time of origin is unknown, and the drink *terremoto* came into existence at the end of the twentieth century. The *arrollado* comes from an acknowledged rural background, while *terremoto* and *choripán* are both urban. Chorizos, pineapple sorbet, and pork used to prepare *arrollado* and *terremoto* frequently come from the food industry. Although artisanal chorizo and *pipeño* exist, they are not highly demanded. Hence, we suggest that these meals and drink cannot be neatly situated on a long historical timeline of the origins of Chile's national cuisine, and they are not exclusively consumed by the working classes. Mass consumption, industrial production, their embedment in mass culture, and their recognition as part of an "authentic" popular urban cuisine are the aspects they have in common.

The characterization just listed allows us to critically reflect on the "authenticity" of these items. Cappeliez and Johnston (2013) observe that the search for food authenticity goes hand in hand with the mistrust of industrial foods, mass production, and foods that are consumed by large numbers of people. From this standpoint, what is perceived as very common would be considered unauthentic, and yet our fieldwork reveals the contrary. Despite the industrial origin of the chorizo and of pineapple sorbet, and also the incorporation of popular urban cuisine into mass culture, *picadas, ramadas,* and the culinary choices they offer are not perceived as unauthentic.

However, certain understandings of popular culture tend to privilege the question of authenticity. Whenever what is considered popular is defined as a "culture of the people for the people," popular culture appears as a pure production, disconnected from commercial activity, untouched by the dominant culture. This kind of approach tends to standardize popular culture with a romanticized version of working-class culture and of popular subjects who are represented as mildly contaminated by foreign customs and removed from modern rationality (Zukin 2008; Lalvani 1995). This romantic social imaginary can be observed in our research when analyzing what is said in reference to the *picadas* and low-income neighborhoods. However, it does not apply to the food itself. The popular dishes that we observed are not perceived as artisanal, nor as exclusive to the working class; it is not seen as ancient, and much less as pure. In fact, *terremoto* is popular because it is impure, because it emerges from the funny and friendly encounter between gringos and locals. Those who are fond of the *chancho* and the *terremoto* are well aware of the industrial origin of these items; they know that *picadas* are shown on television, and that large pork producing companies sponsor the *ramadas*. Nevertheless, this does not result in nostalgia, or into a discourse on cultural appropriation, nor does it become a demand for exclusivity. In this sense, popular urban culture is not differentiated from mass culture, and the latter does not appear as a disgrace that places the working-class traditional ways of life at risk. The case that we have discussed is an invitation to critically think about interpretations of mass culture as a force that, through commodification, *tempt* the working class and pushes it toward standardized ways of cultural consumption (Storey 2009). In contrast, our discussion seeks to encourage reflection on the malleability of tastes, as well as on the relation that exists between popular urban taste and mass culture, without presuming that cultural change entails the loss of authenticity.

Notes

1　*Arrollado* (or *arrollado huaso*) is a meal prepared with different parts of the pig that are chopped up and seasoned, then rolled up in pig skin and cooked in boiling water. *Terremoto* is an alcoholic beverage made of *pipeño* wine (made with ordinary grapes) and pineapple sorbet. *Choripán* is a chorizo sandwich common in Chile and other South American countries.

2　These characteristics are not shared by all of the eating establishments where we studied, and their definition is subject to negotiation among the clientele. For example, the price of some dishes may be considered too expensive for the place to be considered a *picada*. Also, their celebrity beyond working classes may undermine their identity as *picada*. Yet, if they sell *chancho* and *terremoto*, some customers and the press continue referring to them as *picada*. Additionally, the meaning of the term establishes the historical link between these eating establishment, working-class preferences, and a culinary performance that can be locally recognized as "popular."

3　*Ramadas* are short-lived food stands set up during the celebration of Chile's national independence. They are set one next to the other in parks and other open areas in the city, making up a large "fair" where consumers can eat, play, dance, and, of course, drink.

4　*Cuico* is a Chilean term that refers to social classes. *Cuicos* are people who belong to the upper class, the wealthy, and/or people who have refined customs. In the spoken language of our informants and of our secondary sources, they appear as the opposite of the frequent clients that go to the *picadas*; they are the opposite end of popular urban bohemia and, in general, of the working class.

5　Freshness and sweetness tend to be linked to feminized consumption. However, this association is not inferred in the consumption of *terremoto*. On the contrary, it is considered a masculine consumer item.

6　Throughout the twentieth century, Chile was hit by five earthquakes over 7 degrees in the Richter scale. The last major earthquake occurred in February 2010, the strongest registered in history, with a magnitude of 8.8 degrees on the Richter scale (Lawner 2011).

7   Beverage produced from fermented fruit and cereals.

8   According to the study on *Chilenidad* (Chilean Identity) carried out by GFK Adimark in 2006, 70 percent of the survey respondents recognized the *terremoto* as the alcoholic beverage that "best identifies Chileans." https://www.gfk.com/filea dmin/user_upload/country_one_pager/CL/GfK_Estudio_Chilenidad_2016.pdf, last accessed on March 3, 2020.

9   The connection between wine and *cuicos* is such that in a picada in the north of Chile, sellers created a drink they called "*terremoto cuico,*" as it included rosé wine instead of *pipeño.*

10 An endemic grape variety that was popularly consumed in Chile until the introduction of French varieties.

11 http://www.elhoyo.cl/Terremoto (Consulted 15/04/2016). Link no longer available.

12 https://www.tripadvisor.cl/ShowUserReviews-g294305-d807739-r145314122-El_Ho yo-

13 Pineapple sorbet is readily found and industrially produced. It is sold in every supermarket, and there are many different brands and packaging.

14 This is why it is sometimes called "arrollado huaso." *Huaso*, as described by Lenz (1910: 384) is a "Chilean farmer, a farmhand or cowboy, in general it refers to any lower-class man who does not work in the city."

15 https://www.emol.com/noticias/economia/2011/04/14/476004/chile-registro-la-mayor-cifra-historica-en-consumo-de-carne-el-2010.html, last accessed March 10, 2020.

16 http://www.asprocer.cl/industria/analisis-sectorial/, last accessed March 10, 2020.

17 https://www.biobiochile.cl/noticias/economia/actualidad-economica/2018/09/20/vie nesas-son-el-producto-estrella-cada-chileno-come-16-kilos-de-embutidos-al-ano.sh tml, last accessed on March 10, 2020.

18 https://www.odepa.gob.cl/estadisticas-del-sector/estadisticas-productivas/attachment/ cuadro-de-resultados-encuesta-de-industria-de-cecinas-2018s1, last accessed March 10, 2020.

19 The Mapuche are indigenous peoples who inhabited the central-southern area of Chile's current national territory before the arrival of the conquerors.

References

Aguilera, I. (2019), "Guachaquismo: clase, etnicidad y nación. Una mirada desde El Hoyo," in A. Vera, I. Aguilera, and R. Fernández (eds.), *Nación, Otredad, Deseo: producción de la diferencia en tiempos multiculturales*, pp. 31–65, Santiago: Ediciones UAHC.

Bourdieu, P. (1984), *Distinction: A Social Critique of the Judgement of Taste*, Cambridge: Harvard University Press.

Bourdieu, P. (2010), *El sentido social del gusto*, Madrid: Siglo XXI.

Cappeliez, S. and J. Johnston (2013), "From Meat to 'Real-Deal' Rotis: Exploring Everyday Culinary Cosmopolitanism," *Poetics* 41: 433–55.

Cevasco, M. E. (2014), *Diez lecciones sobre estudios culturales*, Santiago: LOM.

Dürr, E. and R. Jaffe (2012), "Theorizing Slum Tourism: Performing, Negotiating and Transforming Inequality," *European Review of Latin American and Caribbean Studies* 94: 113–23.

Gutiérrez, B. A. (2002), *Las prácticas sociales: una introducción a Pierre Bourdieu*, Madrid: Tierradenadi.

Heldke, L. (2003), *Exotic Appetites. Ruminations of a Food Adventurer*, London: Routledge.

Lacoste, P., A. Castro, F. Briones, and F. Mujica (2015), "The Pipeño: Story of a Typical Wine Southern Central Valley of Chile," *Idesia* 3: 87–96.

Lalvani, S. (1995), "Consuming the Exotic Other," *Critical Studies in Mass Communication* 12: 263–86.

Lawner, M. (2011), "Los arquitectos, de terremoto en terremoto," in C. Cares, W. Imilan, and P. Vergara (eds.), *Reconstrucción(es) Sociedad Civil: Experiencias de reconstrucción en Chile post 27F desde la sociedad civil*, pp. 137–50, Santiago: INVI.

Le Breton, D. (2007), *El sabor del mundo. Una antropología de los sentidos*, Buenos Aires: Nueva visión.

Lenz, R. (1894), *Sobre la poesía popular impresa de Santiago de Chile: contribución al folklore chileno*, Santiago: Anales de la Universidad de Chile.

Mato, D. (2009), "All Industries Are Cultural," *Cultural Studies* 3: 70–87.

Maxwell, R. and M. DeSoucey (2016), "Gastronomic Cosmopolitanism: Supermarket Products in France and the United Kingdom," *Poetics* 56: 85–97.

Montecino, S. (2014), *La olla deleitosa*, Santiago: Catalonia.

Montecino, S. (2015), *Mitos de Chile. Enciclopedia de seres, apariciones y encantos*, Santiago: Catalonia.

Oleschuk, M. (2017), "Foodies of Color: Authenticity and Exoticism in Omnivorous Food Culture," *Cultural Sociology* 11: 217–33.

Pereira Salas, E. (2007 [1943]), *Apuntes para la historia de la cocina chilena*, Santiago: Uqbar.

Pino, Y. (1960), *Cuentos folklóricos* en *Chile*, Santiago: Ediciones Universidad de Chile.

Poulain, J.-P. (2012), *Dictionnaire des cultures alimentaires*, Paris: PUF.

Plath, O. (2015), *Geografía gastronómica de Chile. Artículos reunidos 1943–1994*, Santiago: Ediciones Biblioteca Nacional.

Storey, J. (2009), *Cultural Theory and Popular Culture: An Introduction*, London: Pearson Education.

Sutton, D. E. (2010), "Food and the Senses," *Annual Review of Anthropology* 39: 209–23.

Ward, A., L. Martens, and W. Olsen (1999), "Consumption and the Problem of Variety: Cultural Omnivorousness, Social Distinction and Dining Out," *Sociology* 33: 105–27.

Wood, N. T. and C. L. Muñoz (2007), "'No Rules, Just Right' or Is It? The Role of Themed Restaurants as Cultural Ambassadors," *Tourism and Hospitality Research* 3–4: 242–55.

Zukin, S. (2008), "Consuming Authenticity," *Cultural Studies* 22: 724–48.

Web References

Asociación Gremial de Productores de Cerdos de Chile (Asprocer) (n.d.). Available online: http://www.asprocer.cl/industria/analisis-sectorial/, last accessed March 10, 2020.

Canales, A. (2018), "Cuadro de Resultados - Encuesta de Industria de Cecinas 2018S1," ODEPA, November 26. Available online: https://www.odepa.gob.cl/estadisticas-del-sec tor/estadisticas-productivas/attachment/cuadro-de-resultados-encuesta-de-industria -de-cecinas-2018s1, last accessed March 10, 2020.

Diaz, F. (2018), "Vienesas son el producto estrella: cada chileno come 16 kilos de embutidos al año," *Bío Bío*, September 20. Available online: https://www.biobiochile.c

l/noticias/economia/actualidad-economica/2018/09/20/vienesas-son-el-producto-est
rella-cada-chileno-come-16-kilos-de-embutidos-al-ano.shtml, last accessed March 10,
2020.

El Hoyo, "Terremoto," Santiago. Available online: http://www.elhoyo.cl/Terremoto, last
accessed April 15, 2016.

EMOL (2011), "Chile registró la mayor cifra histórica en consumo de carne el 2010."
EMOL, April 14. Available online: https://www.emol.com/noticias/economia/2011/0
4/14/476004/chile-registro-la-mayor-cifra-historica-en-consumo-de-carne-el-2010.
html, last accessed March 10, 2020.

GFK (2016), "Estudio chilenidad 2016," 13 September, Santiago. Available online: https:/
/www.gfk.com/fileadmin/user_upload/country_one_pager/CL/GfK__Estudio_Chil
enidad_2016.pdf, last accessed April 3, 2020.

Lenz, R. (1910), *Diccionario Etimológico*, Santiago: Universidad de Chile.

Tripadvisor (2012), "El mejor costillar de Santiago . . .," Santiago. Available online https
://www.tripadvisor.cl/ShowUserReviews-g294305-d807739-r145314122-El_Hoyo-Sa
ntiago_Santiago_Metropolitan_Region.html, last accessed March 4, 2020.

Part III

The Global-Local Politics of Taste

12

Foreign Influences in Polish Culinary Taste during the Twentieth Century

Katarzyna J. Cwiertka

Introduction

The political landscape of twentieth-century Poland is highly dynamic. Following the annexation of the Polish territory by Austria, Prussia, and Russia in 1795, the country disappeared from the world's map for over a century, only to reemerge as the Second Polish Republic in 1918. It lasted only for a meager two decades, when it fell victim to the German and Soviet invasions, which resulted, once again, in the loss of independence. The westward advance of the Red Army at the end of the Second World War ultimately led to the establishment of the Polish People's Republic (1947–89), a communist satellite state of the Soviet Union. Finally, the Poles left the twentieth century as citizens of the (Third) Polish Republic, with the brand-new constitution approved in the referendum of 1997.

This political hotchpotch did not leave Polish culinary culture unaffected. In fact, as I will argue in the course of this chapter, the developments of the twentieth century functioned as a catalyst in the formation of what we might call "a Polish taste." The quotation marks are necessary, because the now-taken-for-granted idea that food preferences and styles of eating reflect national identity is not a given, but a modern construct, which is closely linked to the rise of the nation-state and nationalism (Anderson 1991; Palmer 1998). After all, the most salient feature of a national cuisine is bridging regional, ethnic, and class differences that had for centuries differentiated eating habits of the population of the national territory. Tied to the conceptions of national history and cultural heritage, national cuisines tend to acquire a sense of permanence and authenticity, which but rarely are confirmed by historical records (Cwiertka 2006, 2020).

Mainstream depictions of Polish cuisine often take the shape of an inventory of flagship food items considered representative (*A Foreigner's Guide to Polish Cuisine* 2014). While historians can delineate the origins of those dishes and link them with specific communities, many of them only relatively recently acquired truly national characteristics, meaning that the entire population willingly identifies them as their own. As historian Błażej Brzostek rightfully pointed out, what we nowadays refer to as "Polish cuisine" is an amalgamation of four strands of distinct culinary traditions, each representing different social groups that had made up the Polish population until the mid-twentieth century: peasantry and the working class, landed gentry, urban middle class, and different minorities, of which the largest one were the Jews (Brzostek 2010: 17).

In an attempt to define Polish cuisine, culinary historian Jarosław Dumanowski underlined another factor—regional differences—that must be taken into consideration when discussing "Polish" taste in its national dimension. Dumanowski (2019) argues that regional variations are often overlooked in mainstream depictions of Polish food and explains that part of the problem is the damage that half a century of communist rule has inflicted on culinary variety. He lists food shortage, forced resettlement of populations from one region to another, and the propagation of ideologically driven, uniform mass-catering formula among the main reasons behind the decline of local culinary traditions across Poland during the second half of the twentieth century.

Another problem that Dumanowski (2019) identifies in mainstream depictions of Polish food is the image of heavy fare centered on meat. It not only is inaccurate but also detracts importance from the age-old practice of eating freshwater fish and crustaceans. To begin with, the majority of the population simply could not afford large quantities of meat on a daily basis, but even among affluent social classes the habit of regular fish consumption was engrained in the fasting calendar dictated by the Catholic faith (Michalik and Łebkowski 1996: 294). If we were to pinpoint common taste denominators that have the long-standing roots across all social strata and across different regions of what nowadays constitutes a Polish territory, it would most probably be extensive use of fermented vegetables and grains, along with dried mushrooms and smoked foods. Originally applied primarily for its practical application aimed at preservation, smoking and fermenting have in time contributed to a distinctive taste that we might identify as "Polish." For example, a distinctive flavor of Polish sausages derives from the application of smoking in the process of their manufacture.

Foreign influences feature prominently in the depictions of Polish cuisine that can be found in culinary encyclopedias and other publications that explore the history of food and eating on the Polish territory (Kuti 2003; Meller 1994a; Szymanderska 2006: 1–3). This is hardly surprising. After all, most national cuisines are grounded on the combination of long-standing practices characteristic of social groups that have occupied the territory for generations and foreign elements carried more recently by traders, immigrants, and aggressors. Still, the most recent chapter of foreign influence on the culinary culture of contemporary Poland deserves more scrutiny. Assessing its impact is the primary objective of this chapter.

Polish Elites and Foreign Tastes

Like elsewhere, the culinary culture of Polish elites had for centuries been enriched by foreign imports. The culinary culture of Byzantium possibly reaching the Polish royal court as early as the tenth century is one of the earliest examples, but the most well-known one is the introduction of Mediterranean fruits and vegetables during the reign of Princess Bona Sforza of Milan (1494–1557), who became queen of Poland in 1518 (Dembińska 1999: 12–14). The flourishing economy during the following century prompted the diffusion of Italian novelties among the affluent Polish gentry (Meller 1994a: 35–7). In the meantime, the culinary refinement at the royal court continued under the influence of Marie Louise Gonzaga (1611–67), the French wife of King Ladislaus IV Vasa (1595–1649), and his brother John II Casimir Vasa (1609–72). An army of French cooks at the employ of the elite households was critical in disseminating French models on the Polish soil (Czaplicki and Długosz 1976: 120). Their impact was reflected in the introduction of French culinary terms into the Polish language and adaptation of French cooking techniques, such as stuffing, jellying, and glazing into Polish recipes (Meller 1994a: 51). German influences also reached Polish elite, after the electors of Saxony occupied the Polish throne during the first half of the eighteenth century. Since the Saxon elite itself had been influenced by the French culinary fashion, the Germanic impact on Polish haute cuisine through this channel was not particularly significant. However, they are attributed with the introduction of potato, which was to become one of the most important elements of Polish diet.

The sixteenth and seventeenth centuries also left the imprint from across the Eastern border on the Polish culinary culture (Meller 1994a: 39). Turkish, Hungarian, and Armenian dishes entered Poland via trade centers in the cities of Lviv, Vilnius, and Cracow. Armenian merchants were the most important carriers of Middle Eastern spices, nuts, and exotic fruits, which continuously appeared on the tables of the Polish elites. Turkish influences increased due to the Polish-Ottoman Wars (1620–1, 1633–4, 1672–6, 1683–99) and became particularly pronounced in confectionery and in the preparation of meat dishes (Meller 1994a: 44).

It must be stressed that the developments described here were primarily relevant for the elites, and only reached the middle orders of society to a very limited degree and, if at all, centuries later. This situation began to change from the nineteenth century onward, when a growing number of French, German, and Austrian cookbooks began to circulate throughout the Polish territory, at the time no longer an independent state, but partitioned among its neighbors, the Habsburg Austria, the Kingdom of Prussia, and the Russian Empire. The increased market for printed cookbooks in nineteenth-century Europe was fostered by several factors, of which an important one was the drop in the prices of books due to the industrialization of paper-making and printing (Eliot and Rose 2007: 579–600). Based on the examinations of the signs of wear found on the copies of the cookbooks that survived in Polish libraries until the present day, material culture historian Beata Meller concludes that they were indeed used in the kitchen (personal communication, August 1996).

Concurrently with the increased circulation of cookbooks written in foreign languages, Polish translations of French and Italian culinary publications became increasingly prominent at the time. The early examples are *Kuchnia Polsko-Francuska* (the Polish-French Cookery) published in 1810 and *Kucharka Doskonała Wiedeńska* (the Perfect Viennese Cook) from 1825 (Meller 1994b: 85). These books foreshadowed the first wave of foreign influence in Polish cookery that continued for nearly a century and, in the long run, contributed to the modernization of Polish diet. This transformation took place in the context of the economic and social changes brought about by the Industrial Revolution. Although far from spectacular by Western European standards—in 1900, nearly 70 percent of the Polish population lived in the countryside (Zamoyski 1987: 310)—urbanization and the growth of the middle class provided fertile ground for foreign innovation. Ultimately, these factors were crucial in the construction of the blueprint for what Poles today consider "traditional food."

The Reinvention of Home Cooking

The agents of change that initiated this process were female culinary reformers—Maria Disslowa (1870–1936), Marta Norkowska (1872–1930), Maria Gruszecka (ca 1850–post-1913), and Maria Ochorowicz-Monatowa (1866–1925)—who strove to provide the urban middle classes with practical solutions to their daily dilemmas of feeding their families on a budget. These resourceful ladies disseminated new ideas about cooking and nutrition through popular and professional publications, public lectures, and cooking courses. During the 1930s, the young generation of reformers, such as Zofja Czerny-Biernatowa (?–1965) and Marja Strasburger (1896–1963), even utilized radio broadcasts to communicate their advice to the public.[1]

The uncrowned queen among them is, undoubtedly, Lucyna Ćwierczakiewiczowa (1829–1901), the author of the bestselling cookbook *365 Obiadów za Piec Zlotych* (365 Dinners for Five Zloty[2]), which was republished twenty-four times between 1860 and 1923.[3] The book provided menu suggestions for each day of the year, divided per month, taking into consideration the seasonal variation of ingredients, including their prices and availability. It relied heavily on foreign borrowings, at times uncredited, but often indicated in the names of the featured recipes. Four different strategies were employed by the author for this purpose: (1) terms such as "à la mode," "à la maître d'hôtel," and "au gratin" were included, indicating their French origins or, possibly, denoting some kind of refinement; (2) geographical names, usually of a city of the alleged origin of the dish were listed, as is the case with chicken soup Orléans Style (Rosół po orleańsku), Herring Hamburg style (Śledzie po hambursku), or Potatoes Lyon-style (Kartofle "à la lyonnaise"); (3) the dish was assigned a particular "nationality," like French dumplings (Kluski francuskie), Chicken Spanish style (Kurczęta po hiszpańsku), Green beans English style (Fasola zielona po angielsku); and, finally, (4) the least recurred method was to include the original name in a foreign language with a short explanation in Polish, for example "Ox-Tail" soup and "Vol au vent" chicken dish (Ćwierczakiewiczowa 1985: 86, 212).

Along with her bestselling book, Ćwierczakiewiczowa provided culinary advice through her cookery column in the progressive women's magazine *Bluszcz* (Ivy), with which she collaborated for nearly three decades, since its launching in 1865 (Kalkowski 1985: 8). Here, again, she regularly included foreign recipes, with their origins clearly signaled by the names she gave them: Karlsbad Cherry Cake (Ciasto karlsbadzkie z wiśniami),[4] Beefsteak Hamburg Style (Befsztyk po hambursku),[5] French Chops (Zrazy francuskie),[6] English Layer Cake with Wild Strawberries (Tort poziomkowy angielski),[7] English Pudding in French Pastry (Budyń angielski w francuskim cieście), and so on.[8] The same pattern was prevalent in cookbooks by other authors that were published throughout the late nineteenth and the early twentieth century, as well as in cookery columns of women's magazines like *Dobra Gospodyni* (Good Housekeeper)— the cheapest women's magazine on the market[9]—and the more exclusive *Pani Domu* (The Lady of the House). In the course of 1938, one year before the outbreak of the Second World War, the readers of the latter were offered quite a geographical variety of foreign recipes to try:

French Omelette with Potatoes and Cheese (Omlet francuski z ziemniakami i serem)
Potato Salad Viennese Style (Sałatka ziemniaczana po wiedeńsku)
Italian Veal Salad (Sałatka włoska z cielęciny)
Swiss Pudding with Ham (Budyń szwajcarski z szynką)
Karlsbad Cookies (Ciastka karlsbadzkie)
Argentinean Dishes: Carbonada, Empanadas, Puchero (Potrawy argentyńskie: carbonada, empanadas, puchero)
Argentinean Dessert "Dulce de Leche" (Legumina argentyńska "Dulce de Leche")
Beans à la Bretonne (Fasolka po bretońsku)
Codfish Hamburg Style (Dorsz po hamburski)
Herrings Greek Style (Merlany po grecku)
Hare Italian Style (Zając po włosku)[10]

While the Argentinian "Dulce de Leche" may still remain largely unknown to most Poles even today, certain foreign recipes that had kept reappearing in Polish cookery columns since the late nineteenth century clearly acquired a permanent position in the home cooking repertoire of Polish urban households. They did not disappear from new cookbooks published after the Second World War, even when the new political climate of the Polish People's Republic (1947–89) deemed refined lifestyle detrimental and foreign influences unwelcome. Rather, their position was strengthened through dissemination beyond urban homes and across the social spectrum. In some publications from the communist era, the references to foreign origins of the featured recipes were removed from their names, but a prevailing trend was to retain them. Let us consider the example of the holy grail of Polish cookery—breaded pork cutlet (*A Foreigner's Guide to Polish Cuisine* 2014).

The recipe was introduced for the first time in Ćwierczakiewiczowa's bestseller under the name of Viennese Cutlet (Sznycle Wiedeńskie). Similarly, Marta Norkowska's *Najnowsza Kuchnia Wytworna i Gospodarska* (The Newest Cookery, Refined and Economical) from 1903 and *Uniwersalna Książka Kucharska* (Universal Cookery Book) by Marya Ochorowicz-Monatowa from 1912 also clearly label this recipe as a Viennese import and list it, as does Ćwierczakiewiczowa, in the veal section (Ochorowicz-Monatowa 1995: 305; Norkowska 1903: 149; Ćwierczakiewiczowa 1985: 185). In a 1948 cookbook titled *Żywienie Rodziny* (Feeding the Family), a reference to the foreign origin of the dish is nowhere to be found (Czerny and Strasburger 1948: 177–8), but only five years later, the publication by one of the two authors referred to it again as "Viennese style" (Czerny 1954: 249).

This is by no means an isolated example. Many of the dishes that entered home cookery under foreign inspiration since the nineteenth century onward have, by the second half of the twentieth century acquired Polish identity. This fact becomes particularly obvious by their inclusion in the 700-page-long postwar culinary compendium *Kuchnia Polska* (Polish cookery). Published for the first time in 1954, and with twenty-nine editions released by 1989, this cookbook is said to have been a favorite gift for newlyweds (Kieszek-Wasilewska 2019). Owing to this high penetration ratio, it de facto codified the boundaries of home cooking in communist Poland. Although by no means a dominant group, the collection did not shy away from recipes with clearly labeled foreign connections. For example, the 1962 edition of *Kuchnia Polska*, which belonged to my grandmother, included twenty such examples (Berger 1962).

> French Patties with Mushrooms (*Paszteciki francuskie z grzybami*)
> French Paste Boiled in Milk (*Kluski francuskie na mleku*)
> French Omelette (*Omlet francuski*)
> Codfish Nelson Style (*Dorsz po nelsońsku*)
> Veal Liver English Style (*Wątróbka cielęca po angielsku*)
> Veal Cutlet Italian Style (*Kotlety cielęce po włosku*)
> Calf's-Foot Viennese Style (*Nóżki cielęce po wiedeńsku*)
> Mutton Brisket Viennese Style (*Mostek barani po wiedeńsku*)
> Roast Mutton English Style (*Pieczeń barania po angielsku*)
> Nelson's Chops (*Zrazy po nelsońsku*)
> Roast Beef Stewed Flemish Style (*Pieczeń wołowa duszona po flamandzku*)
> Sirloin English Style (*Polędwica po angielsku*)
> Roast Beef English Style (*Rostbef po angielsku*)
> Roman Roast (*Pieczeń rzymska*)
> Beefsteak English Style (*Befsztyk po angielsku*)
> Hare French Style (*Zając po francusku*)
> Dutch Sauce (*Sos holenderski*)
> Viennese Cheese Cake (*Sernik wiedeński*)
> French Pastry with Cream (*Ciastka francuskie z kremem*)
> Spanish Layer Cake (*Tort hiszpański*)

A notable difference with similar recipes that have appeared in Polish household literature since the previous century is that they were now clearly recategorized as "Polish food." It goes without saying that considerable differences can be identified between the original foreign recipes and their Polish versions that ultimately became domesticated. I am skeptical, however, whether analyzing them in order to uncover more information about the Polish taste would be warranted, since modifications in recipes tend to be motivated by practical considerations, such as lack of specific ingredients, equipment, or skills, as well as personal preferences of cookbook writers.

The Hidden Legacy of Food Processing

Recipes were not the only channel through which foreign influences reached Polish diet since the mid-nineteenth century onward. Industrial food processing slowly but surely acquired a foothold in the Polish market as well. One of the earliest instances is the confectionery industry, which began to thrive in the early years of the nineteenth century in the hands of Swiss-Italian immigrants who settled in large cities like Warsaw, Cracow, and Lviv (Herbaczyński 1988, Homola-Skąpska 1996; Kozłowska-Ryś 2018). The growth of the confectionery business was stimulated by the dropping prices of sugar, which, in turn, was directed related to the spread of the manufacture of sugar from sugar beets. The very first sugar factory set up by German scientist Franz Karl Achard (1753–1821) in Lower Silesia in 1802 soon found imitators, and by the 1850s the industrialization of sugar manufacture was well underway (Przyrembel 1927). Soon, Polish apprentices of foreign confectioners also began to set up their own workshops, but they had to rely on skilled labor from abroad. One of them was Karol Gronert, who in 1845 hired experienced German confectioner Karl Ernst Wedel (1813–1902) to help run his business. Six years later, Wedel opened his own shop, which in time grew to become a full-fledged chocolate emporium with automated factory employing over a thousand people (Herbaczyński 1988: 234–9; Kuta, Matejun, and Miksa 2017: 99). In 1853, the business expended by hiring skilled craftsmen from Berlin and Vienna and importing steam-powered machinery from Paris (*History of Our Company* 2020). Karl's son Emil Albert Frederick Wedel (1841–1919) took over the control of the business in 1865, and half a century later, under the leadership of his son Jan Joseph Wedel (1874–1960), the brand thrived (Kępa 2018). In 1932, the enterprise became incorporated into E. Wedel Chocolate Factory, and by the end of the decade employed over 1,400 people. A new factory that opened in the city the previous year earlier utilized state-of-the-art machinery for the manufacture of chocolate, along with the automated wrapping equipment (Kuta, Matejun, and Miksa 2017: 99). In 1937, the total volume of production reached 3,500 ton (Lach and Szafran 1987: 73).

Wedel's operations were scaled down after the outbreak of the Second World War, and the consumption of their products restricted primarily to the privileged Germans residing in Poland. After the liberation, the production quickly recovered, and by the late 1940s it had resumed prewar levels. In 1949, the company was nationalized and renamed, and its production portfolio expanded through mergers: in 1960, a merger with one of Wedel's prewar most serious competitors, F. Fuchs and Sons Inc. (F. Fuchs i Synowie S.A.), and six years later with a small factory near Warsaw that specialized in the manufacture of fudge. During the 1970s, the production facilities were thoroughly modernized, relying on cutting-edge machinery imported from West Germany and Italy. Such costly investments were warranted due to an important position of confectionery in Poland's export portfolio, which generated much needed foreign currency. For example, during the 1970s, half of all confectionery exported from Poland was manufactured by the postwar reincarnation of prewar Wedel (Lach and Szafran 1987: 74). Production stagnated during the 1980s, when the economic crisis crippled the supply of cocoa beans and other ingredients (Stępień 1989: 88). In 1991, the Ministry of Ownership Transformation auctioned the enterprise to PepsiCo Foods and Beverages, the highest bidder among the multinational companies that submitted a tender to buy this most famous Polish confectionery producer (Mikołajewska 2014: 74).

While E. Wedel undoubtedly ranked among to top confectionery firms operating in prewar Poland, it is worth pointing out that it acquired the power to shape the parameters of the Polish taste only during the communist era. Since its inception in the mid-nineteenth century, Wedel's success had largely relied on foreign know-how and technology, emulating the famous confectioners of Berlin, Paris, and Vienna. This was a prevailing trend among other confectionery manufacturers operating in other parts of Poland as well. In Lviv, they modeled themselves on the Viennese firms of Kohler, Manner, and Heller. In the city of Cracow, three chocolate factories competed with one another: Lachs brothers who operated directly under a license from the Swiss firm Suchard, a branch of the Viennese firm Pischinger (which in 1933 was pushed out of the market by a local copycat illegally using the Pischinger name), and the enterprise of "Chocolate King" Adam Piasecki (1873–1945), run under the watchful eye of a master-chocolatier from Switzerland (Jakubowski 2012: 128–9; Pintowski 1961: 45–6). In 1949, the three were nationalized, based on the Law on Nationalization of Industry (*Ustawa o nacjonalizacji przemysłu*), passed by the communist government three years earlier. Similarly to the fate of the leading Warsaw firms, Piasecki's chocolate empire was merged with Cracow's Suchard enterprise and the Pischinger copycat, and after 1951 continued under the Wawel brand, named after the Cracow's royal castle (Mazan 2010: 117–18).

The long-standing ties with the foreign chocolate industry were thus abruptly cut off during the second half of the twentieth century. To be sure, foreign machinery continued to be imported. For example, during the 1970s Wedel was furbished with cutting-edge Otto Hansel's evaporators, chocolate-molding equipment by Carle & Montanari, and Werner & Pfleider's automatic production lines (Lach and Szafran 1987: 74). However, a relative isolation from foreign inspiration allowed a specific portfolio of prewar confections to develop further in relative isolation, and gradually acquire a distinctively Polish connotation. Limited supply, which required personal connections or long hours of queuing to get hold of the most popular items, only enhanced their cult status. A noteworthy factor that further contributed to the popularity of socialist confectionery was a very limited availability of foreign products, apart from the exorbitantly expensive hard currency PEWEX stores that enjoyed a semi-magical status, especially among children (Burrell 2011: 150; Cwiertka 2011: 1).

The majority of sweets that today are being promoted to foreigners as "typically Polish"—and perceived as such by the population—have socialist roots, but they often rest on prewar foundations of the factories that made them (Kasprzyk-Chevriaux 2016). For example, the list put together in 2014 by Karolina Kowalska for the promotional portal of the Polish Ministry of Foreign Affairs includes two items from Wedel's merchandise: Torcik Wedlowski (Wedel's layer cake), a round block of thin wafers with chocolate filling in-between, and Ptasie mleczko (Bird's Milk), square pieces of marshmallow covered in chocolate (Kowalska 2014). Both were among the new products that the firm launched shortly after the opening of the new factory in 1932, but the former reveals a striking resemblance to "Original Pischinger Torte" claimed by the Pischinger Company to have been invented in the 1880s by Oskar Pischinger, the son of the founder (*160 years of tradition: Pischinger then and now* 2020).

Foreign food processing businesses moving into the Polish market around the turn of the twentieth century was by no means limited to the chocolate industry. In 1910, ersatz coffee giant Heinrich Franck Söhne Ltd. (est. 1828) set up a factory in the town of Skawina, near Cracow. This was merely another step in the aggressive expansion of the firm toward every corner of the Austrian-Hungarian Empire (*History* 2020). Production in Skawina began the following year, and, by the 1930s, the Polish factory reached a yearly output of 8,200 tons, ranking second among all nine ersatz coffee manufacturers operating across the country (Krupa 2013: 45). Heinrich Franck Söhne's famous brands, such as Enrilo and Karo Franck, were produced here for the Polish consumers. During the early 1940s, the output further increased, since the product was considered by the German occupier as strategic supply for its armed forces (Editorial 1948: 155). In 1949, Skawina factory was nationalized by the newly formed communist government and production portfolio expanded to include noodles, baking powder, and instant soups and Sauces (*100 lat tradycji* 2020). This strategy could already be observed during the 1920s when the chicory factory set up in 1816 by brothers Bohm in the town of Włocławek branched out to the manufacture of baking powder and other ingredients required for home baking (*Fabryka Cykorii we Włocławku BOHM* 2020).

These business strategies were undoubtedly inspired by the phenomenal success of the enterprise of August Oetker (1862–1918). The German pharmacist-turned-entrepreneur hit upon the idea of selling baking powder in small sachets with precisely the right quantity of powder for one pound of flour. The powder itself had been discovered half a century earlier by the British chemist Alfred Bird (1811–78), who is also credited with the invention of egg-free custard—another of Dr. Oetker's signature products, alongside prepackaged gelatin and sugar flavored with semisynthetic vanilla extract, known under the brand name Vanillin. Dr. Oetker's talent laid in the improvement of the already-existing products and their marketing, including detailed instructions about how to use them.

The formal founding of the enterprise is January 1, 1891, when Dr. Oetker became the owner of a pharmacy in Bielefeld, but the business began to grow rapidly toward the end of the decade. By 1899, the sale of the baking powder sachets—after 1902 under its own brand name Backin—reached two million sachets, and soon, one after another, factories were built in order to meet the rapidly growing demand (Wirsching, Finger, and Keller 2013: 28–31). Dr. Oetker also began to expand operations beyond the borders of the Kingdom of Prussia, setting up production facilities in Ústí nad Labem, Baden near Vienna, Brno, Maribor, and Budapest. Yet the largest among all the subsidiary enterprises abroad was the factory in the Free City of Danzig (Wirsching, Finger, and Keller 2013: 101). Created in 1920 in accordance with the terms of the Treaty of Versailles, the area consisted of the Baltic port of Danzig (Gdańsk) and nearly 200 surrounding towns and villages. Dr. Oetker began production here in 1922, and a sales branch in Warsaw was opened in 1933 and a representative office in Katowice in 1935 (Wirsching, Finger, and Keller 2013: 34, 89). By 1938, the turnover of the Gdańsk factory reached 27.8 percent of all foreign branches of the firm; the second largest was the Austrian branch with 21.3 percent, followed by Czechoslovakia with 13 percent, Belgium with 11.9 percent, and France 10.3 percent (Wirsching, Finger, and Keller 2013: 101, 424). The promotional sales strategy followed the tried-and-tested model of free-of-charge leaflets and booklets with recipes using Dr. Oetker's products (Leżyński 2020). During wartime, as was the case with ersatz coffee, the output of the Gdańsk factory contributed to the provisioning of the German troops. Nationalized during the late 1940s, the factory continued production until 1991, when the Oetker family regained control over the business.

What these fragmented data makes undoubtedly clear is that the novel food processing enterprises that emerged at the end of the nineteenth century in the Kingdom of Prussia and the Austrian-Hungarian Empire moved relatively quickly into the Polish market, and by the 1920s even sparked a handful of local competitors. More importantly, these factories provided a foundation for the food industry to thrive in the communist era. For example, the Swiss concern of Julius Maggi (1846–1912) established a sales office in Poland in 1922, and nine years later began manufacture of precooked soups and stock cubes in the new factory of Poznań. In 1932, its German competitor Knorr also launched production in the same city (Engel 1970: 25). While both firms devoted considerable resources to the promotion of their novel products, the production levels remained relatively low—mere 200 tons of stock cubes in 1937–8 (Kwaśnik 1979: 125). It was only after the war, under the backing of the communist regime, that the business began to flourish. In 1946, Maggi and Knorr were nationalized, and five years later formally merged into one enterprise with a small pasta factory run since 1936 by the Italian Alfredo Germanini (Engel 1970: 25). In 1953, a Polish producer of baking powder and custard powder that had operated in the vicinity was also incorporated into the new venture, which was named Poznań Works of Food Concentrates (Poznańskie Zakłady Koncentratów Spożywczych), since 1968 also known as Amino. Between 1945 and 1969, the volume of production increased sevenfold, by far surpassing the prewar levels of all the individual makers combined. This was largely due to investments in automation and innovative packaging methods, along with the development of new products, such as instant soups and sauces. Per capita consumption of instant soups increased from 0.006 kilogram in 1938 to 4.470 kilogram in 1969 (Engel 1970: 28–9). Another signature product was instant coffee Marago, propagated as the Polish version of Nescafe (Mazan 2010: 186–7), and its ersatz version Inka. The latter is not only considered one of the most iconic consumer products of the communist era but also a recipient of the 2016 "Created in Poland Superbrands" award (*Inka honoured with Superbrands award* 2020). Amino brand continues production under the ownership of Unilever, and the company's logo now permanently includes a phrase "Kuchnia Polska" (Polish cuisine).

Support for the food processing industry by the postwar regime was clearly motivated by ideological factors, mainly the Soviet model of efficient communal canteens combined with women's emancipation through their liberation from the drudgery of the kitchen (Reid 2002). However, the support for food processing was shaped by practical considerations as well. Since food was the country's primary export article, effective preservation and transport of perishables to foreign markets was essential. For example, extensive investments in the refrigeration industry during the 1960s and 1970s constituted a lifeline for the export of Polish fruit, vegetables, and mushrooms (Siemiński 1980).

Another incentive in this respect was reducing dependence on imported ingredients, which were often essential for the manufacture of export articles. For example, by the mid-1960s Poland has become nearly self-sufficient in the production of synthetic vanillin—a cheap substitute of vanilla essence—which was an indispensable ingredient for the confectionery industry. Since 1957, vanillin was mass produced by aforementioned enterprise of the Bohm brothers in Włocławek, which had by then been nationalized. The same year, the former Maggi factory in Poznań began producing carotene pigment required in the manufacture of margarine, which had thus far been imported from Denmark (Engel 1970; Stępiński 1962: 334).

In conclusion, similarly to the case of home cooking discussed in the previous section, the communist era was critical in domesticating foreign products that had entered the country during the late nineteenth and the early twentieth centuries. This role was by no means intentional but had twofold consequences. On the one hand, it familiarized the entire population with the products of industrial food processing and the difficulty in acquiring certain items due to shortages only contributed to their cult status. On the other hand, the nationalized enterprises laid the ground for the multinational corporations that flooded the Polish market in the early 1990s by taking over the impoverished state-run enterprises to swiftly establish new production lines. In addition, they could rely on brand recognition of the popular products among the Polish consumers. Today, some of those enterprises may even tap into nostalgia marketing of the communist era products in their promotional activities. For example, a special retro packaging of Calypso brand of ice cream was launched in 2019 on the occasion of celebrating the sixtieth anniversary of the product (Borowski 2019).[11]

Eating Out Foreign Style

Gastronomy was the least-developed sector within the socialist service economy of the Polish People's Republic, and its growth since the 1990s is one of the most visible sites of the changes that the country underwent in the new political-economic context. According to official statistics, the number of establishments offering gastronomic services in Poland increased nearly tenfold between 1950 and 2015, from 7,281 to 68,342, with the most rapid growth recorded between 1989 and 2005, when the peak of 92,072 was reached (Głuchowski, Rasińska, and Czarniecka-Skubina 2017: 119). Along with the expansion of the sheer number of gastronomic units, the growth of ethnic sector—meaning the food marketed as representing a specific ethnic identity—was one of the most distinctive features of this transformation (Derek 2017). The market liberalization of the 1990s prompted a tsunami of foreign culinary trends flooding the Polish gastronomy.

Some of the first and most powerful players that moved into the Polish gastronomic market were McDonald's, Kentucky Fried Chicken, and other American fast-food giants. Today, they remain among the most popular dining establishments in Poland, largely due to their low cost, convenience, and overwhelming presence in shopping malls and in the vicinity of transport hubs (Hebda 2013; Pielak and Czarniecka-Skubina 2016). Their popularity reflects a growing demand, especially among the younger generation, for inexpensive "food-on-the-go" that can be prepared quickly and consumed either at the premises or as a take-out. Precisely the same factors are responsible for the spectacular success of "kebab bars" that are now considered the most serious competitors of the American fast-food chains, with franchised business concepts like Bafra Kebab and Berlin Döner Kebab in operation. They are usually staffed by young male immigrants from Muslim countries (Tunisia, Egypt, Algeria, Syria, Iraq, Palestine, and Lebanon), but the food itself is a Turkish-German invention that simply moved east (Möhring 2010; Nowaczek-Walczak 2011).

With a notable exception of Vietnamese food (Wojtasik 2018), all ethnic cuisines that have taken roots in Poland during the last two decades have something in common. They are not a result of an encounter with a specific ethnic group, but rather represent the influx of trends that had already been spreading globally. In other words, Polish cities have since the 1990s gradually joined the "transnational consumer zone" with ethnic dining as its indispensable component, a "global village" disconnected from geographical, climatic, or historical sense of place. Urban citizens of Poland, and the tourists who come to visit the country, can now fully participate in a postmodern culinary taste characterized by "mixed codes, fragmentation, incoherence, disjunction and syncretism" (Scarpato and Daniele 2003: 309).

A survey conducted by Marta Derek in 2013 revealed that the capital city of Warsaw counted 191 gastronomic establishments claiming to serve ethnic food, revealing a growth rate of 45 percent compared to 2001 (Derek 2017: 227–8). Thirty different cuisines were counted, but as the author points out, the most popular ones—Italian and Japanese (read pizza and sushi)—do not reflect at all Poland's geographical location, or a strong presence of Ukrainians in the gastronomic workforce (Derek 2017: 232; Klimek 2016: 68). The findings are confirmed by another study conducted four years later, which concluded that the three dominant cuisines in Warsaw's gastronomy were Polish, Italian, and Japanese (Głuchowski, Rasińska, and Czarniecka-Skubina 2017: 125).

Nationwide, the ranking is slightly different. Italian cuisine remains in the lead, with pizzerias recognized as the most favorite gastronomic establishments, but instead of relatively high-end sushi, American fast-food, kebab, and Chinese/Vietnamese food emerge as favorites (Pielak and Czarniecka-Skubina 2016 11–13; MAKRO Cash and Carry 2016: 13). The same survey, conducted in 2016 by the wholesale operator MAKRO, confirmed that Polish cuisine was still the most preferred eating out option (MAKRO Cash and Carry 2016: 13). An important detail to add is that despite a remarkable growth that Polish gastronomy has experienced since the 1990s, quantitative data confirms that eating out for the bulk of the population remained is site of celebratory meals, reserved for special occasions. For example, according to the data published in 2015, roughly 82–91 percent of respondents consumed their daily meals at home (Domański et al. 2015: 122–4). Another study conducted nationwide in 2011, over a sample of roughly 1,000 responders, indicated that an average Pole visits a gastronomic unit only once a month (Kowalczuk and Czarniecka-Skubina 2015: 76). However, we might surmise that this trend is subject to change in the future, since the younger generation clearly eats out more often: 76.7 percent of 26 to 35-year-olds and 83.6 percent of 15 to 25-year-olds declared that they frequent a restaurant, while the ratio was 41 percent for those over sixty-five years of age (Domański 2015: 132).

When we consider the foreign impact on the twentieth-century Polish gastronomy in the long run, the communist era cannot be left out. This was not only the period of decapitation of prewar gastronomy but was also marked by the influence of the Soviet model of communal feeding. Anastas Mikoyan (1895–1978), the great architect of Soviet-style gastronomy and consumption more broadly, envisaged it as a science-based industrialized operation focused on hygiene, nutrition, and efficiency. Mikoyan's vision was inspired by his 1935 trip to the United States, where he picked up and implemented the self-service restaurant (Głuszczenko 2012: 81–3). It is, thus, through the Soviet filter that American gastronomic model has become popularized in Polish People's Republic.

Reorganization of Polish gastronomy based on the Soviet model, which also included ideological integration of workers daily routine through commensality, began the early 1950s with investment in employees' canteens that operated at construction sites and factories, as well as schools and dormitories. By 1954, nearly 10,000 of such gastronomic units were set up (and made up 56 percent of gastronomic establishments in Poland, but half of them did not survive the end of the decade) (Czekalski 2011: 80, 83). Historian Tadeusz Czekalski argues that employees' canteens at no point in Polish history were able to compete with other establishments—most of them state owned—that operated outside the mass-feeding system. For example, during the 1970s, a meager 17 percent of Polish workers made use of employees' canteens (of which only 7 percent consumed their main meal of the day), a rather unimpressive number, especially in comparison to 30 percent in Czechoslovakia and Hungary, 40 percent in the German Democratic Republic, and 75 percent in the Soviet Union (Czekalski 2011: 79–82).

An important new trend of the 1970s, which foreshadowed the ethnic food trend of two decades later, was the appearance of restaurants claiming to be serving the cuisine of comrade nations, appropriately named to underline their identity. The capital city of Warsaw boasted several such enterprises: *Trojka*, serving Russian cuisine, *Cristal-Budapest* Hungarian, *Sofia* Bulgarian, and *Szanghaj* Chinese (Brzostek 2010: 245–8). The pride of Szczecin was *Bar Kaukaski*, which served mutton shashliks Georgian style; Tajik dishes were offered in Gdańsk and Ukrainian cuisine in Cracow restaurant *Dniepr* (Czekalski 2011: 87). None of those establishments survived the test of time, and none of the cuisines of the countries that once comprised the Soviet Bloc are popular in Poland today. The other trend, which characterized the 1970s, proved much more durable—the rise of private gastronomic businesses. They have grown from 1,465 in 1970 to 4,044 ten years later, and then doubled by 1988 (Kowalczuk and Czarniecka-Skubina 2015: 76). At the fall of the Berlin Wall, private enterprises accounted for the meager 15 percent of the food service sector, but the ratio was soon reversed. By 2013, 98 percent of gastronomic market was privatized (Kowalczuk and Czarniecka-Skubina 2015: 77).

A question remains whether the diversification and capital investment in the Polish gastronomy influenced Polish taste. It is certain that the quality of food served outside the home significantly increased. The same can be said about variety, in particular in relation to regional products. As Dumanowski (2019) explains in his attempt to define Polish cuisine, half a century of communist rule has inflicted vast damage on regional culinary variety in Poland due to forced resettlement of population from one region to another, food shortages, the propagation of industrial food processing, and other factors. It is only recently that various initiatives to rescue regional specialties produced on a small scale using artisanal methods are taking place. The establishment, in 2004, of the Polish Chamber of Regional and Local Product (Polska Izba Produktu Regionalnego i Lokalnego) was an important step in increasing the visibility of these initiatives, followed in 2007 by the introduction of the Jakość Tradycja (Quality Tradition) label for artisanal food products, a scheme formally recognized by the Ministry of Agriculture and Rural Development (Ministerstwo Rolnictwa i Rozwoju Wsi) and the European Commission. The financial opportunities offered by the EU's agricultural product quality policies, such as Protected Designation of Origin (PDO), Protected Geographical Indications (PDI), and Traditional Specialty Guaranteed (TSG), are critical for the revitalization of regional food products in Poland. According to the data provided by the Ministry of Agriculture and Rural Development (Ministerstwo Rolnictwa i Rozwoju Wsi), as of May 2020, a total of forty-three products were registered under those three schemes (*Produkty zarejestrowane jako Chronione Nazwy Pochodzenia, Chronione Oznaczenia Geograficzne oraz Gwarantowane Tradycyjne Specjalności* 2020).

Food has also been recognized as an important asset by the tourist sector and is extensively utilized for place branding (Kruczek and Krauzowicz 2016; Makała 2013; Plebanczyk 2013). As culinary trails, festival, and other culinary events become tourist attractions in their own right, restaurants serving regional cuisine guide many Poles on their journey toward the rediscovery of Polish taste from the precommunist era (Durydiwka 2020: 218-221).[12] Viewed from this perspective, it is not so much the foreign culinary trends that entered Poland since the 1990s, but rather larger global movements, such as the concerns for sustainability and food safety that often led to a growing of public nostalgia for largely imagined, unidentifiable, authentic past (Caldwell 2002, 2006; Leitch 2003).

Conclusion: Reconnecting with the World

Sociologist Honorata Jakubowska begins her essay on the transformation that the Polish taste preferences underwent since the 1990s with the section titled "The taste of America" (Smak Ameryki). When describing the circumstances surrounding the opening of American fast-food chains in the Polish cities, she argues that their popularity was driven not by gustatory considerations, but rather by hunger for liberation from the constraints of the communist system. "In 1990s Poland McDonald's did not taste of minced meat, Coke and fries," explains Jakubowska, "it tasted of freedom, open borders, and connection with the rest of the world" (2013: 42, my translation). These sentiments were comparable to the experiences of the citizens of Sofia, Moscow, and Beijing, for whom a serving of Big Mac offered an entry, even for a fleeting moment, to the aura of "American dream" with all its illusive promises of affluence and happiness (Caldwell 2004; Krǎsteva-Blagoeva 2001; Yan 2013).

Today the "reconnecting with the world" project seems completed, at least as far as culinary matters are concerned. Big Mac no longer tastes of freedom, kebab and sushi have lost their exotic connotations, and once-unreachable brand names, like Coca-Cola and Mars, are a familiar presence on the shelves of every supermarket. The political and economic liberalization of the early 1990s, and the influx of multinational corporations onto the Polish market, have created an opportunity for every Pole (if only through advertising) to encounter foreign culinary trends to a degree never experienced before, including most recent ones, such as veganism and food trucks (Głuchowski, Rasińska, and Czarniecka-Skubina 2017: 124–5).

A question worth asking is whether the diversification of food supply brought about by capitalist economy have had any tangible impact on the Polish taste, on Polish culinary identity. And how about the other foreign influences discussed in this chapter? To begin with, it seems obvious that the communist era has contributed to a culinary democratization and was instrumental in sealing of what is now considered the canon of Polish cooking. The recent emphasis on local culinary traditions—also visible in newly published cookbooks—has enriched the classic repertoire. Eating Polish food is becoming increasingly a matter of choice, for some more conscious than for others. The rise of "new Polish cuisine" that combines traditional elements with "lighter" ingredients, often inspired by foreign cuisines, not only is a domain of chefs of upmarket restaurants in Warsaw and Cracow in their dog-eats-dog competition for a mention in Gault & Millan and Michelin guides, but is also being recognized by ordinary citizens (Jakubowska 2013: 46–7). Combining adjectives, such as "light" (lekka), "fresh" (świeża), and "healthy" (zdrowa), in relation to the term "Polish cuisine" no longer sounds like an oxymoron, which is a harbinger of change looming on the horizon.

In the meantime, Honorata Jakubowska has made a very potent observation that leads me to the conclusion that despite change, some centuries-old taste preferences may be here to stay. In the last section of her aforementioned essay, Jakubowska brings up the American influence that has proved more powerful than the taste of Big Mac: outdoor grilling (2013: 48). Within two decades since its introduction in the early 1990s, the custom of barbecuing American style, using a Weber-style kettle grill and charcoal, has turned into a national pastime. Poles grill everywhere—on camp sides, beaches, and lake shores, in the woods and parks, in gardens and allotments, even on balconies, whenever the weather condition allows it. It has become the most widespread form of entertainment for the entire population, regardless the income, since the choice of what to put on the grill depends entirely on the individual budget. Still, among the most popular items are (smoked) sausages and the "traditional" innovation: smoked cheese (oscypek), a regional specialty from the Carpathian Mountains, served with cranberry jelly.

Bonfires are among humanity's oldest customs, but are increasingly regulated due to urbanization, environmental regulations, and fire hazard. I recall with a great deal of nostalgia my childhood holidays in the countryside, which always included bonfires and potatoes baked in the ashes. This is the taste that for me was always intricately connected with the memories of summer holidays. However, for most Poles today the taste of summer is yet again composed of centuries-old smoked foods.

Notes

1 *Pani Domu*, vol. 10 no. 12 (1935).
2 A Polish monetary unit.
3 All editions of the book are available online through the National Library of Poland https://polona.pl/search/?query=365_obiad%C3%B3w&filters=public:1, last accessed on April 25, 2020.
4 *Bluszcz*, vol. 3 no. 31 (1867).
5 *Bluszcz*, vol. 5 no. 51 (1869).
6 *Bluszcz*, vol. 6 no. 24 (1870).
7 *Bluszcz*, vol. 3 no. 29 (1867).
8 *Bluszcz*, vol. 8 no. 8 (1872).
9 *Dobra Gospodyni*, vol. 1 no. 45 (1901).
10 *Pani Domu*, vol. 12 no. 2, 3, 15–16, 17, 20, 23, 24 (1938).
11 See the website of the producer for the images of the anniversary packaging. https://www.lodmor.com.pl/
12 The fact that locations without recognizable local dishes/products may resort to fabricating them highlights the potential dangers for the preservation of culinary heritage (Cwiertka 2020). The case in point is *Zygmuntówka*, an almond cupcake filled with chocolate mousse, cranberry jam, and whipped cream, covered with a crown-shaped meringue. It won the 2009 competition announced by the Warsaw City Hall and the Food Craft Guild to remedy the fact that Warsaw did not have a clearly recognizable dish (Głuchowski, Rasińska, and Czarniecka-Skubina. 2017: 127). The name of the cake alludes to King Sigismund III Vasa (1566–1632), who is responsible for transferring the capital from Cracow to Warsaw in 1596. His statue figures prominently in front of the Royal Castle in the Old Town.

References

100 Lat Tradycji. 2020. Available online: https://lajkonik.pl/o-firmie/100-lat-tradycji/, last accessed May 3, 2020.
160 Years of Tradition: Pischinger Then and Now (2020). Available online: https://www.pischinger.at/en/about-pischinger/, last accessed May 3, 2020.
A Foreigner's Guide to Polish Cuisine (2014). Available online: https://culture.pl/en/article/a-foreigners-guide-to-polish-cuisine, last accessed June 3, 2020.
Anderson, B. R. (1991), *Imagined Communities: Reflections on the Origin and Spread of Nationalism*, London: Verso.
Berger, S., ed. (1962 [1954]), *Kuchnia Polska*, Warszawa: Państwowe Wydawnictwo Ekonomiczne.
Borowski, R. (2019), *Lody Calypso mają już 60 lat*. Available online: https://biznes.trojmiasto.pl/Lody-Calypso-maja-juz-60-lat-n135081.html, last accessed June 3, 2020.
Brzostek, B. (2010), *PRL na widelcu*, Warszawa: Baobab.
Burrell, K. (2011), "The Enchantment of Western Things: Children's Material Encounters in Late Socialist Poland," *Transactions of the Institute of British Geographers* 36(1): 143–56.
Caldwell, M. L. (2002), "The Taste of Nationalism: Food Politics in Postsocialist Moscow," *Ethnos* 67(3): 295–319.

Caldwell, M. L. (2004), "Domesticating the French Fry: McDonald's and Consumerism in Moscow," *Journal of Consumer Culture* 4(1): 5–26.

Caldwell, M. L. (2006), "Tasting the Worlds of Yesterday and Today: Culinary Tourism and Nostalgia in Post-Soviet Russia," in R. Welk (ed.), *Fast Food/Slow Food: Cultural Economy of the Global Food System*, pp. 97–113, New York: Rowman & Littlefield.

Ćwierczakiewiczowa, L. (1985 [1860]), *365 Obiadów*, Kraków: Krajowa Agencja Wydawnicza.

Cwiertka, K. J. (2006), *Modern Japanese Cuisine: Food, Power and National Identity*, London: Reaktion Books.

Cwiertka, K. J. (2011), *The Wisdom of the Ordinary: A Prospect for Modern Japan Studies*, Inaugural Lecture, Leiden University. Available online: https://openaccess.leidenuniv.nl /handle/1887/19586, last accessed June 3, 2020.

Cwiertka, K. J. (2020), *Branding Japanese Food: From Meibutsu to Washoku*, Honolulu: Hawai'i University Press.

Czaplicki, W. and J. Długosz (1976), *Życie Codzienne Magnaterii Polskiej w XVII Wieku*, Warszawa: Państwowy Instytut Wydawniczy.

Czekalski, T. (2011), "Przedsiębiorstwa Żywienia Zbiorowego w Realiach PRL: Model Żywienia Zbiorowego w Warunkach Przyspieszonej Modernizacji i jego Realizacja," *Annales Universitatis Paedagogicae Cracoviensis: Studia Politologica* 5: 78–90.

Czerny, Z. (1954), *Książka Kucharska*, Warszawa: Polskie Wydawnictwo Gospodarcze.

Czerny, Z. and M. Strasburger (1948), *Żywienie Rodziny*, Warszawa: Czytelnik.

Dembińska, M. (1999), *Food and Drink in Medieval Poland: Rediscovering a Cuisine of the Past*, trans. M. Thomas, Philadelphia: University of Pennsylvania Press.

Derek, M. (2017), "Multi-ethnic Food in the Mono-ethnic City: Tourism, Gastronomy and Identity in Central Warsaw," in D. Hall (ed.), *Tourism and Geopolitics: Issues and Concepts from Central and Eastern Europe*, pp. 223–35, Wallingford: CAB International.

Domański, H., Z. Karpiński, D. Przybysz, and J. Straczuk (2015), *Wzory Jedzenia a Struktura Społeczna*, Warszawa: Wydawnictwo Naukowe Scholar.

Dumanowski, J. (2019), Co to jest kuchnia polska? Unpublished manuscript.

Durydiwka, M. (2020), "Eating Establishments in Smaller Cities and Towns in Poland (on Selected Examples)," in A. Kowalczyk and M. Derek (eds.), *Gastronomy and Urban Space: Changes and Challenges in Geographical Perspective*, pp. 209–23, Cham: Springer.

Editorial (1948), "Monografie Fabryk i Przedsiębiorstw: Fabryka Środków Kawowych H. Franck i Synowie w Skawinie k/Krakowa," *Przemysł Spożywczy* 2 (5–6): 155–7.

Eliot, S. and J. Rose, eds. (2007), *A Companion to the History of the Book*, Oxford: Blackwell.

Engel, W. (1970), "*Poznańskie Zakłady Koncentratów Spożywczych 'Amino' w latach 1929–1969 (szkic monograficzny)*," *Kronika Miasta Poznania* 38(2): 25–38.

Fabryka Cykorii we Włocławku BOHM (2020). Available online: https://historiawloclawka .pl/historia-wloclawskich-zakladow/25-fabryka-cykorii-we-wloclawku-bohm, last accessed June 3, 2020.

Głuchowski, A., E. Rasińska, and E. Czarniecka-Skubina (2017), "Rynek Usług Gastronomicznych w Polsce na Przykładzie Warszawy," *Handel Wewnętrzny* 4(369): 118–33.

Głuszczenko, I. (2012), *Sowiety od Kuchni: Mikojan i Radziecka Gastronomia*, trans. M. Przybylski, Warszawa: Wydawnictwo Krytyki Politycznej.

Hebda, A. (2013), "Fast Food Nie Tylko Na Szybko," in A. Jawor (ed.), *Paradoksy Ponowoczesności. O Starciach Płci, Religii, Tożsamości, Norm i Kultur*, pp. 149–75, Warszawa: Wydawnictwo Naukowe Scholar.

Herbaczyński, W. (1988), *W Dawnych Cukierniach i Kawiarniach Warszawskich*, Warszawa: Państwowy Instytut Wydawniczy.

History (2020). Available online: https://www.franck.eu/en/history/, last accessed June 3, 2020.

History of Our Company (2020). Available online: http://www.wedel.com/#history, last accessed April 20, 2020.

Homola-Skąpska, I. (1996), "Krakowskie Cukiernie i Kawiarnie w XIX Wieku," *Annales Universitatis Mariae Curie-Skłodowska* 6(5): 43–61.

Inka Honoured with Superbrands Award (2020). Available online: https://www.grana.pl/en/inka-honoured-with-superbrands-award/, last accessed August 7, 2020.

Jakubowska, H. (2013), "Polskie Smaki/ Smaki w Polsce," *Czas Kultury* 5: 40–9.

Jakubowski, K. (2012), *Kawa i Ciasto o Każdej Porze. Historia Krakowskich Kawiarni i Cukierni*, Warszawa: Agora.

Kalkowski, J. (1985), "O autorce '365 obiadów," in L. Ćwierczakiewiczowa, *365 Obiadów*, Kraków: Krajowa Agencja Wydawnicza, pp. 5–16.

Kasprzyk-Chevriaux, M. (2016), *Polish Food 101: Iconic Sweets*. Available online: https://culture.pl/en/work/polish-food-101-iconic-sweets, last accessed June 12, 2020.

Kępa, M. (2018), *The Bitter-Sweet Story of Wedel, Poland's Famous Chocolatier*. Available online: https://znakitowarowe-blog.pl/ptasie-mleczko/, last accessed May 12, 2020.

Kieszek-Wasilewska, I. (2019), *Kuchnia Polska*. Available online: https://kukbuk.pl/artykuly/kuchnia-polska/, last accessed March 25, 2020.

Klimek, D. (2016), "Znaczenie Migracji Zarobkowej z Ukrainy dla Gospodarki, Przedsiębiorców i Rynku Pracy w Polsce," *Zeszyty Naukowe Uczelni Vistula* 47(2): 60–74.

Kowalczuk, I. and E. Czarniecka-Skubina (2015), "Eating Out in Poland: History, Status, Perspectives and Trends," *Scientific Journal of University of Szczecin Service Management* 16: 75–83.

Kowalska, K. (2014), *Sweets Serve as Exquisite Souvenirs from Poland*. Available online: https://poland.pl/tourism/cuisine/polish-sweets/, last accessed March 25, 2020.

Kozłowska-Ryś, A. (2018), *Lwów na Słodko i . . . Półwytrawnie*, Poznań: Liberum.

Krăsteva-Blagoeva, E. (2001), "The Bulgarians and McDonald's: Some Anthropological Aspects," *Ethnologia Balkanica* 5: 207–17.

Kruczek, Z. and M. Krauzowicz (2016), "Turystyka Kulinarna na Podhalu," *Zeszyty Naukowe Turystyka i Rekreacja* 18(2): 17–34.

Krupa, M. (2013), "Przemiany Architektoniczne Skawiny w 2 Połowie XIX i na Początku XX Wieku. Cz. I. Zakłady Przemysłowe," *Wiadomości Konserwatorskie* 35: 41–6.

Kuta, K., M. Matejun, and P. Miksa (2017), "Długowieczność Firm Rodzinnych," *Przegląd Nauk Ekonomicznych* 26: 91–102.

Kuti, K. (2003), "Poland," in S. H. Katz (ed.), *Encyclopedia of Food and Culture*, vol. 1, pp. 349–50, New York: Charles Scribner's Sons.

Kwaśnik, E. (1979), "Przemysł Koncentratów Spożywczych w Polsce," *Przemysł Spożywczy* 33(5–6): 125–7.

Lach, J. and G. Szafran (1987), "Wczoraj i Dziś Zakładów Przemysłu Cukierniczego w Warszawie," *Przemysł Spożywczy* 41(3): 73–5.

Leitch, A. (2003), "Slow Food and the Politics of Pork Fat: Italian Food and European Identity," *Ethnos* 68(4): 437–62.

Leżyński, P. (2020), *Fabryka Środków Spożywczych Dr. Oetker*. Available online: http://www.dawnaoliwa.pl/opisy/firmy/oetker.html, last accessed May 15, 2020.

Makała, H., ed. (2013), *Kulturowe Uwarunkowania Żywienia w Turystyce*, Warszawa: Wyższa Szkoła Turystyki i Języków Obcych.

MAKRO Cash & Carry (2016), *Polska na Talerzu*. Available online: https://mediamakro.pl /pr/313540/jak-ksztaltuja-sie-preferencje-kulinarne-polakow-raport-polska-na-talerzu -2016, last accessed June 11, 2020.

Mazan, L. (2010), *Kraków na Słodko*, Kraków: Anabasis.

Meller, B. (1994a), "Obce Wpływy w Kuchni Polskiej," in J. Łoziński and M. Łozińska (eds.), *Wokół Stołu i Kuchni*, pp. 33–55, Warszawa: Wydawnictwo Tenten.

Meller, B. (1994b), "Książki Kucharskie w XIX Wieku," in J. Łoziński and M. Łozińska (eds.), *Wokół Stołu i Kuchni*, pp. 81–9, Warszawa: Wydawnictwo Tenten.

Michalik, M. and M. Łebkowski (1996), *Mała Encyklopedia Sztuki Kulinarnej*, Warszawa: Wydawnictwo Tenten.

Mikołajewska, K. (2014), "Alienation and Rush towards Change: Introducing Capitalism to a State-owned Polish Enterprise," *Oral History* 42(2): 69–80.

Möhring, M. (2010), "Döner Kebab and West German Consumer (Multi-) Cultures," in U. Lindner, M. Möhring, M. Stein, and S. Stroh (eds.), *Hybrid Cultures Nervous States: Britain and Germany in a (Post)Colonial World*, pp. 151–66, Amsterdam, New York: Rodopi.

Norkowska, M. (1903), *Najnowsza Kuchnia Wytworna i Gospodarska*, Warszawa: Gebethner i Wolf.

Nowaczek-Walczak, M. (2011), "The World of Kebab: Arabs and Gastronomy in Warsaw," in K. Górak-Sosnowska (ed.), *Muslims in Poland and Eastern Europe: Widening the European Discourse on Islam*, pp. 108–25, Warszawa: Faculty of Oriental Studies, Warsaw University.

Ochorowicz-Monatowa, M. (1995 [1912]), *Uniwersalna Książka Kucharska*, Warszawa: Wydawnictwo Graf-Punkt.

Palmer, C. (1998), "From Theory to Practice: Experiencing the Nation in Everyday Life," *Journal of Material Culture* 3(2): 175–99.

Pielak, M. and E. Czarniecka-Skubina (2016), "Kulinarne Preferencje Polskich Konsumentów w Zakresie Kuchni Etnicznych," *Zeszyty Naukowe Turystyka i Rekreacja* 18(2): 5–15.

Pintowski, F. (1961), "Uwagi o Rozwoju Polskiego Przemysłu Cukierniczego," *Przemysł Spożywczy* 15(12): 43–6.

Plebańczyk, K. (2013), "Turystyka Kulinarna w Kontekście Zrównoważonego Rozwoju w Kulturze – Perspektywy dla Polski," *Turystyka Kulturowa* 10(10): 23–38.

Produkty Zarejestrowane jako Chronione Nazwy Pochodzenia, Chronione Oznaczenia Geograficzne oraz Gwarantowane Tradycyjne Specjalności (2020), Ministerstwo Rolnictwa i Rozoju Wsi. Available online: https://www.gov.pl/web/rolnictwo/produkty -zarejestrowane-jako-chronione-nazwy-pochodzenia-chronione-oznaczenia-geografic zne-oraz-gwarantowane-tradycyjne-specjalnosci, last accessed June 10, 2020.

Przyrembel, Z. (1927), *Historja Cukrownictwa w Polsce, T. 1*, Warszawa: Published by the author.

Reid, S. E. (2002), "Cold War in the Kitchen: Gender and the De-Stalinization of Consumer Taste in the SovietUnion under Khrushchev," *Slavic Review* 61(2): 211–52.

Scarpato, R. and R. Daniele (2003), "New Global Cuisine: Tourism, Authenticity and Sense of Place in Postmodern Gastronomy," in C. M. Hall, L. Sharples, R. Mitchell, N. Macionis, and B, Cambourne (eds.), *Food Tourism Around the World: Development, Managment, Markets*, pp. 296–313, Oxford: Butterworth-Heinemann.

Siemiński, J. (1980), "Pięćdziesięciolecie Polskiego Chłodnictwa," *Przemysł Spożywczy* 34(9): 364–6.

Stępień, A. (1989), "'Wedel'- Historia i Perspektywa Rozwoju," *Przemysł Spożywczy* 18(4): 87–9.

Stępiński, M. (1962), "Przemysł Spożywczy Rozwija Produkcję Antyimportową," *Przemysł Spożywczy* 16(6): 333–6.

Szymanderska, H. (2006), *Encyklopedia Polskiej Sztuki Kulinarnej: 2400 Przepisów*, Warszawa: Wydawnictwo REA.

Wirsching, A., J. Finger, and S. Keller (2013), *Dr. Oetker und der Nationalsozialismus. Geschichte eines Familienunternehmens 1933–1945*, München: Beck.

Wojtasik, M. (2018), "Aleja Wietnamskich Barów na Bazarze pod Stadionem Dziesięciolecia jako Miejsce Spotkań Kultur i Klas," *Societas/Communitas* 25(1b): 105–24.

Yan, Y. (2013), "Of Hamburger and Social Space: Consuming McDonald's in Beijing," in C. Counihan and P. Van Esterik (eds.), *Food and Culture: A Reader*, Third edition, pp. 449–71, New York: Routledge.

Zamoyski, A. (1987), *The Polish Way: A Thousand-year History of the Poles and Their Culture*, London: John Murray.

13

Kimchi's Transnational Journey

Tastes of Authenticity and Ambiguity

Sonia Ryang

Tasting Kimchi

Once inside the mouth, that unmistakable heat begins by engulfing your tongue before moving down your throat and your esophagus, finally reaching your stomach and almost setting it on fire for a tiny moment. All the while, that smoky sensation of garlic and chili continues to overwhelm your entire mouth. Intense as this heat may be, it does not dissuade you, the whole experience so special that you cannot resist a second mouthful. That rich aroma, that fermented spiciness, the flavors of garlic, chili, fish preserve, and aged salt come at you all at once in the shape of that red paste clinging to the surface of those chopped vegetables, the entire visual effect unlike that displayed by anything you have ever eaten before—the dish tasting exactly as its rusty red color would lead one to expect. This is kimchi.

The vegetables have given in to the red paste, trading their crisp freshness for long-lasting softness, yet retaining their core resilience, offering an original texture to the eater. The spiciness of kimchi is fundamentally different from that of jalapeño or curry, as it is not as fast and straight heat that jalapeño gives or not as aromatic as curry is, but it nevertheless is so intense that one almost feels it in one's heart. Its hot and pungent flavor comes with a kick, but also a tad of underlying sweetness, its aroma characterized by the strong and distinct scent of fermented garlic. It is raw, yet ripe, rich in unison, yet also complex. Kimchi is a food best shared with others—for there is no way that your after-breath will allow you to hide the fact that you have just had it. The thick trace of its smell, lingering in your own mouth and intruding into the olfactory domains of others, leads one to identify this food as unmistakably unique—and, in this case, unmistakably Korean—many likely to agree that it is one of the most authentic representations of Korean taste.

The most common types of kimchi we see today are made with napa cabbage; when quartered from the root part, its core layers of leaves, shaped just like stacked spoons, offer an ideal receptacle for kimchi paste or *yangnyeom*, a mixture of numerous ingredients, including salt, fish sauce, fish or seaweed broth, fish or shrimp paste, garlic, ginger, chives, radish, carrots, leeks, onions, apples, pears, peaches, rice porridge, some sugar, and of course lots of chili—fresh and dried, powdered and crushed. The tradition of communal kimchi-making in late fall and early winter has a long history in Korea. Called *kimjang*, it is practiced even today in rural and suburban Korea by housewives working together to ensure that each of their neighborhood communities has sufficient condiments to get it through Korea's long, harsh winters. Recognized by UNESCO in 2013 as part of the intangible cultural heritage of humanity, kimjang constitutes a yearlong endeavor for women in these communities.[1]

Also, Kimchi plays an important role in Korea's national pride and identity, Korean commentators stressing its wholesome benefits. For example, the director of the Institute of Traditional Korean Food in Seoul claims that during the severe acute respiratory syndrome (SARS) epidemic of 2002–3, their kimchi diet prevented Koreans from becoming infected by this illness (Yoon 2006). It has also been reported to have protective effects in relation to a number of health conditions, including hypertension (Kim et al. 2018). Recently, Korean scientists have reported that kimchi is effective in preventing influenza during the winter (World Institute of Kimchi 2018). In other words, kimchi and kimchi-making (*kimjang*) are part of Korea's national cultural heritage, but also offer practical health benefits for Koreans and others.

In 1996, the South Korean government registered kimchi in the codex international, locking in its own as *the* authentic recipe (Kim 2016: 44). However, such an action is contrary to the nature of kimchi-making and kimchi-eating as communal activities. The desire for a national culture to be globally appreciated must encourage the adaptation and incorporation of this culture by other nations. But nationalism is a far more complex sentiment, particularly if one considers that the action taken by the Korean government was triggered by the producers of Japanese *kimuchi* (transliterated from Japanese) trying to register their product as an official food for the Atlanta Olympic Games. Indeed, considering the historical backdrop of Japan's past colonization of Korea, the story of kimchi has unfolded in a complex political world in which one may not talk about taste as merely one of the senses with which humans are biologically endowed.

In this chapter, I trace the metamorphosis—or, the lack thereof—of kimchi within the transnational sphere, focusing on its journey across the Japan Strait. In Japan, kimchi—in common with all things Korean—used to be seen as an unsophisticated and unhygienic food belonging to an inferior people. During the past few decades, however, the situation has shifted dramatically. With its spicy, pungent flavor, kimchi has become very popular in Japan, occupying a place on the gourmet food list and enjoying popularity as a home cooking item. We will explore a fascinating story of ambivalence, ambiguity, and contested notions of authenticity, tracing the journey taken by kimchi across this narrow waterway between peninsula and archipelago, a strait which once separated colony from metropolis. First, let us take a close look at kimchi as we know it today, so as to understand and appreciate how it is made, stored, and enjoyed.

Making Kimchi

How much do we know about what kimchi should taste like? Perhaps it should be spicy, hot, a bit tangy, garlicky, stringy, maybe salty, super-salty, and a tad fishy? How about what it should not taste like? One might think it should never be sweet and that it cannot be bland or soothing. It's spicy, but in a different way from jalapeño. It can be tangy, but with a different intensity from pickled cucumber. It is definitely garlicky, but different from garlic that is cooked or roasted. And, most importantly, it should be salty, but too much salt truly ruins it. Many people that I have encountered who make kimchi and eat it themselves say that kimchi has a complex taste and that, depending on when and how you eat it, it can be sweet. But this sweetness is different from that of sugar. Rather, this sweetness comes from the incongruent mixture of fermented fish or shellfish, canned or fresh fruit, and the faint sweetness possessed by vegetables such as cabbage. As such, even though salt is used generously when making the base vegetable, the saltiness must not be overwhelming. In fact, by the time kimchi is ready to be tasted—normally following one week or so in the refrigerator—the flavor of salt should have withdrawn to the background and given way to a concoction of ginger, garlic, chili (both powdered and crushed, fine and coarse), and other secondary vegetables, such as chives, carrots, and onions, all sliced super-thin, minced down to micro size, or grated.

Additionally, the seafood product (tiny shrimps, anchovies, or, rarely, oysters, all raw, salted, sliced or crushed, and fermented) that is used to enhance further fermentation must not overpower the kick of garlic, which is supported by its partner, ginger; in other words, kimchi must not taste fishy. Then, one needs to be careful not to add too much fruit, because fruit quickens the acidification of kimchi, making it too pungent too soon. However, semi-sour kimchi is a delicious delight in its own right, and one needs to seize the moment, kimchi in its semi-sour state offering a whole range of taste-enhancing options to accompany fried rice, pork dishes, tofu, and noodle soups, for example. Some people like to enjoy freshly made kimchi, the vegetables still crisp and the edges of chili chips still coarse, with a bowl of freshly steamed rice, for example, while others prefer it to be weeks-old, mature in its fermentation, and emitting pungent smells all around, mixing it in tofu hotpots or pork stir-fries. Most others say, somewhere in-between is best. In a word, the taste of kimchi is complex yet balanced, generalizable yet highly arbitrary and unique, and, above all, diverse in terms of historical, regional, and, indeed, individual preferences.

The kimchi paste should be prepared while the cabbage is being salted. The base of the paste is made of garlic, ginger, and onions, all minced and mixed together. Many people add rice porridge, or sticky rice powder boiled in water until it achieves a thick consistency, then chilled. Many would refer to this substance as "glue," as in it would generate stickiness ensuring the clinging of *yangnyeom* to the cabbage. Some may add a tad of sugar to this rice porridge or rice water, while many add fish sauce (readily available in Vietnamese grocery stores). Once you mix these (rice porridge/water with minced garlic, ginger, and onions), you add red chili peppers. Some prefer to use only finely powdered chili, while others like to combine it with coarsely crushed dried chili peppers. The choice of seafood products is another critical issue. Whether to use *saeujeot* or tiny raw shrimps, salted and fermented, or *myeolchijeot*, their anchovy counterpart, for example, is a key decision that will determine the fate of a particular batch of cabbage kimchi. Those who are not keen on too fishy a taste might prefer to substitute such items with a small amount of chilled anchovy or tuna broth, or even to do without a seafood product. These seafood products are necessary to promote vegetable fermentation that yields a rich aroma and distinct taste, but again, depending on one's taste, one can make kimchi without any of these. Vegan kimchi lovers can use dried seaweed broth (chilled) in lieu of seafood products.

The use of secondary vegetables is optional, and some proceed to make napa cabbage kimchi without any of these. Some people add fruit, chopped, sliced, or pureed. Many prefer fresh apples, but some use canned peaches or canned pears to enhance the fermentation process. Chopped or sliced fruit should, by the time kimchi has been left to ferment, have dissolved into the kimchi juice, making it bubbly. Many say that adding fruit enhances the fermentation, while others say that it simply adds some sweetness to the kimchi. After the paste has been mixed, it is then distributed between the folds of the cabbage leaves. This part of the work can best be done by hand—no good utensil exists for this task. Today, people commonly wear plastic or latex gloves in order to protect their nails and skin, but, traditionally, Korean women did this work with their bare hands, saying that it generated a handmade taste or *sonmat*.

Once this process is complete, the decision as to how many days the prepared vegetables (i.e., kimchi) should sit in the refrigerator before it is served is entirely a personal one, depending on one's own preferred taste; some people like it fresh, while others like it ripe. Many divide the kimchi they have prepared into two batches, one to be stored in the refrigerator for long-term use and another to be left at room temperature so as to promote faster fermentation. Traditionally, Koreans would store kimchi in large earthen jars with lids, burying the jars in the ground outside so as to keep them for use throughout the winter.

Kimchi, and especially napa cabbage kimchi, has a long shelf life; even after having been served as a side dish, and after its acidity has increased, making it too pungent to be eaten on its own, it retains multiple uses: for example, as an additive for a noodle soup, a pork stir-fry, or a plate of egg fried rice. Kimchi tofu is another popular dish that is best prepared with over-fermented (i.e., old) kimchi, while kimchi pancakes or kimchi dumplings are an easy fix as a nutritious snack or side dish. Some people chop up pungent kimchi and mix it with butter or cream cheese to spread on a bun, while others make pungent kimchi sandwiches. It adds a kick to otherwise bland dishes, such as fried eggs with tomatoes or sautéed potatoes. In a word, the techniques used in the process of making kimchi are only exceeded in their variety by the range of uses to which kimchi may be put during its "afterlife," so to speak.

Kimchi throughout History

In Korea, the first historical documentation of the process of preserving vegetables using salt and fermentation, and the first record of vegetables being fermented in soy sauce, appeared in twelfth-century poetry. Toward the end of the fourteenth century, fermented vegetables were recorded as *chimchae*, a term written using two Chinese ideographs that respectively mean "to soak" and "vegetable." Scholars generally agree that this vegetable condiment, *chimchae*, later came to be known as kimchi (Yi 1988: 41). It was only in the early twentieth century that napa cabbage, as we know it today, became widely available in Korea, thus making cabbage kimchi or *baechu kimchi* very popular; until then, the most common form of kimchi had been made using radishes (Yi 1988: 42). Still, a wide variety of vegetables provided (and continues to provide) the raw materials for kimchi: cucumbers, radishes, cabbages, leeks, chives, eggplant, spinach, squashes, green onions, green chili, sesame leaves, watercress, and so on. Many of them double as secondary vegetables for cabbage kimchi or cucumber kimchi. Depending on the locality and season, kimchi can take on a wide variety of flavors and forms. Examples include *mulgimchi* (literally, "water kimchi"), which is sweet and sour rather than spicy, *dongchimi*, the famous whole-radish water kimchi that is popular in northern Korea, and *baekgimchi*, a type of kimchi made basically using no chili peppers, *baek* denoting the color white; in southeastern Korea, chestnuts and pears are used to make *baekgimchi* (Yi 1988: 44).

Today we know kimchi to be red because of the generous use of chili peppers in its preparation. Originally, however, kimchi was seasoned with salt, cloves, ginger, orange peel, garlic, and other ingredients, and was therefore predominantly white in color, as in *baekgimchi* today (Kim and Jeong 2002: 475). It was the Japanese invasion of Korea at the end of the sixteenth century that brought red chili peppers to Korea; with the ambition of conquering the Ming Dynasty, Japan's strongman, Toyotomi Hideyoshi, sent a massive army to Korea. Along with military occupation, devastation, atrocities, and destruction, Toyotomi's soldiers brought with them chili peppers. According to historical documents, at that time these were referred to as *waegyeja* or Japanese mustard, rather than *gochu*, the term used in Korean today for chili (Jo and Choi 2014: 90). Chili peppers are not native to Japan either; they reached Japan via Iberian missionaries, who, in turn, had sourced them from their South American colonies. Even after chili peppers were transmitted to Korea at the end of the sixteenth century, it still took decades for them to make their appearance as one of the regular ingredients used in kimchi-making. Indeed, it was not until around the seventeenth century that chili peppers began to be used in the making of kimchi (Jo 1994).

It is, then, such an irony to find that it was a Japanese invasion that brought the red chili pepper, in many ways the ingredient that gives kimchi its essential spirit, to Korea, considering that 300 years later Japan would reach Korea again, annexing it in 1910 and governing it as a colony until 1945. It is even more ironic to note that, with Japan's colonization, things Korean came to be seen as inferior to things Japanese—including food in general and kimchi in particular. Calling Koreans *ninniku kusai chōsenjin*, or "garlic-stinking Koreans," was a common derogatory term thrown at Koreans, since in Japan at that time, eating garlic was rare, this food item being associated, in the minds of the Japanese, with the poor and uneducated. Subtle flavors were generally associated with sophistication, evidence of the ability of the eater to identify and appreciate the smallest differences in taste, while strong-smelling food was associated with cheap ingredients and rough eating habits.

Kimchi in Japan was, for a long time, seen as a metonym for things Korean—inferior, barbaric, uncivilized, and filthy. Its spicy and pungent smell was particularly disliked by the Japanese, as garlic was not a common food item among Japanese in the early twentieth century. Referred to as *tōgarashi* or *nanban koshō*, chili peppers were seen as foreign food. *Tō* of *tōgarashi* derives from the Japanese character used to denote Tang China. In this case, however, it carries the meaning of "foreign" and does not denote China itself. The term *garashi* is an elided form of the term *karashi* or mustard. *Nanban* denotes "southern barbarians," meaning "foreigners," and *koshō* is pepper. Today, chili peppers are called *tōgarashi*, and *nanban koshō* has become an archaic term. Still, in Japan, it was not absorbed into the nation's native cuisine after reaching Japan via Spanish or Portuguese missionaries, as was the case for Korea after the Japanese invasion of the sixteenth century.

As Korean colonial immigrants to Japan in the prewar decades clustered together to form shantytowns, they became segregated. In these locales, bizarre kinds of food such as kimchi were eaten, a strange, incomprehensible language was heard, and women strolled around wearing unfamiliar dresses with short bodices and bulky skirts, their gait almost the exact opposite of their Japanese counterparts. Colonial immigrants did just about everything strangely, differently, and wrongly, whether it be wedding ceremonies, breast feeding, children's toilet training, bathing, or, above all, eating. Korean eating habits were viewed by the mainstream Japanese population as unhygienic and ignorant, almost always bad, and at times even evil. This type of judgment aligned with the ideology behind Japan's colonization of Korea. Japan assigned itself the role of providing guiding leadership to its poor, inferior Asian sister, Korea, following the former's emergence as a leading power in Asia with its defeat of China in the first Sino-Japanese War (1894–6) and of Russia, a European nation, in the Russo-Japanese War (1904–5). Thus, by the time it successfully annexed Korea in 1910, in a style akin to the European colonization of Asia and Africa, Japan regarded itself as an unequivocal leader possessing an advanced civilization when compared with its backward neighbors in the hierarchy of Asian racial groups (Duus 1998).

Moreover, traditionally speaking, even from precolonial days, Korea and Japan did not share many commonalities when it came to food, apart from the fact that both nations cultivated rice and enjoyed meals with the staple elements of grains (rice preferred), soup, and side dishes. When it came to meat consumption in particular, Japanese and Koreans had very little in common. Repeated invasions and occupations of Korea by Mongolians during much of the thirteenth century led to Koreans being introduced to a diverse range of meat and dairy products, even though Korea's ruling religion at the time was Buddhism (Ryang 2015). Japan, on the other hand, never had direct contact with the Mongols. In Japan, since medieval times, occupations concerned with the handling of dead animals (leather tanning and butchering, for example) were associated with the untouchables, an outcast group of people who had been excluded from the social hierarchy and were basically seen as not belonging to humanity (see Amino 1994). The untouchables were known as *eta* (filth or pollution) or *hinin* (nonhumans) and were subjected to severe discrimination. The close association between this social group and animal meat led to many taboos coming to be associated with the consumption of meat in Japan, meaning that meat-based cuisine did not develop to the same extent as in Korea. So, for example, while Koreans, in common with Europeans and continental northeast Asians, consumed most parts of a cow, Japanese would traditionally leave out the organs, tail, and other edible parts. During the colonial period, in the 1930s, when poor girls from rural Korea were brought to Kishiwada, near Osaka, Japan, as factory workers, they discovered that butchers would throw away organs, such as kidneys and livers, as waste. Korean girls would ask the butchers to sell them these discarded body parts at very low prices, barbecuing them with spicy marinade using garlic and chili peppers. This became a novel kind of food in the Osaka area known as *horumon yaki*, the term *horumon* derived from the Osaka dialect term *hōru mon* meaning "things to be discarded," and *yaki,* from *yaku,* meaning "to burn" or "to grill" (Kim 1982). Today, *horumon yaki* is a popular Korean barbecue menu item in Japan. But, one can imagine how the Japanese residents of Kishiwada in the 1930s would have viewed the Korean factory girls with utter disgust as they gladly consumed the discarded organs.

With Japan's defeat in the Second World War in August 1945, the occupation of Japan by the Allied Powers began, and so did Japan's reconstruction. Its new constitution designated the emperor as a mere figurehead of the state, and almost every aspect of the lives of the Japanese was touched by the postwar reforms. With the San Francisco Treaty agreed between Japan and the United States in 1952, Japan officially abandoned its former colonies. Yet, this new postwar era did little to improve the relationship between Japan and its former colony, Korea. The Japanese government did not recognize either North Korea or South Korea at the time, both of them having been established in 1948 as independent states. Upon concluding the San Francisco Treaty, Japan unilaterally declared that all of the former colonial peoples who remained in Japan (mostly Koreans and Taiwanese) no longer belonged to Japan, thereby causing them to lose their residential security and other customary rights overnight. When Japan surrendered to the Allied Powers at the end of the Second World War in August 1945, there were more than two million Koreans living in Japan (Morris-Suzuki 2005: 22). They had moved to Japan for various reasons, but mostly to secure better livelihoods than those available in the poverty-stricken colony. Following Japan's defeat (i.e., Korea's liberation), about three-quarters of the Koreans in Japan were repatriated, leaving some 600,000 behind. They became stateless individuals in Japan, having now lost access to state social security provisions on the basis that they no longer belonged to the Japanese nation. Since Koreans had begun immigrating to Japan from the 1920s on, there were already second-generation Koreans in postwar Japan, yet all of them were denied Japanese nationality and citizenship. This is because Japan practices the principle of *jus sanguinis*, right of blood, in its laws dealing with nationality, meaning that regardless of whether an individual is born on Japanese soil or not, he or she is denied Japanese nationality unless at least one parent is of Japanese descent (Ōnuma 1986).

Their difficulties were compounded by the added complication of the internal split into north supporters and south supporters and already suffering from dire poverty and a lack of civil rights and protection, Koreans in Japan faced multifold hurdles in trying to eke out a living in postwar Japan (Ryang 2012). In such circumstances, food was one area in which Koreans did not give in easily to pressure to assimilate and tolerate the ethnocide-like denigration of their culture throughout the colonial and postcolonial periods. As with other immigrants throughout the world, ethnic food businesses served mainly Korean clientele. Slowly and belatedly reflecting Japan's strong economy, however, Korean ethnic food businesses began making inroads into the Japanese mainstream media and other cultural outlets during the 1980s. For example, the Moranbong Corporation, owned by a Korean family in Japan, began advertising its barbecue sauce via televised commercials in 1979. In addition to manufacturing Korean foods, such as packaged kimchi, sauces, and noodles, the corporation now also operates Korean culinary schools and restaurants (Jeon 1993). Moranbong's TV commercials have used mainstream Japanese (and, more recently, South Korean celebrities), replacing the formerly backward image of Korean food with something entirely new—a new status as a shiny object of global capitalism devoid of the old colonial baggage and, thus, something that Japanese customers can enjoy without being mired in complications involving colonial history and unresolved postcolonial settlements.

Such a turn reflected the gradual stabilization of residential status for Koreans in Japan. In 1965, Japan and South Korea achieved diplomatic normalization, Koreans in Japan who supported South Korea subsequently being granted permanent resident status in Japan. However, as stated earlier, large sections of the Korean population remaining in Japan supported North Korea, even though they had originated from the southern provinces of the peninsula. The post-1965 arrangement therefore complicated matters; due to their political allegiance, Koreans who supported North Korea found it difficult to apply for South Korean nationality, and thereby did not obtain permanent resident status in Japan. Such an ethnic divide was further augmented on the ideological level, reflecting intensifying Cold War tensions in East Asia. The Koreans who supported North Korea organized themselves in a much more systematic manner than those supporting South Korea; the former, at the peak of their organizational strength, had a total of 150 independent Korean schools providing Korean-language instruction, their own community credit union, soccer team, performing art theater, publication house, and a network of offices covering every prefecture in Japan (Ryang 1997). The situation changed dramatically when Japan ratified the International Covenants for Human Rights and joined the United Nations Refugee Convention in 1980. From that point on, Koreans in Japan, regardless of whether they had South Korean nationality or not, were granted permanent resident status.

Another factor to consider is the change in Japan-Republic of Korea (ROK) relations during the last three decades. After many decades of animosity due to unsettled postcolonial issues between the two countries, and despite the fact that such animosity in many ways still remains, starting in the 1990s, Japanese immigration law has continued to be reformed, with a shift toward an opening of Japan's doors to foreign nationals of Japanese descent. From around the same time, South Korea began adopting a more lenient overseas travel policy in relation to its own citizens. In contrast with the practices of earlier military dictatorships in South Korea, after the Seoul Olympic Games of 1988, the regime began issuing passports to ordinary citizens. This resulted in an increase in the number of South Korean citizens arriving in Japan; while 515,807 South Korean citizens entered Japan in 1988, the number had doubled to

1,097,601 by 1991; 1,774,872 arrived in 2004 (Immigration Bureau, Ministry of Justice, Japan 2005: 4).

In 2001, during the historic summit between North Korea's Kim Jong Il and Japan's Junichiro Koizumi, Kim revealed that back in the 1970s and 1980s, North Korean agents had kidnapped Japanese citizens from the shores of Japan. This news shocked not only the Japanese public but also those Koreans in Japan who had supported North Korea until that time, resulting in a massive attrition in the number of those adopting such a position (Ryang 2016). Besides, by the early twenty-first century, the Korean population in Japan included fourth and even fifth generations. Even though, due to the *jus sanguinis* principle of Japanese nationality law, no Korean born in Japan was eligible to obtain Japanese citizenship, they enjoyed a more secure form of permanent resident status and were, culturally, basically natives of Japan, not of Korea—either North or South.

At around the same time, law reform in South Korea concerned with the issue of nationality led to overseas Koreans of Korean descent (South Korea also practicing the principle of *jus sanguinis* in its nationality-related law) becoming eligible to apply for South Korean nationality—provided that the applicant did not reside in South Korea nor intend to seek a permanent livelihood there. While being denied voting rights in that country and other civil rights as well as national (domestic) identification, they would be exempt from obligations to pay taxes and undertake military service. This development encouraged many Koreans in Japan, regardless of their political allegiance, to apply for South Korean nationality and passports. By the first decade of the twenty-first century, the majority of Koreans in Japan no longer professed commitment to either of the regimes on the peninsula as they tried to figure out ways to live (and die) in Japan as non-Japanese persons of Korean descent. During the last decade, about 10,000 to 15,000 Korean individuals have been naturalized as Japanese citizens, while more Koreans from South Korea are moving to Japan as students, professionals, and businesspeople—not as colonial immigrants looking for a way to survive (Ryang 2010). Similarly, the majority of (old-timer) Korean residents in Japan today have acquired South Korean nationality, alongside permanent resident status in Japan, allowing them to travel abroad with South Korean passports and Japanese reentry permits. One of the most popular destinations for Koreans in Japan is South Korea, encouraging an ethnic revival and a renewed appreciation of their homeland's culture.

Then came *kanryū būmu*, or the Korean wave, a boom in the popularity of Korean popular culture, whereby Korean television dramas, pop music (or K-pop), films, and other popular cultural products captivated the interest of Japanese and global audiences. Beginning in the early 2000s, Korean cultural products have enjoyed explosive popularity in Japan. Passionate followers of Korean drama series and actors and actresses in Japan would not only passively watch their idols perform on screen but would also actively explore their favorite actors' native culture by traveling to Korea (Ryang 2016). Indeed, during the first decade of the century, Japanese tourists consistently accounted for about 40 percent of all Asian tourists visiting Korea.[2] By the 2010s, things Korean, including food—and, prominently, kimchi—had penetrated Japanese consumer culture, not as products of a former colony, but, collectively, as something cool, global, trendy, and sophisticated. This does not mean that Japanese society has wholeheartedly embraced all things Korean. Far from it. Even to this day, the Japanese government and sections of its society find it difficult to sincerely apologize for the cruelty of the nation's colonial rule and the atrocities and violence that it perpetrated during the Second World War, including the exploitation of thousands of Korean girls and women as military sex slaves (e.g., Yoshimi 2000). Regarding the penetration of Korean popular products in Japan and their appreciation, there are issues that are not entirely unproblematic. Nevertheless, it is safe to say that, compared to the 1960s and 1970s, let alone during the colonial period, things Korean—including kimchi—have gained cultural currency in Japan's consumer market.

Kimchi in Japan

As can be seen from the previous section, the transnational journey of kimchi from Korea to Japan, starting from the colonial period, has waxed and waned, reflecting Japanese-Korean historical relations. From the postwar period up until the 1970s—that is to say, during the period before Korean ethnic food businesses began advancing into Japan's mainstream market—kimchi in Japan was known as *chōsenzuke, chosen,* denoting "Korea" and *zuke* derived from *tsuke* or pickles. According to Sasaki (2009), a kimchi researcher in Japan, during the 1960s, kimchi, under the name *chōsenzuke,* was sold in food stores in Japan and eaten, albeit in small quantities, in ordinary households. A few years before Moranbong, a Korean ethnic food corporation in Japan began selling its product under the name "kimchi" and popularizing it in the mainstream Japanese media (see previous section). The Japanese food producer Momoya used the term "kimuchi" (kimchi according to the Japanese enunciation) when it rolled out a product called *kimuchi no moto,* meaning "kimchi base" in 1975, a packaged instant sauce mix that generated a kimchi-like flavor when mixed with chopped vegetables ("Tsukemono ichiban ninki jitsuwa kimuchi" 2017). One can be rather certain that this instant sauce had a much milder garlic and chili flavor than the kimchi we know today. Today, according to one source, kimchi ranks among those varieties of *tsukemono* or pickles produced in the largest quantities in Japan: 47,000 tons of kimchi were produced in Japan in 1985, the volume rising to 249,000 tons in 2000, and reaching 384,000 tons in 2003, around the peak of the Korean popular culture boom in Japan. Japanese consumers would eat kimchi both at home and at restaurants, many of them eagerly awaiting the arrival of new kimchi products on supermarket shelves in Japan ("Tsukemono ichiban ninki jitsuwa kimuchi" 2017). In 2003, the Japanese public television station, NHK, broadcast kimchi cooking classes and published an accompanying cookbook introducing fifteen easy-to-prepare recipes (Asakura and Chae 2003).

In cyberspace, various online kimchi recipes circulate in Japan, each site boasting the authenticity of its own recipe and insisting that it was provided directly by a Korean chef. Many of them also emphasize the health benefits of kimchi, with its rich probiotics due to fermentation. The popularity of kimchi and kimchi-making in Japan seems to cross class divides. For example, a high-end department store's food website introduces a recipe for making kimchi in two hours, a creation of its chef (Nara 2017). While advertising the ingredients that are sold at this department store, the recipe does not hold back in its use of chili and garlic, emphasizing the authenticity of its taste—that is to say, an authentically Korean taste—rather than modifying it to please Japanese consumers, who might have preferred a subtler taste some decades before. Seen in this way, that distinct smell, that strong taste, and that radical difference that kimchi gives, in sharp contrast to traditional Japanese cuisine, with its emphasis on subtle tastes, has acquired transnational currency, this also being a distinctly postcolonial development.

When we compare this data with the micro data that I collected from seven Korean women in Japan belonging to the second and third generations in Japan (all aged fifty-nine to sixty), all of whom make their own kimchi at home, an interesting contrast emerges. The women come from families that used to support North Korea. Consequently, they received a Korean-language education and, by and large, possess a clear and secure sense of self-identification as Koreans living in Japan. Even though they are able to understand Korean, they are more at home with the Japanese language, which they speak as native speakers. Except for one woman who grew up in Tokyo but moved to rural Japan after marriage, all of the women were born and raised in the Tokyo metropolitan area and currently reside there. They live in Japanese neighborhoods with Japanese families as their immediate next door neighbors. Only one lives in a stand-alone home and the rest live in condominiums. All of the women are married to ethnic Korean husbands and have children; about half of the women also have grandchildren. About half of their children are married to Japanese spouses, while all of their grandchildren attend Japanese schools. Two out of seven work full-time, while the rest have either retired from full-time employment or only worked part-time in the past.

According to the women, interest in kimchi among their Japanese neighbors has risen dramatically since the *kanryū būmu* or Korean wave of the first decade of the century. Some of these Japan-born Korean women learned how to make kimchi from their mothers-in-law after marriage, but many of them are self-taught. Factors that have facilitated this process include the dissemination of the internet, the stabilization of their residential status in Japan, and their subsequent acquisition of South Korean passports allowing them to frequent South Korea's marketplaces themselves. A few of the women refuse to use Japanese chili powder, traveling to South Korea every three to four months to obtain local supplies. They patronize stores in Seoul's main markets, where they ask for the chili to be freshly crushed or ground right in front of them. But, all of them use vegetables that are produced in Japan. Some even said that they preferred to use Japanese napa cabbages (especially those produced in Ibaraki Prefecture) because of their water content, many of them telling me that Korean cabbages contained less water than their Japanese counterparts. Accordingly, they believe that different methods are used in Japan and Korea for the initial salting, with differences also existing in the quantity of salt used, Japanese cabbages not requiring too much salt. Also, many of them use Japanese rather than Korean salt, claiming that Korean salt is too coarse. Some women refrain from using shrimps or anchovy paste for fermentation, because they consider that these create too fishy a flavor, while others insist on using them, demanding that these ingredients be imported from Korea. Some may opt for a compromise, substituting shrimp paste with *katsuo dashi*, the tuna stock that is readily available in Japan and used in a vast array of Japanese cooking. Some do without rice porridge/water, sugar, or fruit; one woman told me these would make the kimchi taste too complicated. Still, all of them use garlic, ginger, and chili, mixing them with thinly sliced secondary vegetables to produce *yangnyeom* or kimchi paste.

All of the women have had the experience of sharing their kimchi with their Japanese neighbors, while a few of them have also had the experience of receiving kimchi made by their Japanese neighbors themselves. All agree that they find their Japanese neighbors quite enthusiastic about kimchi and have not detected any signs of disdain or surprise, even when sharing kimchi, despite the fact that their neighbors know fully well that this is a Korean food, a food that the Japanese general population used to look down upon. This presents a sharp contrast with the experience of their mothers and grandmothers. Korean women in Japan of their mothers' generation (in their eighties and above) would have strictly managed the issue of "kimchi breath" by, for example, restricting the dish's appearance at the family meal table to Saturdays. This was because Koreans in Japan, keenly aware of the Japanese dislike of the smell of kimchi, tried to mitigate its effects by timing the consumption of kimchi so that it took place well before any interaction with Japanese people, be it at work or on public transport. Even today, Koreans in Japan are careful not to eat kimchi for lunch, for example, and some of the women whom I interviewed, who are office workers in Tokyo, have been surprised to see their younger Japanese colleagues happily eating Korean food for lunch and then returning to their offices afterward. It is almost ironic to see that Koreans are now more aware of this issue than some Japanese, the latter seemingly no longer sensing much stigma to be attached to kimchi at all.

When asked about the sentiment or emotion that accompanies kimchi-making, however, the Korean women in Japan whom I contacted did not display particularly nationalistic responses, nor were they emphatic about the notion of kimchi as Korea's signature food. All of them said they kept making it because they had gotten so good at it and that it was fun to make. When pressed about their ethnic identity and its connection to food, they admitted this link, only to quickly generalize their response by saying that such links existed for every food in every culture. They did remember, however, growing up feeling that kimchi was something that they only ate at home with their families and not something that they would share with their Japanese neighbors. In that sense, they were all in agreement in recognizing the change represented by the current celebration of kimchi in Japan. They pointed out, however, that this was the case for most other things Korean as well, including television dramas, films, music, and so on, all of these having been rejected or looked down upon in Japan prior to the Korean wave. Hence, many of them said, there was nothing special about kimchi, save for one point—that it could not be substituted with something Japanese, as none of the Japanese pickled vegetables used garlic or chili. Whereas one could have K-pop *and* J-pop, Korean dramas *and* Japanese dramas, the women stressed, kimchi had no Japanese counterpart. But, when asked whether they regarded their kimchi to be authentic, all of them denied that this was the case. They cited the fact that they had learned how to make it online or from their mothers-in-law, who were also raised in Japan, showing that their idea of kimchi's authenticity had a physical connection with Korea itself and not with their immigrant upbringing. Even those who traveled to

Korea to obtain local chili claimed that they did so not because the use of ingredients sourced directly in Korea would make their kimchi authentic, but simply because it would improve the taste. Besides, they added, they loved traveling to Korea, and buying chili was a great excuse for purchasing an airline ticket.

When asked if their kimchi was more Korean or more Japanese, one woman said: "*yoku wakaranaikedo, kekkyoku dochirademo iinjanai?*" (in Japanese), which means, "I don't really know, but in the end, I don't think it matters much, do you?" This type of perspective contrasts sharply with Japanese recipes found online that make enthusiastic claims concerning their authenticity. By way of contrast, the Korean women in Japan that I interviewed, all of whom make kimchi themselves, regard their creations as far more hybrid, and do not insist on their authenticity. For them, kimchi is something that exists concretely in their world as their everyday creation, yet they immediately display ambiguous responses when prompted to think about the cultural authenticity of the kimchi that they make. Clearly, it is part of their ethnic identity as Koreans living in Japan, while it is but one of the many things which they claim to be Korean. And, insofar as they are conscious of their ambiguous status as Korean women living in Japan with South Korean passports and Japanese permanent resident status (and, therefore, as members of a group that will not be "returning" to South Korea), they renounce the authenticity of the kimchi that they make. Furthermore, conscious that they themselves were born in Japan and grew up there, living there and speaking Japanese, they self-select themselves as being unable to create Korean kimchi with an authentic taste.

Kimchi in the World

Today, kimchi travels across the globe, widely accepted as one of the most representative examples of Korean cuisine. In order to promote kimchi, the South Korean government established the World Institute of Kimchi or *Segye kimchi yeonguso* in 2010, its mission being the promotion of kimchi's cultural uniqueness and health benefits to the world (Pak 2010). Still, not all Korean kimchi is Korean made. Currently, Korea both exports and imports kimchi; most of its imported kimchi comes from China, with the majority of its exports going to Japan. In both cases, volumes are increasing, one data source pointing to a 5.5 percent increase in imports and a 15.9 percent increase in exports between 2018 and 2019 (Park 2019: 4).

However, this increase in kimchi imports to South Korea may not necessarily point to an increase in consumption there. Lower prices are behind the nation's dependence on imported kimchi. Moreover, kimchi produced in China may not differ as much from the Korean-made product as one might imagine. In northeastern China, home to a large concentration of Korean Chinese, kimchi-making is registered as an intangible traditional art and skill by local municipalities, accorded extra attention as an example of cultural heritage; kimchi experts are certified, providing formal instruction in kimchi-making in institutionally supported settings (Noh 2019). Moreover, in South Korea, recent years have seen a substantial fall in kimchi consumption among young people in urban areas and among women nationwide (Park and Lee 2017).

When all of these factors are considered, then, to what extent is kimchi still Korean? What does it mean, at any rate, for kimchi to be Korean? Furthermore, should the authenticity of food, even in the case of a signature food such as kimchi, be measured first and foremost by its national identity? According to Sidney Mintz, the notion of "national cuisine" is problematic, as cuisines are defined by region, and not nation (Mintz 2002). Considering that cuisine, cooking, food, and eating, for that matter, existed way before humanity came to be divided according to the borders of nation-states, Mintz's view makes complete sense. Furthermore, regional cuisines also display an infinite number of variations, all the way down to the cooking and eating habits of particular families and individuals. And yet, even family heritage, in and of itself, does not guarantee the authenticity of cuisine—as in the case of the Korean women in Japan characterizing the kimchi they make as being not quite authentic. The fact is that no one can be completely confident that their kimchi is authentic, the process of assessing the authenticity of food, itself, being a subjective undertaking. As such, one might say that kimchi's authenticity can only ever be ambiguous, the only thing certain being that spicy, burning sensation as it kicks, burns, and then warms your stomach.

Notes

1 https://ich.unesco.org/en/RL/kimjang-making-and-sharing-kimchi-in-the-republic-of-korea-00881.
2 Calculated from https://kto.visitkorea.or.kr/eng/tourismStatics/keyFacts/KoreaMonthlyStatistics/eng/inout/inout.kto.

References

Amino, Y. (1994), *Chūseino hininto yūjo* [Women and Non-humans in Medieval Japan], Tokyo: Akashi Shoten.

Asakura, T. and S.-M. Chae (2003), *Kimuchino tabi: Tsukutte, tabete, shiru* [Kimchi's Journey: Cook, Eat, and Know], Tokyo: Nippon hōsōkyōkai.

Duus, P. (1998), *The Abacus and the Sword: Japanese Penetration of Korea, 1895–1910.* Berkeley: University of California Press.

Immigration Bureau, Ministry of Justice, Japan (2005), *2005 Immigration Control.* Tokyo: Ministry of Justice, Japan. Online: http://www.moj.go.jp/content/000007268.pdf, last accessed March 20, 2020.

Jeon, J.-S. [Zen, Chinshoku] (1993), *Waga chōsen watashino nihon* [Our Korea, my Japan], Tokyo: Heibonsha.

Jo, J.-S. (1994), "Kimchiui yeoksajeok gochal" [Historical Review of Kimchi], *Dongasia siksaenghwal hakhoeji* [Journal of the East Asian Society of Dietary Life] 4(2): 93–108.

Jo, J.-S. and I.-S. Choi (2014), "Kimchi jaeryoui byeoncheone gwanhan munheonjeok gochal" [A Historical Study of the Ingredients of Kimchi], *Wesiksaneop gyeongyeong yeongu* [Research into Management in the Food Service Industry] 10(1): 83–98.

Kim, B., E.-G. Mun, D. Kim, P. Doyeon, L. Yongsoon, H.-J. Lee, and Y.-S. Cha (2018), "Kimchi mit kimchiyurae yusangyunui geonghang ganeungseonge daehan yeongudonghyang josa" [A Survey of Research Papers on the Health Benefits of Kimchi and Kimchi Lactic Acid Bacteria], *Journal of Nutrition and Health* 51(1):1–13.

Kim, C. (1982), *Chōsenjin jokōno uta: 1930nen kishiwada bōseki sōgi* [Songs of Korean Female Factory Workers: The 1930 Labor Dispute in the Kishiwada Textile Industry], Tokyo: Iwanami shoten.

Kim, C.-H. (2016), "*Kimchi* Nation: Constructing *Kimjang* as An Intangible Korean Heritage," in C. M. K. Lum and M. de Ferrière le Vayer (eds.), *Urban Foodways and Communication: Ethnographic Studies in Intangible Cultural Food Heritages Around the World*, pp. 39–54, Lanham: Rowman & Littlefield.

Kim, E. and H. Jeong (2002), *Hanguk eumsik* [Korean Food], Seoul: Munjisa.

Mintz, S. (2002), "Eating American," in Carole Counihan (ed.), *Food in the USA: A Reader*, pp. 23–34, New York: Routledge.

Morris-Suzuki, T. (2005), *Exodus to North Korea: Shadows from Japan's Cold War*, Lanham: Rowman and Littlefield.

Nara, T. (2017), "Tsukekomi 2jikan, igaina umamishokuzaide tsukuru 'jikasei kimuchi' reshipi" [Only Two Hours to Pickle: "A home-made kimchi" Recipe using Surprising Umami Ingredients], *Foodie* Mitsukoshi Isetan, January 13, 2017. Online: https://mi-journey.jp/foodie/31981/, last accessed March 20, 2020.

Noh, Y.-K. (2019), "Jungguk geoju joseonin kimchimunhwaui yangsanggwa uimi" [The Outlook of Kimchi Culture and Its Meaning among Koreans in China], *Tongil inmunhak* [Journal of the Humanities for Unification] 79: 107–33.

Ōnuma, Y. (1986), *Tanitsu minzoku shakaino shinwao koete—zainichi kankoku chōsenjinto shutsunyūkoku kanritaisei* [Beyond the Myth of the Single Ethnic Nation-State – Koreans in Japan and Japan's Immigration Control System], Tokyo: Tōshindō.

Pak, W.-S. (2010), "Kimchiui segyehwa bangan" [Directions of Kimchi's Globalization], in *Hanguk sikpum yeongyang gwahakhoe saneop simpojium balpyojip* [Proceedings from the Symposium of the Korean Society for Food Science and Nutrition], pp. 13–26, May 2010.

Park, J. and H.-J. Lee (2017), "Choegeun 10nyeongan hanguginui jiyeokbyeol sodeuksujun kimchiseopchwi byeonhwa" [Shifts in Kimchi Consumption among the Korean Population by Region and Income Level during the Past Ten Years], *Daehan jiyeok sahoe yeongyanghakhoeji* [Korean Journal of Community Nutrition] 22(2): 145–58.

Park, S.-H. (2019), "Kimchi saneobui hyeunhwanggwa jeonmang" [The Current Status and Future Prospects of the Kimchi Industry], *Sikpumsaneopgwa yeongyang* [Food Industry and Nutrition] 24(1): 1–8.

Ryang, S. (1997), *North Koreans in Japan: Language, Ideology, and Identity*, Boulder: Westview Press.

Ryang, S. (2010), "To Be or Not to Be—In Japan and Beyond: Summing Up and Sizing Down Koreans in Japan," *Asia Pacific World* 1(2): 7–31.

Ryang, S. (2012), "The Denationalized Have No Class: The Banishment of Japan's Korean Minority: A Polemic," *The New Centennial Review* 12(1): 173–202.

Ryang, S. (2015), *Eating Korean in America: Gastronomic Ethnography of Authenticity*, Honolulu: University of Hawaii Press.

Ryang, S. (2016), "Rise and Fall of Chongryun: From Chōsenjin to Zainichi and Beyond," *Asia-Pacific Journal/Japan Focus* 14, Issue 11, no. 11 (August 1, 2016). http://apjjf.org/2016/15/Ryang.html, last accessed March 20, 2020.

Sasaki, M. (2009), *Kimuchino bunkashi: Chōsenhantōno kimuchi, nihonno kimuchi* [The Cultural History of Kimchi: Kimchi in the Korean Peninsula and Kimchi in Japan], Tokyo: Fukumura shuppan.

"Tsukemono ichiban ninki jitsuwa kimuchi" [The Most Popular Pickle Is in Fact Kimchi] (2017), *Sankei shinbun* [Daily Sankei], April 4, 2017. Online: https://www.iza.ne.jp/smp/kiji/life/news/170404/lif17040416470008-s1.html, last accessed March 14, 2020.

World Institute of Kimchi (2018), "Kimchi, A Well-known Traditional Fermented Korean Food, Has Proven Effective Against Influenza," *Cision PR Newswire*, July 26, 2018. Online: https://www.prnewswire.com/news-releases/kimchi-a-well-known-traditional-fermented-korean-food-has-proven-effective-against-influenza-virus-300687023.html, last accessed March 30, 2020.

Yi, S.-U. (1988), "Kimchiui munhwa" [The Culture of Kimchi], *Sikpumgwa saneop* [Food Science and Industry] 21(1): 40–5.

Yoon, S.-Y. (2006), *Good Morning, Kimchi: Forty Different Kinds of Traditional and Fusion Kimchi Recipes*, Seoul: Hollym International.

Yoshimi, Y. (2000), *Comfort Women*, New York: Columbia University Press.

14

Tasting Quinoa

From Indigenous Food to "Healthy" US Dining

Christina Morris and Clare A. Sammells

Introduction: Tasting Quinoa in the United States and Bolivia

"Taste" emerges from engaging with specific cultural worlds in active ways. Individuals not only are aware of the "tastes" of those around them but also embrace, play with, criticize, ridicule, or reject those tastes (Bourdieu 1984). Tastes are dialectically produced by social groups for which they have meaning, as practices that simultaneously constitute both the boundaries of those groups and the tastes that define them (Ayora Díaz 2019). We will consider these processes through the example of quinoa—a grain with deep roots in the Andes, and now heralded as a "superfood" in the United States. While there is no consensus about what a "superfood" is, a quick internet search reveals that the popular US press and food bloggers do seem to agree that quinoa clearly is one. It is the very lack of any accepted definition for the term "superfood" that gives it such symbolic (and marketing) power. In the United States, superfoods are elevated above everyday foods as ingredients that break the boundaries of ordinary nutrition. One health journalist labeled this the "superfood fallacy": the belief that consuming a small number of fetishized foods is more important than improving one's overall diet (Davis 2008: 35–42). But there is a deeper question: Why do some foods become touted as "superfoods" at all?

In this chapter, we bring together ethnographic observations from two very different contexts—a rural Andean village in Bolivia and a liberal arts college cafeteria in the United States—to ask how "taste" is created around global commodities, and how specific foods come to be understood as "super" or superior in terms of nutrition and taste. We argue that quinoa allows its consumers to "play" with concepts of nutrition, healthiness, economic class, and gender, and that this play is made possible by the fact that quinoa plays very different roles in different cuisines. While foods may be de- and recontextualized in new cultural contexts, meanings are not replaced, but rather accrete. This is certainly true of quinoa as it moves from being a rural grain associated with Bolivian indigenous farmers, into being a superfood for wealthy, white, female college students in the United States who are concerned about "healthy" eating.

As Sidney Mintz (1985) demonstrated in his work on sugar, in anthropology a "commodity chain" analysis allows an investigation of how groups of people—even those who may never meet directly—are linked through chains of production, distribution, and consumption chains (see also West 2012). Thus, intersecting ideas surrounding quinoa play out through the commodity chains linking Bolivian and North Americans as both producers and consumers, turning quinoa into a politically charged food in both contexts. The polysemic nature of this little grain gives it an outsized importance in conversations about nutrition, sustainable agriculture, and food security. Quinoa isn't just good to eat—it is clearly "good to think" for many people.

When people in the United States talk about eating quinoa, they tend to focus on questions of taste, in a literal sense. They describe the grain as tasting "nutty," compare it to other grains, and think about its impact on particular bodies as a gluten-free "superfood." There are other sensory aspects of the taste of quinoa that they do not remark on, but that still distinguish quinoa consumption in the United States from that in Bolivia, such as the dryness of its presentation. In Bolivia, however, when rural indigenous people talk about the nutritional value of quinoa, they are often discussing their perceptions not just of the grain itself, but the impacts of a global system on their individual well-being.

Quinoa in Bolivia

Quinoa is native to the Andes of South America; its tiny spiral seeds are often described as having a "nutty" taste and are high in protein. The plant is hardy in saline soils, arid conditions, and cold temperatures, although it is susceptible to be damaged by hail. It is well adapted to the harsh climate of the Andean mountains (Hellin and Higman 2005) but also requires intensive manual labor to harvest and clean it. Although widely farmed in pre-Columbian times (Bruno and Whitehead 2003), quinoa was gradually displaced by grains such as wheat and barley, first through the systematic devaluing of indigenous foods under Spanish colonialism, and later by an influx of foreign food aid, largely from the United States under the PL480 program (Skarbø 2015; Weismantel 1988). Ingredients in Andean cuisines that are highly marked as indigenous are simultaneously marginalized and symbolically useful elements in national and touristic culinary projects (Colloredo-Mansfeld 2011; Sammells 2010, 2014, 2018). These seemingly contradictory associations are actually two sides of the same coin, which mutually reinforce each other (Trouillot 2003). Indigenous peoples are assumed to be poor farmers, connected to isolated landscapes (even though the majority of people who identify as indigenous in Bolivia live in towns and cities). Foods particularly associated with indigeneity, such as quinoa, are therefore marginalized as the food of the poor, rural, and ethnically marked people (Orlove 1998). But this association of "indigenous" foods with the land means that these foods also can become "good to think" about local culinary practice and essential in projects of presenting culinary localness to both citizens and visitors. As such, they can become elevated as ingredients that are believed to possess the qualities of nutrition, of naturalness, and of unprocessed, and uncommercialized foods—the very qualities that in the United States are used to describe "superfoods."

In the Bolivian highland village of Tiwanaku where Sammells has done ethnographic research since 2000, Andean farmers certainly know the value of quinoa, but did not use terms like "superfood." There, quinoa was a secondary crop and not a "staple" in the sense of providing the majority of local calories (that role was played by the potato), nor was quinoa grown for export (as it is in other regions of Bolivia). Quinoa was grown largely for personal consumption and was highly valued and considered an essential part of local cuisine. It was prized for many of the same reasons it was later to become popular in the United States—its taste, its nutritional qualities, and its "healthiness." Rural Tiwanakeños credited quinoa and other "traditional" foods as the reason their own grandparents and great-grandparents had lived long, healthy lives. They often talked about the ages these ancestors lived to—90 or even over 100 years of age—as due entirely to their healthy diet. In contrast, younger Tiwanakeños attributed their own diets—which they perceived as far less healthy—to a decline in consumption of these "traditional" foods and a rise in the intake of purchased foods such as sugar, pasta, and soda. These two broad categories of food were often presented as binary opposites. "Traditional" foods (not to be confused with "pre-Columbian" crops) included quinoa, potatoes, fava beans, *tarwi* (an Andean legume, *Lupinus mutabilis*), homemade wheat bread (baked in homemade adobe ovens for *Todos Santos*), and meats such as llama and guinea pig. Store-bought foods, however, were viewed as nutritionally suspect: sugar, soda, pasta, rice, store-bought bread, and cooking oil.

There were obvious tensions here. Although store-bought foods were seen as less "healthy," they were also "normal," expected, and desired parts of a rural family's diet. Even in rural villages, store-bought breads, pasta, rice, and oil were common in everyday diets to varying degrees. Schoolchildren would often buy processed cookies and crackers as snacks at school. Parents would worry about what their children were eating, and whether it was good for them. But these concerns and discourses on "healthiness" were not the fetishized discourse of individual ingredients that we see in US conversations about "superfoods." Instead, it was a discourse about the entire food system, and the relationship of people to their own food either directly, or as mediated through capitalist networks.

In this context, the nutritional value of "traditional" food was connected to an understanding of the relationships between an individual's food production and sustenance and the larger economy. For example, food acquired through the work of planting, tending, and harvest (even if performed on someone else's field in exchange for part of the crop) was believed to last longer than the same amount of food acquired through money. In other words, "traditional" foods are healthier not only because they are better for the body than sugar but also because they are obtained directly through work rather than bought with money.

Although Tiwanakeños were not directly part of the commodity chain producing quinoa for export to the United States (Ofstehage 2010, 2011, 2012), they were well aware of quinoa's growing reputation and popularity in urban Bolivia and abroad as a healthy grain. This cosmopolitan network transformed quinoa from a grain that was consumed largely where it was grown, into a global commodity. But the ways that people in the United States prepare quinoa seemed strange to Tiwanakeños. Sammells once brought boxes of gluten-free quinoa pasta from the United States to share with her compadres. Although they were familiar with both quinoa and pasta, the idea of making the latter from the former was a novelty. While they found it totally understandable that wealthy US consumers would want to buy quinoa, they didn't recognize these new ways of eating it as entirely "grammatical." As Douglas (1972) demonstrated in her study of English cuisine, culinary systems are structured in how dishes are put together. There are rules that govern the use of ingredients, spice combinations, timing of meals, and the order of dishes. Culinary grammar (like its counterpart in language) structures the logics of how foods become cuisines, while at the same time providing the flexibility for accommodations and creativity. Nevertheless, the rising sale value of quinoa on the commercial market bolstered Tiwanakeños' belief in the value of their grain. That rising value not only was reflected in price however, but also shifted the ways that quinoa was prepared.

In rural Bolivia, quinoa is prepared in several ways. The three most common are in soups, as *quispiña*, and as *pesq'e*. *Quispiña* are salty biscuits made from quinoa flour and steamed; they are served as an alternative to (or with) potatoes and other tubers. Soups and *pesq'e* (quinoa porridge), by contrast, are both wet dishes. In soups, quinoa supplements potatoes and vegetables. In *pesq'e*, quinoa is served as a moist, savory porridge with milk or melted cheese. In poor urban markets, one also sees *quinoa con manzana*, a thick morning drink of cooked apples and quinoa, waterier and sweeter than *pesq'e*. It is sold on cold mornings from small carts pushed by indigenous market women. What these rural/indigenous preparations of quinoa have in common is that they are "wet," a category that has importance in Andean culinary grammar. In Andean cuisines, *sopas* (soups) and other wet dishes are contrasted with "dry" *segundos* ("second plates" or "main dishes"), which are usually centered around potatoes and/or rice and meat. (*Quispiña* is an exception; it is not wet, but it is prepared and served in such a way as to make it equivalent to a potato, the staple of rural cuisine.) This wet/dry distinction maps onto other divisions in Andean cuisines. In urban Andean spaces, main meals (lunches and, to a lesser extent, dinners) usually include both a soup and a *segundo*. In most restaurants, a set lunch menu includes both for a single price. But in rural households, many domestic meals are just sopas (which are hearty enough to be meals in themselves), and *segundos* are served only on Sundays and special occasions. The distinction between *sopa/segundo* is one of wet/dry in terms of taste, but also mirrors social distinctions of rural/urban, indigenous/nonindigenous, and poor/not poor.

In its transformation to an urban commodity, quinoa was also turned from a grain served "wet" into one served "dry." Quinoa in elite Bolivian restaurants, and in the United States, is usually served in *segundos* or main dishes as a substitute for rice—as a cooked, but relatively dry, grain. In the rural Andes, rice has a higher social status than the potato; adding rice alongside potatoes is one way to make a meal more "special." In this context, the moisture content of the food involving quinoa shows how the "food's sensory qualities [are] embodied forms of social distinction" (Sutton 2010: 213). Consumers in the United States who treat quinoa as a substitute for rice or pasta are unwittingly reinscribing a set of social hierarchies through cooking practices.

Quinoa in the United States

Quinoa may have been once framed as only part of rural, indigenous, Andean diets, but it now seems to be everywhere in the United States. Imported from Bolivia, Peru, and Ecuador in increasing quantities, quinoa now appears on restaurant menus and college cafeterias as a marker of healthy, cosmopolitan lifestyles. While in a few places it is still showcased for its connection to indigenous cultures (e.g., the *Mitsitam Cafe* of the National Museum of the American Indian in Washington, D.C.), for the most part quinoa has taken on an entirely different set of associations for those living in the United States. From high-end restaurants to Panera grain bowls, quinoa seems to be unavoidable on US menus, but little of it is served in a way that would be "grammatical" in the daily food practices of rural indigenous Bolivians.

Quinoa was first imported to the US market as a specialty grain for gluten-free diets. It was sold as the "lost crop of the Incas," grown by "traditional" indigenous peoples. It offered ancient nutritional value while being untainted by the corrupting influence of modern capitalism. When NASA classified quinoa as a "complete food" for astronauts, US marketing companies used this to market quinoa as a healthy, high-protein option for vegetarians (Caceres, Carimentrand, and Wilkinson 2007: 182). Due to the increase in popularity of quinoa and the "organic" label, the price of quinoa has risen since the 1990s (Caceres, Carimentrand, and Wilkinson 2007: 194–5). Quinoa gained popularity in the United States, and its consumption became "Americanized" through recipes and methods of cooking. This is displayed through gluten-free and weight-loss recipes, and the use of words such as "ancient" and "organic" to portray quinoa as the ultimate health food, tying it to its domestication and production by indigenous Andeans—often portrayed in traditional dress doing agricultural work by hand. In the process of being redefined as healthy food, quinoa's identity as specifically Andean sometimes fades into the background. For example, Morris found a French product marketed in a US supermarket called *Le Pain des Fleurs*, which was a quinoa cracker. The box displayed a generic landscape with rolling hills in the background and fields of quinoa in the forefront. The box was placed between organic nut bread and baked beans and above gluten-free/vegan snacks. Quinoa has become a symbol of organic, vegetarian, vegan, and healthy diets, rather than something linked to a particular group of producers.

"Healthy eating" in the United States has been linked to classed identities in many contexts. Discourses of obesity in the United States had focused on processed foods that tend to be more frequently available in food deserts. Increased sugar and soda consumption have been linked to diabetes (Gálvez 2018). In the US context, "healthy eating" is not class neutral; on the contrary, it often becomes a way to mark classed food consumption. "Superfoods" are part of the obsession with healthy eating, by fetishizing the role of specific ingredients—often imported and/or expensive. These foods are assumed to contain "more" nutritional virtues, although the specifics are often left undefined. Some examples of superfoods include blueberries, acai and goji berries, kale, turmeric, avocado, and salmon.

Around 2012–13, quinoa rose to "superfood" status, with the Food and Agriculture Organization of the UN declaring 2013 "The International Year of Quinoa" (FAO n.d.). At the same time, the sudden rise of the popularity of quinoa in the United States, combined with its previous relative obscurity, became a source of humor. A 2013 commercial for *Bud Lite* beer features a football fan at a tailgate party eating a quinoa burger even though "it tastes like a dirty old tree branch" because it might be good luck, while his friend asks: "What is that, a loofah?!" The ad ends by honoring "the fans who do whatever it takes." But largely, quinoa became a symbol of self-righteous conspicuous "healthy" consumption. On Pinterest, "Quinoa" was the fictional star of "My Imaginary Well Dressed Toddler Daughter." Started in 2012 by Tiffany Beveridge, this collection of advertisement photos, paired with original captions, pillories high-end children's fashion ads, aloof philanthropic charity, and obsessions with organic food. Less humorously, around this same time, a series of news articles in US and UK newspapers suggested that rising exports of quinoa was starving farmers in the Andes, taking vegans to task for their supposed self-righteousness in avoiding animal products in favor of quinoa (Blythman 2013; Evans 2013; Romero and Shahriari 2011; Sherwin 2011). These examples show the inherent ambiguities of quinoa's movements between different "tastes." It embodies many contradictory things at once: poverty and wealth, rustic healthiness and self-righteous eating, indigeneity and whiteness. To see these contradictions in action, we now turn to Morris' ethnography of the role of quinoa in the cafeteria of a US liberal arts college.

Eating on Campus: Quinoa as a "Rich White Girl's Food"?

Even in US college cafeterias, quinoa mirrors the tensions of economic class divisions within the larger society of which they are a part. Although quinoa is common enough to be sold in Walmart, eating it is still seen as a class-marked activity. These contradictions allow quinoa to be used to strategically communicate—sometimes playfully—consumers' class identities. Unlike Bolivia, where quinoa was not particularly gender-marked, but was associated with poor indigenous people, in this new context quinoa is seen as food for wealthy white women. College women use quinoa to communicate about themselves in subtle ways, using consumption as a way to mark class, or aspiring class, while often remaining largely unaware of the racialized "whiteness" of their quinoa consumption. Quinoa's reputation on campus as a "rich white girl food" became strategically useful for some, off-putting for others, and sometimes invisible to those consuming it.

As part of an undergraduate honors thesis project in anthropology, Morris conducted observations and in-depth interviews to understand how college students understood quinoa's symbolic importance, both as a health food and as a marker of social and economic class. During the academic year of 2014–15, she conducted ethnographic research on and off campus, focusing on where quinoa was sold, purchased, cooked, and consumed. This included observing the college cafeteria for three to five hours a week for twelve weeks, completing fourteen semi-structured interviews with students, faculty, and staff and local residents. She also conducted an online survey in Spring 2015 with 147 individuals associated with the college, 59 of whom were students (Gonzalez [Morris] 2015). This college is located in a small town in central Pennsylvania. Its main street has small boutiques and restaurants, and the area has a federal prison, a Farmer's Market frequented by locals, a major medical center, and the liberal arts college described here. The 2013 US Census shows that 14 percent of the residents aged twenty-five years and older obtained a graduate or professional degree, which was only slightly higher than the national average at that time (about 12 percent). The college is residential, with a small number of students living "downtown" a few mere blocks from campus. This college traditionally attracts a predominantly aged student population. About 70 percent of these students live in the region. Approximately 40 percent attended a private school before college, compared to 10 percent of US students as a whole (Council for American Private Education 2015). Tuition at the time of this research was approximately $63,000 a year, and about a third of students received no financial aid. Only 15 percent of the college's total students identified as nonwhite.

Students were required by the college to have one of several meal plans. First-year students were required to have an "all access" plan, allowing unlimited access to a buffet space. Second- through fourth-year students could choose between the "all access" plan and some combination of "dining dollars" for purchasing a-la-carte items and "swipes" allowing one-time entrance to the buffet space. For wealthier students, campus dining was supplemented by take-out and local restaurants. For those of more limited means, or with restricted diets, cafeteria food was often complemented by grocery shopping and cooking for oneself or a small group of friends. The main sources of cooked meals for students were two cafeterias operated by a subcontracted dining service. One was an all-you-can-eat buffet-style dining hall geared toward first-year students and athletes, although other students could use "swipes" to access it for particular meals. The other was an a-la-carte-style dining area geared toward second-through fourth-year students and university employees, where meals were ordered and paid for individually. Additionally, some second- through fourth-year male students ate in separate fraternity houses which were generally not open to other students, leading to a somewhat gendered separation of dining spaces.

During the period of this research, this college cafeteria had a dedicated "quinoa bar," which was the first thing one saw on entering the cafeteria. This quinoa bar has since been repurposed, although we believe the class-marked nature of consumption on this campus that we describe remains largely the same. As students lined up at the bar, a dining services worker—standing behind the bar in a white chef's jacket, clear latex gloves, and a hairnet or baseball cap—would guide students through the topping options, starting on the left side of the bar. Holding a plastic rectangular take-out container in the left hand, the worker would first scoop cooked quinoa from large metal containers, then move to the middle of the bar with smaller metal containers to add ingredients at the request of the student—protein options (chicken, smoked salmon, and tofu), vegetables (tomatoes, cucumber, red onion, and edamame), feta cheese, and dressings in plastic bottles (Italian, balsamic vinegar, and olive oil). These dishes would definitely qualify as "dry" in the Andean binary described earlier, although in the US context they might be equated to "grain bowls." Once orders were complete, workers would hand the students their closed plastic container, and students would move toward the checkout lines to pay.

The quinoa bar was more expensive than other cafeteria options. Full meals, such as a burger, fries, and a drink, or a quesadilla and a drink, generally cost between US$5 and US$7. In contrast, a container of quinoa cost about US$9. The price rose to US$10 if smoked salmon, chicken, or tofu was added. The salad bar, where students could select their own lettuce, toppings, dressings, and quantities, had a cost per weight, but the total cost of a salad with similar toppings to the quinoa bar (minus the quinoa) and a drink ranged from US$4 to US$7. Given this price differential, and the public nature of eating in a cafeteria, ordering quinoa was a multivalent class marker. Students' dietary habits, and their ability to pay for them, are put on display for all to see. Quinoa was therefore seen as both a high-protein nutritious food and a luxury good. The following conversation between several college students shows some of these tensions highlighted by the consumption of quinoa:

> I [Morris] was sitting in the student space [on campus] eating lunch. The place is marked by an aura of casualness, as it is home to group meetings, friendly gossip sessions, and individual students completing their work. I noticed Zheng eating quinoa with tomatoes and salmon. Zheng is from China, and he was wearing a light grey hoodie marked with the college symbol and colors, Levi's jeans, and sneakers. Zheng was sitting with two girls, and he told them "I feel really cool eating quinoa right now," pronouncing quinoa as "quin-OH-ah." One of the girls, K., was a white American and was wearing a red T-shirt, jeans, and black riding boots. She looked uncomfortable and never made direct eye contact with her friends. She asked Zheng, "Why are you eating it?" and before he could reply she said dismissively, "Quinoa is for rich people."

This understanding that quinoa was for rich people, and, in the context of this college, specifically for rich, white women, was shared among students. When Morris presented the results of her research in several of Sammells's undergraduate classes, the reactions of students showed this was common, if often implicit, knowledge. When a black male student told Morris after her presentation that quinoa is for "white sorority girls," his comment was met with laughter and humorous applause by many students, although others seemed abashed by having this so explicitly stated. No student challenged this claim; while it might be uncomfortable for white women to find their consumption patterns so clearly marked by quinoa, all appeared to recognize the gendered association of the grain.

This gendering of quinoa was also evident in the survey results. Among the fifty-nine students who answered Morris' survey (in response to an email request sent to the entire student body), 91.5 percent (fifty-four) were women. Since the sample was self-selecting, this suggests that women, far more than men, were interested in quinoa enough to even participate. All these students had heard of quinoa, and 85 percent (forty-six) had tried it. While 20 percent (eleven) said they "never" ate quinoa, over half ate it at least once a month. Given this shared cultural understanding on campus, students strategically used quinoa to communicate something about themselves. Consider the following two cases of college women, "Jocelyn" and "Rachel," who were both frequent customers at the college cafeteria quinoa bar. Morris approached both of them for interviews because she had observed them there frequently. It turned out, however, that their reasons for eating quinoa were quite distinct.

Jocelyn. Jocelyn is a white woman who Morris had seen in line for quinoa every single day of her research, during both lunch and dinner. Each time she got the same toppings: edamame, feta cheese, tomatoes, and oil. From observations, Morris noted that Jocelyn was wearing a rose gold Michael Kors watch she estimated to be priced at about $400, a custom embroidered sorority tee ($45), a Barbour jacket ($450), black Lululemon leggings ($98), and Frye boots with a buckle ($278). In an interview, however, Jocelyn suggested to Morris that her clothing was an attempt to portray herself in a very deliberate way. She did not view herself as upper class, but rather as lower-middle class. The wealth of other students on her campus made Jocelyn "extremely uncomfortable" and gave her "a sense of feeling worthless around the rich." Jocelyn's long-term boyfriend, also a college student, was wealthy; he had bought her the luxury clothing she was wearing so she could "feel more comfortable at a rich school."

Jocelyn experienced college as a competitive space where she needed to perform a certain class identity in order to "fit in." Because of this, she ate quinoa in order to "be seen as one of the cool kids for once." But she also experienced this kind of healthy eating, and the performance of healthy eating, as inherently competitive: "they've made eating a competition at this school too. I just want to be able to eat what I want and not feel judged. Is that so much to ask?" Jocelyn's self-understanding of her own class position tied into the way that she interacted with the staff working in the cafeteria. She saw wealthy students being rude to the workers, so Jocelyn tried "to brighten their day by being courteous" because she knew "how it feels to be on their side of the divide." Throughout her interview, the tension was clear; Jocelyn did not like displays of wealth, and yet she felt forced to participate in them. She ate "healthy" food but felt this was part of a competition she didn't really wish to be part of. For Jocelyn, clothing, food, and behavior were linked in complicated ways to her self-presentation at a college where she felt out of place, and where she felt she needed to perform an aspirant class position.

Rachel. On first glance, Jocelyn and Rachel might have appeared to be inhabiting the same classed position. Rachael was also a thin, white woman who dressed in designer clothing and who Morris observed eating quinoa almost daily. Like Jocelyn, Rachael was in the quinoa line just about every day, ordering edamame, cucumber, and tofu to accompany her quinoa. And yet, Rachel had a completely different understanding of her own situation and the meaning of quinoa within it. Rachel focused on quinoa as a healthy food, rather than a class or a status symbol. She was very concerned about the other ingredients at the quinoa bar and how they might impact her health, noting:

[S]ome of the things they put in [at the quinoa bar] make it less healthy, so you do have to be kind of choosy if you're trying to eat it for the lack of calories or for the health benefits. . . . There's feta cheese, which in small quantities is very good, but they do kind of put heaping spoonfuls, so that is something to be conscious about. Edamame is full of protein and definitely very good for you, but it does have high calories, so people who are looking at it for calories, they might not recognize that. Sun-dried tomatoes (any kind of dried fruit like that) have a higher concentration of sugar to volume.

Rachael self-identified as upper class. Her clothing flaunted numerous brands and logos that suggested this, but she seemed unaware of the class markings of her clothes. She said that she and her friends simply dressed comfortably and casually: "just your normal everyday outfit." She didn't really think much about what she wore, because "everyone else dresses the same." While Jocelyn felt that quinoa explicitly marked a class position—one she did not feel she truly inhabited—for Rachel, quinoa was simply "healthy food." Of course, quinoa is both these things, shifting between meanings in ways that Jocelyn hints at when she notes that even eating healthily seems like a classed competition to her. Interestingly, neither Jocelyn nor Rachael seemed aware of any racialized associations for quinoa. When Morris asked them (separately) about the type of people they see in line for quinoa, they replied: "girls." When she asked specifically the race of the girls, they each emphasized, "just girls." Neither of them seemed to notice that white women ordered quinoa the most often.

The contradictions shown through the examples of Jocelyn and Rachel also appear in the survey data. The survey asked the open-ended question "How would you describe your socio-economic class." From the fifty-nine respondents, the majority self-identified as "Upper Middle Class" (thirty out of fifty-three), twelve identified as "Middle Class," and ten gave answers indicating they were below middle class (e.g., "working class" and "lower class"). In general, the students who self-identified as wealthier also ate quinoa slightly more often. But when asked (again as an open-ended question) *why* they ate quinoa, survey participants did not mention cost or economic class at all. Instead, they either said it was tasty, healthy, or nutritious. While some said it made a nice alternative to grains such as rice or couscous, none remarked on its relative cost compared to those grains. In other words, while as anthropologists we may analyze quinoa as part of a class-marked cuisine, for those eating it, quinoa is understood through the lens of "health." But as discussed earlier, "healthy eating" is not class neutral. This makes quinoa a polysemic symbol and a sometimes subtle way to communicate about economic class. Much like the aforementioned students who were uncomfortable talking about the gendered and classed nature of quinoa consumption, talking about "healthy eating" is a way to highlight social distinctions while not directly attributing them to status.

Conclusions

In this chapter, we have demonstrated how a food associated with marginalized, "third-world" populations (rural, poor indigenous farmers) is able to do the work of marking conspicuous consumption for wealthy white residents of the industrialized North. Yet, quinoa is not the only example of this shift, either. In the last twenty years we have seen similar trajectories for foods such as acai berry and other "superfoods." This is not (just) about quinoa per se, its flavor, texture, or nutritional qualities. There is something else about foods perceived to be like quinoa, for affirming a certain identity. Foods such as quinoa have become part of the culinary scene of the cultural and economic elite in the United States and elsewhere, even as it maintains its origins, both in terms of domestication and contemporary production, in the indigenous Andes. For this reason, quinoa marks social class in divergent, even contradictory ways. In other words, "taste" is performed through consumption, but consumption of particular items often evokes multiple meanings at once and, therefore, how these performances are read are not always how they are intended.

In his classic study of class formation, Veblen (1899) wrote about the presence of "conspicuous consumption" and "conspicuous leisure," and how individuals of higher social statuses consume goods and partake in activities to enact their own social class. People also use food as one of these marked items to create "boundaries" and separate themselves from those who do not fit into the social situation (Wilk 2006). But in the case of quinoa, a luxury food may also connect elites to marginalized indigenous peoples elsewhere (West 2012). However, for US diners this connection is usually doomed to be infelicitous—just like tourism, elite consumption of indigeneity does not create true linkages with the "Other." Much like the tourist who believes that the "authentic" culture is only visible outside the bounds of the very tourist encounter they feel confined to (MacCannell 1994), eating quinoa can never create an "authentic" link to Andean peoples for those eating it in a US college cafeteria. Nor did any of the students Morris interviewed say that was their primary motivation for eating it. Instead, their consumption is meant to be read by members of one's own society, and they use symbols of indigeneity toward that purpose. While indigenous peoples are important symbols of the "healthiness" of quinoa, the very same discourses surrounding "healthy eating" and "superfoods" allow quinoa to elide questions of class, ethnicity, and global inequalities that are inherent to how quinoa came to be in the US diet in the first place.

References

Ayora Díaz, S. I. (2019), "Introduction. Matters of Taste: The Politics of Food and Identity in Mexican Cuisines," in S. I. Ayora Díaz (ed.), *Taste, Politics and Identities in Mexican Food*, pp. 1–18, London, New York: Bloomsbury Academic.

Blythman, J. (2013), "Can Vegans Stomach the Unpalatable Truth about Quinoa?" *The Guardian*, January 16, 2013, sec. Opinion.

Bourdieu, P. (1984), *Distinction: A Social Critique of the Judgment of Taste*, Cambridge, MA: Harvard University Press.

Bruno, M. C. and W. T. Whitehead (2003), "Chenopodium Cultivation and Formative Period Agriculture at Chiripa, Bolivia," *Latin American Antiquity* 14(3): 339–55.

Caceres, Z., A. Carimentrand, and J. Wilkinson (2007), "Fair Trade and Quinoa from the Southern Bolivian Altiplano," in L. T. Raynolds, D. L. Murray, and J. Wilkinson (eds.), *Fair Trade: The Challenges of Transforming Globalization*, pp. 180–99, New York: Routledge.

Colloredo-Mansfeld, R. (2011), "Work, Cultural Resources, and Community Commodities in the Global Economy," *Anthropology of Work Review* 32(2): 51–62.

Davis, R. J. (2008), *The Healthy Skeptic: Cutting through the Hype about Your Health*, Berkeley: University of California Press.

Douglas, M. (1972), "Deciphering a Meal," *Daedalus* 101(1): 61–81.

Evans, P. (2013), "Quinoa Boom Offers Hard Lesson in Food Economics," *CBC News*, January 18, 2013.

FAO (n.d.), "Quinoa," *Food and Agriculture Organization of the United Nations*. http:// www.fao.org/quinoa/en/, last accessed May 15, 2020.

Gálvez, A. (2018), *Eating NAFTA: Trade, Food Policies, and the Destruction of Mexico*, Oakland: University of California Press.

Gonzalez, C. R. (2015), "Is Quinoa 'For Rich People'? The Consumption of Quinoa in Central Pennsylvania," B.A. Honors Thesis, Department of Sociology & Anthropology, Bucknell University.

Hellin, J. and S. Higman (2005), "Crop Diversity and Livelihood Security in the Andes," *Development in Practice* 15(2): 165–74.

MacCannell, D. (1994), *The Tourist. A New Theory of the Leisure Class*, Berkeley: University of California Press.

Mintz, S. W. (1985), *Sweetness and Power: The Place of Sugar in Modern History*, New York: Viking Books.

Ofstehage, A. (2010), "The Gift of the Middleman: An Ethnography of Quinoa Trading Networks in Los Lipez of Bolivia." Available at SSRN: https://dx.doi.org/10.2139/ssrn .1866330

Ofstehage, A. (2011), "Nusta Juira's Gift of Quinoa: Peasants, Trademarks, and Intermediaries in the Transformation of a Bolivian Commodity Economy," *Anthropology of Work Review* 32(2): 103–14.

Ofstehage, A. (2012), "The Construction of an Alternative Quinoa Economy: Balancing Solidarity, Household Needs, and Profit in San Agustín, Bolivia," *Agriculture and Human Values* 29(4): 441–54.

Orlove, B. S. (1998), "Down to Earth: Race and Substance in the Andes," *Bulletin of Latin American Research* 17(2): 207–22.

Romero, S. and S. Shahriari (2011), "Quinoa's Global Success Creates Quandary in Bolivia," *The New York Times*, March 19, 2011.

Sammells, C. A. (2010), "Ode to a Chuño: Learning to Love Freeze-Dried Potatoes in Highland Bolivia," in H. R. Haines and C. A. Sammells (eds.), *Adventures in Eating: Anthropological Tales of Dining Around the World*, pp. 101–25, Boulder: University Press of Colorado.

Sammells, C. A. (2014), "Haute Traditional Cuisines: How UNESCO's List of Intangible Heritage Links the Cosmopolitan to the Local," in R. Brulotte and M. Di Giovine (eds.), *Edible Identities: Food as Cultural Heritage*, pp. 141–58, Farnham: Ashgate.

Sammells, C. A. (2018), "'Local-Politan' Gastronomy and Bolivian Cuisine: How the Cosmopolitan Is Forged from the Local," in R. Shepherd (ed.), *Cosmopolitanism and Tourism: Rethinking Theory and Practice*, pp. 163–77, Lanham: Lexington Books.

Sherwin, A. (2011), "The Food Fad That's Starving Bolivia," *The Independent*, March 22, 2011.

Skarbø, K. (2015), "From Lost Crop to Lucrative Commodity: Conservation Implications of the Quinoa Renaissance," *Human Organization* 74(1): 86–99.

Sutton, D. E. (2010), "Food and the Senses," *Annual Review of Anthropology* 39(1): 209–23.

Trouillot, M.-R. (2003), "Anthropology and the Savage Slot: The Poetics and Politics of Otherness," in M.-R. Trouillot (ed.), *Global Transformations: Anthropology and the Modern World*, pp. 7–28. New York: Palgrave Macmillan.

Veblen, T. (1899), *The Theory of the Leisure Class*, New York: Modern Library.

Weismantel, M. J. (1988), *Food, Gender, and Poverty in the Ecuadorian Andes*, Prospect Heights: Waveland Press.

West, P. (2012), *From Modern Production to Imagined Primitive: The Social World of Coffee from Papua New Guinea*, Durham: Duke University Press.

Wilk, R. (2006), *Home Cooking in the Global Village: Caribbean Food from Buccaneers to Ecotourists*, New York: Berg Publishers.

15

The Taste of the Mediterranean Diet

Food, Taste, and Identity in the Campania Region, South Italy

Rossella Galletti

Introduction

Our journey to discuss the taste of the Mediterranean Diet starts in Naples, the capital of the Campania region, in South Italy. The community of Cilento, recognized by UNESCO, is located in the south of Campania. It is a social, cultural, economic, and political point of reference for the entire region, despite the existence of competing localist identities (*campanilismo* in the developmentalist language of the 1950s) (Benjamin 2001; Braudel 2006; Chambers 2007; De Seta 1999; Ginsborg 1990; Lewis 1993). Naples is a Mediterranean city overlooking the basin of the Mediterranean Sea, a sea that contemporary Europe has delimited by clear, definite, safe lines, establishing its southern and eastern borders (Chambers 2007; Montalbàn and Gonzàlez 2002; Said 1996; Sayyid 2003). However, as Edward Said (1978) has suggested, we all move within imaginary geographies, built ad hoc through a process of continuous inclusion and exclusion.

The Mediterranean is inarguably an enduring construction, and this is also evident in the most "natural" and "cultural" act: eating. Let's imagine walking through the streets of the ancient center of Naples, studded—as they are—by numerous restaurants with various vocations. Among examples of cultural food mobility, in the current gastronomic offering of the city we find Neapolitan pizza. By eating pizza, we would taste a gastronomic icon of Naples self-represented as "authentic" and "popular." The main ingredient of the "Neapolitan" pizza invokes the *memory* of a cuisine that privileges wheat flour, the staple food of the peninsula and symbol of "Italian" cuisine. Housewives use it to prepare food to eat with bread, as well as breads, pizzas, and pastries of various kinds, which at least until the first half of the 1900s constituted, for the populations of Southern Italy, a remedy against hunger and a supply of caloric energy (Montanari 2005, 2006; Niola 2009, 2012a; Teti 1999, 2002). De Boucard, Duamas, and Serao (Puzzi 2016) suggest that in its origin pizza was eaten by "common people" who dwelt in warehouses with no kitchens. It was a street food that appeased the sense of material and symbolic hunger, sold by *pizzaioli* that kept it in a cart. In the first versions of pizza, the use of lard is attested, while the tomato is associated with it only later, at the beginning of the nineteenth century. In the 1900s, oral tradition was written with the institution of the *Associazione Verace Pizza Napoletana* in 1984 and the *Associazione Pizzaioli Napoletani* in 1998. These associations were constituted by pizza masters to defend and valorize pizza made "in observance of the ancient Neapolitan traditions and practices." The norms prescribe the raw material to be used: type "00" soft wheat flour, natural water, brewer's yeast, peeled tomatoes or fresh cherry tomatoes, sea salt, and extra virgin olive oil. One could add garlic and oregano only if preparing *marinara*, and mozzarella, fresh tomato, and basil for the *margherita*. These two were defined as the authentic "traditional" pizzas. However, tomato is not a native fruit: it arrived in Europe from Mexico during the 1500s and only a couple of centuries later it became "native." This adaptation illustrates how the exchange of products between countries are the ground of every "locality," "identity," and "authenticity." The tomato went from a deterritorialized product to a characteristic element of the lands surrounding Mount Vesuvius, and it has further acquired organoleptic peculiarities there, so much that today there are several "typical" tomato varieties from Campania: *Piennolo*, *San Marzano*, and *Sorrento*. To be "authentic," Neapolitan pizza must use only fresh or peeled tomatoes from the region.

By eating pizza, Neapolitans adhere, more or less consciously, to the need for recognition of a local, gastronomic, and cultural identity, which today seems to be a dominant imperative. Locals will tell you that true Neapolitans love pizza, almost viscerally, and if they don't, they are not true Neapolitans. To sanction popular wisdom, local people invoke the institutional recognition from UNESCO, which listed the Art of Neapolitan Pizzaioli as Intangible Cultural Heritage of Humanity in 2017. This added onto the 2010 European Union recognition of pizza as traditional specialty guaranteed (TSG),[1] and pizza is listed among the traditional products of Campania. On the other hand, the main ingredients for its preparation—mozzarella, olive oil, and tomato—are also considered "traditional" products by the regional government. Only recently pizza has been promoted as a Mediterranean food because it represents the meeting of wheat with tomato and olive oil from the territory, three symbolic foods in the collective imaginary on the Mediterranean Diet. Today, the Cilento UNESCO community is promoting their pizza as a typical dish of the area different from Neapolitan pizza mainly because they use goat cheese instead of cow's milk mozzarella, and it also differs in the kneading of the dough.

The question of food belonging to a group, a community, or a nation today is a recurrent, redundant, and compelling discourse in the spaces of media and politics both, when they are expressed through the poetics and rhetoric of valuation, affirmation, and communication of *local identities*, and when it deploys a rhetoric of "immunization" and "security" underscoring the political and symbolic significance of *local identity*. These discourses frequently make use of the notion of "food tradition" as a symbolic operator and creator of modes of locality (Appadurai 1996), of place, peoplehood, or community. The purpose of these discursive formations seems to be to produce and, at the same time, legitimize the naturalization of belonging (Fabietti 1995, 2001, 2004; Kilani 1994, 1997; Robbins 2009). On the one hand, they have an extremely localistic tendency; on the other, they aim to exploit international awards, in particular the UNESCO listing of the Mediterranean Diet that created a hyper-community encompassing different countries unified by unique gastronomic "principles." The gastronomic system and the sense of "taste" of Cilento, as those of Campania, are actually very different from those of the other UNESCO countries of the Mediterranean Diet: the different landscapes, religions, societies, economies, and histories of Mediterranean countries have led to the preference for certain foods, spices, cooking methods, and preparation and production of foods very different from each other. For example, if we examine how pork is used in Campania, we find it as sausages, lard, the stuffing of pizzas and cakes, and as an essential ingredient for *ragù* (another typical preparation of the region). Pork is completely absent in all the Islamic countries bordering the Mediterranean. Also, red wine, a cult drink in many European countries, and banned by Islam, is not included in the UNESCO Mediterranean Diet, thus excluding France. In addition, parsley and basil, recurrent herbs in many dishes of Campania, and paprika, widely used in Spain, rarely appear in "typical" dishes from Campania. These differences and particularities can help us understand the issues addressed in this chapter and reveal a scenario characterized by the encounters of peoples, foods, tastes, and identities moving within global and local contexts, chiefly that of the Mediterranean Diet in the Campania region. Thus, I examine the relationship between identity and the taste of the Mediterranean Diet.

The Mediterranean Diet Coast to Coast

Food defines our everyday life and, in addition to a nutritional function, it has an important cultural role. It motivates people to find something to eat and renders the body a political object (Foucault 2005; Goody 2012: 171–83, 205–25). The Mediterranean Diet is a good illustration of this statement: Ten years after UNESCO's recognition that listed it as Intangible Heritage of Humanity, it is possible to trace the identitarian policies triggered by UNESCO and their repercussions on three dimensions: political national, regional, and local actions; the sense of identity founded on social practices in the communities involved; and the international imagination kindled by media and by international intergovernmental organizations.

To understand the ways in which UNESCO has sparked identity movements, we must read between lines the Application Dossiers presented in 2010 (the year of the first registration in the Representative List of Intangible Heritage of Humanity) and in 2013.[2] In the Nomination file of 2010, the Mediterranean Diet is presented as a *musealized* and *simplified* nutritional model. The authors affirmed that it has not changed over the centuries, maintaining the same structure and the same proportions, making it fixed, impervious to any form of change, and, therefore, musealized. In this regard, Sanità (2016) has clarified that the definition of the Mediterranean Diet presented to the Nairobi Committee in 2010 is essentially static, focusing on continuity rather than transformation. In listing food categories (wheat, fruit and vegetables, nuts, olive oil, and, in small quantities, fish, dairy products, and meat) and condiments, spices, tea, and wine, the file simplifies the complexity of food systems of the cultures mentioned, purifying them from the diversity of ingredients, techniques, technologies, and the vastness of combinations of foods that characterize the cuisine of the countries involved. In short, the food cultures of different countries were reduced to a nutritional pyramid, much closer to medical health standards than to cultural ones. In fact, even if we focus on the proportions and shape, the model does not reflect the "food pyramid" of Campania, where dairy products, especially fresh cheese produced in the region—absent in other Italian regions except as variations of Campania products—such as mozzarella, *provola*, and *fiordilatte* cheeses, constitute the everyday food of the population. Also, in recent decades, meat is consumed three to seven times a week on average, as shown by a MedEatResearch[3] study, and as I have observed during fieldwork I conduct in Campania since 2012.

Subsequently, in the Nomination file of 2013, the definition of Mediterranean Diet has been modified as

> the set of skills, knowledge, rituals, symbols and traditions, ranging from the landscape to the table, which in the Mediterranean basin concerns the crops, harvesting, picking, fishing, animal husbandry, conservation, processing, cooking, and particularly sharing and consuming the cuisine. It is at the table that the spoken word plays a major role in describing, transmitting, enjoying and celebrating the element. Served for millennia, the Mediterranean Diet, the fruit of constant sharing nourished as much by internal synergies as by external contributions, a crucible of traditions, innovations and creativity, expresses the way of life of the basin communities [. . .]. With regard to its utilitarian, symbolic and artistic popular expressions, it is important to highlight the craftsmanship and production of ancestral domestic objects linked to the Mediterranean Diet and still present in everyday objects, such as receptacles for the transport, preservation and consumption of food, including ceramic plates and glasses, among others. As a unique lifestyle determined by the Mediterranean climate and region, the Mediterranean Diet also appears in the cultural spaces, festivals and celebrations associated with it. These spaces and events become the receptacle of gestures of mutual recognition and respect, of hospitality, neighborliness, conviviality, intergenerational transmission and intercultural dialogue. They are opportunities to both share the present and establish the future. (p. 6)

Compared to the 2010 Dossier, the nutritional model has disappeared, the Mediterranean Diet has become exclusively a social practice and the simplification process is now accompanied by that of *generalization*. There are no specific characteristics that would distinguish the Mediterranean Diet lifestyle from others. Only the Mediterranean climate and landscape are mentioned as if they would explain a unique lifestyle, and the "distinctive" characteristic of conviviality. The list of rituals, celebrations, symbols, traditions, and knowledge, that go from the earth to the table, is without any specific cultural content.

To fully understand how "generalization" emerges from the 2013 definition of the Mediterranean Diet, it is useful to compare it with that of Traditional Mexican

Cuisine, which also became an Intangible Cultural Heritage in 2010. The candidacy Nomination file no. 00400 describes it as follows:

> Traditional Mexican cuisine is a comprehensive cultural model comprising farming, ritual practices, age-old skills, culinary techniques and ancestral community customs and manners. It is made possible by collective participation in the entire traditional food chain: from planting and harvesting to cooking and eating. The basis of the system is founded on corn, beans and chili; unique farming methods such as milpas (rotating swidden fields of corn and other crops) and chinampas (man-made farming islets in lake areas); cooking processes such as nixtamalization (lime-hulling maize, which increases its nutritional value); and singular utensils including grinding stones and stone mortars. Native ingredients such as varieties of tomatoes, squashes, avocados, cocoa and vanilla augment the basic staples. Mexican cuisine is elaborate and symbol-laden, with everyday tortillas and tamales, both made of corn, forming an integral part of Day of the Dead offerings. Collectives of female cooks and other practitioners devoted to raising crops and traditional cuisine are found in the State of Michoacán and across Mexico.[4]

In addition to mentioning "typical" foods of Mexico, the Dossier on Traditional Mexican Cuisine gives specific content to agricultural methods (*milpas* and *chinampas*), cooking techniques (nixtamalization), and gastronomic preparations (*tortillas* and *tamales*). A similar content is missing in the dossiers on the Mediterranean Diet.

But unlike traditional Mexican cuisine, the aspirations of the Mediterranean Diet are universalistic: "The singular and universal character of the element will not only strengthen this dialogue at the level of the basin, but also at the global level" (Nomination file 2013: 8). Also highlighted are transversality, intra and intercultural exchange, and respect for Others. These values are certainly commendable and testify the spirit of openness and dialogue of the compilers' dossier, who sought not to essentialize the diet as a substance from which identities and cultures emerge. The same file, however, is ambivalent, as it underlines the "unique" character of this lifestyle determining the "natural" identification and sense of belonging of the populations of the communities involved. There is, however, a generalizing inclination leading to wonder if the Mediterranean Diet could (theoretically) include the lifestyle of all the different populations that inhabit the Earth. This question, which may seem confrontational, is not far removed from the aspirations of some international or extra-Mediterranean organisms that embrace its universalistic vocation and underscore its nutritional value, alluded at UNESCO in 2013. Since 2010, the American dietary guidelines include the Mediterranean dietary style as an example of a healthy diet; FAO believes it to be one of the most sustainable diets in existence and an exemplary model that would greatly contribute in alleviating the serious problem that globalization generates with its consumption models undermining the environment. In turn, WHO defines it as the healthiest possible diet and recommends governments of all countries to implement consumer awareness policies and measures. As Moro (2016) pointed out, these assessments spurred WHO to promote Mediterranean nutrition to improve global health and to use the Food Pyramid as a pedagogical tool to highlight its basic rules, turning it into a symbol of the Mediterranean lifestyle during the last twenty years (Moro 2014: 28–36; Willet et al. 1995). The Mediterranean Diet seems, in short, a sort of *tabula rasa* on which it is possible to write numerous stories: stories of "cultures," peoples, communities, regions, countries, and also nutrition science and public health.

While the universalist push prevails on the international scale, on the national side Italy has declared the Mediterranean Diet a National Cultural Heritage (Decree No. 8–9 April 2008), and in 2015 the Italian government drafted the *Charter of values of the Mediterranean Diet* providing for the development of national and local measures to ensure its transmission to younger generations and promoting awareness within the same communities seeking to identify an operational network to guarantee the transmission of these values (Sanità 2016: 32). On a regional level, Campania promulgated the law on the "Promotion of the model of sustainable development focusing on the Mediterranean Diet as intangible heritage of humanity" (RL2013—No. 00884). Subsequently, other regional laws and decrees sought to promote this "cultural heritage" as an engine for the development of the territory, as well as a tourist attraction. At the same time, a series of actions to safeguard local gastronomic specialties were implemented in Campania, all characterized by a strong identity mark, distinct from the homogenizing Mediterranean Diet. In this context, to date, there are 37 Slow Food Presidia in the region, 14 DOP (Protected Denomination of Origin) products plus 1 in the process of recognizing, 10 IGP (*Indicazione Geografica Protetta* or Protected Geographic Denomination) products plus 4 in the process of recognizing, 2 STG (Specialità Tradizionale Guarantita or Guaranteed Traditional Specialty) products, and 552 traditional agri-food products (PAT).

Sanità (2016) highlighted that while UNESCO tends to configure an open, virtual, abstract, and deterritorialized heritage community, and presumes a Mediterranean that takes on the connotations of an expanded terroir, the national trend is to define restricted communities in which identities are located making use of iconic foods linked to terroir. During this process, the identity of Campania people is strengthened through the representation of traditional food, safeguarded by various brands guaranteeing its authenticity, and reaffirming their "autochthony." Even though this autochthony is a construct—because food is always far from being an autochthonous product (Geertz 2001; Herzfeld 2003; Niola 2012b: 13–18; Palumbo 2009)—the need to defend a "restricted" identity seems to run contrary to what I would call the "expanded" identity promoted by UNESCO.

Precisely for this reason, many countries could claim their cuisine as Mediterranean—something that already happened within UNESCO when the four countries (Spain, Greece, Italy, and Morocco), initially identified in 2010 as representative of the good diet, were joined by three more (Portugal, Croatia, and Cyprus) in 2013. In all probability, UNESCO cannot prevent leaving the registration doors open to other potential applicants who could be added to the seven countries in the coming years since the Mediterranean Diet represents a sort of *floating signifier*, a linguistic concept in itself, empty of meaning, and, therefore, suitable to be loaded with any meaning (Lévi-Strauss 1965). The creation of an expanded identity runs counter to the sense of identity within the archetypal communities recognized as "patrimonial expressions" (Moro 2016) of the Mediterranean Diet, who strengthen their roots in their territories. In the writing of the dossiers, there is an ambivalence between an identity too broad and inclusive and the idea of a restricted identity. The strategy inherent in the *musealization* process generated by UNESCO has the effect of making the communities' identification process bound to the construction of an unchanging identity, closed, not subject to flow and change, and therefore rooted in the places' "nature." This has the effect of turning communities into living museums, remaining unchanged despite the passage of time.

The Mediterranean Diet would constitute "the element of identity par excellence of the Mediterranean peoples" and "today, it continues to be the characteristic element that accompanies the personal history of each individual in this community" (Nomination File 2010: 3). The 2013 file highlights how these communities "rebuild their sense of identity, belonging and continuity, enabling them to recognize this element as an essential component of their common and shared intangible cultural heritage" (p. 6). For the compilers of the Nomination file, the Mediterranean Diet would be a strong identity foundation determined by the climate and by the Mediterranean area. The identification was clearly exposed as fictional when in the 2013 Dossier it was stated that the communities have committed themselves to safeguarding the good by teaching their members the Mediterranean Diet, to educate them into its values, principles, and traditions. It is not just an effort to recover the "culture" of a lost practice, but to acculturate into a practice and identity made up by a team of doctors, based on external viewpoints legitimized by UNESCO—a *super partes* organism, supranational, despite the application being submitted along with partner states. Notwithstanding references to "innovation" within countries, the reference to "ancestralization" is repeated and perpetuated throughout the dossier and in media communications about the Mediterranean Diet (Moro 2014). It is no coincidence that the epigraph of the Nomination file is attributed to Plutarch: "We do not sit at table to eat but to eat together." This quotation underlines that eating is a millenary aspect of daily life, and that the conviviality and solemnity of eating together remains untouched in the communities. Again, the risk here is to ignore the dimension historical change (Prosperi 2016: 9).

Additionally, the FAO director Qu Dongyu says regarding traditional healthy diets such as the Mediterranean Diet, they "contain the wisdom of our ancestors and the cultural essence of generations"; he also argues that traditional and indigenous diets, such as the Mediterranean Diet, can stop hunger in the world and achieve the goal of the *2030 Agenda for Sustainable Development*.[5] The concept of "tradition," as enunciated by the director of FAO, refers to the type of diet practiced, and therefore of widespread use, among poor, peasant populations, in certain areas that until not long ago, like Southern Italy, suffered from hunger. What emerges is the paradox that the diets that once characterized poor "starving" populations could today fight hunger in the world. Therefore, we must ask ourselves whether the indigenous and traditional diets cited by Dongyu correspond to the reality of the living and feeding conditions of those people, or are they rather edulcorated and mythologized reformulations only useful for this contemporary romantization of sustainable diets which find its raison d'être and its validation in a mythologized past. As Hobsbawm and Ranger (1987) have argued, the invention of tradition is part of a process of projection into a "common" past of collective bodies that feel so united in the present. Iain Chambers wrote: "Neighboring identities are brought into relation in an extraterritorial space, where traditions are shattered to become the site of continuous translations" (2007: 50). Traditions are continuously updated, reformulated, and innovated in order to serve narratives and actions in a specific historical and sociocultural context.

Behind this "Mediterranean" turning point, acknowledged by UNESCO and other organizations, likely, there is a desire to show a fair and just diet that "can now be seen in the UNESCO communities." The Mediterranean Diet could be regarded as a category that takes contemporary humans, within the context of "nature," closer to a practice of food consumption connected to an image of "tradition" which takes us closer to a mythical past when people and food were better and more genuine. The sense of bewilderment and modern humans' identity crises is placated by nostalgic rhetoric and poetry.

The Taste of the Mediterranean Diet

All discourses on the Mediterranean Diet that I have examined, and their identitarian implications foster a dialogue between local and global. They have very specific effects on the notion and perception of taste brought into play. The identitarian policies and rhetoric I have examined shape food acquisition and food preferences in the communities involved and those aspiring to join the UNESCO List. I now highlight some properties of the "taste of the Mediterranean Diet" which contribute to forge the sense of identity in their communities: (a) The Mediterranean Diet is homogenizing, skirting national, regional, or local identity marks, and, instead, highlighting the sharing of a rather indeterminate set of communal practices. (b) The Mediterranean Diet is territorial, as it is imagined closely tied to landscapes where there is a tight relationship between communities, their lands, and their common sea. In fact, in Chefchaouen, Cilento, Koroni, or Soria, "the landscapes announce the cuisine, and the cuisine evokes the landscapes" (Nomination File 2010: 6); this eventuality constructs the diet as close to nature and contributes to its representation as a "natural" expression of the people of the communities, becoming naturalized. (c) The Mediterranean Diet is sustainable, because it consists of "the management of natural resources, the unique efficiency in the traditional use of water, the safeguarding of species and varieties, the achievement of harmony on a fragile land and sea in a demanding climate." In other words, the Mediterranean Diet is a system rooted in the respect for the territory that "ensures the conservation and development of traditional activities and crafts linked to fishing and farming in the four communities, thereby guaranteeing the balance between the territory and the people" (Nomination File 2010: 6). (d) The Mediterranean Diet is simple and frugal, as it privileges simple, unprocessed preparations, which recall the values of a so-called 'poor cuisine,' which comes from below, shaped by the daily practices of land- and sea-workers of the past decades and centuries. In this regard, the star chef Ernesto Iaccarino of the Don Alfonso 1890 restaurant, in Sant'Agata sui Due Golfi (Sorrento), declares himself a promoter of Mediterranean cuisine. Once, he pointed out to me a mackerel, a fish he qualified as "of very poor origins," to illustrate how foods considered poor are now part of haute cuisine. (e) The Mediterranean Diet is ancient, as it preserves the knowledge, practices, traditions, production, and consumption processes of ancestors. Finally, (f) the Mediterranean Diet is healthy, as it has beneficial effects on health, all demonstrated by numerous studies on human nutrition, which are derived from the Seven Countries Study led by Ancel Keys, who coined the label "Mediterranean Diet" in 1975 in the informational book he wrote with his wife Margaret Haney: *How to Eat Well and Stay Well. The Mediterranean Way.*

Of Fieldwork and Memory in Cilento

When I started doing fieldwork, I always kept in mind what anthropologist Luigi Maria Lombardi Satriani told me during an interview: "Every human being is a heritage of humanity."[6] This maxim prompted me to consider every person I meet during fieldwork not a mere object of research, but as heritage of humanity. The memories they keep tell their life story—which is also a family, social, cultural, "national," local, and global history—and allow me to observe an exemplary path, individual and collective at the same time, for the understanding of a slice of humanity, a protagonist of what I would call "cultural" and "historical" epochs. During my fieldwork in Cilento,[7] I collected the stories, tales, and gastronomic autobiographies of individuals aged between 80 and over 100 years. The elderly, subjects of the survey, explained the "nature" of what I call the "taste of the Mediterranean Diet," highlighting its contradictions and fictional essence.

Memory was the key to their stories. This red thread connecting with the past serves to establish an identity, a story, made unique. Food, traditions, and eating habits, banquets on festive days, special dishes have marked our childhoods or particular moments in our lives and become an important part of our memory. Proust's *madeleine* is the quintessential illustration of this tie to the past, the mother of all the foods. Memory affects the way we perceive smells and tastes, the way we "taste" a particular food. The anthropologist Douglas Harper wrote: "Memories created by smells and tastes are not rational collections of places and events, but connections to things of the past"; therefore, they are mostly emotional connections. In contrast, the "importance of nutrition is not in the memory that one has of food, but in the memory of the people who made it and in the circumstances in which it was shared together" (2010: 71). Memories rooted in smells and tastes are not an "objective" list of the series of dishes consumed in the course of one's existence, but rather the selective memories that we keep of our food "experiences" including, above all, emotions and feelings founded in the act of sharing them with other people. Memory is shaped by narration, poetics, and rhetoric, through which experiences are remembered. Holtzman noted that the sensuality of food makes it a particularly intense *medium* for memory and that the experience of food evokes memories that are not simply cognitive, but also emotional and physical (2006: 365). One must hear their stories to gain access to the world of the "centenarians" of the Mediterranean Diet's taste, who according to UNESCO are the main custodians of "millenary" practices and reveal the mechanisms they use to build their own identity and cultural taste. Here I focus on some of their narratives, especially as they focus on their experiences and memories of taste.

Family Affects and the Memory of Taste

The strongest food-related memory of Pasqualino, a 91-year-old man born in a small town in Cilento close to a hill a few kilometers from the sea, is his mother's homemade pasta. He said: "The flavors of childhood remain impregnated in the flesh." As soon as he can, he eats some homemade pasta with gusto. Pasqualino moved as a young adult to Naples to carry out his medical profession, but he returned every two weeks to his native town to stock up on food supplies he would bring to the city. During his account, a certain nostalgia emerges that would mark his existence: nostalgia for village life, for the countryside and the vegetable garden, for the food and drinks shared with family members and fellow villagers. City life, which nourished his way of being in the world and identified him as a "good doctor," could not erase his memory of country life. He has eaten countryside foods most of his life to bring the country into the city. Today, old and retired, he remains tied to his youthful world by maintaining through food his bond with his mother and the world she represented. That explains his taste and his preference for homemade pasta. Taste is not only the result of human biology, genetic predispositions, and physiology or chemistry of food but also has a precise cultural determination (Ayora-Diaz 2012, 2019; Sutton 2010; Korsmeyer and Sutton 2011).

The "*madeleine*" of Pia, the taste of the past of a 93-year-old woman who has always lived in Cilento, is the "antipasto" prepared by her mother on the first Sunday after Easter, when she was a child, when all the relatives gathered, including those who came from elsewhere. It was a piece of boiled meat cut into very thin pieces and flavored with grated goat cheese and beaten eggs, all mixed with broth. "It was delicious!" she repeated to me several times, lamenting that she had never been able to replicate the taste her mother achieved.

If it is true that cultural memory perpetually constructs and remodels identities and, therefore, the sense of one's raison d'être, as Lévi-Strauss would say, it is equally true that it remodels both the taste and, better, the gustatory perceptions both of individuals, and therefore draws on their individual and collective histories. The memory of these two witnesses during my fieldwork is also meaningful for the way eating is experienced (Korsmeyer and Sutton 2011). The past world and time interact with the present of Pasqualino and Pia. I thus suggest that they taste the present thanks to their memory of the past. Their taste seems to be conditioned by the visual image of an event that is located in the past—the mother who prepares homemade pasta—and acts on the gustatory perception of the present evoking a specific dish (homemade pasta) as "good to eat" (Ayora-Diaz 2012; Korsmeyer and Sutton 2011). This is true for most of the Cilento seniors who have informed my field of study. Everyone remembers a dish prepared by the mother during childhood, as their favorite dish, still today.

The taste of the elderly in Cilento is the result of two different but connected "memories": the memory of "hunger" and of "vegetable gardens." The first makes food choices and preferences evocative of the foods that they were deprived in the past. The second tends to emphasize those foods that remind of the main way of obtaining food resources during their youth, that is, "working the land," and are cultivated today in their own gardens. This second "memory" leads to a preference for "poorer" foods, simple, deriving from the earth, mostly vegetables, which they consider "genuine." It is from the intersection between these two memories that the taste of the elderly of Cilento is made (Ayora-Diaz 2012).

Hunger

Hunger pervades their memories, and it determines the perception of the tastes of the present. Remembering the most solitary and personal events is always a collective process because our memory is always shaped by social environments, people, objects, and the institutions that create them (Halbwachs 1980; Korsmeyer and Sutton 2011). Pia told me that when she was young she was constrained to eat what nature offered and she didn't have access to "the variety of artificial fruits and vegetables found in today's supermarkets." Michele declares that in his home, as a child, "sometimes there was no salt, sometimes no bread and sometimes no olive oil." Until the 1950s, food was scarce, and "hunger" was not just a rhetorical expression, emphasizing a life of poverty. As Mauro said, a meal was often made of wild herbs that grew spontaneously in the land.

"When I was young?" Giovanna asks me with a surprised air,

> We had almost nothing! Pasta with beans, polenta with beans! What did we eat? In the evening, mom gave us a piece of bread and sent us to sleep. We couldn't sleep because we were hungry. We would get up, there was a bag of red flour, we would go up to it, put a pan on the fire, brown an onion, stir it and eat it. We couldn't sleep. But what do you know about our youth? My mom would have some garlic, she would take it, roast it on the grill and then we would eat it. What do I miss from the past? Today we are rich! At the time we were poor!

In many of their stories, hoeing the earth was equivalent to "killing oneself" and "starving." But because there was no bread, it was the only way to survive: "there were no pensions," and what you grew in a land that was not yours, you had to give the owner, "he was so rich while we were poor and starving," adds Maria. The mother often did not eat at all to be able to give some bread to all of her children.

All subjects in my study recall the difficulties and deprivations of the past, when meat was rarely eaten, mostly on some festive occasions such as celebrations dedicated to the Madonna or the patron saints of the village, on Easter and Christmas. There was no choice; one had to feed oneself on what one could afford, and what mothers put on the table was often the same soup. The deprivations of youth led them to mythologize and emphasize the taste for sweet foods, elaborate preparations, and meat, consumed both as a filling for pasta and pizzas and as main course. The memory of ricotta cake with yellow cream and a layer of chocolate, of whole meal flour donuts twisted and covered in honey made during the first week of December to consume and gift on Christmas days, and of sweet pizzas with milk cream or chocolate bars, reminiscences of the period of Italian economic boom, make their mouth water. The preparation of the dishes was quite elaborate and described with great emotional involvement.

Evelina, for example, explained to me how she prepared, and still prepares, lasagna: "We make the dough, similar to *fusilli* dough but kneaded in such a way that it remains softer, then we roll out the lasagna, this wide (she indicates with her hands a width of about eight to ten centimeters), heat it, and then season it. We used minced meat to make the sauce. Earlier, when I was young, I also made small meatballs, and we also put these meatballs, beaten egg on top, a little cheese, parmesan and mozzarella and baked them. We made it of substance."

Later, when the economic boom reached Cilento, meat, rich pastas, and desserts became accessible and became part of their daily meals. Today, Alessandro, ninety-seven, eats meat almost every day. On Sundays, his table is a triumph of chops, meatballs with meat sauce, and fusilli with goat meat. He begins: "In the past meat was eaten only if you had enough savings to be able to buy it." Many valued the memory of events in which meat was eaten because finally it was possible to eat "as God commands." Giovanni, 101, told me about the expectations for Sunday *chianga*, a country butcher where people went to get meat, coveted by all members of the family, for the main Sunday dish. Regarding drinks, red wine is still the absolute favorite and, especially during their youth, it was not consumed in moderation at all. In the countryside, people drank starting in the morning during breakfasts and when they rested from working the land during the hottest hours of the day.

The Vegetable Garden

Most of the elders said they own a garden where they grow a variety of products. Pia takes care with her own hands of the garden where she grows the fruits and vegetables that she consumes every day, and the olives to make the oil she uses to dress the tomato salad she eats almost every evening at dinner. Pia's garden's olive oil is special; she also uses it for frying, and despises the various sunflower or peanut oils commonly used for frying because, in her opinion, they have no flavor. As if to say that she has never been impressed by the wave of industrialized food, she continues to eat seasonal and zero-kilometer fruit and vegetables.

Luigia hates fertilizers and only puts manure in her garden: she learned the lesson of her father, who grew olives, fruits, and vegetables without chemicals. Everyone remembers the past, when food was wholesome and tasty, and the family was large and united. Antonio tells me how the 1950s marked an epochal change for his village, Pioppi: most of the population moved from the countryside to "built" towns. Since then, the peasant and gastronomic culture of the area has gradually changed with industrialization and with the distancing of ordinary people from the food production process. The coast of Pioppi was the landing place for *cianciole* (the fishing boats of Cilento); plenty of fish was unloaded, but today almost nobody in town wants to fish. The times and ways of food have radically changed for Antonio, and he and his peers are left with bitterness veiled with melancholy. He often repeats that food used to be genuine:

With a natural sense [he affirms] because it was all stuff we made. It was actually cooked with a different flavor because it was seasoned with our olive oil and in short, everything was tastier: the sauce for the pasta was made with our beautiful, red tomatoes. I still make it so. That is why I say today has changed. Fish is no longer what it used to be, wine is no longer what it used to be because you drink powdered wine, but I still make wine myself, I don't buy it. When I buy something in the store it is because I want to eat a vegetable that I don't have, and I don't eat it with pleasure because it doesn't taste the same. I prefer, when I lack vegetables, to pick in my garden the plants we do not plant (the wild ones) the ones we know are good to eat, instead of buying cabbage or something else.

Giovanna echoes him: "Even if I used to roast it on the grill, I would never use frozen products. I have always preserved food with a drop of vinegar, a little bit of salt and soaked them. You can preserve it for eight days without a freezer. What they sell is always frozen; if we freeze it again it is unhealthy." It seems evident that taste, like other senses, can be considered an embedded knowledge, and in the taste of food there is, in reality, a cultural value that the body expresses through the sense of taste, pleasant or unpleasant (Csordas 2003).

Conclusion

During my fieldwork, I noticed that the industrialization and homogenization of contemporary taste has made its way into the lives of the subjects I interviewed, although in the local narratives they tend to gloss over it: the meat they eat with so much pleasure, for example, comes mostly from industrialized and mechanized slaughterhouses. Some eat mainstream food products every day, like cookies and other sweets or beverages based on fermented milk with added plant sterols. However, the nostalgia for food-related practices of the past leads them in the present to cultivate their own vegetable garden and to prepare homemade food. This is seen as a resistance that opposes the McDonaldization of food, a culture that marks food as individualistic and hedonistic. This battle pits the globalization and industrialization of food against a culture that struggles to maintain its identity by means of a deep connection between food and humans. Here local poetics meet UNESCO values around the Mediterranean Diet behind Western society's nostalgia (Herzfeld 2003; Palumbo 2009).

Throughout this process, the construction of the Mediterranean Diet and its taste seems to have informed only a small part the practices and imagery of this generation of Cilento people. This is because since they are no longer hungry and can eat sweets, meat, and hearty and elaborate dishes every day, they believe that their diet has changed for the best over time. From this point of view, their practices contradict the indications of all international organizations that fear the risks of a diet rich in animal fats, sweets, and cheese. At the same time, they embrace the rhetoric about the sustainability of the Mediterranean Diet, preferring fruit and vegetables grown by them, or at zero kilometer and resisting, at least in their words, food homogenization. However, the whole narrative on the Mediterranean Diet, which can be considered an "ideology of language" (Irvine and Gal 2003) or a moral economy (Asad 2003), does not take into account the complexity of the identitarian process of the Cilento people and promotes the Mediterranean Diet as one idyllic lifestyle, which has been passed down from generation to generation for millennia, despite the fact that there have been cultural and commercial exchanges in the Mediterranean that have innovated this "diet" and made people dialogue.

What the policies and rhetoric on the Mediterranean Diet have not taken into account are the conflicts that have affected this area to date and the suffering of peasant people. Are they also to be preserved? Are these also traditions to be protected? Faced with the statements from the people I have encountered in my fieldwork, which highlight the hunger and social inequalities they experienced, one cannot but question the idealization of the traditional and indigenous diets expressed by the FAO director, who uses them as examples of an Eldorado of nutrition, shining examples to follow in order to fight hunger in the world and be the new frontier for a more just and egalitarian future. What I mean is that this is a dangerous omission in the discursive orders I discussed, as it erases historical, cultural, economic, political, and social processes, telling only one part of the "story," the "good, clean and right" which creates uncritical collective images, unable to evaluate and, therefore, to overcome the global criticalities that find their center in the Mediterranean. I agree with UNESCO when it states that the "Mediterranean Diet" is not just a diet, it can actually be the litmus test for some important future scenarios, provided that the other half of the story is also told.

As Korsmeyer and Sutton (2011) state, taste is a total social fact. And the taste of the "Mediterranean Diet" comes close to the definition of total social fact that emerges from the Lévi-Strauss interpretation of Mauss' work: it is not the simple reintegration of discontinuous aspects (family, technical, economic, juridical, religious) but "it presents itself with a three-dimensional character. It must make the properly sociological dimension coincide with its multiple synchronic aspects; the historical or diachronic dimension; and finally, the physio-psychological dimension. Well, this triple juxtaposition can only find its place in individuals" (Lévi-Strauss 1965: XXX), that is why it can only be embodied in a concrete experience. The concrete experiences of all human beings of the peoples of the Mediterranean area, which cannot be hidden.

Notes

1 COMMISSION REGULATION (EU) No 97/2010 of February 4, 2010.
2 Nomination file no. 00884 for Inscription in 2013 on the Representative List of the Intangible Cultural Heritage of Humanity approved in Baku, Azerbaijan, in December 2013, and Nomination file no. 00394 for Inscription on the Representative List of the Intangible Cultural Heritage of Humanity approved in Nairobi, Kenya, in November 2010, located at http://www.unisob.na.it/ateneo/c002_i.htm?vr=1:
3 The MedEatResearch—Centre of Social Research on the Mediterranean Diet, University of Naples Suor Orsola Benincasa, has been conducting research on the Mediterranean Diet since 2012. More information and some of the research work can be found at the following web address: https://www.unisob.na.it/ateneo/c002.htm?vr=1
4 See https://ich.unesco.org/en/RL/traditional-mexican-cuisine-ancestral-ongoing-community-culture-the-michoacan-paradigm-00400
5 See at: http://www.fao.org/news/story/en/item/1253018/icode/

6 My interview with the anthropologist Luigi Maria Lombardi Satriani is published on
   the website www.granaidellamemoria.it in the *Granai del Mediterraneo* archive edited
   by MedEatResearch and on the website Mediterranean Diet Virtual Museum www
   .mediterraneandietvm.com.
7 I conducted this research in Cilento during the years 2018–20 among people aged 80–103.

References

Amselle, J. L. (1999 [1990]), *Logiche meticce. Antropologia dell'identità in Africa e altrove*,
   trans. M. Aime, Torino: Bollati-Boringhieri.
Appadurai, A. (1996), *Modernity at Large*, Minneapolis: University of Minnesota Press.
Asad, T. (2003), *Formations of the Secular: Christianity, Islam, Modernity*, Stanford:
   Stanford University Press.
Ayora-Diaz, S. I. (2012), "Gastronomic Inventions and the Aesthetics of Regional Food:
   The Naturalization of Yucatecan Taste," *Etnofor* 24(2): 57–76.
Ayora-Diaz, S. I., ed. (2019), *Taste, Politics, and Identities in Mexican Food*, London:
   Bloomsbury Academic.
Benjamin, W. (2001 [1924]), "Napoli," in *Opere Complete: II Scritti (1923–1927)*, pp.
   34–46, Torino: Einaudi.
Braudel, F. (2006 [1979]), *Civiltà materiale, economia e capitalismo*, Torino: Einaudi.
Chambers, I. (2007), *Le molte voci del Mediterraneo*, Milano: Raffaello Cortina Editore.
Csordas, T. J. (2003 [1999]), "Incorporazione e fenomenologia culturale," in *Antropologia
   III*, pp. 19–42, Roma: Meltemi.
De Seta, C. (1999), *Napoli*, Bari: Laterza.
Fabietti, U. (2001), *Storia dell'antropologia*, Bologna: Zanichelli.
Fabietti, U. (2004), *Elementi di antropologia culturale*, Milano: Mondadori Università.
Fabietti, U. (2012 [1995]), *L'identità etnica*, Roma: Carocci.
Foucault, M. (2005), *Nascita della biopolitica*, trans. M. Bertani and V. Zini, Milano: Feltrinelli.
Geertz, C. (2001 [1973]), *Antropologia interpretativa*, Bologna: Il Mulino.
Ginsborg, P. (1990), *Storia d'Italia dal dopoguerra ad oggi*, Torino: Einaudi.
Goody, J. (2012), *Cibo e amore. Storia culturale dell'Oriente e dell'Occidente*, Milano:
   Raffaello Cortina Editore.
Harper, D. and P. Faccioli (2010), *The Italian Way: Food and Social Life*, Chicago:
   University of Chicago Press.
Herzfeld, M. (2003), *Intimità culturale: antropologia e nazionalismo*, Napoli: L'Ancora del
   Mediterraneo.
Hobsbawm, E. J. and T. Ranger, eds. (1987 [1983]), *L'invenzione della tradizione*, Torino:
   Einaudi.
Holbwachs, M. (1980 [1983]), *The Collective Memory*, New York: Harper and Row.
Holtzman, J. (2006), "Food and Memory," *Annual Review of Anthropology* 35: 361–78.
Irvine, J. T. and S. Gal (2003), "Language Ideology and Linguistic Differentiation," in P.
   V. Kroskrity (ed.), *Regimes of Language: Ideologies, Polities, and Identities*, pp. 35–83,
   Santa Fe: New School of American Research.
Kilani, M. (1994), *Antropologia. Dal locale al globale*, trans. A. Rivera and V. Carrassi, Bari:
   Dedalo.
Kilani, M. (1997), "La théorie des deux races: quand la science repète le mythe," in J.
   Hainard and R. Kaher (eds.), *Dir les autres. Refléxions et pratiques ethnologiques*, pp.
   31–45, Lausanne: Payot.

Korsmeyer, C. and D. Sutton (2011), "The Sensory Experience of Food," *Theory, Culture and Society* 14(4): 461–75.

Lévi-Strauss, C. (1965), "Introduzione all'opera di Marcel Mauss," in M. Mauss, *Teoria generale della magia e altri saggi*, pp. xv–liv, Torino: Einaudi.

Lewis, N. (1993 [1978]), *Napoli '44*, Milano: Adelphi.

Montalbàn, V. and E. Gonzàlez (2002), *Rappresentare il Mediterraneo*, trans. G. Varghi, Messina: Mesogea.

Montanari, M. (2005), *Il cibo come cultura*, Bari: Laterza.

Montanari, M., eds. (2006), *Il mondo in cucina. Storia, identità, scambi*, Bari: Laterza.

Moro, E. (2014), *La dieta mediterranea. Mito e storia di uno stile di vita*, Bologna: Il Mulino.

Moro, E. (2016), "Politiche patrimoniali e sviluppo sostenibile. La dieta mediterranea UNESCO," in M. Niola (ed.), *Antropologie del contemporaneo*, pp. 11–30, Lecce: Pensa MultiMedia.

Niola, M. (2009), *Si fa presto a dire cotto. Un antropologo in cucina*, Bologna: Il Mulino.

Niola, M. (2012a), *Non tutto fa brodo*, Bologna: Il Mulino.

Niola, M. (2012b), "Le primarie del fast food: kebab vs. big mac," *Italianieuropei* XII(10): 13–18.

Nomination file no. 00394 for Inscription in 2010 on the Representative List of the Intangible Cultural Heritage of Humanity. Available online: http://www.unisob.na.it/a teneo/c002_i.htm?vr=1, last accessed August 5, 2020.

Nomination File no. 00400 for Inscription in 2010 on the Representative List of the Intangible Cultural Heritage of Humanity. Available online: https://ich.unesco.org/en/ RL/traditional-mexican-cuisine-ancestral-ongoing-community-culture-the-michoaca n-paradigm-00400, last accessed August 5, 2020.

Nomination file no. 00884 for Inscription in 2013 on the Representative List of the Intangible Cultural Heritage of Humanity. Available online: http://www.unisob.na.it/a teneo/c002_i.htm?vr=1, last accessed August 5, 2020.

Palumbo, B. (2009), *Politiche dell'inquietudine. Passioni, feste e poteri in Sicilia*, Firenze: Le Lettere.

Puzzi, A. (2016), *Pizza. Una grande tradizione italiana*, Bra (Cuneo): Slow Food Editore.

Prosperi, A. (2016), *Identità. L'altra faccia della storia*, Roma: Laterza.

Robbins, R. H. (2009), *Antropologia culturale. Un approccio per problemi*, Torino: Utet.

Said, E. (1996), *Covering Islam: How the Media and the Expert Determine How We See the Rest of the World*, New York: Vintage.

Said, E. (2013 [1978]), *Orientalismo*, trans. S. Galli, Milano: Feltrinelli.

Sanità, H. (2016), "Identità patrimoniali fra radici e ali: la dieta mediterranea," in M. Niola (ed.), *Antropologie del contemporaneo*, pp. 31–45, Lecce: Pensa MultiMedia.

Sayyid, B. (2003), *A Fundamental Fear: Eurocentrism and the Emergence of Islamism*, London: Zed Books.

Sutton, D. E. (2010), "Food and the Senses," *Annual Review of Anthropology* 39: 209–23.

Teti, V. (1999), *Il colore del cibo. Geografia, mito e realtà dell'alimentazione mediterranea*, Roma: Meltemi.

Teti, V. (2002), *Mangiare meridiano: culture alimentari del Mediterraneo*, Catanzaro: Abramo.

Willet, W. C., F. Sacks, A. Trichopoulou, G. Drescher, A. Ferro-Luzzi, E. Helsing, and D. Trichopoulous (1995), "Mediterranean Diet Pyramid: A Cultural Model for Healthy Eating," *The American Journal of Clinical Nutrition* 61(6): 1402S–1406S. https://doi.org /10.1093/ajcn/61.6.1402S, last accessed August 5, 2020.

16

Soylent

The Cultural Politics of Functional and Tasteless Food

Andrew Ofstehage

Introduction: Nutritionism and Nontaste

A Silicon Valley work regime with twelve- and fourteen-hour workdays affords little time for sustenance for executives and workers alike, yet many have found a solution—not take out food but take out the food. In a 2018 *TechRepublic* article, CEO and founder of *Kiwi* for Gmail Eric Shashoua is quoted as saying "I'd been searching for something like Soylent for ages, ever since I could imagine how convenient it would be if you could just drink food . . . I'm not a foodie guy. For me, it's more convenient during the day." In the same piece, anthropologist Jan English-Lueck reflects, "As functional food is seen as an answer to the dilemma of 'What do I eat?,' it's going to become increasingly important. . . . It takes the processed food model to its final expression" (Rayome 2018). The founder and one-time CEO of Soylent described the design of Soylent as trying to create just that kind of functional food: "We're designing for function. . . . A lot of meals seem to have this trade-off. You can have something healthy, but it's going to be costly or inconvenient. You can have something quick and easy, but it's not going to be very healthy" (Robinson 2015).

Soylent, defined by its nutrition and efficiency, calls for a reconsideration of taste itself, along with the connection between taste and tastelessness with political identity. Taste, even in a seemingly vacant taste landscape of Soylent, is social and cultural (Højlund 2015), as well as physiological, yet Soylent brings certain assumptions into question. We do not usually eat (or drink) Soylent together. Højlund argues that taste as an individual, physiological experience does not address symbolic meanings of food, food taboos, or the symbolic power of food. We can understand how taste is social in terms of food sharing, preparation, and conversations about food, or in cultural terms of how we externalize taste (2015), but how do we do this with a food that is *seemingly* asocial and acultural? While Soylent seems to be distant from society, I argue that it is both reflective of a social context of work and life and socially reproduced via online sharing of experiences that defend Soylent consumption and celebrate their foresight in eschewing traditional notions of taste, food, and consumption—demonstrating their superior food consumption.

Taste is a socially codified marker of distinction, and a matter of politics as we affirm our associations and identities through our choices (Ayora-Diaz 2019). Roasters, baristas, and marketers of coffee tie coffee to narratives and values of provenance and exclusivity in their pursuit of symbolic distinction, leaving small coffee farmers unable to plug into high-end coffee markets despite their ability to grow high-quality coffee and act as stewards of the land (Fischer, in Press)—taste separates and is tied to sites of production, even if tenuously. Taste is devalued in Western tradition as a lower sense, but a shift toward slow food has placed renewed emphasis on the tasting experience and the multisensory experience of foods as well as attention to terroir (Sutton 2010). Soylent can be considered a counterwork (Arce and Long 2000) to that process. It is known for being tasteless and without a backstory, but this does not mean that it is separate from identity building (Wilk 1999), but rather that it is building identity from tastelessness.

Miracle foods are not defined by taste as much as nutrition. Soylent represents a counterpoint to what Otero et al. call a neoliberal diet, or the calorie dense, highly processed junk food that stems from overabundance of US agriculture (Otero et al. 2015). It is indeed calorie dense and highly processed, but lacks the flavor, texture, and even packaging of junk food. Junk food is calorie dense as a consequence of the high-fat, high-sugar ingredients and highly processed to manufacture the desirable balance of salt, sugar, and fat (Moss 2013). Soylent is designed in reverse; the ingredients are chosen in order to make the final product calorie dense, but with only secondary regard for taste. In this, it follows the miracle food narrative (McDonell 2015). Like high-lysine corn, Golden Rice, and quinoa, Soylent is touted as the solution to hunger, but Soylent is a unique solution to a unique hunger—it is designed to solve the problem of busy tech workers needing sustenance but lacking the time and energy to procure, prepare, and consume traditional meals. Soylent and other food replacements stand in a unique position of adding by subtracting to consumers' lives. It does not promise good taste, good times, or good feelings, but rather the basic necessary nutrients and time. It's a miracle in that it frees the consumer from food as a matter of concern. In this pursuit of adding by subtracting, Soylent supports transhumanist desires (Pilsch 2017) to optimize the individual human condition.

As documented in a special issue of *Gastronomica* on critical nutrition, inspired by a collective concern regarding the consequences, politics, and practices of nutrition science and their relation to broader biopolitical projects, reentrenchment of class and race, and the commodification and appropriation of nutritional science by global food companies (Guthman 2014), Biltekoff points to the increasing dominance of nutritionism in the field of nutritional science (Biltekoff et al. 2014). Nutritionism uses neutral, objective language of science to evaluate relative food values in terms of nutritional content. It simplifies or erases biological processes, ingredients, additives, and processing techniques and reduces food to nutrients (Scrinis 2013). Nutrition acts as a project for social reform, colonial practice, and subject making (Kimura et al. 2014); but what I propose here is that Soylent acts as a kind of grassroots nutritionism, powered not by research and state agencies, but by demand from overworked tech workers who have both embodied and enforced pressures to work long hours, not leave their desks, and optimize their time. Workers, for a variety of reasons, are asking for nutritionist solutions to food. Additionally, nutritionism offers a masculine way out (or weigh out) from concerns about feminine dieting. Weight Watchers depicts its women consumers as self-actualizing and empowered people taking control of their health and body, but men consumers as losing weight easily, not distracting from masculine foods, activities, or lifestyles (Contois 2017). Like black packaging to make shampoo and yogurt acceptable for the male gaze and subtle marketing, Soylent reframes dieting as bio-hacking—optimizing the body through nutritionism and transhumanism.

Taste intersects with food aid in a similar way. Nutritionism is increasingly incorporated into food aid delivery (Kimura 2013). Food aid recipients are expected to forego tastes of "liberty" and "luxury" and adapt "tastes of necessity," which are divorced from flavor preference and cultural cooking traditions (Trapp 2016). Nutrients not only gain significance but also become the only matter of concern in food. Fortified blended foods began as a humanitarian product from the mid-twentieth century, before being adopted by consumers in search for compact and efficient diet, then supported by science and tech as improvement on traditional food, until later enmeshed in state-led industrialization oriented to protein gap and productivist agricultural economies in the United States (Scott-Smith 2015). Soylent, in different ways, refers back to each of these moments in fortified food history—it has been proposed as the ideal food aid, it is connected to nutritionist fads of high protein, and its founder and supporters link it explicitly to productivist and efficient agriculture, proposing even that Soylent could be the last farmer as family farms become obsolete and fields move indoors.

Soylent is designed to deliver nutrients to the body as a primary goal, taste, along with enjoyment, social life of consumption, and tradition were afterthoughts (McQuaid 2016). Rob Rhinehart, founder and CEO of Soylent, makes this clear in his origin narrative of the meal replacements:

> What if I consumed only the raw ingredients the body uses for energy? Would I be healthier or do we need all the other stuff that's in traditional food? If it does work, what would it feel like to have a perfectly balanced diet? I just want to be in good health and spend as little time and money on food as possible.

The setting is not clear from the narrative; we might assume it is from his home kitchen, but in my imagination it's a sort of experimental laboratory kitchen with bright lights (Rhinehart 2013). "There are no meats, fruits, vegetables, or breads here. Besides olive oil for fatty acids and table salt for sodium and chloride nothing is recognizable as food." Here, he draws our attention to the definition of Soylent by what it is not—it is not whole foods, it's not even recognizable as food: "I researched every substance the body needs to survive, plus a few extras shown to be beneficial, and purchased all of them in nearly raw chemical form from a variety of sources. The section on the ingredients ended up being quite long . . .." When describing what it is, both the ingredients and process are scientific—raw chemicals, research, and survival.

> The first morning my kitchen looked more like a chemistry lab than a cookery, but I eventually ended up with a thick, odorless, beige liquid. I call it "Soylent." At the time I didn't know if it was going to kill me or give me superpowers. I held my nose

and tepidly lifted it to my mouth, expecting an awful taste. It was delicious! I felt like I'd just had the best breakfast of my life. It tasted like a sweet, succulent, hearty meal in a glass, which is what it is, I suppose. I immediately felt full, yet energized, and started my day.

Again, the nutrients came first, then the chemistry lab work, and then, tepidly, a taste. Thus, Soylent encourages us to think about what food is in a digital food culture that is "hackable" (Miles and Smith 2015) and anthropological notions of food are turned on their head (Dolejšová 2020, 2016; Dolejšová and Kera, 2017). I argue in this chapter that Soylent is mobilized to support identities and politics of nutritionism in both individual consumer choices and food aid discourse.

Why Tho?

Research on the marketing, production, and trade of quinoa in Bolivia has demonstrated that food can be intimately connected to kinship, ecology, soil, political action, and history (Ofstehage 2012), and research on transnational industrial soy production in Brazil shows how food can be disconnected from history, ecology, and social life, but only ever partially (Ofstehage 2018). My fourteen months of digital ethnographic work on Soylent, along with my digital research of "Soy Boy" discourse, is working toward an understanding of the limits, possibilities, and consequences of disconnecting food from social and ecological life. Using digital ethnography (Caliandro 2018), I have combed Reddit forums, Twitter posts, podcasts, and YouTube videos, as well as public posts and marketing by Soylent, much in the model of others (Potts and Parry 2010).

According to Rob Rhinehart, Soylent has

> Everything the body needs . . . vitamins, minerals and macronutrients like essential amino acids, carbohydrates and fat. For the fat, I just use olive oil and add fish oil. The carbs are an oligosaccharide, which is like sugar, but the molecules are longer, meaning it takes longer to metabolize and gives you a steady flow of energy for a longer period of time, rather than a sugar rush from something like fructose or table sugar. (Heisey 2013)

On being asked about the taste, he said, "It tastes very good. I haven't got tired of the taste in six weeks. It's a very 'complete' sensation, sweeter than anything." But that "Eating to me is a leisure activity, like going to the movies, but I don't want to go to the movies three times a day." The benefits of a "food-free lifestyle" include not worrying about food:

> No groceries, dishes, deciding what to eat, no endless conversations weighing the relative merits of gluten-free, keto, paleo or vegan . . . I save hours a day and hundreds of dollars a month. I feel liberated from a crushing amount of repetitive drudgery. Soylent might also be good for people having trouble managing their

weight. I find it very easy to lose and gain precise amounts of weight by varying the proportions in my drink. (Heisey 2013)

Taste is secondary for Soylent consumers, and they're proud of that. An IAmA Reddit post (in which a verified person is available to answer questions) by a person who acquired 80 percent of their calories from Soylent over three months drew heavy interest and a significant amount of questions on taste, enjoyment, and pleasure of consuming Soylent, along with questions about bowel movements. One of the most frequently asked questions was a series of queries, "What are some positives of eating Soylent that you have seen effect your daily life? What are some negatives? What does it taste like? Do you actually like eating Soylent?" The response was that the subject of the AMA felt "more energized," had "less food cravings," and had lost twenty-six pounds. The drawbacks were that it had to be ordered online and thus one had to keep an eye on food stock and "the after taste." The subject explained, "The flavored kind gives me an 'I haven't brushed my teeth yet' taste in my mouth. It comes in two flavors, cocoa and nectar as well as plain. Cocoa tastes like milk chocolate, nectar tastes like lucky charms, and plain tastes like pancake batter. The plain flavor is the cheapest . . . I actually do enjoy drinking Soylent."

Later, in the Q&A, a poster asked, "why tho?" to which the subject responded by explaining that they had an eating disorder throughout their life and wanted to reduce the amount of sugary and fattening foods that they consumed: "My goal is to teach myself to see food as a survival mechanism and not an emotional outlet." As they "progressed" in their Soylent diet, they found that "I am not as interested in eating a variety of things like I used to." This was not only because they had come to prefer "bland and healthy things" but also because "food is such a chore for me now and I might switch to only Soylent in the near future but with the occasional meal with friends . . . I'm also finding myself getting disgusted with food ads."

Soylent is about progress, not conservatism. Soylent and Reddit forums are a site of defense for that progress, derision of other food practices, and evangelism for new forms of food consumption. A poster responded to coworkers' discomfort about their food consumption. The poster writes that he "went through the whole speech . . . showed him a few videos, he seemed quite intrigued." But the coworkers had questions. They asked about digestive issues, digesting large amounts of protein, and now "tries to convince [the poster] to stop." The poster ends by opening up the discussion: "Has anyone else had this experience?"

A poster began their response much like a cultural anthropologist might. "Food is a biological necessity that everyone to ever live has considered every day of their life. Food is culture. Food is habit. Food is life. After sleeping it's probably the single biggest expenditure of time on average." But they mobilized this culture, habit, and life as backward:

Before civilization that was just about all anyone did. Procuring and consuming food is how many animals spend most of their time. Food is a Big Deal. Soylent is a very radical change to food and some people may feel threatened or upset by that. I find that reaction stupid but it's not the first time I've said that about a common action.

Another poster echoed this:

> He's angry because his belief system is being challenged . . . most people are groupthinkers. independent minds are threatening to them. I find that the concept of powdered food really brings out most people's instinctual conservatism and highlights their (in)ability to independently evaluate the value in something— think they just have difficulty overriding their instinctual reaction against a new food. We're evolved to eat what we know from experience is safe to eat. recognizing the value in powedered [*sic*] food requires bypassing that instinct which comes easier to some people than others.

A similar post opened up discussion from the beginning. "Let's share. Who is getting mocked at work/school over soylent." And a poster characterized the typical conversation:

> Q: "So why do you drink those shakes?"
> A: "I get hungry and it's too much effort to make something for work every day."
> Q: "But they don't taste very good do they?"
> A: "They're not bad but they're not good either."
> Q: "But good food!"

Several posts on the Soylent Reddit forum ask for or provide advice on how to speak to friends, family, and coworkers about the diet:

> Sadly, it appears the only one (approach) that's simple and where everybody reliably leaves the conversation on good terms is when you shrug them off with a "it's a protein shake." This is because most people that will try to initiate talks on this subject will not *actually* be curious and be open to challenge their views on food: people are very sensitive about nutrition, so they'll be on their guards and kinda spooked by the fact you're eating something different, and thus will be primed for defaulting to "sounds like it's not healthy, and totally not food: I wouldn't eat that."

Others had more elaborate approaches:

> I try to relate -lents and things they are accustomed with. This can vary depending on who I'm talking with, but the most common introduction is when I say that it's like a soup powder, except that it's not only vegetables. I then explain that I mix it with water, and that it has the texture and flavor of a smoothie. Even if that's not true, I usually "lie" and say that I then eat an apple for dessert or something. All this should be sufficient to establish that -lents are a form of dried powder food that make up the main course. This is very important as it tells them it's not a supplement, nor a dessert, nor a multivitamin mix. It's food, plain and simple.

The poster went on to outline different scenarios that stem from that conversation including questions about being hungry, why they don't prep meals instead, if it's a weight-loss strategy, and if it's healthy with go-to responses for each question. If the person is receptive to these arguments, the poster would then expand on other perks of Soylent, including that it is "reasonably healthy," is "reasonably cheap," "saves time," "can be stored for a very long time, perfect for emergencies," and is environmentally friendly. To end the discussion, they offer a sample pouch. Others in the same conversation wrote about convincing their workplace to stock up on Soylent despite having a fully stocked kitchen, "they couldn't really argue with the fact that this was a great alternative for a busy tech company, especially those who were running in between meetings all day and hardly had a chance to sit down. With the price and more importantly, health benefits compared to, not eating at all, it was an easy sell at the time." What's particularly notable about this, beyond the espoused benefits and Soylent evangelism, is the frame of comparison. Soylent here is not compared to the other food in the kitchen, but to "not eating at all."

Other posts address the need to avoid specific words. "Be careful with the use of the word chemical. I know you're using the word correctly, but I came a cross [*sic*] some folks who only know the word with the negative connotation, one guy didn't know that all natural foods were made up of chemicals." But this response drew disagreements:

> Seriously? I can't even imagine someone with that problem. We are biological machines: this complex chemical need is our fuel source . . . I think it says a lot about someone's personality and how open-minded and independent-minded they are whether they can see the value in it or not. Most people are sheep and won't use their brain to arrive at their own conclusion about something new. They wait for the bandwagon to ride by before they jump on board.

This in turn drew criticism for using "sheep" unironically and sounding arrogant, but none challenged the poster's central position—that Soylent is fuel for the machine that is the human body, a better way to power the body, available for those open-minded and independent-minded enough to forego the cultural aspects of food. This to say that Soylent is celebrated for having not bad taste at best, but, more importantly, for being smart, efficient, and nutritious.

Soylent marketing promotes a similar view. A clean, crisp billboard in Los Angeles shows two bottles against a bright sky blue background. On the left is a brown-orange liquid in a bottle and on the right is a bottle of original flavor Soylent. It reads, "Juice is sweet. Soylent is complete." A YouTube ad for Soylent titled "Soylent: Donuts are Great!" opens with a shot of a glazed donut on a tissue, zooming in slowly, and a robotic woman narrator says in a flat monotone: "Donuts, they have no nutritional value, but they make me feel good momentarily. Ninety seconds of enjoyment is worth the shame I will feel later. I am so alone." And the commercial is over.

Soylent is framed as an optimal superfood and its users are concerned about taste only as a secondary characteristic. Taste is romantic, not that important, and social eating is rarely even mentioned; together, this challenges the anthropological concept of food as a social, shared, cultural experience, and yet my research on Reddit and other social media shows that this food experience is indeed shared, cultural, and political, but that this experience is more often shared via online communities than across a dinner table. This shared meaning of food and identity as food consumers who are interested in nutrition and efficiency over taste and joy speaks to the competing frames of care in Silicon Valley in which tech workers are expected to work intense and long hours. Tech companies attempt to balance this demand for intense work by providing care in the form of yoga, massage, and cafeteria food—this care is meant to help workers manage stress and illness, but as much to support the investment of stock holders by keeping the workforce content and busy (English-Lueck and Avery 2017). The tendency of some Silicon Valley companies then is to provide healthy, flavorful, and sustainable food to meet worker demands (English-Lueck and Avery 2017), while Soylent works on the other end of the spectrum. It meets these intense work demands by not meeting demand but by eliminating demands. As demonstrated in the "seeds of disruption" framework, Soylent is a counterwork to foodie culture in Silicon Valley and a move to redefine the future of food (Avery et al. 2013). Both marketing and consumers are promoting a higher elevation of food consumption, one that foregoes enjoyment, taste, and pleasure in favor of nutrition and convenience. For some, this also makes Soylent the ideal disaster relief food.

Soylent as Disaster Relief

Soylent has been proposed by consumers and the company itself for use for disaster relief and food aid. In an interview with CNN, Rob Rhinehart says that he has envisioned Soylent as a tool in ending world hunger from the beginning (Russell 2013):

> Being able to produce calories very cheaply at scale, in a form that is very shelf-stable and comparatively easy to store and transport, alleviates many issues around food aid and security . . . I think we can focus on food security—that's something that's been on my mind from the very beginning—but we have to be profitable first.

The company reports regularly donating to food pantries, but their goals of food aid are larger than that. Rather than sending bottles or packets of consumer-ready Soylent, they have tested "algae paste" as a more appropriate food delivery system.

A writer and lecturer builds on Rhinehart's statement that "In some countries people are dying of obesity, others starvation" to build toward a Soylent-based food aid strategy (Hodge 2015). Since Soylent has been open-sourced as database of meal replacement recipes, the writer proposes that for $1.50 per meal optimal nutrition could be sourced locally by aid recipients. He recognizes that the cost remains higher than recipients can afford, but since they can already not afford them, it's a nonissue, "Bottom line: Soylent is cheaper than indigenous foods." Rhinehart rejects underproduction as a cause of hunger and identifies waste as the main culprit, without mentioning distribution as an issue. Thus, the fact that Soylent doesn't spoil is for him the main benefit. Soylent has an ongoing collaboration with the World Food Program, but this is apparently not based on distribution of Soylent as a product, but rather a "fast growing hydroponics program" for refugees to grow grains in water and land scarce areas (World Food Program USA 2020).

Turning back to Soylent consumers on Reddit, there is also a debate on whether Soylent can be an optimal food aid source, or even an ideal prison food. A user started a post titled "Would it be unethical to use Soylent as prison food? What about for disaster relief/emergencies?"

> Although many of us would have no problem with a year's supply of Soylent being bequeathed unto us, those who haven't fully accepted the Soylent overlords have quite bit of an adverse reaction to Soylent. A friend of mine got one of the free bottles of 2.0 and absolutely hated it (describing it as "like a mix between wheat and elmers glue . . ."). I'm sure it could have tasted like that to me when I first tried it, but I was so sold on the concept of Soylent that I didn't really pay it much mind. So it got me thinking, would it be ethical (or just nice in general) to essentially force other people to consume Soylent?

Users responded that it wouldn't be nice, but ethically it may be no different than forcing aid recipients or prisoners to eat any other food. "Practical matters aside, I wouldn't expect either prison or disaster victims to have a lot of say in the matter. But again, that goes for literally any food you're providing." Users found the cost, not taste, might be the limiting factor for Soylent as prison food or food aid, but one poster wrote that

> i really like the idea of serving nutriloaf/prison loaf/totaloaf to prisoners [*sic*] and then they can be upgraded to different food for good behavior. the community here might disagree with me, but i dont expect everyone to enjoy what i eat/enjoy plus i mix other food stuff in with it. however in a prison context i think it is perfectly fine to feed the prisoners the same thing day after day if they are causing trouble.

Kimura writes on the use of nutrition in development work to support aid and agricultural research that can disrupt local food economies (Kimura 2013). Golden Rice, or rice engineered to contain Vitamin D, supplements food with nutrients. Soylent as food aid works in the other direction—it delivers nutrients, but not food.

Covid-19

I am finishing this chapter from my kitchen table as Covid-19 spreads globally, and my state has ordered a shelter in place directive. Out of precaution we have been working from home for more than two weeks already. It's a precarious, anxious, and chaotic time, and perhaps a time when Soylent will appeal uniquely to people. On March 15, Soylent published a blogpost to announce that their workers are working from home, but their sales have increased since January due to high demand; they warn consumers to avoid stockpiling so that "everyone has access to needed nutrition." The company reports donating 150,000 bottles of Soylent to food banks across the United States and reports working with Feeding America to address hunger. They inform the consumer that it is okay to live on Soylent entirely and that Soylent can be stored without refrigeration, and they state that their international supply chain is safe so far. Three days earlier, a poster on Reddit wrote that they felt liberated from stress and anxiety of shopping because they had a six-month supply of Soylent at home. Responses were overwhelmingly favorable—people were either glad that they had a stockpile or regretting that they didn't.

It's no surprise. Reports that Covid-19 originated in a "Chinese wet market" may only deepen interest in Soylent. Xenophobia surrounding global food supplies has transformed food systems in the past and may do so again. White bread exists in part because of such xenophobia and a preference for industrial-made, and fortified, safe foods (Bobrow-Strain 2012). Further, the image of a "wet market" as a dirty, chaotic space may even be a source of backlash against farmers' markets, food cooperatives, and other alternative food sources. If proximity to farms, farmers, and food becomes a worrisome connection, then consumers may likely flock to safe, industrial foods such as Soylent. Soylent Reddit forums today are full of posts about fridges stocked with Soylent, just-arrived boxes of Soylent bottles, and appreciation for not having to go to grocery stores, markets, or restaurants.

Conclusion

A new meal replacement drink has become a staple of Silicon Valley diets: Soylent. The marketing of Soylent promises that by replacing meals and snacks with five servings of Soylent per day will meet a person's daily nutrient requirements without demanding food preparation time, time away from work, or time procuring food. It frames other foods as unhealthy, time consuming, distracting, and "rotting." Soylent stands as an anti-food, without socialized eating or preparation, enjoyment, or history, but rather a nutrient delivery system to optimize nutrition and work. Taste, for the consumers of Soylent, is of little consequence. Most report the texture to be unpleasant and the flavors unremarkable. Marketing campaigns for Soylent focus on its functionality and convenience. As a "functional food," Soylent seems to fall outside of social relations of food procurement, preparation, and consumption and yet it is tied to socioeconomic class and identity through its relationship with work and life. It supports a work regime in which workers can remain at their desks through lunch break and minimize unpaid labor (e.g., food preparation and procurement). This work regime supports worker identity formation as workers demonstrate their value in terms of efficiency, focus, and dedication by foregoing lunch breaks in favor of quick, tasteless meals at their workstation.

References

Arce, A. and N. Long (2000), "Reconfiguring Modernity and Development from an Anthropological Perspective," in A. Arce and N. Long (eds.), *Anthropology,*

Development and Modernities: Exploring Discourse, Counter-Tendencies and Violence, pp. 1–30, London: Routledge.

Avery, M. L., B. Hamamoto, B. Kreit, and S. Smith (2013), *Seeds of Disruption: How Technology Is Remaking the Future of Food*, Palo Alto: Institute for the Future Publication SR-1618B.

Ayora-Diaz, S. I. (2019), "Introduction: Matters of Taste: The Politics of Food and Identity in Mexican Cuisines," in S. I. Ayora-Diaz (ed.), *Taste, Politics, and Identities in Mexican Food*, pp. 1–18, London: Bloomsbury Publishing.

Biltekoff, C., J. Mudry, A. H. Kimura, H. Landecker, and J. Guthman (2014), "Interrogating Moral and Quantification Discourses in Nutritional Knowledge," *Gastronomica: The Journal of Critical Food Studies* 14(3):17–26.

Bobrow-Strain, A. (2012), *White Bread: A Social History of the Store-Bought Loaf*, Boston: Beacon Press.

Caliandro, A. (2018), "Digital Methods for Ethnography: Analytical Concepts for Ethnographers Exploring Social Media Environments," *Journal of Contemporary Ethnography* 47(5): 551–78.

Contois, E. (2017), "'Lose Like a Man': Gender and the Constraints of Self-Making in Weight Watchers Online," *Gastronomica: The Journal of Critical Food Studies* 17(1): 33–43.

Dolejšová, M. (2016), "Deciphering a Meal through Open Source Standards: Soylent and the Rise of Diet Hackers," *Proceedings of the 2016 CHI Conference Extended Abstracts on Human Factors in Computing Systems*, pp. 436–48.

Dolejšová, M. (2020), "From Silicon Valley to Table: Solving Food Problems by Making Food Disappear," in D. Lupton and Z. Feldman (eds.), *Digital Food Cultures*, pp. 193–208, London: Routledge.

Dolejšová, M. and D. Kera (2017), "Soylent Diet Self-Experimentation: Design Challenges in Extreme Citizen Science Projects," *Proceedings of the 2017 ACM Conference on Computer Supported Cooperative Work and Social Computing*, 2112–23.

English-Lueck, J. A. and M. L. Avery (2017), "Intensifying Work and Chasing Innovation: Incorporating Care in Silicon Valley," *Anthropology of Work Review* 38(1): 40–9.

Fischer, E. F. (In Press), "Quality and Inequality: Creating Value Worlds with Third Wave Coffee," *Socio-Economic Review*. https://doi.org/10.1093/ser/mwz044

Guthman, J. (2014), "Introducing Critical Nutrition: A Special Issue on Dietary Advice and Its Discontents," *Gastronomica: The Journal for Food Studies* 14(3): 1–4.

Heisey, M. (2013, March 13), "This Man Thinks He Never Has to Eat Again," *Vice*. https://www.vice.com/en_uk/article/yv59ab/rob-rhinehart-no-longer-requires-food, last accessed March 20, 2020.

Hodge, K. (2015, February 8), "Soylent and the Future of World Hunger," *Nextographer*. https://medium.com/the-nextographer/soylent-and-the-future-of-world-hunger-e127c 3a6c91a, last accessed March 20, 2020.

Højlund, S. (2015), "Taste as a Social Sense: Rethinking Taste as a Cultural Activity," *Flavour* 4(1): 1–3.

Kimura, A. H. (2013), *Hidden Hunger: Gender and the Politics of Smarter Foods*, Ithaca: Cornell University Press.

Kimura, A. H., C. Biltekoff, J. Mudry, and J. Hayes-Conroy (2014), "Nutrition as a Project," *Gastronomica: The Journal of Critical Food Studies* 14(3): 34–45.

McDonell, E. (2015), "Miracle Foods: Quinoa, Curative Metaphors, and the Depoliticization of Global Hunger Politics," *Gastronomica: The Journal of Critical Food Studies* 15(4): 70–85.

McQuaid, J. (2016), *Tasty: The Art and Science of What We Eat*, New York: Scribner.

Miles, C. and N. Smith (2015), "What Grows in Silicon Valley? The Emerging Ideology of Food Technology," in H. L. Davis, K. Pilgrim, and M. Sinha (eds.), *The Ecopolitics of Consumption: The Food Trade*, pp. 119–38, Lanham: Lexington Books.

Moss, M. (2013), *Salt, Sugar, Fat: How the Food Giants Hooked Us*, New York: Random House.

Ofstehage, A. (2012), "The Construction of An Alternative Quinoa Economy: Balancing Solidarity, Household Needs, and Profit in San Agustín, Bolivia," *Agriculture and Human Values* 29(4): 441–54.

Ofstehage, A. (2018), "Farming Out of Place: Transnational Family Farmers, Flexible Farming, and the Rupture of Rural Life in Bahia, Brazil," *American Ethnologist* 45(3): 317–29.

Otero, G., G. Pechlaner, G. Liberman, and E. Gürcan (2015), "The Neoliberal Diet and Inequality in the United States," *Social Science & Medicine* 142: 47–55.

Pilsch, A. (2017), *Transhumanism: Evolutionary Futurism and the Human Technologies of Utopia*, Minneapolis: University of Minnesota Press.

Potts, A. and J. Parry (2010), "Vegan Sexuality: Challenging Heteronormative Masculinity through Meat-Free Sex," *Feminism & Psychology* 20(1): 53–72.

Rayome, A. D. (2018), "Meal Replacements make Tech Workers more Productive: Can they also Solve World Hunger?" *TechRepublic*. https://www.techrepublic.com/article/meal-replacements-make-tech-workers-more-productive-can-they-also-solve-world-hunger/, last accessed March 20, 2020.

Rhinehart, R. (2013, February 13), *How I Stopped Eating Food | Mostly Harmless*. http://robrhinehart.com/?p=298, last accessed March 20, 2020.

Robinson, M. (2015), "You Can Replace an Entire Meal with a $2.50 Bottle of Soylent," *Business Insider*. https://www.businessinsider.com/soylent-2-bottled-food-replacement-2015-8, last accessed March 20, 2020.

Russell, L. (2013, December 13), "Could Soylent Solve World Hunger?" *CNN*. https://www.cnn.com/2013/12/13/health/soylent-hunger/index.html, last accessed March 20, 2020.

Scott-Smith, T. (2015), "Beyond the 'Raw' and the 'Cooked': A History of Fortified Blended Foods," *Disasters* 39(s2): s244–s260.

Scrinis, G. (2013), *Nutritionism: The Science and Politics of Dietary Advice*, New York: Columbia University Press.

Sutton, D. E. (2010), "Food and the Senses," *Annual Review of Anthropology* 39: 209–23.

Trapp, M. M. (2016), "You-Will-Kill-Me Beans: Taste and the Politics of Necessity in Humanitarian Aid," *Cultural Anthropology* 31(3): 412–37.

Wilk, R. R. (1999), "'Real Belizean Food': Building Local Identity in the Transnational Caribbean," *American Anthropologist* 101(2): 244–55.

World Food Program USA (2020), "Soylent," *World Food Program USA*. https://www.wfpusa.org/organizations/soylent/, last accessed March 20, 2020.

Postface

Heritage-Making after the US Century

Krishnendu Ray

It is August 2020, and Covid-19 has ravaged lives and livelihoods across the world. More than twenty million have been infected and almost one million are dead, and by now the virus of ethnocentrism has spread everywhere. In Delhi, for instance, the fight against the virus has been stymied by Hindu nationalist mania for temple-building during a moment of peril to the body politic. From Ayodhya to Hagia Sophia, the clarion call of majoritarian religious nationalisms is ricocheting from the minarets, church spires, and temple domes, egging each other into misdirected Armageddon in response to a microscopic enemy leaching everywhere. Lives have come to a standstill, while the pace of history has hurried up. As a result, questions about the relationship between the current moment and the past have reemerged with scorching intensity. A heritage is a view of the past from the present. Lives are being lost and heritage is being reinvented.

It is in this context that I draw upon the empirically rich chapters on national heritage-making—among other themes such as restaurants, indigeneity, street foods, and popular urban tastes—to articulate what the evidence makes clear: that every national gastronomic heritage is built on ethnic cleansing, expressed as regional unevenness and class domination. There is no national cuisine without the violence of exclusion and repression.

*　*　*

The process of excision, simplification, and amplification in Japan is powerfully illustrated by Yoshimi Osawa in this volume (in Chapter 2), where *dashi* and umami appear not only as a thing and a taste "but also . . . a source of national pride." It illustrates at the extreme end how taste has become the locus of a new science of nationalism, with the nationalization of sensory science. The quest here hinges on the perfectly nationalist soup stock. *Dashi* itself is varied and multiple. Its excessively venerated and standardized modern form derives from dried bonito and kelp. In its current shape, it is a twentieth-century invention pushed by corporations and the state, which have added *dashi*-making to the school curriculum. The emerging script of making *dashi* appears to be an upper-class clean-up of a lower-class act of adding soy sauce and sugar. The adding of *kombu* (a type of edible kelp) to the soup stock also came late, in one assessment, as a transfer from the Kansai region—Kyoto and Osaka—to Tokyo among connoisseurs. There is some evidence that it might be an unacknowledged borrowing from the indigenous Ainu of Hokkaido (Cobb 2020). Nevertheless, there is little doubt that the final phase of *dashi* standardization emerged from an upper-class restaurant favored by critics and commentators. The naturalization of *dashi* as a part of the domestic art of female home cooking—*katei ryori*—is an even more recent invention, where the phrase first appeared in 1903. Before that it might be more accurate to identify hegemonic Japanese home cooking with servant's cooking, as it is in India today: unacknowledged, unnamed, and mostly written out of history (de St. Maurice 2018).

We witness here the sobering process by which "great" culinary culture is fabricated, akin to the making of hotdogs—unseemly if you pay close enough attention to it. The manufacturing—real and representational—of the quintessential Japanese cuisine, where *dashi* is illustrative, disabuses us of the easy myth-making that everything Japanese is of great antiquity. Looked at long and hard, and without sentimentalism, it appears as nothing more than the conjoined effort of the Japanese state, its local bureaucrats, and Western professionals (in their recent appreciation of anything Japanese, after securely consecrating French and Italian cuisines) to assuage themselves of long-enduring processes of racism and exclusion by composing the portfolio of a global elite heritage. Consecration by UNESCO has set off a destructive clamor between nations to standardize, ethnically purify, class stratify, and accentuate their own greatness in the eyes of cultural bureaucrats and marketers of tourism. There is no way to avoid the conclusion that UNESCO tangible and intangible heritage is at best ahistorical and at worst another form of national self-aggrandizement, often racially imagined. Thankfully in practice there is continuing diversity of making, tasting, and preferring *dashi* that is regional, using a mix of industrial and homemade processes. This is food at medium speeds, as Sidney Mintz once put it, neither fast, nor slow, and surely not safely national.

The unevenness of the standardization process within Japan is nicely illustrated by Shingo Hamada's chapter on fermented mackerel sushi (*heshiko-narezushi*). Connoisseurs and producers are specific about the source of the mackerel, which can be local Japanese or Norwegian, winter or spring caught, and vary by fat content. They are also quite specific about the provenance of the rice *koji* (*Aspergillus oryzae*) which came to be added at some point of time to give the product a sweeter, sake-like taste compared to steamed rice, which makes it sour. But local folks are not particularly invested in the provenance of the salt, which is industrial and constitutes almost 20 percent of the production process by weight. Fortunately for the preservation of variety, and all that makes food interesting, there is no agreement on a standard taste for *heshiko-narezushi*: it differs by household and generation and residence. The taste and the texture changes from cask to cask, and from household to household. An old lady sweetens it by adding rice wine to accommodate the palate of her grandchildren and their friends, escaping the homogenizing control from above wherever there is cultural contact and local tastes are made public.

From *nga-pi* of Myanmar, *patis* of the Philippines, to the *nam-pla* of Thailand, we see the widest range of fish sauce across South and East Asia. Each illustrates the basic principle of prolonging the availability of fat, protein, oil, and salt in fish as condiment, seasoning, or side dish. Much of India too, is hot, wet, and tropical, where most of the people eat rice and fish. Half a billion people eat fish in India. A continuous line from the southwestern part of the peninsula from Goa to Bihar along a line at about 45° NE cuts the map of India into almost two equal halves, establishing the wheat/rice and vegetarian/nonvegetarian line. In contrast, only six states are majority vegetarian: Punjab, Haryana, Himachal Pradesh, Rajasthan, Madhya Pradesh, and Gujarat (Yadavar 2018). The latter are on the edges of the dry zone of India, many of them well irrigated with capital- and water-intensive Green Revolution projects. The fact that most of India is fish-eating gets so overwhelmed by the presumption that India is the home of vegetarians that even Indians buy that canard. Of course, India is exceptional by global standards in terms of ritual (rather than necessary) vegetarianism, but still the picture of vegetarianism is overdrawn and plays into the hands of ethnic cleansers.

Much of the fish there is saved across the seasonal cycle as fermented fish sauce but there is no known Indian fish sauce—that is, branded by state or company—and no one is clamoring to mark them as part of Indian heritage. Most outsiders, and many Indians from the heart of the subcontinent, would have a hard time identifying any dried or fermented fish as a substantial part of national culinary culture. Kikon, Tamang, and Thapa have shown how Indians "prepare and consume different types of traditionally processed smoked/sun-dried/fermented/salted fish products. *Suka ko maacha* and *gnuchi* are ethnic smoked and dried fish products; *sidra* and *sukuti* are sun-dried fish products; *ngari*, *hentak*, *tungtap*, and *shidal* are fermented fish products; and *karati*, *bordia*, and *lashim* are sun-dried and salted fish products" (Kikon 2015; Tamang 2010; Thapa 2016). These are only a few of many locally available variants. All these are homemade or market-based comestibles of non-hegemonic cultures that have not, and I doubt ever will, draw the consideration of corporations or national bureaucrats, the consecrators of culture. In the national gastronomic project of Hindu-Hindi-Hindustan, there is an implication that these are not real Indian foods because they are the local practices of communities marginalized by caste, religion, language, and location, valorized neither by the East nor by the West. For Indian and global elites, a fish sauce from the margins of India is unimaginable no matter how many people use it and how artisanal, local, and sustainable it is.

In Chapter 13, Sonia Ryang shows us kimchi's heroic transformation from a poetic figment in a twelfth-century text, through everyday ubiquity, foreign disdain and disgust, to a pillar of "Korea's national pride and identity." Another cheap, fermented, tasty, unevenly standardized product—ranging from the sweet and sour *mulgimchi*, the whole-radish *dongchimi*, the original *baekgimchi* without chili peppers—now has to carry the weight of a nation's anxiety about its own greatness and radical upward mobility in the interstate system. Minor historical inconveniences, such as the introduction of Napa cabbage in the twentieth century and red chilies (originally referred to as Japanese mustard *waegyeja*) at the end of the sixteenth century, brought along by invasion, can no longer despoil its nationalist credentials. The normalization in Japan began around 1975 when the Momoya Corporation began using the term "kimuchi" to market an industrialized base that when mixed with vegetables would give a kimchi-like flavor. Here again is the happy marriage of company and culture.

Yet separate from national propaganda of the state, more subaltern Korean diasporic citizens in Japan, long treated as second-class residents, hold it in a complex embrace of love, longing, and embarrassed self-consciousness.

Analogously, we see Cwiertka's analysis (in Chapter 12) of Polish cuisine as the work of various acknowledged and unacknowledged classes and ethnicities, sometimes in conflict (over pork) and sometimes in congruence (on dumplings and sour cream), with added differences brought about by regionalism. Class difference is highlighted in the distinct imagination of Polish food as meat-heavy against one that in reality has lots of pickled vegetables, grains, and mushrooms. The collation of a Polish national cuisine includes aspects unrelated to food directly but with the power of the print media, as cookbooks from Austria, France, and Germany flooded the market. Foreign entrepreneurs also reshaped the Polish palate in the nineteenth and twentieth centuries with sugar, chocolate, baking powder, and soup stock. Each claim of what constitutes a cuisine and who made it so is shaped by a series of inclusions, exclusions, repressions, and subordinations that have changed over time. The Polish state, taste-makers, and tourism boards are desperately trying to catch up once again to the league of nations of good taste by inventing a contingent cuisine culled from its conflicted history.

Lyra Spang's discussion of divergent nationalist models of nationalism in Belize (in Chapter 9) is particularly productive here. She distinguishes between Afro-Caribbean and Euro-Kriol on the one hand and pre-Colombian Maya and Mestizo identities on the other, with the latter considered somehow less than national, although they predate the black-and-white post-Colombian populations. This mirrors the exclusion of Native American indigeneity from "Americanism" in the United States and Indian culture's silencing of Adivasi heritage in India. With power on their side, longevity is no obstacle to national heritage exclusion. A general theory of gastronationalism (deSoucey 2010) must be attuned to such local conditions and contentions. The purification of national, regional, provincial, and ethnic traditions also challenges the reality of everyday practices. As Ayora-Diaz shows in the case of Mexican cuisine: "it hides, on the one hand, the political tensions and negotiations at work between the ideology of a purported national cuisine . . . and, on the other hand, the actual local, ethnic and regional cuisines in which hybridity thrives" (Ayora-Diaz 2019: 1).

There is a bifurcation of attitudes toward the nationalization of culinary canon: in the scholarly academic world, there is deep skepticism about both the nature and the standardization of Japanese cuisine, to take the case best developed in this volume, in contrast to the Western institutional gaze of chefs and critics (Assman 2017, 2019; Bestor 2018; Cwiertka 2020; Rath 2015). Nipponese heritage-making is enabled by a naïve celebration of *umami*, *dashi*, and everything Japanese by US chefs and food writers, entailing a form of self-congratulation by the latter for their own belated multiculturalism, having selectively admitted Japan to the Western pantheon of great cooking.

There is also a lifecycle of such claims-making and their academic sanctification. Drinking tea in China (Chapter 4) is a place-making practice of a very particular kind of social class, which has a specific conception of the world and a relationship to the "ontological property of being a hegemonic group." The process connects high aesthetic and ethical theorization to everyday practices of drinking a stimulant and connecting it to well-mannered gentlemanly behavior where mind and body are one. There is a fascinating traffic between high concept and the local practices of an elite, which has been revived by funding from recently rich diasporic Chaozhouese capitalists in Hong Kong. Here again there is the marriage of capital and culture. Since 2008, the process has been reinvented as a Chinese way of drinking tea, rather than a local neo-Confucian elite practice. This particular chapter is a more optimistic reading of cultural reinvention, compared to the pieces by Japanese scholars, as the Chinese enter the self-consciously modern competitive world of culture making and great power assertion. That is not very far from the work of the Korean state on behalf of K-pop and kimchi, similarly positioning itself to make claims on a global culture. So here we have professionals of aspirant nations with different degrees of scholarly distance from their respective nationalist project.

That is comparable to the Italian case, which reveals a similar aspiration to join the league of cultured nations by showing evidence of having stayed apart from the corporate, industrial, "Americanization" of the world. As the ethnographic work by Cristina Grasseni (Chapter 5) shows, entrepreneurs marketing a mountain cheese are aware that what they are selling can be invented by others, hence argue for its protection. It is part war-of-positions, part theater, part quotidian labor, where cheesemakers of Val Taleggio perform the activities of hand milking, milk curdling, and cheese tasting for local, touristic, and bureaucratic audiences, invoking both narrow local ecologies and wide worlds of global sentiment.

*   *   *

Capital and nation-states are the twin products of the modern world and heritage is their misbegotten child. It seems that everyone is into the heritage-making business now. It has always been there as a quieter, almost subterranean, process of nation-state and culture-making project, and sometimes a regional-provincial one (as in the cases of Lyonnaise cuisine or *narezushi* from Uchitomi Bay). It has now been fed a new accelerant by the scope of intergovernmental activity from organizations such as UNESCO. The process itself is a subtle and complicated one of "community" making (which must by necessity exclude others), place-based protections, intellectual property claims, and legal protections and intergovernmental negotiations, along with a substantial amount of bullying by strong nation-states (DeSoucey 2010; Parasecoli 2017). None of it can work without the power of the state in the interstate system. Heritage is supposed to be a retort to the homogenization of the world of commodities and an attempt to challenge the apparent vulgarity of market-based, mobile, placeless, commercial brands such as Coca-Cola, Pepsi, and Levis. But it reproduces the evils of its modern universalizing twin, the arbitrary power of states, and the acute inequalities between them, to herald a different type of homogenization. Each one of the above chapters points to a hesitating, complicated way out of grappling with this conundrum in an attempt to evade the grasp of big corporations, big states, and big intergovernmental organizations. Scale is the enemy of good food, most of the time, regardless of the organization, be it company, state, or interstate. Upscaling is good for money-making in great quantities and power-hoarding, but destructive to vernacular food cultures of local shifting repute.

We have known for a generation now that the US model of feeding people, with input-intensive production of cheap carbohydrates and animal proteins, while externalizing the costs of environmental and social reproduction, is unsustainable. Soylent, as the last chapter shows, is the ultimate culinary expression of this model where food is reduced to a narrow function—as a unit of energy, muscle-builder or micronutrient, a superfood—"sweeter than anything" else in its potential for making money. This system is still in place because of large agro-industrial corporate interest, their handmaiden states, and the unfocused Malthusian anxieties of multilateral organizations about the coming ten billion people. We have long known that the green revolution is no longer green.

On the cultural front, heritage has been the counterweight of Anglo-US forms of commodification and imperialism for the last quarter of the twentieth century. The US system was built on imported migrant labor and micro-entrepreneurs and exported commodities. Almost all the food in the Unites States' public domain is produced by migrants; nearly all farmworkers and more than one-half of restaurant and cafeteria workers in the United States today are foreign-born. The Soviet model was no different in terms of scale, input intensity, and unsustainability, but it was different in its recruitment of labor, which was often via forced internal resettlement (Scott 1999). The real counterpunch to US food commodification was the Western European response of terroir, at its heart an argument about people in place. This is the anti-system to the system of "Americanism." The terroir strategy does produce local food that internalizes some of the costs of production, but it is structurally and inescapably anti-immigrant, because immigrants are people out of place and terroir is all about some people in place for a very long time (Laudan 2004). The strategy sometimes protects local livelihoods but is done in aggregate by excluding immigrants and milking the citizenship premium that ultimately increases global inequality (Milanović 2016). In much of Europe, the making of national heritage has been little more than anxious forms of consolidating soft, white nationalism to bar migrant practices from the patrimony. Presently, the locus of those concerns has shifted to Hungary, Poland, Italy, and Greece.

That chiasmus of the commodity system and the terroir-based anti-system was a product of the US century. But the US century is over. This moment has echoes of both the dangers and possibilities of the interwar years in Europe. The United States after the US century is a weakened, dangerous, unraveling giant. Unimaginable things have become possible. The concern now is how destructive the US state will be in addressing sustainability, natural and social, on its way out of dominance. Which opens up the real question for the future: What will be the next hegemonic vision of food culture, and what will be its anti-system?

References

Assmann, S. (2017), "Global Recognition and Domestic Containment: Culinary Soft Power in Japan," in A. Niehaus and T. Walravens (eds.), *Feeding Japan*, pp. 113–37, Cham: Palgrave Macmillan.

Assmann S. (2019), "Mediating National Identity, Practicing Life Politics: Visual Representations of a Food Education Campaign in Japan," in J. Dürrschmidt and Y. Kautt (eds.), *Globalized Eating Cultures*, pp. 53–68, Cham: Palgrave Macmillan.

Ayora-Diaz, S. I., ed. (2019), *Taste, Politics and Identities in Mexican Food*, London: Bloomsbury Academic.

Bestor, T. (2018), "Washoku, Far and Near: UNESCO, Gastrodiplomacy, and the Cultural Politics of Traditional Japanese Cuisine," in N. Stalker (ed.), *Devouring Japan: Global Perspectives on Japanese Culinary Identity*, pp. 99–117, Oxford: Oxford University Press.

Cobb, E. (August 11, 2020), "Japan's Unknown Indigenous Cuisine," BBC. http://www .bbc.com/travel/story/20200810-japans-unknown-indigenous-cuisine?, last accessed August 21, 2020.

Cwiertka, K. J. (2020), *Branding Japanese Food: From Meibutsu to Washoku*, Honolulu: University of Hawaii Press.

DeSoucey, M. (2010), "Gastronationalism: Food Traditions and Authenticity Politics in the European Union," *American Sociological Review* 75(3): 432–55. https://doi.org/10 .1177/0003122410372226

de St. Maurice, G. (2018), "Making the Multi-Dimensional Taste of Japanese Cuisine Public," in C. Counihan and S. Højlund (eds.), *Making Taste Public: Ethnographies of Food and the Senses*, pp. 113–25, London: Bloomsbury.

Kikon, D. (2015), "Fermenting Modernity: Putting Akhuni on the Nation's Table in India," *South Asia: Journal of South Asia Studies* 38(2): 320–35. https://doi.org/10.1080/008564 01.2015.1031936

Laudan, R. (2004), "The French Terroir Strategy and Culinary Modernism," *Food, Culture and Society* 7(2): 133–44.

Milanović, B. (2016), *Global Inequality: A New Approach for the Age of Globalization*, Cambridge, MA: Harvard University Press.

Parasecoli, F. (2017), *Knowing Where It Comes From*, Iowa City: University of Iowa Press.

Rath, E. (2015), "The Invention of Local Food," in J. Farrer (ed.), *The Globalization of Asian Cuisines: Transnational Networks and Culinary Contact Zones*, pp. 145–64, New York: Palgrave MacMillan.

Scott, C. J. (1999), *Seeing Like a State*, New Haven: Yale University Press.

Tamang, J. P. (2010), *Himalayan Fermented Foods*, London: CRC Press.

Thapa, N. (2016), "Ethnic Fermented and Preserved Fish Products of India and Nepal," *Journal of Ethnic Foods*, Korea Food Research Institute, Elsevier. https://doi.org/10.1 016/j.jef.2016.02.003, last accessed August 21, 2020.

Yadavar, S. (May 22, 2018), "Over 70% Indians Are Non-Vegetarian," *The Quint*. https ://www.thequint.com/news/india/many-indians-are-non-vegetarian-most-meat-ea ters-in-, kerala#:~:text=Overall%2C%2042.8%20percent%20Indian%20women,16%20 (NFHS%2D4), last accessed August 21, 2020.

Contributors

Isabel Aguilera is Professor at the Sociology department, Universidad Católica del Maule, Chile. Her main research interest is the relationship between food, nationalism, and indigenous people in Latin America. She has been part of different anthropological research projects exploring culinary exotism, national cuisines, and food heritage. She is the author of *De la cocina al Estado Nación* (From the kitchen to National State), 2016.

Alejandra Alvear M. is a social anthropologist at the University of Chile, and holds a master's degree in Historical Sciences from the University Francois Rabelais de Tours (France). She is currently a PhD student in American Studies IDEA-University of Santiago (Chile). Her research focuses on food and colonialism among the Rapanui people in Chile. She is member of the Indigenous Chair at the University of Chile as a researcher specialized on food heritage.

Steffan Igor Ayora-Diaz (PhD McGill University, 1993) is Full Professor of Anthropology at the Autonomous University of Yucatan and Member of the National System of Researchers (Level II). He has been doing research on Yucatán's gastronomy and regionalism, on food changes and technology, and, more recently, on taste and innovation. Since 2016, he has been conducting research in Seville, Spain. He is the author of *Foodscapes, Foodfields and Identities in Yucatán* (2012) and edited *Taste, Politics and Identities in Mexican Food* (2019).

Ishita Banerjee-Dube (PhD Calcutta University, 1994) is Professor of History at the Centre for Asian and African Studies, El Colegio de México in Mexico City, and a member Level III of the National System of Researchers (SNI, Mexico). Her work focuses on religion and power, gender and nation, food and emotion, and democracy and justice in South Asia. She has authored six books and edited twelve volumes.

Rachel Black is Assistant Professor of Anthropology at Connecticut College. She has done ethnographic and historical research on open-air markets in Italy and France; cooperative wine production in Italy; urban agriculture in Italy and Canada; and female culinary professionals in France. She is the author of the book *Porta Palazzo: The Anthropology of an Italian Market* (2012) and editor of *Alcohol in Popular Culture: An Encyclopedia* (2010).

Katarzyna J. Cwiertka (PhD Leiden University, 1999) is Chair of Modern Japan Studies at Leiden University. She holds an MA degree in Japanese Studies from Warsaw University, Poland (1990), an MA degree in Area Studies from Tsukuba University,

Japan (1994), and a PhD from Leiden University (1999). Her most recent book is *Branding Japanese Food: From* Meibutsu *to* Washoku (2020).

Rossella Galletti (PhD Anthropology) is Adjunct Professor and Research Fellow of Cultural and Symbolic Anthropology at the University of Naples Suor Orsola Benincasa, and Adjunct Professor of Sustainable Food and Wine Tourism at the University of Naples Federico II. She is currently writing the book *Le vie del cibo. Cibo, identità e globalizzazione tra Campania e Minnesota.*

Cristina Grasseni is Professor of Anthropology at the Institute of Cultural Anthropology and Development Sociology at the University of Leiden and Principal Investigator of the European Research Council-funded project "Food Citizens? Collective Food Procurement in European Cities: Solidarity and Diversity, Skill and Scale" (2017–22). Her most recent monograph is *The Heritage Arena* (2017).

Shingo Hamada (PhD Indiana University, Bloomington, 2014) is Associate Professor at the Faculty of Liberal Arts, Osaka Shoin Women's University, Japan. His publications include *Seafood: Ocean to the Plate* (2018, coauthored with Richard Wilk), "Future of Food Studies" (2015), "Ainu Geographic Names and a Multiethnic History of Coastal Hokkaido" (2015), and "Herring and Merroir" (2019, in Japanese).

Lanlan Kuang (PhD Indiana University, Bloomington) is Associate Professor at the University of Central Florida's Philosophy Department and CEFLA distinguished fellow appointed by China's Ministry of Culture and Tourism for her contributions to safeguarding folk arts and heritage culture. Her monograph *The Dunhuang Performing Arts in Global Context* (2016) is available in Harvard-Yenching Library, Princeton-Marquand Library of Art and Archaeology.

Walter E. Little (PhD University at Illinois, Urbana-Champaign) is Professor of Anthropology at the University at Albany, SUNY. He is the author of nine books, and has edited volumes and published over ninety articles and reviews. His monograph, *Mayas in the Marketplace: Tourism, Globalization, and Cultural Identity* (2004), won Best Book of 2005 from the New England Council for Latin American Studies.

Christina (Gonzalez) Morris (BA in Anthropology, Bucknell University) has conducted ethnographic fieldwork in a rural community in Central Pennsylvania and currently works as a project manager for a central laboratory in New York, focusing on global clinical trials.

Andrew Ofstehage (PhD in Anthropology, University of North Carolina-Chapel Hill, 2018) studies agrarian change in Bolivia, Brazil, and the United States, and currently is a postdoctoral associate in Development Sociology at Cornell University. He is presently working on a monograph on transnational soy farmers in Brazil and pursuing new research on the social life of soy.

Yoshimi Osawa (PhD in Ethnobiology, the University of Kent) is an assistant professor at Aoyama Gakuin University (Tokyo). Her publications include "The Cultural Cognition of Taste Term Conflation" (with Roy F. Ellen) in *The Senses and Society*, "Glutamate Perception, Soup Stock and the Concept of Umami" in *Ecology of Food and Nutrition*, and "We Can Taste but Others Cannot: Umami as Exclusively Japanese Concept" in the edited volume *Devouring Japan*.

Krishnendu Ray is Chair of the Department of Nutrition and Food Studies at NYU. He was a faculty member and the Associate Dean of Liberal Arts at the Culinary Institute of America. He is the author of *The Migrant's Table* (2004), *The Ethnic Restaurateur* (2016), and the coeditor of *Curried Cultures: Globalization, Food and South Asia* (2012).

Sonia Ryang (PhD in Anthropology, the University of Cambridge) is TT and WF Chao Professor of Asian Studies and the Director of Chao Center for Asian Studies, Rice University. Her books include *Reading North Korea: An Ethnological Inquiry* (2012) and *Eating Korean in America: Gastronomic Ethnography of Authenticity* (2015). She is also the editor-in-chief of *Transnational Asia: An Online Interdisciplinary Journal*.

Clare A. Sammells is Associate Professor of Anthropology at Bucknell University. She has conducted ethnographic fieldwork among Aymara speakers in the Bolivian Andes and among Bolivian migrants in Spain. She is coeditor (with Helen R. Haines) of the volume *Adventures in Eating: Anthropological Experiences of Dining from Around the World* (2010).

Lyra H. Spang (PhD Indiana University Bloomington, 2014) consults on Belizean cuisine, culinary tourism, and other anthropological matters, and is Chair of the Research Group on Gastropolitics, Food and Identity at the Open Anthropology Institute. She owns and operates Taste Belize Tours, a culinary and cultural tour company. She is the author of *Bite Yu Finga! Innovating Belizean Cuisine*.

Gabriela Vargas-Cetina (PhD McGill University, 1994) is Professor of Anthropology at the Autonomous University of Yucátan (UADY), in Merida, Mexico, and member of the National System of Researchers in Mexico (SNI II). She specializes in organizations and anthropological representations. Her most recent book is *Beautiful Politics of Music: Trova in Yucatán, Mexico* (2017). She is currently working on technology, sound, and music in Mérida, Yucatán and in Seville, Spain.

Index

Polish 179
pork 161
regional 127
saba-narezushi 47
Seville 122
swan 35
traditional 120
weight-loss 217
regionalism 25, 91, 124, 257
restaurant
 aesthetic 156, 157
 Belizean 140
 big hotel 92
 Bolivian 216
 ethnic 122
 experimental 156, 157
 fifth gama 121, 131 n.5
 fusion 122
 high-end 217
 Maya food 155
 quality 87
 self-service 189
 tapas 118
 traditional 119, 122, 156,
  157
 upmarket 191
 upper-class 37, 255
 upscale 95, 120, 121, 122
Rosanjin, K. 36, 41 n.9

SARS-CoV-2 2, 122, *see also*
 Covid-19
SARS epidemic 198
sattvik 105
 upper class and 106
scandal
 rotten-meat 108, 113, 114
 and social media 103–4
seasonality 45, 48, 96, 129
Seville International Expo 121, 124–5,
 126, 127, 128
Slow Food
 Japan 64
 Presidia 82, 231
 Turin 80, 81
social media 3, 15, 104, 107–11,
 248
 Facebook 103, 108, 109, 110, 114,
  115, 122

Reddit 245, 248–9, 251
WhatsApp 103, 108, 109, 110, 114,
 115
spatial permissiveness 151–2
stracchino 73–5
strachitunt 73–5, 78–83
street vendors, *see* food vendors
superfood 213–5, 217, 222, 248,
 259
sustainable diet 230
Sutton, D. E. 15, 17, 18, 144, 163
synesthesia 18

Tagarasu 44, 45–6
 artisans 49, 52
 local crafters 50
Taleggio cheese 73–5
tamasik 105, 113
taste
 intersubjective 1, 2, 5, 9
 "naturalized" 2, 21, 123, 130
 popular 162, 170
 three gains 62–3
tasteless 105, 243, 251
terroir 4, 23–4, 25, 45, 49, 53, 89, 231,
 243, 259
three teachings 70 n.4
time-space (in *gongfu cha*) 68
tipicità 73, 78–80
tourism
 automobile 87, 88, 90
 and cheesemaking 80
 culinary 22, 87, 155
 gastronomic 89, 90, 96, 155
 heritage 147
 slum 164
 in Spain 121, 124, 129
tourist 80–1, 89, 126, 164
 bourgeois 90
 brochures 77
 foreign 153
 gastronomic 88
 in Guatemala 148–9
 Guatemalan 156
 Japanese 205
 nonlocal 43, 52, 53
 in Poland 188, 190
 and tapas 131 n.3
transhumance 76–7

www.ingramcontent.com/pod-product-compliance
Lightning Source LLC
Chambersburg PA
BHW071354290326
932CB00045B/1808